INGA-BRITTA SUNDQVIST

The Vegetarian's Bible

350 Quick, Practical, and Nutritious Recipes

TRANSLATED BY LISA LINDBERG

Skyhorse Publishing

Skyhorse Publishing books may be purchased in bulk at special discounts for sales promotion, corporate gifts, fund-raising, or educational purposes. Special editions can also be created to specifications. For details, contact the Special Sales Department, Skyhorse Publishing, 307 West 36th Street, 11th Floor, New York, NY 10018 or info@skyhorsepublishing.com.

Skyhorse® and Skyhorse Publishing® are registered trademarks of Skyhorse Publishing, Inc. ®, a Delaware corporation.

www.skyhorsepublishing.com

10 9 8 7 6 5 4 3 2

Library of Congress Cataloging-in-Publication Data is available on file.

Paperback ISBN: 978-1-63220-309-0
Hardcover ISBN: 978-1-62087-244-4
Ebook ISBN: 978-1-62087-777-7

Printed in China

Table of Contents

Foreword

By the end of the '70s I started writing down recipes that I wanted to use for my study circles in vegetarian cooking. This material eventually turned into the *Vegetarian's Bible*, which with time, to my great delight, came to be both a best seller and a classic. In the beginning of the 2000s, it was time for a revision of the book, since so many new things had happened in the field of health. Most of the new research from scientists was confirming the enormously important role that vegetables and fruits play in our health.

The new version of the *Vegetarian's Bible* came out in 2001 and was called the best Swedish literature by Culinary Academy Awards in Grythyttan 2002, with the praise: "With great authority the *Vegetarian's Bible* turns into a current standard work, it has everything." The book also received an international award the same year from Gourmand World Cookbook Awards for "Best in the World, Honorable Mention." In addition, it has received the award for 2005 Best Carrot (Årets morot) from the Swedish Vegetarian Society 2005 as well as Health Promotion Award 2010.

Now it is once again time for an extensive revision of my classic. Scientists are continuing to reveal new research about our health. Among other things, they show how extremely important every single little nutrient—for example, vitamin D—is for our bodies to develop and function optimally. All nutritional information in the book is, of course, up to date. Particularly interesting is the new research about the important fatty acids and what kind of fat is best suited for cooking. A new chapter, "Your inner doctor," with detox as well as anti-inflammatory diets and superfood with ORAC-values for both fruit and vegetables, has been added.

It is also particularly fun to be able to state that vegetarian food is more topical today than ever before. People are increasingly taking responsibility for their own health and for the planet by eating eco-friendly vegetarian food. To those who wish to live more climate-consciously, there is a new chapter, "Eco-friendly guide," with everything from tips on how to grow and store your food to how to make a compost. There is also a seasonal guide for fruits and vegetables, where you easily can see what vegetables and fruits are in season.

I myself thought that I was living a fairly climate-smart life. I did not think I would be able to affect my carbon dioxide emissions as much as I could, with relatively small changes in my life. I do not consider it to be a sacrifice to live green. It is the complete opposite; I feel much more at peace with both myself and my life. I have more free time now that I shop less often. I enjoy the food more when I eat by season, and my cooking is even more varied and creative.

The base of the book is, of course, all the delicious vegetarian recipes. The new version of the *Vegetarian's Bible* consists of GI-customized vegetarian recipes, and most recipes have completely new pictures. I have added more raw food and a symbol next to each recipe that indicates if it is part of a raw food, vegan, lacto, or lacto-ovo vegetarian diet. A four-seasonal customized meal plan and suggestions of winter and summer buffets have also been added.

Finally, I would like to take the time to give my warm thanks to the photographers Kent Jardhammar, Karin Westerlund, and Inger Nordell for their lovely work with all the beautiful pictures in the book; editor Gunilla Wagner; and also Ulla Rosander for reviewing the nutritional information.

I hope that both old and new readers will be as inspired by the book as I have been by writing this new material.

Do not forget to enjoy the tasty food in good company!

Inga-Britta Sundqvist

Vegetarian diet

Vegetarian food is more popular than ever. More and more people are choosing to eat vegetarian food for the sake of the environment. In addition, one researcher after another has confirmed how important it is to eat vegetables that are filled with antioxidants and other nutritional agents that are good for us.

That vegetarian food is the purest food we can eat—since vegetables are found at the bottom of the food chain—is just a bonus. Above that, vegetarian food is fresh, beautiful, and, most of all, tasty.

THERE ARE MANY REASONS to choose a vegetarian diet. Today, more and more people want to eat vegetarian food because of environmental reasons. A lot of people choose a vegetarian diet for ethical reasons and others for health reasons. Vegetarians are reported to suffer less from heart and vascular diseases, diabetes, lung cancer, and colorectal cancer. Vegetarians—in particular, vegans—generally weigh less than people of a mixed diet and have lower blood pressure and cholesterol values.

Purer food. Since vegetables are at the bottom of the food chain, they collect less environmental toxins than animals that are higher up in the chain. In other words, a vegetarian diet contains fewer heavy metals and toxins like PCB and DDT.

Ethical reasons. Many people, especially young people, refuse to take part in other creatures' suffering or deaths for our sake. Most animals today live under terrible conditions in animal industries.

Economical reasons. If you mainly cook food from beans, grains, root vegetables, and seasonal vegetables and fruits, stay away from processed goods, and sprout and create your own source of protein, like tempeh (see p. 110), it will turn out a lot cheaper to eat vegetarian food.

VEGETARIAN DIETS

A "super diet" that is right for everyone does not exist. Each and every person has to feel and try out a diet that fits them the best. A person who does not eat meat and fish is generally called a vegetarian. But there are different types of vegetarian diets.

A vegan diet only includes nutrients from the plant kingdom like grains, beans, vegetables, and fruits. Many people become vegans because they choose to not participate in killing animals. They also avoid all products that in any way derive from exploited animals, like wool and honey as well as the leather found in shoes, boots, and jackets. All vegan recipes in this book are marked with Vegan.

Frugivore diet. Frugivores are vegans that let the plants live through their whole cycle. They only eat the plants' own harvest, like fruit, berries, grains, and nuts and also vegetable fruits, like tomatoes, bell peppers, peas, and cucumbers.

Raw food is becoming increasingly more popular. This diet is restricted to berries, fruit, vegetables, root vegetables, seeds, nuts, algae, green shoots, sprouts, and cold pressed oils as well as spices that are heated to a maximum of 107.6°F (42°C). Sweetening is only done with dried fruit and small amounts of agave syrup and honey.

This makes the food very nutritional and allows all of the enzymes to remain in the food. Raw food is easy to digest and does not burden your body as much as "regular food." Raw food enthusiasts also claim that the food contains more "life energy," and it makes them feel more alert and energized. All the raw food recipes in this book are labeled with Raw.

Lacto-vegetarian diet. Lacto comes from *lac*, which means "milk" in Latin. In addition to all vegetables, this diet also contains dairy products, like milk, butter, and cheese. All lacto-vegetarian recipes are labeled with Lacto.

Lacto-ovo vegetarian diet. *Ovum* means "egg" in Latin. The diet contains the same food as above, but also eggs. All lacto-ovo vegetarian recipes are labeled with Lacto-ovo.

Demi-vegetarians are a growing group of people that are not really "vegetarians." Their diet consists of the same food as above, but they also eat fish and seafood.

Macrobiotic diet. "Macrobiotic" means "big life" and has its origin in the Far East. It is based on the principle of yin and yang, which are the universe's opposite yet interdependent forces, and the key is to find balance between them through diet. Grains are considered to be the most balanced nutrients.

A macrobiotic diet is 50 percent cooked grains and whole wheat products, 25 to 30 percent vegetables and root vegetables, 10 to 15 percent legumes, and a small amount fruit, algae, and fish.

The Ayurvedic diet is about 3,000 years old and comes from the Indian Vedas. According to Ayurvedic thinking, we are born with a certain elementary constitution. The three basic types are vata, pitta, or kapha. You can also be a combination of two or all three basic types.

A vata and pitta have a high metabolism and need to eat a steady breakfast and more cooked food. Vata and pitta get easily excited and easily get an "upset stomach." It is particularly important for them to eat in a peaceful environment. A kapha has a slower metabolism and should eat a light breakfast and more raw food. A kapha also needs to drink more to speed up the circulation in their body.

Eco-friendly guide

Food does not need to be one of our biggest climate villains. Food represents over one-fourth of our climate impact. If we all threw away less food, bought less junk food and bottled water, and ate more seasonally, we could easily affect our food impact on the climate by half.

To eat seasonally is not a limitation but rather the opposite; it enriches the creativity and makes the food more exciting and varied. In this chapter, you will find a seasonal guide for vegetables as well as berries and other fruit. There are also several tips for indoor and outdoor cultivation.

EVERY PERSON IN SWEDEN CONTRIBUTES almost six tons of carbon dioxide every year. If the whole world's population lived the way we do here in the West, we would need three planets. Luckily, most of us have very good opportunities to make important contributions to decrease emissions without any greater sacrifice. Food alone stands for 25 to 30 percent of our climate impact, including transport to and from stores. It is a matter of having knowledge and making conscious decisions. As a bonus, we gain better health and economy.

According to the Swedish EPA, beef generates about 25 times more greenhouse gas per kilo of edible food compared to an equivalent amount of beans. A five to ten times larger area is used for cultivating meat production, compared to the equivalent amount of vegetable protein. On 2.5 acres you can produce 616 pounds of beef or 24,640 pounds of beans. The United States is the world's largest producer of soybeans, and a large amount of the soybean harvest is used as cattle food.

Junk food, mostly candy and chips, also affects carbon dioxide emissions. One bag of marshmallows affects the climate as much as one portion of pork. About 2.2 pounds of chips leads to 4.8 pounds of greenhouse gas emissions, which is 20 times what the production of 2.2 pounds of potatoes does.

FOOD AND ECOLOGY

When the sun's rays hit the earth, they are transformed into heat that radiates back into space. There are greenhouse gases in the atmosphere around the whole globe that will prevent some of the heat from leaving us. Without the greenhouse gases, the world would be ice cold. But if the amount of gases becomes too great due to human emissions, the earth will become too hot and cause the climate to change. Food production contributes to nearly a third of the global greenhouse gas emissions.

According to the United Nations' climate panel, the increased amount of carbon dioxide in the atmosphere over the past 20 years is caused 75 percent by the burning of fossil fuels (coal, oil, and natural gas), and 25 percent by using land, mostly clearing of forests.

Eat more eco-friendly
- Eat more vegetarian meals
- Throw away less food and use the leftovers
- Eat according to season
- Eat organic and local produce
- Avoid bottled water!
- Buy less junk food!

The atmosphere's methane content is currently increasing. Some types of farming cause large emissions of methane, such as animal farms and rice paddies.

Today we speak of "climate dieting in an environmentally adapted way." More people think we should choose more green options, and if you choose animal products you should choose organic or pasture-raised meat. Organic and pasture-raised animals contribute to biodiversity by keeping the landscape open and supporting the flora, insects, and small animals.

We throw away an average of 25 percent of our food. That is almost one million tons of food in Sweden alone. Half of the food would have been edible if only treated the right way, according to Konsumentföreningen, Sweden's largest consumer association, in Stockholm. On average, Swedes buy 5.3 gallons of bottled water a year. Besides that, Swedes buy junk food like candy, soda, and snacks for about 35 to 40 percent of food costs.

Biodiversity

Today, the landscape in the West mostly consists of large monocultures. That often leads to illnesses in animals and pests on plants. As a result, biodiversity decreases, and both flora and small insects disappear. The most alarming effect is that bees are dying around the whole world, and our food chain is in danger. If there are not enough bees, pollination will not take place, and that makes it impossible for us to have large harvests of fruit, vegetables, grains, nuts, or seeds. Most scientists claim that it has to do with all the toxic pesticides that are used in conventional cultivation. Organic cultivation supports biodiversity.

In poor developing countries, there are usually several different species cultivated in the fields, just like people did in the old days. The diversity is a way of spreading risks and it contributes to important ecosystem services like insect pollination, natural pest control, cleaning water, and creating fertile soil.

Sesam is a nonprofit organization that wants to maintain the diversity that can be found in the plants of the garden or in fields. The members preserve old cultural plants by seed cultivating them and then spreading the seeds among the members. There are also smaller seed companies that sell the seeds of old cultural treasures.

Organic produce

More and more people are choosing to buy organic produce for both environmental and health reasons. Organic produce usually has a lot more flavor and stays fresh longer. "Organic" is a generic word for ways of cultivating in which gene manipulation, irradiation, pesticides, toxins, and fertilizers are not allowed. In organic produce, there cannot be any substances that may do harm to people or nature.

Organic produce is also proven to be more nutritional. The EU's extensive research project (Quality Low Input Food Project) shows that there are 40 percent more antioxidants in eight kinds of organically produced fruits, vegetables, and grains. Several studies show that children who eat a lot of organic food run a lower risk of developing different kinds of allergies. A British study of rats that only ate organic feed showed that they remained slimmer, slept better, and had a better immune system. The University Hospital in Lund, Sweden, has shown that people who do not eat organic food have higher levels of pesticides in their urine than people who eat a lot of organic produce.

Organic labeling

There are several different brands for organic produce. The EU symbol for organic food demands the product to have at least 95 percent ecological raw material. Demeter and KRAV (a Swedish issuer of organic standards) have stricter rules—among other things, they demand 100 percent organic raw material. KRAV also has a climate label. In addition, KRAV accepts only a few food additives.

KRAV-approved animal breeding demands that the animals have a good life, that the calves can suckle their mother for a longer time, and that the animals can eat outside as much as possible. That, in turn, keeps the landscape open; flora, insects, and small animals are supported and carbon storage in the ground is increased.

KRAV-approved farmers grow their own feed and do not use any imported feed. That makes the farm self-sufficient using manure, and no fertilizer needs to be bought. Conventionally bred animals in Sweden are given feed that contains soy that contributes to the devastation of rain forests and the spread of extremely toxic chemicals.

Environmental labeling

There are several different environmental brands for different types of products, including everything from food, clothing, household products, and IT-products to services like hotels and restaurants. There are both national and international brands. EU has its branding; Nordic countries have international brands as well as various chain stores with their own brands. They all have their own different norms. The brands with the strictest demands in Sweden are KRAV and Nature Conservationist's own brand, with the swallow.

Fair trade is an ethical and social branding with a focus on human rights. By buying fair trade products, you help give both producers and workers reasonable pay for their work, prevent child labor, and contribute to a better and more free existence for both children and adults in poor countries. The branding also encourages organic produce.

Eco-friendly pantry

The selection of vegetables and fruits in our grocery stores is enormous and almost the same all year round. It can even be difficult to see what is in season. That is when a seasonal guide comes in handy.

There are surprisingly many varied products in a climate-conscious pantry. To eat vegetables and fruits of the season has a lot of advantages. Usually they are more locally produced, which leads to shorter transport distances, and that is good for the environment.

Besides that, vegetables and fruit that are allowed to ripen by themselves are richer in aroma and flavor. Another benefit is that cooking will be much more varied and exciting. When you can eat lovely strawberries during the summer, you enjoy it so much more than if you have unlimited access to them all year round.

Best buy for imported goods:
Autumn: October to December is the season for outdoor-grown fruits and vegetables like clementines, lemons, pomegranate, persimmon, and kiwi, as well as cauliflower, broccoli, fennel, celery, sweet potatoes, and zucchini.

Winter: January to March is the season for fruit and vegetables like oranges, lemons, and pomegranate, as well as avocado, fennel, celery, sweet potatoes, and zucchini.

Spring: April to June is the season for fruits and vegetables like lemons and melons as well as avocado, eggplant, fennel, bell peppers, asparagus, cucumber, celery, sweet potatoes, tomatoes, and zucchini.

Summer: July to September is the season for fruits and vegetables like lemons, peaches, nectarines, grapes, and melons, as well as avocado, eggplant, artichoke, bell peppers, and sweet potatoes.

The worst buy you can make is everything that is transported by plane and products that are grown in oil-heated greenhouses. Avoid tomatoes, eggplant, and bell peppers from November until March. Use tomato concentrate, tomatoes in a can or paper box, or dried tomatoes during the winter season.

Rice is not a climate-smart option since it also creates methane gas during cultivation. Climate-smart alternatives are oats, spelt, barley, kamut, quinoa, and bulgur.

INDOOR GROWING

Sprouts have everything. They are nutritious, fresh, and tasty. No matter where you live, you can grow your own vegetables. They are cheap, too. About one tablespoon of alfalfa seeds will give you a big jar of sprouts. Sprouts are perfect during the winter and spring when we have a limited supply of other vegetables. In Asia, sprouts have been used for thousands of years. In Europe, they were introduced during the 1500 to 1600s.

All seeds have a concentrate of the nutrients that are needed for the future plant to grow. As long as the seed is not harmed and stored in a dry place, it can keep its ability to grow for a very long time.

Tips! Use sprouts in raw food, on your bread, in salads, in energy drinks, stews, and soups. If you have too many sprouts, you can mix them and use them when baking bread or in vegetarian sauces.

How to sprout:

1. Place a few tablespoons of seeds in a regular big glass jar. Attach a piece of mosquito netting with a rubber band over the jar. All seeds can be sprouted, such as alfalfa, lentils, mung beans, broccoli, radishes, red clover, and sunflower seeds, as well as all grains like quinoa, barley, wheat, spelt, rye, and oat.
2. Rinse the seeds a few times and then leave them to soak in water overnight.
3. Pour off the water they soaked in and water your plants with the nutritional water. Carefully rinse the seeds in running lukewarm water. Turn the jar upside down until it is drained from all water.

4. The sprout grows best in the dark. If the jars are standing on the kitchen sink, you can place a towel over them. Rinse the sprouts well, both morning and night, then let them drain. After three to five days, the sprouts will be done. Alfalfa needs the longest time. Delicate sprouts are usually the tastiest. That goes especially for mung beans. Peeled sunflower seeds will be done in one day.

When the sprouts are done, you rinse them several times. When it comes to alfalfa sprouts, it is important that you rinse off most of the brown seed peel. Drain the sprouts. Store them in jars or plastic bags in the refrigerator. They stay fresh for three to six days. Sprouted wheat grows small, white, hairy roots that are completely harmless.

Do not eat slimy sprouts that smell bad!

Tip! If you let sprouted alfalfa stand in the window for a few hours, they turn beautifully green, and the level of antioxidants increases considerably. It is important that you rinse the sprouts well and that all the fluid is gone. Spread the sprouts on a plate and cover with plastic wrap. Rinse the sprouts afterwards.

Green shoots:

Fresh nutritional and chlorophyll-rich green shoots are very tasty to eat as a snack, mix in salads or energy drinks, or sprinkle on food.

1. Sprout whole seeds with peel of sunflower (bird seeds), radish, fenugreek, buckwheat, mustard, or turnip for a few days. See above.
2. Divide 1 to 1.5 inches of soil in a regular sowing box. Water the soil until moist, flatten the soil, and spread the sprouts on top of the soil. Place the box in a dark place or cover with black plastic for a few days.
3. Take off the plastic and let stand in a light window for a few days until the shoots have grown. Spray the grass with water every day.

While sprouting, the enzymes' activity increases and many changes take place:

• The vitamin content increases substantially, especially when it comes to vitamin C. But carotenoids, vitamin E, as well as some B vitamins increase, especially folic acid. Vitamin B12 is formed but in very small amounts.
• Phytic acid is broken down, and that way we can absorb the minerals in the seeds more easily.
• The protein changes and becomes more easily digested.
• The gas-generating ability in beans is reduced.

Ecological cycle

In nature, plants that have grown during summer fall down to the ground and decompose into nutritional soil that naturally fertilizes new plants. If we want to live in harmony with nature, we should let our food and vegetable waste be decomposed into a nutritional compost.

It is easy to make a compost. Choose a shady place outside. There, you place a big box with three sections. In the first section, you place all the dry waste from your garden like leaves and sticks. In the other section, keep placing moist waste from the kitchen and garden in layers with the dry garden waste. It is important to keep the compost thoroughly moist all the time. Sometimes you have to water it. When the section is filled, you place a layer of dry garden waste on top. Then you leave the compost to decompose into soil.

That is when it is time to start from the beginning with the third section and place layers of moist and dry material in it.

The compost is done when the material smells and feels like soil. The compost is full of life and nutrition, and it is an amazing way to improve your soil and to fertilize your garden. Today there are also good organic aids that are approved by health authorities (see p. 339), if you want to create a completely odorless compost in an apartment.

Tip! If the decomposing process in the compost is slow, you can add a shovelful of soil from the garden. There are also composting aids you can buy.

SEASONAL GUIDE FOR FRUIT AND VEGETABLES

Local variations occur depending on where in the country you live. Make sure to choose local produce when possible.

● Secure supply   ○ Insecure supply or self-grown

VEGETABLES AND ROOT VEGETABLES	Dec	Jan	Feb	Mar	Apr	May	Jun	Jul	Aug	Sep	Oct	Nov
Asian leafy vegetables	●				●	●	○	○		●	●	●
Cauliflower							●	●	●	●	●	○
Broccoli							●	●	●	●	●	○
Brussels sprouts	●	●	●							●	●	●
Beans, fresh								●	●	●		
Fennel							●	●	●			
Kale	●	●								●	●	●
Cucumber						●	●	●	●	●	●	●
Iceberg lettuce						○	○			●	●	
Jerusalem artichoke	●	●	●	●						●	●	●
Chanterelles							●	●	●	●		
Artichoke									●	●		
Kohlrabi								●	●	●	●	
Turnip	●	●	●	●	●	●	●	●	●	●	●	●
Onion yellow/red	●	●	●	●	●	●	●	●	●	●	●	●
Chard									●	●	●	●
Yellow turnip	●	●	●	●		●	●			●	●	●
Corn								●	●	●		
Carrot	●	●	●	●	●	●	●	●	●	●	●	●
Parsnip	●	●	●	●	●	●	●	●	●	●	●	●
Parsley							●	●	●	●	○	○
Parsley root	●	●	●	●						●	●	●
Potato	●	●	●	●	●	●	●	●	●	●	●	●
Pumpkin/winter squash	●	●	●	○	○	○	○			●	●	●
Leek	●								●	●	●	●
Celery root	●	●	●	●	○	○	○	●	●	●	●	●
Arugula					○	●	○		●	●	●	
Radish							●	●	●	○		
Daikon	●	●	●	●	●	●	●	●	●	●	●	●
Beetroot	●	●	●	●	●	●	●	●	●	●	●	●
Red cabbage	●	●	○	○			●	●	●	●	●	●
Lettuce					○	●	●	●	●	●	●	○

VEGETABLES AND ROOT VEGETABLES

	Dec	Jan	Feb	Mar	Apr	May	Jun	Jul	Aug	Sep	Oct	Nov
Chinese cabbage	●						●	●	●	●	●	●
Savoy cabbage	●								●	●	●	●
Peas							●	●	●	○		
Asparagus						●	●					
Spinach						○	●	●	●	●		
Celery								●	●	●	●	●
Squash/zucchini								●	●	●	●	
Mushroom									●	●	●	○
Black salsify										●	●	●
Tomato							○	●	●	●	●	○
White cabbage	●	●	●	●					●	●	●	●
Garlic	○	○	○	○	○	●	●	●	●	●	○	○

FRUIT AND BERRIES

	Dec	Jan	Feb	Mar	Apr	May	Jun	Jul	Aug	Sep	Oct	Nov
Chokeberry (aronia)										●	●	
Blueberry								●	●			
Blackberry									●	●		
Raspberry								●	●			
Raspberry, autumn										●	●	○
Cloudberry								●				
Strawberry							●	●	●	●		
Cherry									●	●		
Lingonberry										●		
Wild strawberry, garden							●	●	●		●	
Cantaloupe									●	●		
Plum										●	●	
Pear										●	●	○
Rhubarb					●	●	●	●	○			
Wild strawberry							●					
Currant, black/red								●	●			
Apples	●	●	●	●	○				○	●	●	●

Storing and preservation

We have a lot to learn from old, proven knowledge. The most environmentally friendly and best method of storing both vegetables and root vegetables is a good old-fashioned root cellar and a well-functioning pantry. Back in the day, you always built the pantry on the north side of the house so it could stay cool.

What you could not store in the root cellar during wintertime you either dried or fermented in lactic acid. Despite our modern techniques, like deep freezing, there is no method that matches fermentation with lactic acid. Not only are all the nutrients preserved, but new, healthy nutrients like many B vitamins, enzymes, and acetylcholine are formed.

THE MOST ECO-FRIENDLY and often the best storage area for most fruits, vegetables, and root vegetables is an old-fashioned pantry. In the pantry, the fruits and cucumbers keep from getting ice cold like they would in a refrigerator and that makes them taste so much better. If the pantry is well ventilated, it has an entirely different humidity than a refrigerator, and it also prevents vegetables from quickly drying out and shriveling up.

Warm and dry air causes fruits, vegetables, and root vegetables to shrivel up or decay more quickly, and that also decreases the nutritional value. If you do not have a pantry, an entryway or porch would be a better option for most vegetables. Many things can also be stored in boxes in the balcony, like, for example, apples that can cope with several degrees below zero.

There are a few exceptions; for example, all onions except for leeks and scallions should be kept dry and preferably cool. When an onion is kept in a moist place, it starts to mold, and if it is too warm, it starts to grow.

If you have larger amounts of root vegetables, the best place for storage would be a root cellar with good ventilation. Keep the root vegetables in boxes with sand so they stay damp and do not dry out.

FERMENTATION

All over the world, people have fermented with lactic acid. It is a great way of refining and storing vegetables, beans, fruit, and milk. Lactic acid is a fantastic method of preserving food. Not only are all the nutrients preserved, but new ones are also formed, like B vitamins, enzymes, and acetylcholine, which the lactic acid bacteria need to grow.

In Germany, Russia, and the Balkan countries, fermented vegetables and sourdough bread are still a part of the everyday diet. In Southeast Asia, soy products, like tempeh, miso, and tamari are fermented. In Sweden, dairy products are mostly fermented, like processed sour milk and yogurt.

Tip! You can use fermented vegetables and broth instead of lemon juice in most dishes. It is especially tasty in salads with a yogurt-based dressing.

Lactic acid bacteria create a lactic acid coat on skin and mucous membranes, the mouth, intestines, and genitals. This protective coat of acid surrounds all living things in humans, animals, and plants. Pesticides and fertilizers can disrupt this balance. For that reason, all vegetables that are fermented should be organic.

Most lactic acid bacteria can be found on the outer green parts of vegetables. Because of this, the amount of bacteria can be smaller during rain. Do not harvest vegetables for fermentation right after rain; wait a few days. Green leaves are especially rich in lactic acid bacteria, like raspberry or black currant leaves.

Almost all vegetables and fruit can be fermented, like all kinds of cabbages, carrots, beetroots, celery, onions, peas, cucumbers, tomatoes, bell peppers, mushrooms, and beans. All vegetables except for beans are fermented when fresh. Beans should be parboiled before the process.

Spices that prevent decay are juniper, garlic, chili, horseradish, and yellow mustard seeds. Feel free to season with other spices too, like cumin, coriander, dill, bay leaf, and other leafy spices. All spices are used whole.

During the fermentation, the lactic acid bacteria transform the raw material's sugars to organic acids, mostly lactic acid. As the fermentation progresses, the pH levels are lowered, and no decay can occur. After that, the product has to mature and that is when the aroma is created.

A successful milk acid fermentation needs:
- organic vegetables
- a certain amount of salt. The salt prevents decay and incorrect fermentation before enough lactic acid has formed.
- an acid-free environment, otherwise yeast is formed on top
- right the temperature so that the fermentation gets started properly. The fermentation demands a warm place while fermenting and a somewhat cooler place while maturing.
- Whey (see p. 115) is not necessary but gives the lactic acid bacteria good nutrition and will help the fermentation to start.

How to ferment:

- Use glass jars with tight-fitting lids—preferably French preservation jars with a rubber seal. The size of the jar should be at least 1 quart.
- It is important that jars and bottles be very clean. Wash them in hot water and rinse carefully. Then place them in a cold oven. Heat the oven to 212°F and turn it off right when the temperature is reached. Let the jars cool.
- Boil the rubber seal in water.
- Press the vegetables into the jar with your fist so that the fluids are pressed out. (When you make cabbage, you first press or bang the cabbage with your fist in another bowl.)
- The jars can only be filled up to four-fifths of the jar. There must be space left for fermentation.
- Place the jars in a warm spot, protected from light. You can place a paper bag upside down over the jars.
- When the fermentation is finished, the jars are placed in a cool spot, and the temperature should preferably be between 32 and 46.2°F. If it is warmer than 46.4°F, the fermentation process will not stop.

Storage: Anything that has been fermented should be kept at a temperature of 32 to 46.4°F after fermentation and maturing. Fermented products has a good durability: up to two years in cool places like a root cellar.

If you have a problem with storing the fermented products, you can freeze them. Cold will not destroy the lactic acid bacteria. All vegetables except for cucumbers, which soften, can be stored in the freezer.

Sauerkraut

PER 2.2 POUNDS CABBAGE:
1–2 tbsp sea salt (12.5–25 g)
1 tsp juniper (3 g)
½ tsp cumin (1 g)
½ sliced apple (optional)
1 tbsp whey (optional) (12.5 g)

- Clean the cabbage and shred finely. Also shred the core of the cabbage coarsely and mix with other cabbage. Layer cabbage with salt and spices, and, if you choose, some apple slices and whey in a separate bowl.
- Press the cabbage with your fist until it becomes juicy. Continue to layer cabbage, salt, and spices, and press with your fist in the same way until all cabbage is thoroughly moist.
- Fill the jar to four-fifths and press the cabbage down until it is under the vegetable juice.
- Place the jar at room temperature (64.4–68°F) for 10 to 12 days. If it is warmer than 68°F, about 8 days will be enough. After this, the cabbage has to mature in a cool place of about 32 to 46.2°F for at least another 6 to 8 weeks.

Fermented carrots

FOR ONE 1½ QUARTS GLASS JAR:
about 2.2 pounds carrots and onions
1–2 bay leaves
2 peeled garlic cloves
1 tbsp sea salt (12.5 g)
1 tsp coriander seeds (3 g)
1 tsp mustard seeds (3 g)
fresh dill
2 tbsp whey (optional) (25 g)

- Peel and grate the carrots coarsely. Peel and cut the onions in big pieces.
- Layer salt and spices (and optional whey) directly into the jar. Press everything down as hard as possible with your fist, in order for the vegetable juice to cover the vegetables.
- Fill the jar to four-fifths.
- Let the jar stand at room temperature, about 64.4–68°F for 10 to 12 days.
- Leave the jar in a cool place of 32 to 46.2°F and let the root vegetables mature for at least 7 to 8 weeks.

Fermented beetroots

Fermented beetroots is a delicacy. Follow the above recipe but replace the carrots, dill, and mustard seeds with beetroots and five whole cloves. Only fill the jar to two-thirds since beetroots ferment and become larger than other vegetables.

Fermented pickles

FOR ONE 1½ QUARTS JAR:

about 1.1–2.2 pounds mixed vegetables, for example cucumbers, tomatoes, cauliflower, bell peppers, and onions
2 peeled garlic cloves
2 bay leaves
1 tsp coriander (2 g)
1 tsp mustard seeds (3 g)
dill
¼ cup whey (30 g)

■ Rinse and clean the vegetables. Place them in the jar whole or divided in big pieces.
■ The cucumbers should be whole. Poke a few holes in the cucumber with a needle, to make sure they don't turn out soft on the inside.
■ Layer the vegetables with spices. Stuff them in the jar and fill with boiled and cooled off water (with 2 tbsp salt per quart of water) as well as whey.
■ Leave the jar at room temperature (64.4–68°F) for 10 days. If it is warmer than 68°F, it will be long enough after 6 to 8 days. Then place the jar in a cool place for maturing at 32–46.2°F for 2 to 3 weeks.

Fermented beans

Fermented green beans turn out very tasty.

Boil water with 2 tbsp salt per quart of water and let the beans boil until tender, about 5 minutes. Pour off the broth and save it. Rinse the beans with cold water in a strainer.

Place the beans together with the broth when it has cooled off, according to the recipe above. Add a little extra dill.

Fermented cucumber

Pick small, firm cucumbers. Poke a few holes in the cucumber with a stick.

Follow the basic recipe above, but add black currant leaves and a small oak leaf. The tannic acid in the oak leaf prevents the cucumbers from turning soft.

DRYING

Since time immemorial, food has been preserved by drying. Drying has mostly been done by using the heat of the sun. Legumes and rice are still dried in the sun in southern countries. Here in the north, we have dried food with the help of wood stoves or other sources of heat.

Since only the fluid disappears during drying, the plant regains its original volume after soaking. Unlike deep freezing, this method does not harm the plant's cell structure. The method is environmentally friendly and gentle with the raw material. Dried vegetables are ideal food to bring when hiking.

Everything can be dried: wild plants, spices, vegetables, root vegetables, mushrooms, seeds, fruits, and berries.

Sliced fruit, rose hip, mushrooms, herb spices, and different kinds of leaves can be dried at room temperature. For vegetables that are richer in fluid, you need a heat source to achieve a good result.

There are very good drying machines that you can buy, often online. It will make the drying process both faster and easier.

▶ ON THE DRYING RACK, at the bottom are celery leaves, then mint, then slices of zucchini, then marigold petals, then salvia as well as chanterelles. On the hanging drying rack are dried apples. Hanging to the left are dried sliced oranges and lime fruit as well as chanterelles. In the basket to the left are dill, mint, and marigold.

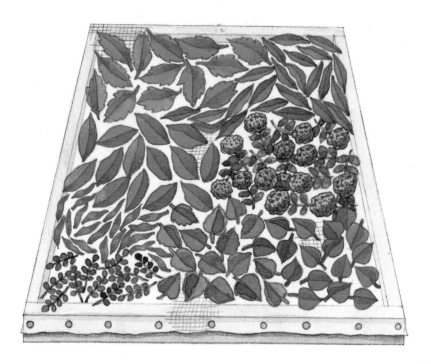

▲ A DRYER can be easily created by attaching a fine net—a mosquito net, for example—and nailing it onto a wooden frame. Nail several wooden frames, about two inches high, which you can stack on top of each other. But if you want to stack several dryers on top of each other, you need a source of heat under them, like a lukewarm wooden stove or an electric heater.

Air drying. Many plants can be dried at regular room temperature both indoors and outdoors. Choose a warm, dry, and preferably dark place with plenty of circulation. This method is suitable for green leaves and herbs, spices, sliced apples, and mushrooms.

You either spread what you want to dry on a paper without ink, a basket tray, or dryer, or you can attach slices of fruit or mushrooms to threads or sticks that you hang in the air (see picture on p. 23).

The drying rack with baskets of several different heights is both beautiful and practical. It is easy to fold together when the season is over. The other drying rack on the picture is easily created by hanging two coarse strings with a knot at the end. Mark with a pen every four inches. Place regular flower pot sticks at the markings or tie open knots where the flower pot sticks should be attached.

Wooden oven. Place the dryers or the basket on double bricks on a not-too-hot wooden oven and leave without adding more wood to the fire.

Oven drying. A convection oven is ideal for drying. To dry in a regular oven is too energy-consuming, and there is a large risk of cooking the product instead of drying it, since the circulation is poor.

Sun drying. On dry and sunny days, you can dry outside, preferably on a hot balcony. Be careful to take your food inside when the air starts getting cold and moist at night.

Harvest

All plants contain different amounts of water depending on how high the humidity is when they are harvested. That makes the drying time varied. It is best to harvest on a dry and sunny day at noon, preferably a few days after rain when the plants are cleaned of dust. Only use high-quality products for drying. Pick young leaves off wild herbs and plants, since the flavor gets more bitter the bigger the leaves are.

All green leafy vegetables, herbs, spices, and mushrooms should be dried until they are thoroughly dry and easily crumble. Root vegetables should be dried until they are really hard. Fruit rich in sugars, like pears, apples, and plums, on the other hand, should not be dried too hard. They are done when they have a chewy, leather-like texture.

Tip! In the beginning, it is better to dry too long than vice versa. If there is any moisture left in the vegetables, they can turn moldy while storing them. Cut a slice of the dried product and check the color in the middle. If it is darker in the middle, it means it could still have fluids in it.

Storing

Most products shrink to about one-third of their original size, and that way they will not take up a lot of space when storing. Dried food can be stored at room temperature. Dried products need to be protected against moisture and pests. If the air is moist, the dried material will absorb moisture again, the vitamin content will decrease faster, and the product will deteriorate.

Package the dried foods in small packages in a size that is easy to consume right after opening. Use jars with air-tight screw-caps or small paper bags. Package the dried food very tightly and try to press out as much air as possible. Carefully tape the bag and label it with the contents and date. Place one or more bags in a bigger plastic bag or a large jar with a lid. Close the bag or jar carefully.

When it comes to wild plants and spice herbs, the aroma is better kept if you store the leaves as whole as possible. Fill a jar or a paper bag with leaves but do not press them together. If you use paper bags, you can place several small bags in a bigger plastic bag that is carefully sealed.

Store dried goods in the dark or use brown paper bags or colored glass jars. The ideal storage place is dark, cool, and dry. Packaged and stored in the right way dried vegetables, mushrooms, fruit, and berries can stay fresh for many years.

Drying vegetables and herbs

Spices and wild herbs should be dried indoors or in the shade. Package the plants as soon as they are dry since the aroma quickly disappears. For the same reason, you should not store spice herbs longer than a year.

Pull the leaves off the stems and spread them wide apart on clean paper without ink or dirt. Stir it around from time to time. Spices can also be dried in the shape of small bouquets that are hung on a taut string, a curtain rod, or similar.

Tip! Save leaves from celery and parsnip and use as a spice.

Flowers. Dried petals from marigolds, roses, and malva are beautiful and give a nice aroma to tea. Sprinkle dried marigold over food. Spread the petals on trays or dryers and leave to dry in a warm place for about one day.

Mushrooms. Most mushrooms have a richer and better taste after drying, like chanterelles, yellowfoot, porcino, and boletales, especially velvet boletes. Many dried mushrooms—in particular, velvet boletes, black trumpets, parasol mushroom's, and even regular sheep polypores—are fantastic to use as spices if you mix them to a powder. Only a small amount of the mushroom's powder gives a nice flavor to sauces, soups, and stews.

Dry mushrooms, like chanterelles, can be strung on thread or placed on dryers or trays. Shred big chanterelles lengthwise. They dry in a few days in a warm place. Stir occasionally.

Thick mushrooms can be cut in slices or pieces and are preferably dried at 104°F for 5 to 6 hours.

When cooking: Let the dried mushroom soak 10 to 15 minutes in lukewarm water before cooking. A ½ cup dried mushroom should be soaked in 1.5 to 2 cups water and is equivalent to 0.75 to 1 quarts fresh mushrooms.

Leeks, as well as yellow and red onions are shredded or sliced and dried in 95 to 113°F for about 5 hours. From yellow onions, you can make a useful onion powder. Mix the dry onion together with different spices and possibly celery leaves. This way you can create different kinds of herb spices.

When cooking: Let the onion boil in water a couple of minutes and then soak 10 to 15 minutes when cooking.

Spinach, chard, lettuce, and leaves of beetroots should be dried at 95°F for about 3 hours. Shred larger leaves and remove all the larger nerves.

When cooking: Let the dried leaves soak for 5 to 10 minutes in boiling water before cooking.

Cucumbers, bell peppers, small squash, and tomatoes are cut in thin slices or strips and should be dried at 112°F for 6 to 10 hours. Mix with dried paprika and/or tomato to spice it up.

Parboiling. All other vegetables and root vegetables, like beans and peas, should be parboiled before drying. The parboiling makes the vegetables dry faster and they stay fresh longer.

Cut vegetables and root vegetables in slices, sticks, and pieces or grate them coarsely. Parboil them in plenty of boiling water with salt for ½ to 2 minutes. Do not boil the vegetables too long. They should still be chewy. Rinse with cold water and let them drain in a colander.

Spread the parboiled vegetables over dryers and dry for 4–5 hours at 104 to 122°F.

When cooking: Boil all root vegetables and vegetables for 2 to 5 minutes in water and let soak for 5 minutes.

Drying fruit and berries

Only dry high-quality fruit and berries. They should not be overripe since they ripen during the drying process. The finest aroma and the highest nutritional value is right under the peel, which makes it unnecessary to peel the fruit before drying.

All dried fruit and berries, especially strawberries, turn out very tasty and can be used as candy. They also give a good aroma and sweetness to dessert and tea. The taste becomes sweeter and the aroma richer after the drying process.

Apples. Winter fruits give the best result in both flavor and durability. The aroma is improved if the fruit is allowed to mature a couple of weeks after harvest. Apples dried at home do not turn out as light in color as the ones you buy. Packaged dried apples are treated with sulfur.

If you dip the apple slices quickly in salted water, 1 tsp for 1 quart of water, they remain relatively light.

Apples can be cut in slices or in pieces and dried on dryers or strung onto a strong string or thin sticks. If you want apple circles, you remove the core with a special core remover. Cores can also be dried to make a good fruit tea. Apple rings are usually dry after 3 to 4 days at room temperature.

Citrus fruit. Sliced oranges, lemons, and limes should be dried in a dehydrator, but they can also be strung onto a string and dried above a heat source. They will dry within a few days. The lemon slices are beautiful as decoration and give a lovely taste to tea, drinks, and desserts.

Cherries, whole or seeded, are dried at 104 to 122°F for about 15 hours.

Pears are dried in pieces or wedges at 122°F for 5 to 6 hours.

Plums are cut in halves and seeded. Large plums are cut into slices and dried at about 122°F for 10 to 12 hours.

Blueberries, lingonberries, and currants are dried at 104 to 122°F for about 15 hours.

Strawberries, raspberries, and wild strawberries can be sliced, halved, or cut into smaller pieces and dried preferably in 122°F heat for 8 to 9 hours.

Rosehip is halved, but don't take out the seeds. Dry them in 122°F heat for 6 to 8 hours.

FREEZING

Freezing is an easy way to store food for a long time. The deep freezing process stops microbial development. Despite the cold, the rancidity process with atmospheric oxygen continues, though at a much slower rate than normal. During freezing, there will be no major loss of nutritional value but any parboiling before making the water-soluble nutrients will cause some of them to be left behind in the water. The cold allows food cells to rupture, and that texture rapidly deteriorates after thawing. Well-packaged and frozen goods have high shelf durability. Vegetables, fruits, and berries can last in the freezer about one year.

Freezing Tips:
- Rapid freezing at low temperatures, at least 213°F (225°C), gives the best results. Typical storage temperatures are 20.4°F (218°C).
- To facilitate rapid freezing, it is helpful to make the packages airy and not freeze too much at once.

Vegetables. Unless the vegetables will be consumed relatively quickly, they should be parboiled prior to freezing. By parboiling food, it prevents the enzymes from altering the flavor.

The process begins by blanching the vegetables in plenty of water. Immerse them in a colander or muslin in boiling water, see parboiling times, and then cool the vegetables quickly, preferably under cold running water. Wrap them when they have cooled and freeze immediately. It is important that the freezer packs are tight enough so that moisture does not escape from the food.

Parboiling Times

1–2 minutes
cauliflower, small florets
small green beans
cut string beans
small peas
whole leaf spinach

3–4 minutes
cauliflower, large florets
broccoli
brussels sprouts
diced kohlrabi
carrots, whole
diced carrots
asparagus, whole
wax beans

5–6 minutes
cauliflower, whole
corn cobs
new potatoes

All herbs, peppers, and horseradish are best without parboiling. Roots such as horseradish, turmeric, and ginger are best if you freeze them peeled, but in whole pieces. When you later use the root, grate it once it has been thawed.

Chopped herbs should be stored compressed in small freezer containers made of plastic.

Berries and fruit can be frozen without sugar. Strawberries and other berries retain flavor best if they are frozen throughout. If you want to pour in syrup, you can sweeten with honey or agave syrup.

Juice of chokeberry (aronia) or black and red currants can be frozen into single portions. Use a chinois or a juice extractor and distribute juice in small ice cube molds. Freeze the juice quickly and then pack the frozen cubes together in freezer bags.

An aware consumer

There are many who care about their own health and that of the planet's. Today, it is more important than ever to have the knowledge to choose pure and healthy food. It is impossible to eat food that is completely free of toxins in today's contaminated world. Many toxins, pesticides, heavy metals, and dioxins are spread all around the world. Food additives and bioengineered and irradiated food are also a concern.

IN RECENT YEARS, the health concerns surrounding food additives and trans fat have been heavily debated and questioned. The Swedish national food agency has approved about 320 additives. According to KRAV, there is scientific proof that only 32 of the additives are completely harmless. Out of these 32 additives, most come from nature—like E 162, which consists of natural color from beetroot.

Choosing KRAV-approved products is an easy and good way to avoid harmful additives in your food. The most questioned additives are the sweeteners Aspartame E 951, Cyclamate E 952, and Sucralose; flavor enhancer glutamate, especially Monosodium glutamate E 621; AZO-compounds and soy lecithin.

When it comes to trans fat, the EU is working to set new regulations to lower the levels of trans fat in food. In reality, there is still ambiguity, and trans fat may still be found in fried food, crackers, and cookies.

PESTICIDES, IRRADIATION, GENETICALLY MODIFIED FOOD

Pesticides can give a cocktail effect. There are about 450 registered products to fight weeds and pests in Sweden alone. Conventionally grown fruit is sprayed often with pesticides; for example, our best-selling potato King Edward is sprayed 8 to 14 times just for late blight. In banana plantations in Costa Rica, 97 pounds of pesticides are used per every 2.5 acres each year.

Even if a product is forbidden in Sweden, like the anti-mold agent carbendazim, it can frequently be found in imported goods like orange juice since it is still approved in the EU. Carbendazim has mutagenic properties and can cause fetal and reproductive changes.

Tests for residual pesticides in vegetables are regularly done. The tolerance values for residual pesticides usually exceed maximum limits in 3 to 5 percent of the tests. The values for remaining pesticides are generally considerably lower in Swedish food than in imported food.

The most serious risk for pesticides is in food from tropical countries.

Different types of pesticides are frequently found in many products. Trace amounts are usually low and below the standard set by the EU. However, many scientists deem there to be a risk of a "cocktail effect," a collected effect that has a greater impact than one single pesticide has. The national food agency of the EU is researching this, but there is still no good model for doing a risk assessment when it comes to the cocktail effect.

Genetically modified food. "Genetically modified" means that you change the genome in plants and thus change their attributes. This is called genetically modifying or manipulating (GMO) a plant.

The most common reason to genetically modify plants is to make them more resistant to chemical pesticides and insects. Economic interests are the main reason for doing this.

Nobody knows if genetically modified plants can have negative effects on humans, animals, and plants in the long run. What happens if GMO plants are crossed with regular plants growing next to them and genetically manipulated genes are spread in all of nature?

The most genetically modified crops in the world are soy, corn, rapeseed, cotton, and rice. So far, the EU has approved sales of genetically modified corn, soy, and rapeseed, but it has to be labeled on the product. But there are exceptions: If the product contains less than 1 percent of genetically modified material, the product does not need to be labeled. Nor is it necessary to indicate that an animal ate GMO feed.

According to the Swedish national food agency's report "GMO project 2002," almost a third of 44 investigated raw materials in Sweden contained GMO materials. Studies on 68 ready-made products from the grocery store showed that GMO materials could be found in almost 20 percent of the products. KRAV-labeled products are not genetically modified.

Dioxins, which occur in processes in paper and metal factories and incineration, have had a very large spread in nature and can be found all over the world. The name stands for polychlorinated dibenzodioxins (PCDD) and polychlorinated dibenzofurans (PCDF). There are over 200 known compounds. This group includes a few compounds that are extremely toxic.

Dioxins that gather in fat tissue are carcinogens and inhibit the immune system. Fish rich in fat, like herring, are the largest source of dioxins. Crab, lobster, and crayfish butter also contain high levels of dioxins. Smaller amounts are found in dairy products.

Breast milk also contains dioxins. Although the baby has a large intake relative to its weight, the advantages of breast milk are considered to outweigh the disadvantages. Dieting while breastfeeding is ill-advised as it raises the levels of dioxins in the mother's milk.

Phthalates are emollients that are used in PVC plastic. More than 2.5 million tons of phthalates are produced every year in the world and used for plastic articles, packaging, toys, car seats, waterproof shoes, body and hair products, and so on. Phthalates have been largely debated since they can have an effect on the reproductive ability as well as on the kidneys, lungs, and liver. In 1999, the EU forbid the use of phthalates in toys and products for children under three years old.

When it comes to food, the PVC plastic wrapping is mostly used in grocery store packaging, and then the phthalates are transmitted to fatty foods like cheese and grilled meat. Plastic labeled with a glass and a fork or the words "food" shows that the material is safe to use with food.

Radioactive decay that was spread into the atmosphere by the winds after the Chernobyl accident in 1986 caused increased levels of cesium in freshwater fish, meat from wild animals, wild berries, and mushrooms from locally stricken areas. Sweden was mostly affected in the area around Gävle and the northern parts of the country.

Different kinds of fish, berries, and mushrooms absorbed cesium in varying degrees. Porcinoand *Agaricus* mushrooms had low levels, while, for example, chanterelles absorbed large amounts. During the years, the levels have dropped, but increased levels are still expected to be found in reindeer meat and freshwater fish in stricken areas. According to the national food agency's research, most food today contains very low amounts of cesium.

Many cleaning detergents, body and hair products, and cosmetics that are used daily in our households can contain subtle toxins; for example, deodorants and medication can contain aluminum. Everything that we breathe in or have skin contact with goes right into the body.

Many hair products are based on mineral oils that come from the petroleum industry. They clog the pores of the skin cells and reduce the skin's ability to breathe. Nail polish and nail polish remover contain strong chemicals. The list is long. Health food stores have several environmentally friendly alternatives.

TOXIC METALS

Cadmium is naturally present in varying levels in our soils. However, the cadmium content is increasing due to acidic atmospheric deposition, contaminated fertilizer, and sewage sludge. Cadmium is present in most food, particularly liver, kidneys, crab, and wheat. The snowball mushroom and the prince mushroom can also contain very high levels. Cigarette smoke contains very large amounts of cadmium. Smokers are calculated to have about double the amount of cadmium in their organs compared to nonsmokers.

Cadmium causes damage to the bones, brain cells, and liver, but especially to the kidneys. It takes a very long time for the body to break down the poison. The metal is mostly stored in the kidneys and parts of the intestinal track.

Mercury accumulates in the body and can damage the central nervous system. Today, dental amalgam (mercury alloy) is no longer used by dentists. But there are many who still have old amalgam fillings in their teeth. High levels of mercury can be found in our bays, lakes, and waters because of emissions from the logging and cellulose industries. This causes fish to sometimes contain large amounts of mercury.

As a result, the Swedish Food Administration advises pregnant and nursing women to not eat tuna, pike, zander, burbot, eel, and the Atlantic halibut.

Lead is ubiquitous in the environment—in air, soil, and water. The spread of lead has been reduced because we use unleaded gasoline today. Lead can also be found in food, but in low concentrations. Lead can cause damage to the central nervous system. Fetuses and small children are particularly susceptible.

Be careful with lead-glazed pottery. Acidic food may precipitate the lead during storage in glazed ceramics. Stoneware, on the other hand, is burned at such high temperatures that no lead can precipitate. Crystal glasses also contain lead, and the amount can increase significantly if you store drinks in crystal decanters.

Tin is present in low levels in food. In the past, Sweden obtained most of it's tin from the United States through imported tin cans, but today all cans are varnished. However, we should not store food in open tin cans since tin can be released. A high intake of tin can cause nausea, vomiting, and diarrhea but does not cause any chronic damage.

Aluminum can be found naturally in our soil. The more the acidification is spread out, the more the metal is released. This causes the levels of aluminum to increase in both plants and groundwater. The intake of metal also can increase if acid food is dried and kept in aluminum pans.

NATURALLY OCCURRING TOXINS

Mold spores exist everywhere in our environment and even in our food. Depending on the product's aging, temperature, pH, and oxygen availability, mold spores may begin to grow and form a network of threads, known as mycelium. Usually it looks like off-white fluff, but it can also be green, black, and blue. These spores can produce toxic compounds known as mycotoxins.

The most dangerous mold toxin is aflatoxins that can damage your liver and cause liver cancer if you eat a high dosage. Aflatoxin is almost exclusively found in imported foods, such as rice, nuts (peanuts, especially, can be moldy in the middle), corn, figs, and melons that grow in tropical countries.

Generally you should avoid eating any moldy food at all, especially discolored and shriveled nuts and fruit—most of all, figs. For small mold infestations on fresh fruit and cheese, it is OK to eat if you cut off the mold with a good margin. When heating and baking, mold spores can be killed, but most mold toxins can withstand high heat and remain in the cooked food, such as jam or juice, if it became moldy.

Nitrate is normally found in plants. It is a necessary part of the circulation of the plant. Nitrate can react with other substances, such as amino acids, and convert to carcinogen nitrosamines in the human gastrointestinal tract or, for instance, if cooked spinach is left out for too long at room temperature.

Lower your nitrate intake

- Eat C and E vitamin-rich vegetables. Nitrosamine formation is inhibited by vitamins C and E.
- Do not store spinach stew or cooked beetroots at room temperature.
- Cool down the dish immediately after cooking if it is not eaten at once.
- Also cool down any leftovers directly after the meal, and then store them in the refrigerator.
- When parboiling, you should pour off the boiling water and immediately cool the vegetables with cold water.
- Do not give vegetables that are rich in nitrates to children under six months. Infants have special intestinal bacteria that accelerates the conversion of nitrate to nitrite.

The more fertilized the soil is, the more nitrate is formed in the plant. Alternatively, according to an EU survey, organically cultivated vegetables only contain about half as much nitrate as conventionally grown ones, since they do not have easy access to nitrogen from fertilizers. However, nitrate is also found in wild plants that have not been fertilized—for example, stinging nettles.

All green leaves contain moderate to high amounts of nitrate, especially beetroots, spinach, chard, nettles, and goosefoot. Nitrate concentration is the highest after periods of bad weather and as autumn approaches with shorter days. Preferably harvest what you believe to be nitrate-rich vegetables in the afternoon and after a period of sunny weather; that gives the plant time to convert the nitrogen.

Oxalic acid is a by-product of photosynthesis and can be found naturally in plants. It binds calcium in an insoluble compound that prevents the intake of calcium. However, excessive amounts of oxalic acid may cause kidney damage and a special form of anemia. Rhubarb, goosefoot, spinach, chard, and sorrel usually contain high doses of oxalic acid. When parboiling, most of the water-soluble oxalic acid is left in the boiling water.

Normal consumption of vegetables does not significantly affect our calcium supply. But it is good to offset the oxalic acid in a meal by also eating something rich in calcium, such as dairy products, tofu, sesame, or sunflower seeds.

Good advice

Clean water. Throughout history, water has been considered a source of life energy. Austrian Viktor Schauberger (1885–1958) studied the movement of patterns in streams and found that the cycloidal spiral movement that comes from the outside and moves inwardly toward the center of motion works to oxygenate the water. This is a life-giving cycle, whereas water flowing in ordinary pipes has a destructive movement that makes water lose its vitality.

Water filters constructed following Schauberger's theories can be purchased today. When regular pipe water is refined in this way, the water is revitalized and gives us life energy. In addition, the "living water" facilitates the kidney's work. There are also nice natural water sources with "living water" in many places in the country where you can collect water.

Since our bodies consist mostly of fluid and we need to drink 1.5 to 2 quarts of water per day, it is important that the water we drink be of good quality. The more the acidification spreads and the lower the pH levels, the more metals, such as aluminum, are absorbed by the water. Water may also contain high levels of radon, iron, and manganese. Water often contains copper that leaks out from old pipes. Test the water you drink and buy a filter if needed. There are many good solutions, whether you live in an apartment or in a house. If you have municipal water, it contains chloride that will disappear if you let the water stand in a carafe.

Tip! Do not use warm water from the faucet for cooking or drinking. Let the water run from the faucet for a few minutes before using it.

Be an aware consumer!
- Read the contents of packaged food and minimize the intake of food and drinks with synthetic sugar, additives, and color agents.
- Buy mostly labeled organic products.
- Use glass, porcelain, stoneware, and stainless steel in your household. Avoid plastic and aluminum.
- Use natural household products like soap, tooth paste, and environmentally friendly detergents. Use smaller amounts.
- Choose natural and environmentally friendly body and hair products and cosmetics.
- Use natural pesticides, compost, and cut-grass natural fertilizer in the garden.

Our inner doctor

When we give ourselves and our bodies what we need—love, a good night's sleep, positive thoughts, harmony, a stimulating social life, nutritional food, and enough fluids—the body has a chance to heal itself. The healing force of nature is immense and our "inner doctor" always strives to keep the body in balance.

WE ALL WANT TO FEEL GOOD and live our lives to the fullest. Most people know how they should live, but the difficult part is actually leading your life in a positive direction. Most of us feel burdened by all "musts" that make you feel like time is never enough.

Luckily it is enough to make one small positive change in your life, like deciding to take a brisk walk every day. This will in turn generate impulses to continually add good habits to your routine, resulting in a positive cycle. The important thing is to do something you enjoy doing. It is the small changes that eventually lead to permanent results.

We need to train ourselves to listen to our inner voices and create a connection with ourselves. At all times, we should ask ourselves what strengthens us and what takes energy away from us. It is important to avoid what steals energy from us.

We need to develop what strengthens us and treat ourselves by doing things we like. Or maybe allow ourselves to just "be" and not do anything at all.

What we do is not very important. The important thing is that it feels good for us and gives us joy and well-being.

Carpe diem! Seize the day!

ENJOY YOUR BODY

Think about the enthusiastic life power, energy, and curiosity that all children have. They really enjoy being in their bodies. What happens while growing up that causes us to all of a sudden start considering out bodies to be stiff and "annoying"?

The more we move, the more endorphins and other substances are formed that make us happier. Our bodies are built for movement and hugs. Without movement, the body clogs up, muscles atrophy, and skeletons turn brittle.

Exercising in all forms and physical touch builds and strengthens the whole body, as well as the heart and immune system. The best exercise is the one we enjoy doing, like dancing, garden work, riding a bicycle, swimming, or playing. Try to take advantage of all the free exercise you can get, like taking the stairs instead of the elevator, or biking or walking to work.

The power of thought

Often we spend too much time worrying about what will happen in the future or brooding about what already happened. Often we are too busy with everything else and and do not think about what is happening right now. All the thoughts we think and all information from the outside affect us either positively or negatively. Positive thoughts increase serotonin levels. That makes us feel happier and the whole body functions better.

Negative thoughts cause the body to produce stress hormones. That means that if we keep feeding ourselves negative information, our inner selves are affected by the message, whether we like it or not.

*If you want to know what your
thoughts were yesterday,
look at your body today.
If you want to know what your body
will be like tomorrow,
look at your thoughts today.*
—Old Indian proverb

Train yourself in thinking as positively as possible. Positive thoughts are nutrients for the soul. When a negative thought comes to mind, turn it to its opposite. Eventually you will achieve a positive thought pattern that makes you feel much better. Learning techniques in mindfulness helps us to not think too much about the things behind us and live in the present. (Also see reference list, p. 339.)

Rest in yourself

We are all exposed to stress. Sometimes it is caused by too little stimulation but often it is because we have too much to do. Sometimes stress is good. We get a energy kick, which in turn makes it possible for us to "step on the gas" in a very demanding situation.

But when we constantly walk around and feel stressed, we are only burning out our bodies.

When we feel stressed, the body produces the stress hormones adrenaline and cortisol. Cortisol controls the fat storage in the abdomen area and that increases the risk of obesity.

Adrenaline demands more oxygen, and that can lead to oxygen deficiency. When we feel stressed, our breathing is less deep and the oxygen supply is even worse. In general, our breaths are too shallow in the West. Oxygen is the fuel for your body's energy production (ATP). If the body does not get enough oxygen, it cannot function like it should; as a result, we can get headaches, have problems sleeping, and become chronically tired.

When you have been in a big hurry
you have to stop and wait for your soul.
—Chinese proverb

It is important to be aware of the fact that most times stress is something that is created inside of ourselves and not outside of us. If you expose different people to the exact same situation, some are enormously stressed and others not all. Eating food that isn't nutritious, smoking, some medication, sugar, dehydration, too much caffeine, and alcohol also put our bodies through stress.

Throughout the ages, people have used herbs for different conditions. Adaptogens is a generic name for generally strengthening, performance-enhancing, and stress-reducing herbs like Siberian ginseng, schisandra, roseroot, and ginseng. Adaptogens supports the body's self-healing ability and have no harmful side effects whatsoever if you follow the recommendations.

Take control over your life!

Do not feel like a victim. Take control of your life instead:

- Practice taking long and deep breaths with the diaphragm. If you breathe deeply, it is difficult to get stressed.
- Practice thinking positive. It is our thoughts that stress us the most. Do not worry about all possible problems. Encourage yourself: "This will work out," instead of "This will never work out."

- See possible problems as challenges where you can learn and change something.
- Also think about how we never make any mistakes but only learn new experiences.
- Take a break sometimes!
- Relax directly after a stressed situation. Breathe deeply, meditate, rest, close your eyes, or take a walk. Five minutes can do miracles. It is better to take a five-minute break and think clearly than remain stressed and not be able to think at all.
- Demand less from yourself. Separate what has to be done now from what is less important. Learn to say NO. Be happy about what has been done instead of being stressed about what is not done yet.
- Make a time plan about what has to be done today, a week plan, and a plan for the future. Only spend energy on what has to be done right now. Only do one thing at a time and finish it before you start something new.

We do not make any mistakes. We only gain experiences!

Relaxation

After any tension, whether physical or mental, we need relaxation. This is obtained by sleeping and resting. But many of us have such intense bodily stress that sleep does not give enough rest. Tense muscles can be the cause of headaches as well as aches in muscles and joints.

To wake up in the morning and feel energetic and well rested is wonderful. It is something everyone should get a chance to experience. But unfortunately more and more people suffer from insomnia. We can never escape the fact that our bodies act the same way that they have for thousands of years. We have to accept that our bodies have not kept up with the technological development.

If we turn the day around, the whole biochemistry in our body will be off balance. If we stay up all night and are surrounded with light, not enough of the sleep hormone melatonin is produced, which results in trouble falling asleep.

Melatonin comes from the pineal gland that controls our circadian rhythm. Evening darkness stimulates the melatonin production and when the light comes in the morning the production is lowered and we wake up.

Melatonin can be naturally found in oats, pearl barley, rice, corn, ginger, tomatoes, and bananas. Stress, smoking, alcohol, too much caffeine, big meals at night, and strong electromagnetic fields, like from a clock radio near the bed, negatively affect the production.

Meditation

In addition to enough rest and sleep, we can achieve relaxation through meditation. The basic idea behind meditation is to free your senses from spinning thoughts and reach a state of consciousness beyond thought. Regular meditation lowers the levels of stress and improves sleep. Also the levels of the "youth hormone" DHEA increase.

Meditation can be done in many different ways. In old farming culture, people would normally sit and relax in the dusk after a hard day's work. It was and is a form of meditation. Some people meditate when they walk in nature, work in the garden, or listen to music. There are

different meditation techniques to learn. Other things that bring relaxation and harmony are qigong, yoga, and deep breathing.

Nobody escapes aging, but there are no reasons to age prematurely. Even in old age we can keep our vitality, flexibility, strength, hair color, and sexual appetite.

We have seven glands in our body that affect most of our bodily functions. All glands are connected to each other and affect each other if one or several glands are out of balance. Nothing affects the glands so negatively as stress does. Excessive weight and age also affect the glands' productivity in a negative way.

Enough sleep, meditation, yoga, qigong as well as regular exercise and a diet rich in minerals and micronutrients stimulate the glands' function.

Our glands

- **Ovaries and testicles** give energy to all the glands. They also control the sex steroids, reproduction, and sexual activity. A good way to stimulate these glands is to do "pelvic floor exercises" several times a day.

- **Adrenal glands** help the kidneys, skin, bone marrow, and spine to work like they should. The adrenal glands also produce DHEA, dehydroepiandrosterone, which many scientists call the "youth hormone." DHEA strengthens the immune system and increases the levels of endorphin.

  Many scientists think that DHEA also prevents cancer, heart disease, and decomposition of bone and skin structure. In addition, DHEA is believed to protect the brain's ability to work and thus prevents Alzheimer's disease and dementia. Regular exercise and meditation increase the levels of DHEA. To stimulate the adrenal glands, make sure the body is kept warm and massage daily around the area of the kidneys.

- **The pancreas** controls the body temperature, digestion, and blood sugar levels. Eating regularly and moderately sized meals, as well as a diet with a low GI, facilitates the work of the pancreas. Being overweight, as well as having high blood sugar and insulin levels, induces inflammation in the pancreas that contributes to aging.

- **The thymus** is important to make the heart, circulation, and immune system work properly. There is a spot on the breast bone between the breasts, at the height of the nipples, that you can stimulate daily by pressing on the sensitive spot. If the spot is sore, the thymus is not working like it should.

- **The thyroid gland** controls metabolism and cell growth. If you massage both sides of the larynx every day, the thyroid gland is balanced.

- **The pineal gland** is placed between the eyes in the middle of the head and controls the circadian rhythm. According to Taoists, the pineal gland is the body's spiritual and mental center.

- **The pituitary gland** is located in the brain and controls other glands, but it is also connected to intelligence and memory.

Eat according to the seasons

In order for our body to function optimally, the body temperature should be 98.6°F. It is especially important that the stomach be warm enough to be able to digest food properly. When we eat food that is cold from the refrigerator and drink water with ice throughout the meal, the whole stomach and genitals are cooled down and you can even start to freeze.

It is actually strange that people in cold climate often eat cold yogurt and drink ice-cold drinks all year round, while people in Asian countries with a considerably warmer climate always eat warm food. In Japan, miso soup is often eaten for breakfast and hot green tea is drunk with meals.

The Chinese qigong master PU Gang has, after 15 years in Sweden, noticed that Swedes often have a weakened kidney function that is negatively affected by both outer and inner cold. Unbalanced kidney function makes it, according to Chinese medicine, difficult for Swedes to digest the fluid they drink and that causes them to become swollen and create fluid build-ups

Live young longer!
We have seven glands in the body that affect most of our bodily functions. Enough sleep and rest, meditation, yoga, and qigong, as well as regular exercise and a diet rich in minerals and micronutrients, stimulates the glands' functions.

in their bodies. Swedes can also suffer from lowered sleep quality which in turn makes them constantly tired. Besides that, they can suffer from constipation, bad hearing, tinnitus, bladder problems, menstrual problems, a less active sex drive, and a difficulty becoming pregnant.

The Chinese say that "kidneys dominates the skeleton and manifest in the hair on your head." That means that an unbalanced kidney function lowers the quality of hair, skeleton, and teeth. The risk for brittle bones (osteoporosis) can, in other words, increase. People in the Nordic countries have one of the world's largest intake of limestone and dairy products, but at the same time have the highest frequency of brittle bones. In China, this disease is very rare.

To stimulate kidney function:
- Massage the kidney area (lower back) every day.
- Make sure the body is warm, especially the lower back, stomach, and genitals, by wearing warm clothes and eating food that is room temperature or warmer.
- Drink plenty of water at room temperature or more preferably, warm water. Take in about 1.5 to 2 quarts a day. It is easier for the kidneys to digest spring water or revitalized water.
- If you have sensitive kidneys, you should also avoid standing still for too long.

"Pehle et pooja-phir kaam dooja."
(First take care of your stomach, then everything else.)

—*Indian proverb*

A healthy intestinal environment is the Alpha and Omega

In a healthy bowel, there are thousands of billions of useful bacteria, and they fill several important functions. Among other things, they produce vitamin K, folic acid, and choline and activate the immune system. About 70 percent of the immune system's condition depends on the intestinal bacteria. If we have a healthy GI, it is likely that the risk of colorectal cancer is reduced. The useful bowel bacteria prevent infectious farm bacteria and heal inflammations in the intestinal mucous.

Water-soluble fiber functions as food to useful bacteria in the large intestine, like lactobacilli and bifidobacteria, and are important for a healthy and strong gut flora. Treatments with antibiotics and stress, on the other hand, reduce the number of healthy bowel bacteria.

Water-soluble fibers are found mostly in fruit, oats, and artichokes. Especially important fibers are found in beans and artichokes. If you eat beans and artichokes and then suffer from problems with gas, it is probably because your gut flora are not functioning like they should. Lactic acid bacteria start working and growing, and our stomachs will feel upset and swollen and we have gas. One suggestion is to eat bowel bacteria supplements.

When we are constipated, the intestinal contents stay for too long in the bowel, and harmful decomposing bacteria grow. If unwanted bacteria outnumber the good ones, it is usually shown by gas, stomach ache, and diarrhea. In addition to lack of dietary fiber, constipation can be caused by dehydration and stress.

Even if you have regular defecation every day, it does not guarantee that the bowel is working like it should. If a long pipe is filled in one end, an equivalent amount must sooner or later come out the other end.

The easiest way to control your bowel function is to eat a good portion of something that colors the waste—for example, beetroots. Within 24 hours the red-colored waste should have come out.

Tips for upset stomachs:
- Make sure that the intestinal bacteria are balanced. Eat lactic acid vegetables and eat supplements with lactic acid bacteria sometimes.
- Chew the food properly! Digestion starts in your mouth. In the saliva there is amylase, which is an enzyme that starts the digestion of carbohydrates.
- Enjoy your food and do not eat overly large meals, especially not at night.
- Many people with a sensitive stomach feel better if they do not eat fruit together with cooked food.
- Vinegar, lemon juice, bitter lettuce, artichoke, ginger, chili, cinnamon, pineapples, or papayas stimulate the digestion.
- Drink lemon water with your food.
- Anise, fennel, and savory reduces the production of gas.

Gluten intolerance

Celiac disease or gluten intolerance means that you are intolerant to gluten that can be found in the grains wheat, rye, and barley. The gluten found in oats has a different structure and recent recommendations say that oats can be included in a gluten-free diet for adults. Rice, corn, millet, amaranth, quinoa, and buckwheat are also gluten-free.

Gluten causes the mucous in the small intestine to become completely or partly inflamed, and you lose intestinal villi. The damaged bowel does not function normally and causes a deficiency of iron, zinc, limestone, and folic acid. One child out of every 250 has celiac disease. Among adults, the number is one out of 500. The actual frequency of gluten intolerance is probably greater.

Symptoms of gluten intolerance: mostly diarrhea, weight loss, gas, and stomach problems. Tiredness, irritability, depression, low levels of hemoglobin as well as skeleton, muscle, and skin problems can be caused by gluten intolerance. When you exclude gluten from your diet, all problems disappear, but the intolerance is still there.

Lactose intolerance

Intolerance to milk and dairy products can be caused by an intolerance for milk protein or by the lack of an enzyme that breaks down milk sugar.

Most people who are lactose-intolerant can eat fermented milk products and aged cheese, where the milk sugar has already been broken down. Many immigrants lack this enzyme. Symptoms of lactose intolerance include stomach ache and long-lasting diarrhea.

Stressed stomachs

More and more people suffer from problems with their stomachs, like gas, aches, and alternating constipation and diarrhea. The reason could be sensitivity to food or lactose and gluten intolerance, but the cause is often stress, lack of dietary fiber, irregular food habits, or not enough physical activity. If you suspect that you are intolerant, get headaches, tiredness, or stomach problems from some type of food, you can exclude that particular food from your diet for 3 to 4 weeks and see if you feel better. Foods that often cause intolerance are sugar, dairy products, wheat, citrus fruits, eggs, peanuts, and hazelnuts.

Enjoy the food!

To eat good food is one of life's big highlights. We often spend time with friends over a meal.

As important as the meal being beautiful, good, and nutritious is enjoying it in a nice and relaxed company. Only then can we talk about true food joy and health. If you have little time and feel stressed, it is better to drink a couple of smoothies than "gorging" food under stress.

To get into the right mood at a beautifully set dinner with flowers and candlelight during the weekend is easy. But it is equally important to enjoy the weekday meals. If someone at the table is feeling stressed and eats the food in a hurry, answers the phone, watches TV, or discusses serious problems, the meals end up being stressful. Light candles and set the table nicely even if it is a weekday meal. Play calm music in the background and enjoy the food.

What happens when you eat?

Digestion works the most effectively during the day. At night, the body sets itself to rest and sleep mode, and digestion is slowed down.

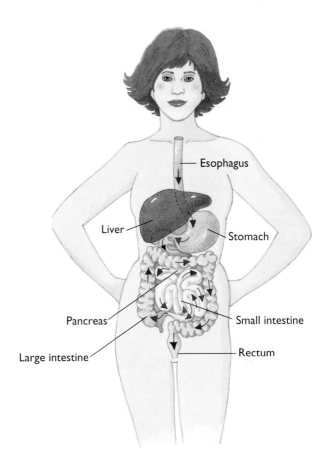

The food is decomposed in the mouth mechanically by chewing and chemically through enzymes, which start the decomposing of carbohydrates to monosaccharides. It continues to pass through the esophagus, which is 10 to 12 inches long.

The stomach, which fits 1 to 1.5 quarts, continues to decompose the food mechanically through muscles contractions, and chemically through gastric acid, which contains gastric and hydrochloric acid, which make the stomach contents sour and make bacteria passive. Enzymes start the digestion of proteins.

The liver has many functions in the body. It transforms or stores many substances, like glucose, some vitamins, minerals, and fatty acids, and takes care of most toxins and harmful substances.

The gallbladder contains bile that is emptied into the small intestine and dissolves fat.

The pancreas that is located in the duodenum secretes pancreatic juice with enzymes.

The gland produces insulin and glycogen that regulates the glucose metabolism.

The small intestine is 13 to 19 feet long. Its upper part is known as the duodenum. There the food is mixed with bile from the liver, pancreatic juice from the pancreas, and intestinal juice from glands in the bowels. These intestinal juices contribute to the food's decomposition into more simple components, which in turn are absorbed by the blood and the lymph nodes.

In the large intestine, there is mostly an intake of water, sodium, and other minerals. There is also bacterial activity there.

The rectum, which is 6 to 8 inches long, makes sure we get rid of the waste.

Water and fluid balance

The water level in the body varies from person to person. As we get older the water level is reduced. Women have a lower level than men. If the body contains a lot of fat, the water level is lower.

We use about 2.5 quarts of fluid a day that is lost through sweat and urine. If we sweat a lot when exercising or sauna bathing, or if it is very warm, we use more fluid.

We need to drink 1.5 to 2 quarts of fluid a day. A third of the fluid is normally absorbed through food; the rest we obtain through drinks. It is better to drink a little too much than too little, since the body easily gets rid of the excess.

But exaggerated intake of fluid is also not good. The color of the urine should be like cider. If the urine is dark despite a plentiful intake of water, you should have a medical checkup.

Tip! It is easier to drink enough if you always have a bottle or jug of room temperature water ready. Flavor the water with lemon juice or fresh herbs if you want to.

Detox

It has been common for people to do vitalizing detoxes. Today the detox is needed more than ever since the exposure to dangerous substances is constantly increasing. There are more than 100,000 chemicals on the European market. About 30,000 of these are produced in amounts

amassing to more than 1 ton per year, according to the Swedish Nature Conservation Association.

Each day we are exposed to hundreds of xenogeneic substances just from hair and skin products, toothpaste, hair styling, cosmetics, washing detergents, clothes, plastic products, medicine, and more, as well as pesticides in the food. The organ that takes the most beating is the liver, which we should take care to guard from all the harmful substances.

Waste products are always produced during normal metabolism. These substances are normally secreted through skin, lungs, kidneys, and bowels. But even though the body has several ways to take care of the waste products, this cleaning process does not always work like it should—especially if we stress, eat too much or the wrong things, and exercise too little.

According to alternative medicine, the waste products that the body cannot take care of are stored in the connective tissue and block the life process. Many people get a headache, are constantly tired and stressed, sleep poorly, have digestion problems, feel body ache, and feel stiff. It also shows on the outside, since the skin swells and gravity takes its toll.

To only eat raw food and/or change all meals to nutritional drinks gives your stomach a well-needed rest, and somewhat of a cleansing occurs. It is also vitalizing and does not affect your muscle mass like a regular fast does. You can detox for a day now and then, once a week, or several days in a row like a course.

Do a two-week detox every autumn and spring. That lets all of the organs rest, and they work better after the detox. There are also special liver

Time for detox?
Let all the inner organs rest from time to time. That gives all of the organs a well-needed rest, when they can rejuvenate and revitalize. Only eat raw food or replace all meals with smoothies. You can detox for a day now and then, once a week, or several days in a row like a plan.

detoxes (found in health food stores or at a nutritionist.) Milk thistle is a fantastic herb for revitalizing the liver.

Other advantages with detoxing is that you lose weight, and above all, you gain energy as well as become more responsive to your body. It is important to listen to what your body wants. If you have an infection or fever in your body, you are usually not very hungry. Then it is better to drink revitalizing drinks instead of eating regular meals, which demand that your body work harder digesting. The same thing applies to having too little time. It is much better to drink a couple big glasses of nutritional drinks instead of skipping a meal or "gorging" the food while feeling stressed.

Detox course

Replace regular meals and snacks with smoothies, and eat fresh fruit, berries, fresh herbs, and raw food. Drink plenty of water, juice without sugar from cranberries or pomegranate, green drinks, ginger drinks (p. 321) as well as cleansing herb teas (p. 325). Avoid sugar, coffee, black tea, and alcohol.

Stimulate your body's cleansing:

- Use psyllium husk in drinks. They absorb waste products in the bowel and work well as a bulk-producing agent.
- Fresh air and exercise increase the intake of oxygen and your body's metabolism. Choose forms of exercise that you enjoy, like walking, dancing, aerobics, bicycling, or swimming.
- Dry brushing stimulates circulation and lymph in the body. Use a brush or sponge made from natural materials. Start by brushing the feet, including the bottoms of the feet, and continue up with small circular movements. Work toward the heart at all time.
- Sauna bathing stimulates skin cleansing by sweating.
- Natural materials. Wear clothes that can breathe, like silk, cotton, linen, or microfibers.

Food as medicine

"Let your food be your medicine and your medicine your food," said Hippocrates 2,000 years ago. Today's research on how our diet affects our health confirms how right he was. Plants are filled with tens of thousands of plant nutrients. In recent years, scientists' interest is more and more focused on these substances, and new ones proven to be important for our health are still being discovered.

WHY DO WE NEED protecting substances? One reason is that we need antioxidants to protect us from free radicals. Oxygen is vital to us and needed in order for the cells to extract energy. During this process, free radicals are produced. They are small molecules that lack one electron. They are aggressive and want to find a electron somewhere else. Oxygen radicals steal electrons from other molecules that are often found in cell walls and mostly come from fatty acids. One single cell can be attacked by free radicals 10,000 to 100,000 times a day.

Oxygen radicals can also damage the DNA, which can lead to cancer. If our vasculature is attacked, the risk for heart and vascular diseases increases. If the brain cells are attacked, the risk for dementia increases.

The more we expose ourselves to this oxidative stress, the more damage on our cells and the acceleration of the aging process. Almost all the usual signs of aging that occur too early are because of increased stress from free radicals.

The production of free radicals is increased by:
• stress
• UV rays from the sun
• alcohol
• infections
• inflammations
• physical training
• toxins
• overdosing iron and copper (pills)

To prevent the free radicals, you need antioxidants. They are substances that can give one electron to the oxygen radicals without being damaged themselves. They are produced in our bodies and can also be found in plants.

The most powerful antioxidants like glutathione, alpha lipoid acid, and Q10 are produced in our bodies. But lack of sleep, illness, and aging decrease the production. In order for the body to be able to create these antioxidants it needs enzymes which in turn need enough selenium, zinc, manganese, and copper.

In vegetables we find the antioxidants vitamin C and vitamin E. There are also many protective substances in plants that work like antioxidants.

Phytochemical

Each plants consists of hundreds of different substances. In addition to vitamins, minerals, amino acids, fatty acids, and fibers, there are a great amount of interesting plant chemicals. Mostly they are substances that also have a protective effect on humans. Many work as powerful antioxidants. Most antioxidants are found in the color of vegetables, fruit, and berries. The more color, the more antioxidants.

Many of these substances are also used like a concentrate in natural medicines and are synthetically produced in some conventional medicines. But plants can also contain substances that are harmful to us—for example, phytic acid makes it more difficult for us to absorb minerals and micronutrients from the plant.

Carotenoids

The possibly most well-known antioxidant is beta-carotene that is found in carrots. Beta-carotene is included in the family of carotenoids that consists of over 600 protective substances found in yellow-red vegetables and fruits like carrots and apricots. Green vegetables also contain carotenoids, but they are hidden under the green chlorophyll.

About 50 of these carotenoids—for example, beta-carotene and astaxanthin—are transformed into vitamin A in the body. Carotenoids are fat-soluble and are quite strongly connected to the vegetables. Using fat in the meal, as well as finely grinding or slightly heating them, increases the absorption.

About 2.5 to 2.8 oz of carrots eaten in a meal gives you the daily required amount of vitamin A.

Some common carotenoids are:
• Astaxanthin, a powerful antioxidant mostly found in algae and yellow bell peppers.
• Beta-carotene, the most well-known carotenoid, found in apricots, winter squash, and carrots, but also in dark green vegetables.
• Lutein, sensitive to heat and found in green leafy vegetables, mostly in kale, blueberries, and black currants. The substance seems to

protect the eyes from bright sunlight and lower the risk of cataracts and age-related damages to the macula.

- Lycopene, an antioxidant that can lower the risk of prostate cancer. New findings indicates that lycopene also protects against heart and vascular diseases. The substance is not sensitive to heat, but just the opposite; we absorb more lycopene if the vegetable is heated. Lycopene can be found in tomatoes and tomato sauce, but also in watermelon and blood grapefruit.

Flavonoids

Another big group of plant chemicals are flavonoids, which consist of hundreds of closely related substances that are found in almost all vegetables, fruit, and berries. Most flavonoids are produced in vegetables that grow above the soil as well as in fruit and berries. The flavonoids are usually found in the outer parts of the plants. Flavonoids are sensitive to heat and destroyed if cooked. Quercetin, anthocyanin, rutin, catechin, and tangeritin are a few examples of flavonoids. Anthocyanin is found in dark red vegetables. All flavonoids work as antioxidants and also contain anti-inflammatory substances with an effect similar to aspirin. They can also prevent blood clots.

Vegetables that contain the flavonoids isoflavones and lignans produce plant estrogens from intestinal bacteria. Plant estrogens—or phyto estrogens, as they are also called—have a similar effect to estrogen, but considerably weaker.

Plant estrogen also has an anti-estrogen effect before menopause and an estrogen effect after menopause. That means the total estrogen effect in the body is lowered in women before menopause, which in turn can lower the risks of breast cancer. After menopause, when the body's own estrogen production is lowered, the plant estrogens will instead give the body a little additional estrogen, which can ease menopause symptoms.

Estrogens are a group of steroid hormones that are also important to men, according to recent research, for semen production, among other things. Plant estrogen can lower the risks of cancer in the breast, prostate, and large intestine, as well as prevent growth if you already have a tumor. Flax seeds, red clover, fennel, and legumes, most of all soy beans, are examples of vegetables that can be transformed into plant estrogens.

Other protective substances

There are thousands of protective substances in plants, and we are far from done with research. Allyl sulfides are sulfur compounds found in all onion plants. They can protect against heart and vascular disease in different ways. Most are proven to lower cholesterol, but they also seem to lower blood pressure and the risks of blood clots. Some studies also indicate a cancer-preventative effect. Garlic has the greatest effect.

In all types of cabbage you can find isothiocyanate, which is among a group of very powerful antioxidants. Most well known is sulforaphane, found in broccoli and broccoli sprouts, that both strengthens the body's ability to defend itself from cancer and is said to prevent cancer cells from metastasizing, thus slowing down the growth of tumors. Scientists still do not know what doses are needed to reach a positive effect.

There is no fruit or vegetable that contains all the protective substances; instead, a well-balanced diet with a rich and varied intake of vegetables, fruits, and berries is what will protect you the most. Often it is shown that the food in its entirety has a completely different effect than if you isolate each substance. The old belief that "the whole is greater than the sum of its parts" still works.

Colorful antioxidants
Eat vegetables, fruit, and berries in all colors like green, yellow, red, blue, and purple every day! Different kinds of antioxidants have a synergic effect and enhance each other's positive qualities.

ORAC values

ORAC is an abbreviation of oxygen radical absorbance capacity that shows which vegetables contains the most antioxidants. To find out the ORAC value of a vegetable, which is measured per 100 g (3.5 oz), the vegetable is first ground and then exposed to a great deal of free radicals. This makes it possible to see how many free radicals they can neutralize.

The ORAC value can differ in individual fruit, berries, and vegetables depending on growing conditions. The tests are performed by Human Nutrition Research Center on Aging at Tufts University in Boston. They recommend you to eat from 3,000 to 5,000 units every day. There are many plants that have high ORAC values not found in these tables, like edible wild plants. Wild portulacaceae is one of the most nutritious lettuce plants we can eat and they are especially rich in omega-3.

Fruit, berries, and vegetables

Cranberry	9,584	Blood grape	495
Blueberry	6,552	Pink grapefruit	483
Blackberry	5,100	Kidney beans	460
Pomegranate	3,307	Yellow onion	450
Raspberry	1,800	Corn	400
Kale	1,770	Aubergine	390
Strawberry	1,540	Cauliflower	385
Spinach	1,515	Green peas, frozen	375
Apple	1,400	Potato	300
Broccoli	1,362	Cabbage	295
Asparagus	1,241	Sweet potato	295
Yellow squash	1,150	Lettuce (not iceberg lettuce)	265
Brussels sprout	980		
Plum	949		
Alfalfa sprouts	930	Cantaloupe	250
Steamed spinach	909	Carrot	210
Beetroot	840	Tomato	195
Avocado	782	Zucchini, green	176
Oranges	750	Apricot	175
Red grapes	739	Peach	170
Bell pepper, red	710	Pear	134
Cherry	670	Watermelon	100
Kiwi	610	Cucumber	60
Banana	500		

Chocolate, dried fruit, and spices

In this table are foods that we eat less of the alternative, their dried and more concentrated form.

Raw cacao	59,700	Basil, fresh	4,800
Acai berry	18,400	Raisin	2,830
Ginger	14,800	Watercress	2,223
Dark chocolate	13,120	Garlic, fresh	1,662
Prunes	5,770		

IFD, Inflammation-Free Diet

Inflammations constantly arise in our bodies. Too many inflammations and swellings are, by most scientists, considered to cause heart and vascular diseases, Alzheimer's disease, and disease of the pancreas, liver, and lungs.

Many scientists today recommend certain foods to eat that prevent inflammations. IFD stands for Inflammation-Free Diet and is starting to become a term of its own. This food does not only prevent inflammation but is also believed to increase both life span and life quality.

Almost all vegetables and fruit contain flavonoids, which have an anti-inflammatory effect. Most flavonoids are produced in vegetables that grow above the soil, as well as fruit and berries. Often the flavonoids are found in the outer parts of plants. Eat apples with the peel and keep the white skin on the oranges. Flavonoids are sensitive to heat and destroyed if cooked.

The main foods recommended in an inflammation-free diet are mostly vegetables and berries as well as fruit in moderate amounts, omega-3, olive and canola oil, herbs and garlic, onions, chili, ginger, turmeric and curry, nuts and seeds, whole grain products, legumes, and whole grain bread in moderate amounts.

Food for the brain

Everything we eat affects our body and the brain function. It decides how we feel and function in our daily life. With the help of signal substances the brain does its job. Certain food stimulates increased production of a few important signal substances:

- Dopamine regulates blood pressure, metabolism, and digestion and also contributes to memory function and focus. The amino acid phenylalanine that is broken down to tyrosine is a building block for dopamine. Found in cacao, soybeans, walnuts, eggs, and cream cheese.
- GABA is involved in endorphin production, the body's own "feel-good hormone." GABA makes sure we are relaxed, in harmony, and sleep well. GABA is found in bananas, citrus fruit, broccoli, lentils, potatoes, walnuts, almonds, and spinach.
- Serotonin is needed in order for the sleep hormone melatonin to be produced and contributes to balance in life. Lack of serotonin causes depression, hormone imbalance, and eating disorders. Serotonin is created from the amino acid tryptophan. Found in chocolate, eggs, bananas, cream cheese, cheese, yogurt, and avocado.

Functional food

The term was created in Japan in the 1980s. Some food has developed so that it has a stronger effect on health or medicinal attributes than other foods of the same sort.

One example is acidophilus products, which contain an extra high level of vital lactic acid bacteria. In regular sour milk and yogurt there are natural lactic acid bacteria, but only one of ten bacteria survive in the digestion system to the large intestine. From the acidophilus milk bacteria, nine out of ten make it all the way. If you have problems with your intestinal bacteria, the acidophilus products can be a good addition, provided you are not lactose-intolerant.

The "green revolution"

We all want to be healthy and avoid aging faster than necessary. Where do we find the "superfood"? Definitely in an inflammation-free diet filled with antioxidants, nutrients, and signal substances.

It is interesting to look at groups of people with a long life span like the Japanese island Okinawa. The habitants there have the longest life expectancy in the world. The secret is believed to be their simple and nutrient-rich diet and the small portion size of each meal. Traditionally the Okinawa population eat a lot of soybeans in different forms, like tempeh, tofu, and miso. In general they eat about 2 to 4 oz of soy products every day.

Today it is trendy to eat raw food and enthusiasts claim that the "life energy" is lost when heating the food. In addition to eating food and drinking nutritional drinks that are easy for the body to absorb, raw food eaters' meals are full of enzymes. Enzymes are found naturally in all vegetables but are destroyed when heated over 107.6°F.

Enzymes are vital to us and needed for all chemical reactions that happen in our bodies. All of our organs, tissues, and cells work with the help of enzymes, most of all digestion. No vitamins, minerals, or hormones can work without enough enzymes. We produce our own enzymes, but the enzyme production is decreased by stress, lack of sleep, and aging. In reality, it means that the enzyme production is low in most adults.

Superfood
Food that affects the brain's function, our mood, and our bodies' function:
- Eat organic food that has as little industrial processing as possible.
- Eat at regular hours.
- Eat with moderation and not too much at night.
- Make sure to keep your weight in good proportion to your body size.
- Eat nutritional food that gives you enough antioxidants, omega-3, and protein.
- Make sure you have a good digestion system and intestinal bacteria.
- Eat a diet rich in enzymes with a lot of unheated vegetables.
- Eat a diet that prevents inflammation.
- Eat food that contains neurotransmitters.
- Drink enough pure water, 1.5 to 2 quarts of water every day.

Learning about nutrition and planning meals

Today's increasing problems with obesity, diabetes, cancer, and heart and vascular diseases have raised the interest and awareness of diet and way of life. Life expectancy is longer, and that naturally leads to a desire for knowledge about how to keep our bodies strong and healthy even at an old age.

OUR BODIES ARE MADE up of billions of cells. The cells look different; the smallest are the red blood cells and the longest are the nerve cells in our legs. The different types of cells shape organs that have various functions in the body. Each second, about 50,000 new cells are produced and about as many die. A big part of the cell's activity is to copy the DNA so that the cell receives the doubled new DNA and can split it into two new identical cells.

If the old cell is not healthy it cannot produce a new cell. In other words, we cannot feel any better than what our cells feel. If the cells do not get the nutrients they need and are burdened for too long by free radicals, changes in blood sugar, stress, and biologically unknown substances, they will not work well. Eventually the whole body is imbalanced. Our whole life and health is dependent on how our cells are feeling.

We all know it is important to live a healthy life, but we also know how difficult it can be to live the type of life that makes us feel good. Many factors play a role in your general health—metabolism, physical activities, age, sex, stress, and environmental toxins. Most harmful of all to our health are environmental toxins, stress, and too little sleep, all of which also increase the need for nutrients.

There is a clear connection between lowered sensitivity to insulin and heart and vascular diseases and some types of cancer. When the pancreas cannot produce enough insulin, you can develop type 2 diabetes.

The structure affects the GI

It is most of all the structure of the food that affects the GI and not whether it is whole grain or not. However, whole wheat products are richer in dietary fiber and nutrients. Porous rice cakes and whole grain bread that is baked from finely ground flour have about the same GI as white bread, with few fibers. The more finely processed a product is, the higher the GI value. For instance, carrot juice and cooked carrots have a high GI while raw carrots have a medium GI.

Cooked root vegetables have a higher GI, while cooked potatoes (root vegetables) that have been kept in a refrigerator have a lower GI since the starch in the root vegetables is transformed into a firmer structure. The firmer fresh summer potato has a somewhat lower GI also when just cooked, compared to winter potato. When you cook a vegetable al dente, the GI value is a little lower than if the same root vegetables are "overcooked." If you

GLYCEMIC INDEX

Glycemic index (GI) is a measurement of the amount of carbohydrates out of 50 g (1.75 oz) carbohydrates, from different food, that goes out into the blood under two hours. When you measure GI, you either use white bread or glucose as a scale, since the GI of white bread has been measured to be 100. When measuring the blood sugar after eating other food, this is the scale we use.

The body's base level is set at having an even level of glucose in the body. It is harmful to have too little or too much glucose. In order for the excess of glucose to be stored in the cells, insulin is needed. If you are overweight it takes more insulin to store glucose as well as fat and some amino acids in the cells. That can lead to blood sugar peaks and is known as lowered sensitivity to insulin.

Energy
In order for our bodies to function we need energy. Our fuel comes from energy (glucose) that the body absorbs mostly from carbohydrates in the food, but also from fat and protein. There must always be a certain minimum amount of glucose in order for the body to work well. Energy is measured in kilojoules or kilo calories. 1 calorie is the energy it takes to heat 1 gram of water to 1°C. 1 kilocalorie = 4.19 kilojoules.

Fiber gives 2 kcal/gram
Carbohydrates give 4 kcal/gram
Protein gives 4 kcal/gram
Alcohol gives 7 kcal/gram
Fat gives 9 kcal/gram

▶ ONE BAG OF CHIPS contain as many calories as 10 clementines, 5 apples, and 5 pears.

mash the root vegetables like mashed potatoes, the GI value is higher.

Berries and tart fruit like apples or oranges have low and medium GI compared to sweet tropical fruit like bananas and mangoes that have a high GI. The greener the banana its lower is the GI value.

High and low GI

Food with high GI gives a short saturation and leads to major fluctuations in blood sugar. Food with low GI, on the other hand, makes the blood sugar even and thus the feeling of fullness is longer.

After an intensive workout in which the storage of glucose is used, it is good to eat a small meal of higher GI to make the construction of muscles easier.

High GI
Puffed rice
Rice cookies
Cornflakes
Oatmeal + milk
Cooked potatoes
White bread (for reference)
Bread and oatmeal from whole grain flour
Oat flakes
Bananas

Medium GI
Sourdough bread
Oat bran bread
Bread with 40 percent whole grain
Cooked barley
Pasta, both regular and whole grain
   (boiled for at least 7 minutes)
Oranges

Low GI
Apples
Beans, lentils
Milk, yogurt
Barley (whole or crushed)
Bread with 80 percent whole grain

Factors that affect the GI value
To make the most out of GI you should think in meals and not focus too much on single food products. It is the total amount of carbohydrates in a meal that is important.

- **Beans, seeds, and whole grains** have a low GI value and thus lower the GI value in the meal. Oatmeal made of crushed or whole barley has a lower GI value than oatmeal made of whole grain flour or whole grain cereals.
- **Acids** like lactic acid vegetables, sourdough bread, and vinegar lower the stomach's discharge rate which lowers the GI.
- **Fat lowers** the stomach's discharge rate which contributes to a lower GI.
- **Cinnamon lowers** the GI value in the whole meal, maximum 1 to 2 teaspoons of cinnamon per day.
- **Mushrooms** have a very low GI and lower the GI value in the meal.
- **Exercise** reduces the risk of insulin resistance.

Protein, the building stones of the body

Our bodies are made up of one-fifth protein. We need protein to build up and maintain all the cells in our body. Protein is also needed to produce enzymes, hormones, and antibodies.

Protein is made up from about 20 amino acids. Eight of these cannot be produced by the body itself, but must be taken in through food. These essential amino acids are isoleucine, leucine, lysine, methionine, threonine, tryptophan, and valine. Infants also need histidine.

Complete protein

If a product contains all the essential amino acids in a good balance, the protein is called complete. Protein in food deriving from animals like meat, fish, eggs, milk, and cheese are complete. Soybeans, todo, or soy milk are generally equally good.

If you combine grains, nuts, and seeds with beans and lentils, you end up with a combination of amino acids that are equivalent to the body's need. Canihua seeds, chia seeds, and hemp seeds make a very good addition to protein. It is enough if you get all the amino acids during one day.

Green leafy vegetables and potatoes contain complete protein, but in very small amounts. But if you eat a lot of dark green leaves or mixed green drinks (see the Green Super Smoothie, p. 319), you will get a good protein supplement. This is especially important for those who eat a lot of raw food.

All people have a different requirement for protein. Children and teenagers have a bigger need for protein than adults. The recommended daily protein intake is about 0.8 g per kilo of bodyweight (0.02 oz/35 lbs). That is about 50 grams of protein per day for a person who weighs 70 kilograms, or 1.75 oz per 154 lbs.

Vital fatty acids

Fat protects nerves and skeleton, as well as the body from heat and cold. Fat is also needed to absorb fat soluble vitamins like A, D, E, and K. We also need fatty acids like linoleic acid and alpha-Linolenic acid that the body cannot produce by itself.

The fat we find in food consists of three groups of fatty acids—saturated fat, monounsaturated fat, and polyunsaturated fat. All fat that we eat is made up of various amounts of these three fatty acids. The fatty acids that dominate the food decides to what group it belongs—for instance, butter, which for the larger part consists of saturated fat, we consider saturated.

- Saturated fat usually has a firm shape at room temperature.
- Monounsaturated fat is liquid at room temperature.
- Polyunsaturated fat is liquid at room temperature.

Saturated fat

Saturated fat has simple bonds that make the structure stable and more resistant to heat. Saturated fat can mostly be found in animal products like butter, milk, and dairy products, as well as coconut. Coconut fat has a higher heat resistance than butter.

Monounsaturated fat

Monounsaturated fat, omega-9, has a double bond and is found in olive, canola, and peanut oil and avocado and almonds. In recent research it has been proven that monounsaturated fats lowers blood fat as well as polyunsaturated fats.

Monounsaturated fat is more resistant than polyunsaturated fat and is more heat-resistant. But when you stir-fry or fry, it is better to choose butter or coconut oil that can resist a higher temperature. Canola oil contains somewhat more linoleic acid and alpha-Linolenic acid than olive oil. Olive oil, however, contains more antioxidants.

Polyunsaturated fat

Polyunsaturated fat can be found in almost all seeds and vegetable oils like sunflower seed, corn, thistle, walnut, and grape seed oil. If you want to use polyunsaturated oils, only use them in dressings and cold dishes, since they oxidize easily when in contact with oxygen and light as well as when heated.

Polyunsaturated fatty acids are divided into two groups: omega-6 fats and omega-3 fats. These are divided into different subgroups depending on how long they are; if they have 18 carbon atoms, the omega-6 fat is called linoleic acid and omega-3 fat alpha-Linolenic acid.

Omega-6 fats (linoleic acid) are abundant in most seeds. Omega-3 fat (alpha-linolenic acid) in contrast is only abundant in a few vegetables like canihua seeds, chia seeds, hemp seeds, and flax seeds, but canola oil is also a good source. In addition, omega-3 can be found in small amounts in dark green leaves like purslane. For alpha-linolenic acid the liver can elongate the fatty acids to EPA and DHA (EPA has 20 carbon atoms and DHA has 22 carbon atoms). EPA and DHA is mainly in fatty fish.

Usually our liver can manage to create this extension of EPA and DHA, but in some cases with hepatic impairment, a lot of stress, and with age, the body may fail to make it. This means you run the risk of "fat deficiency," even if you eat enough fat. That is when a supplement of algae oil or fish oil containing EPA and DHA can be a good idea.

EPA and DHA reduce the blood fats and make the blood thinner, which decreases the risk of blood clots. If you use blood-thinning medicine, a doctor should be contacted. These fatty acids are also important to eyes, the immune system, regulation of blood pressure and production of protein, the nervous system's function, and it also prevents rheumatic diseases, arteriosclerosis, type 2 diabetes and some types of cancer.

DHA also affects the serotonin production as well as several functions in the brain like memory and learning. Many common health problems—for instance, low stress tolerance, depression, fatigue syndrome, dyslexia, and ADHD and DAMP—can be improved or helped with supplements of omega-3 acids.

What fat should we choose?

- Eat natural fat like nutritious avocado, almonds, nuts, and seeds!
- Use canola oil and eat walnuts, canihua seeds, chia seeds, and hemp seeds that are rich in omega-3!
- Use olive or canola oil in cooking and use low temperatures when heating.
- Use butter or coconut oil when frying or stir-frying!

Trans fat

In order to make firm margarine from liquid oil the oil has to go through a process in which trans fat is produced. One of these trans fats (Elaidic acid) is harmful to us. Elaidic acid is removed from the type of margarine that we buy in stores to use at home, but in fast-food restaurants it is usually still there; this is also true for a part of the fat used in cookies or microwave popcorn.

In general, you should be careful with all heating of fat, especially polyunsaturated fat. The ideal frying temperature is around 302°F. If the fat reaches a higher temperature than 365°F, it will oxidize quickly and the flavor will diminish. Butter changes color and shows when it is time to lower the temperature. Oil, however, will not change color and starts to smoke around 482°F and it is then too late and the oil is destroyed and harmful substances are created.

Vitamins

Vitamins are chemical substances that cannot be produced in a large enough amount in the body. They all have different tasks in the body (see vitamin guide, p. 326). Although vitamins are needed in very small amounts, they are vital and cannot replace each other. Vitamins regulate the body's different metabolic processes, either instantly or combined with other substances. Without vitamins, neither normal growth nor health is possible.

Growth conditions, harvest methods, transports and storing time affect the content of vitamins. The water-soluble vitamins B and C are particularly sensitive. Most fruits and vegetables are harvested when green and unripe and are then left to mature in storage spaces. That means that the fruit has not had time to develop all the nutrients they would have if they were allowed to ripen in a natural way.

Tips!
- Eat fruit and vegetables when they are in season.
- Eat vegetables and root vegetables freshly cooked! Keeping vegetables warm for a long time destroys most of vitamin C and some B vitamins.

Minerals

Our body is made up of 4.5 percent minerals. They are necessary for the health of our cells, bone tissue, and fluid balance. Many minerals regularly disappear from the body through urine and sweat. We need a daily supplement of a large amount of phosphoric, calcium, magnesium, potassium, sodium, and sulfur.

Increased need for nutrients:
- Stress increases the need for all B vitamins and magnesium.
- Being burned out mostly increases the need for magnesium, all B vitamins, and fatty acids.
- Some medicines. When you eat cortisone and painkillers with acetylsalicylic acid (for example, aspirin), you need to eat more vitamin C.
- Contraceptive pills. If you take birth control pills, the body can require supplementary vitamins A, B1, B2, B6, B12, C, and folic acid. The need for B6 can increase up to ten times the normal need.
- Environmental pollutions. It is important that our cells be in good condition to have the strength to resist all the harmful chemicals and toxins we absorb through air, water, food, and medication. Vitamin A is considered to give a certain protection against DDT and vitamin C against cadmium and several other harmful substances.
- Hard physical exercise produces free radicals and it increases the need for antioxidants.
- Tobacco smoke creates many extra free radicals, and more vitamin C is needed to disable them.

Minerals differ from vitamins because they are not made from living organisms. They are stable chemical elements, and they are found in the ground. The plants absorb minerals and bind them so they are more easily accessible to humans. So far, there are 92 known natural chemical elements. These substances form all matter that exists, either alone or combined with each other through different chemical compounds. Most of these substances are minerals.

If the soil is unbalanced and lacking some nutrients, the plant will not grow strong. If conventional fertilizer is used, that contains phosphorus, potassium, and far too much nitrogen. In organic cultivation, natural fertilizer is used, rich in minerals and micronutrients.

Micronutrients

Minerals that we only need in very small amounts are called micronutrients. That group includes iron, manganese, copper, zinc, molybdenum, cobalt, chromium, nickel, silica, boron, tin, fluoride, chloride, bromine, iodine, and selenium.

All of these substances need to be added through food and cannot replace each other. Micronutrients are included as necessary parts of the enzymes that control metabolism. Between each single substance and groups of substances (vitamins, minerals, micronutrients), there has to be a certain connection.

Minerals and micronutrients are not as sensitive as vitamins but remain unchanged after harvest. The biggest and most common mineral loss happens when refining raw material for production of white flour, sugar, and rice.

Minerals are not sensitive to heat, but they are water-soluble and easily end up in the cooking water. If you do not use boiling water, some of the minerals and micronutrients are lost. (Read more about minerals and micronutrients in the mineral guide on p. 330.)

Iron and iron deficiency

Iron deficiency is considered to be one of the most common forms of malnutrition in the world. According to recent research, about 30 percent of all fertile women in Scandinavia suffer from iron deficiency. But it could be even more common among young girls. Many teenage boys also suffer from iron deficiency. Symptoms of iron deficiency are little different from normal tiredness and lethargy. Other signs could be headaches and paleness as well as being irritable and having reduced efficiency.

A problem with iron deficiency is that it is not always discovered in a regular blood test, which measures the amount of hemoglobin in the blood (Hb). The body tries hard to keep the levels of iron up, and that can cause the iron storage to be emptied before the Hb value is lowered and a lack of blood is caused (iron deficiency). It is not until the iron reserves are emptied that it shows in the test. You can ask your physician to measure the serum ferritin level as well, which is a storage protein in the blood.

There are two forms of iron in food: heme iron found in meat and non-heme iron mostly found in vegetables, but also in meat. Normally there is enough iron in the diet like in whole grain products, legumes, and dark green leaves. But several factors can inhibit the uptake of non-heme iron, like phytic acid, eggs, tea, coffee, calcium, milk, and dairy products.

How to increase your intake of iron:
- Eat vitamin C-rich fruit or vegetables like kiwi, oranges, bell peppers, cauliflower, and cabbage with all meals. Vitamin C can more than double the intake of non-heme iron.
- Eat lactic acid vegetables and soy sauce, which also increases the intake.
- Choose sourdough bread that has been fermented for a long time, filled with whole grain which increases the uptake.
- Cook food, preferably something tart, in an iron pot.
- Do not drink coffee or black tea after any meal, since it inhibits the uptake of iron.

Phytic acid
Phytic acid is a phosphoric substance found in shells and sprouts and in all seeds like peas, beans, grains, almonds, and nuts. Phytic acid binds some metals like iron, zinc, and calcium, which makes it more difficult for the body to absorb these minerals.

Normal amounts of food rich in phytic acid does not affect our total mineral uptake to any greater extent. Seeds are also rich in minerals. But if you eat a lot of vegetables rich in phytic acid, you have to pay attention.

Phytic acid is decomposed by an enzyme called phytase, and that can be found in the same seeds that contain phytic acid. The amount varies. Phytase is activated by lukewarm and warm water (under 176°F) as well as low pH. When seeds sprout, the phytase that breaks down phytic acid is activated.

MEAL PLANNING

The key is to keep blood sugar on an even level and eat three main meals as well as 3 to 4 snacks every day. Besides that, we need enough fat, omega-3, and fluids.

If you want to lose weight you should choose food with low or medium GI. If you are very physically active, you can increase the amount of carbohydrates rich in starch like root vegetables and whole grain bread.

The plate model
The plate model shows an easy way to put together a nutritious meal:
- Half the plate is vegetables
- Hardly ¼ whole grain products, root vegetables, and whole grain bread
- About ¼ protein-rich food like legumes, tofu, tempeh, ready-made soy products, corn products, cheese, and eggs

Good snacks:
Always carry around a couple of snacks to avoid low blood sugar.
- Whole grain bread with sourdough and egg/cottage cheese/cheese/tofu/hummus and vegetables and sprouts
- Hard-boiled egg
- Cottage cheese or soy cream cheese and berries or fruit
- Carrots, cucumbers, and cauliflower
- Avocado
- Smoothie
- Energy bars
- Fruit, berries and nuts, almonds, or seeds

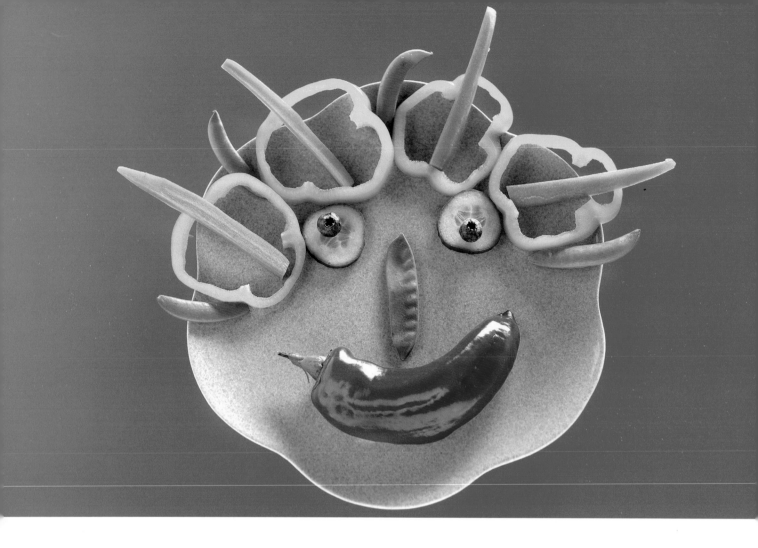

Vegetarian diet

If you are a vegan and eat according to the plate model, you will not have a problem with the intake of protein. The key is to eat legumes of some kind in several meals a day. On the other hand, it is important to make sure you get enough of vitamin D and B12 as well as calcium, iron, zinc, iodine, and selenium. Lacto-vegetarians should think about eating enough iron, zinc, iodine, and selenium.

• Vitamin D is a common deficiency in Scandinavia, since they are not exposed to enough sunlight during November to March.
• B12 cannot be found in vegetables, and vegans are recommended to take supplements.
• Vegans should pay attention to their calcium intake and use calcium-enriched products.
• Iron deficiency is fairly common.
• Zinc deficiency is fairly common.
• Iodine is found in iodine-enriched salt, but if you use sea or rock salt you should pay attention to your intake.

• Selenium is something to pay attention to, since Swedish soil belongs to one of the most selenium-deficient in the world.

Read more on pages 326–335.

VEGETARIAN DIET FOR CHILDREN AND TEENAGERS

During the past three decades, the recommendations for what small children should eat have changed. Today it is about carefully introducing new food, higher fat, small amounts of dietary fiber, and most of all the importance of a long period of breastfeeding.

Breast milk is the best food for a little child. The longer you can breastfeed, the better. Not only is breast milk valuable in itself, but it is important for the closeness the child experiences to its mother.

Breast milk does not contain any dietary fiber and today it is recommended that you slowly increase the amount of fiber in small children's diet.

Pregnancy and breastfeeding

During pregnancy and breastfeeding, the need for all nutrients, mostly protein, folic acid, vitamin D, calcium, iron, selenium, and zinc is increased. The future mother should also be observant of the intake of fatty acids.

Iron deficiency can increase the risk of miscarriage. Folic acid deficiency can mean a risk of birth defects like spina bifida. Zinc deficiency can give the child skeletal malformations. It is good to increase the intake of iron and folic acid even before planned pregnancy. It is important that the mother is not on a diet or fast while she is pregnant and breastfeeding. Dieting increases the levels of environmental toxins like dioxins in the breast milk.

Be careful with deep-fried food. New studies show that fry-mutagens (carcinogenic substances) can pass through the placenta to the child as well as secrete into the breast milk. If any of the parents are allergic, it is wise to avoid peanuts during pregnancy and breastfeeding.

Avoid allergies

According to Swedish diet recommendations, children should start eating baby food at 4 to 6 months of age.

From an allergy standpoint, it is important to introduce new food together with breast milk. The breast milk contains protective substances from the mother's immune system. If there are allergies in the family, the child should be breastfed as long as possible.

If any of the parents are allergic there is an increased possibility that the child is allergic. It is then good to avoid peanuts, eggs, fish, and citrus fruit during the first year and also be careful with cow milk products.

Samples at 4 to 6 months

Sometime between 4 to 6 months is usually a good time to start with small samples of puréed vegetables or root vegetables. Mainly choose organic-labeled products. Some children quickly accept the new food while others are more doubting and need more time.

The noon meal is usually the best time to start when switching to solid food. The child is well rested and this meal will eventually become the main meal. Good foods to start with include avocado, potatoes, parsnip, carrots, broccoli, corn, and alfalfa sprouts. Children under one year should not eat spinach, chard, or beetroot because of the high amounts of nitrate, and neither should the child eat honey, considering the risk of botulism bacteria.

Start by giving a teaspoon of mashed vegetables, and then extend it to a few tablespoons. At the beginning, you can mix the sample with breast milk. When the samples are bigger, you can mix it with a teaspoon of oil.

Try each kind for at least 4 to 5 days. The child has so far only had one dish on its menu, and the need for variation is not very big. Eventually you can give samples of sour milk as well as fruit like mashed bananas, berries, mangoes, apples, and pears in the afternoon.

Baby food

From 5 to 6 months the child needs iron-enriched drinks, purée, or gruel. At 6 to 8 months the breast milk is eventually replaced at noon with a regular meal, like mashed potatoes, vegetable purée, and quark or cottage cheese as well as carrot juice and regular milk.

If the child is allergic to cow milk products, a doctor and dietitian should be consulted. Eventually you can vary with quark or cottage cheese with mashed green peas. The most important thing is that the child feels well and is growing properly.

Slowly increase the levels of fiber in the meal. You should be careful with all whole grain products, even whole grain gruel, when the child is under three years old.

From 8 to 12 months the child needs bigger portions and food that takes more chewing. Give children as pure and unprocessed food as possible and avoid both fried and salted food until the child is at least one year old. From three years old the child can eat the same food as the rest of the family, with a recommended fat level of 30 percent.

Smoothies are superfood for both young and old. Do not give children processed products and other food that contain questionable additives, like margarine, cheap oils, strongly colored candy, and drinks sweetened with synthetic sugar.

Children need much more energy during the first years of life. During its first year the child triples its weight. About 60 percent of the energy from the breastmilk derives from fat.

When the child is 6 to 12 months, 35 to 40 percent of energy from fat is needed, and between 1 and 3 years, 30 to 35 percent of energy from fat.

Children up to two years should have 1 teaspoon of oil in every portion of cooked food. Give vegetarian children cold-pressed canola.

Cook the baby food yourself!

Cooking baby food is easily done with a hand blender. Avocado and fruit is mashed or mixed right before the meal. Cook a larger amount of vegetables and root vegetables and freeze as a purée in ice cube molds. That makes it simple to just take one cube out and defrost it.

Tasty smoothies, fruit, and berry ice cream is easy to make. Gruel and possibly breastmilk formula should be bought.

Stimulate older children's interest in vegetables:

- Never force a child to eat something that they do not want.
- Children often like to eat each vegetable separate instead of in a mixed salad.
- Do not give whole green peas and corn to children under three years. They can get stuck in their throat.
- Give the children raw vegetables like carrot sticks, cauliflower, cucumber sticks, pieces of fennel, green peas, and corn to snack on while they are waiting for the food to be done.
- Let the children prepare imaginative raw food plates for the whole family.
- Always keep a big bowl with different fruit for the children to eat from.
- Let the children help to cook sometimes. Then take the opportunity to introduce new vegetables or fruit.

Teenage food

All of a sudden, there will be a day when your teenager comes home and says that she or he refuses to eat meat and fish. The parents are confused and naturally worried that the teenager will not get enough nutrition, especially if the teenager wants to become vegan.

Many people think that it is complicated and time-consuming to cook vegetarian meals, especially when the rest of the family wants traditional food. Then it has to be two kinds of dinners. But turn it around. Consider your teenager's vegetarianism as an asset. Vegetarians generally eat a better and more complete diet than people who eat a mixed diet. It is only if the vegetarian diet is too one-sided that there are risks.

Let the vegetarian food be the base of the family's diet and serve meat or fish as sides. It does not have to take longer time to cook vegetarian food. Imagine all the new taste sensations you can have with new dishes. When everyone in the family begins to eat a greener and more nutritional diet, the whole family gains. Pay attention to how your teenager is feeling and growing as well as developing normally (see meal planning, p. 57). Stimulate the new vegetarian to learn more about a vegetarian diet both when it comes to practical cooking and nutrition as well as meal planning. Smoothies and energy bars are popular and nutritional snacks.

In many online vegan communities, the teenager can gain knowledge and contact with people of the same age and interest.

SEASONAL MEAL SUGGESTIONS FOR FOUR WEEKS

Vegetarian food is climate-smart, and vegetarian food adapted to season is even better and the dishes more varied and tastier as well as affordable. Here are one or two suggestions for the main meal for each day of the week, one week for each season.

Complement the dishes with salad, vegetable sides, raw grated root vegetables, beans of some kind, as well as bread or cooked bulgur, couscous, quinoa, spelt, oats, or potatoes.

Eco-friendly tips for summer and autumn can be found on page 152, and for winter and spring on page 159. Also look at the seasonal guide for fruit and vegetables on page 16 to 17.

SPRING

Monday Avocado Soup, page 202, or Lentil Soup, page 209.

Tuesday Root Vegetable Lasagna, page 218, or Salad with Sesame Marinated Tofu, page 164.

Wednesday Filled Wraps with Falafel and Hummus, page 232.

Thursday Beetroot Stew with Horseradish Yogurt, page 240.

Friday Root Vegetable Hash with Halloumi or Tofu, page 256.

Saturday Grilled Tzay Skewers (Frozen) with Avocado Sauce, page 172, and Peanut Sauce, page 175.

Sunday Kidney Burger, page 268, with Oat with Apple and Ginger, page 219, and Carrot Tzatziki, page 170.

AUTUMN

Monday Borsht (beetroot soup) with Horseradish Yogurt, page 204. (Boil a few beetroots separately for the Friday's beetroot patties.)

Tuesday Thai Stew with Coconut, page 236, or Greek Salad with Feta or Tofu, page 166.

Wednesday Mushroom Burger, page 276, with Bean Salsa, page 162.

Thursday Pasta with Greek Pasta Sauce, page 216, or Tomato Sauce with Vegetarian Mincemeat, page 216.

Friday Breaded Beetroot Patties, page 269, with Wax Beans in Parsley Sauce, page 196.

Saturday Chile con Quorn, page 239, or Fried Soy Mincemeat with Taco Spices. (Serve with tortillas and tortilla chips as well as bowls or finely chopped red onions, tomatoes, avocado, corn, and crème fraiche/yogurt and optional grated cheese.)

Sunday Moussaka with Zucchini, page 249.

SUMMER

Monday Gazpacho, page 202, or Zucchini Soup, page 207.

Tuesday Salad with Tandoori Marinated Tofu, page 164.

Wednesday Zucchini Patties with Feta, page 271, or Kidney Burger, page 268, with Tzatziki, page 170, and Lingonberries, page 199.

Thursday Pasta Salad with Feta or Tofu, page 166.

Friday Stir-fry Vegetables with Halloumi or Tofu (onions, sugar peas, broccoli, zucchini, bell peppers, and tomatoes), page 262.

Saturday Grilled Marinated Quorn Fillets and Zucchini, page 266, or Grilled Tzay Skewers with Potato Salad with Asparagus and Cocktail Tomatoes, page 163.

Sunday Lemon Marinated Green Beans with Potatoes and Capers, page 161.

WINTER

Monday Indian Lentil Soup with Coconut, page 206, or Green Pea Soup with Horseradish Yogurt, page 207.

Tuesday Cabbage Stir-fry, page 265.

Wednesday Roasted Root Vegetables, page 254, with Hummus, page 176, or Sesame Marinated Tofu, page 164.

Thursday Spinach Lasagna, page 218, or Potato Gratin, page 258, and Kidney Burger with Olives, page 268, or Grilled Tzay Skewers.

Friday Stir-fry Vegetables with Halloumi or Tofu, page 262 (apples, cabbage, kale, carrots, and onions).

Saturday Inger's Quorn Stew with Banana and Curry, page 239, or Chickpea Stew with Algae, page 239.

Sunday Falafel, page 271, is with Coleslaw with Apple, page 159.

Fruit, berries, and flowers

Is there anything more tasty than a sun-warmed strawberry or a fragrant wild strawberry? Besides the lovely flavor, they are loaded with antioxidants. The Swedish native berries are like a goldmine filled with treasures. Both fruit and berries are healthy delicacies.

Throughout history, flowers have also enriched our food. Even the ancient Greeks ate marigolds and carnations. The Chinese have always eaten day lilies and chrysanthemums. Here are some suggestions of wonderful and colorful flowers both to enjoy and for decoration.

raspberries

strawberries

kiwi

orange

fresh dates

cactus fruit

satsuma orange

galia mellon

grapes

apples

WE HAVE EATEN FRUIT AND BERRIES throughout history. Fruit cultivation has existed in the Mediterranean since the beginning of our history. In Scandinavia, monks developed fruit cultivation in their monastery gardens and from there the knowledge about growing fruit spread.

SWEDISH FRUIT AND BERRIES

In folk medicine, apples have been used raw and grated to help with diarrhea and other intestinal problems. Who has not heard the expression "A apple a day keeps the doctor away"? The apple tree originated from the area between the Caspian Sea and the Black Sea. From there it spread all across Europe about 5,000 years ago. Today, over 20,000 different kinds of apples are said to exist.

Swedish apples usually have thinner peel and a sweeter, more aromatic taste than foreign kinds. Tasty native apples are Gravensteiner, James Grieve, Katja, Lobo, Cox Oselection, Signe Tillisch, and Ingrid Marie. Swedish apples are not waxed. Foreign apples are often sprayed with beeswax or wax from palm leaves.

Pears have been cultivated in the country since the Middle Ages. Ripe pears stay fresh for a limited time and are generally sold unripe. If you press gently at the top of the pear and it is soft, it means that it is ripe. Swedish pears can be found from October to December.

Plums are a stone fruit and have somewhat of a laxative effect. Ripe plums are very sensitive to both pressure and high temperature. The plum season is between August and October.

Cherries are actually a stone fruit related to plums. Originally the cherry tree comes from the Black Sea coast. It grows wild in almost all of Europe and Asia. There are sweet cherries that taste best fresh. The sour cherries are better suited for juice, lemonade, and compote and are rich in beta-carotene. Sweet berries are rich in anthocyanin, which is a flavonoid. The Swedish season lasts from June to August.

Chokeberries ripen in the autumn and are very rich in antioxidants. In Eastern Europe the berries have been used in folk medicine for their preventative and healing abilities. The berries grow on big bushes and are easy to grow, with sheer white flowers in the spring and flaming bright colors in the autumn. There is also a smaller variant that is perfectly suited as a hedge.

Strawberries are related to wild strawberries. They are primarily rich in vitamin C, folic acid, and ellagic acid. Light strawberries taste the best when fresh. Dark red is most suited for jam and lemonade. The Swedish strawberry season starts by the end of June and some strains grow berries all the way into autumn.

Raspberries are mainly rich in vitamin E and egallic acid. The raspberry season occurs from July to August. There are also autumn raspberries that are harvested throughout autumn.
   Tip! Young raspberry leaves can be used for tea during all of summer.

Blackberries grow wild in the middle and south parts of Sweden. The blackberry bush is related to the raspberry but has black raspberry-like berries. They are somewhat firmer in the texture and the flavor is freshly tart. The berries ripen from August to September.
   Tip! Young leaves can be used for tea during all of summer.

cumquats

lime cumquats

limes

lemons

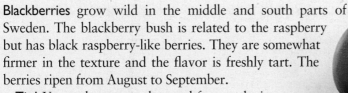

plums

fresh figs

pears

blood grapefruit

pomelo

Buckthorn grow wild along our coasts and are more and more common in our gardens. The yellow-orange berries are tricky to pick, but have a exquisite flavor similar to passion fruit. They are very nutritious, since they contain beta-carotene, vitamin C and E, as well as many B vitamins.

Cloudberries are related to raspberries and blackberries. They grow wild on bogs and wetlands in most of the country and ripen in July. The berries are very rich in beta-carotene and vitamin C. They also contain ellagic acid and natural benzoic acid that keeps them fresh.

Lingonberries grow all over the country. They are rich in vitamin E and contain natural benzoic acid to keep them fresh.

Cranberries are related to lingonberries and grow on wetlands. These vitamin E-rich berries are larger and less tart than lingonberries. Cranberry juice reduces the risk of urinary infection.

Blueberries are related to lingonberries and grow all over the country. In folk medicine, the berries are believed to have a healing and strongly disinfecting ability. Cooked or dried berries used in blueberry soup stops diarrhea, and fresh berries in larger amount or fresh blueberry juice prevents constipation. The color in blueberry comes from a very powerful antioxidant, anthocyanin. Blueberries also contain lutein, an antioxidant that can lower the risk of age-related blindness.

Rose hips grow wild and are cultivated in almost all of the country. They are very nutritional and primarily contain a great deal of beta-carotene, vitamin C, calcium, potassium, magnesium, and iron.

Fresh, deep-frozen, or dried rose hips go well with tea or soup. Dried rose hip flour is easy to use as enrichment in muesli and oatmeal. Rose hips ripen during the month of September.

Currants are grown in the whole country. The black and red currants are the most common. There are also white currants that are similar to the red ones but milder in flavor. Black currants are mostly rich in vitamin C, but also in vitamin E and calcium. The seeds contain gamma-linolenic acid, GLA. But it is doubtful whether or not we can use the fatty acid since the seeds must be crushed first. Currants start ripening in the end of July.

Tip! Leaves from currants make a good tea.

Gooseberries are related to currants and there are many strains. The berries can be green, yellow, or red, small or big, and have a smooth or hairy surface. The gooseberries start ripening by the end of July.

Rhubarb has been used as a medicinal plant for over 2,000 years in China, among other places. The root has a strongly laxative effect and is also considered to have a cooling effect. From the beginning of the 1700s, tender rhubarb stems were used in British kitchens for both tart and sweet dishes. Since it is easy to grow and delicious, it quickly gained popularity.

In most old Swedish gardens at least one rhubarb plant is growing. There are hundreds of edible rhubarbs, even strains with low amounts of oxalic acid. With a little care, you can easily harvest the plant many times. Fertilize the plant early in spring and harvest it a few times during the spring. Then leave the plant to rest and harvest it another few times during late summer. It is easy to split old plants and make several new ones.

Tip! Harvest rhubarb stems by breaking them at the base. If you cut them with a knife, you can damage the root.

Storage! Let unripe fruit sit out and ripen in order for aroma and sweetness to develop. Not only does the flavor change during the ripening process but the levels of antioxidants also increase. Store all ripe fruit except for bananas and tropical fruit in the refrigerator or a cool pantry (41–50°F). Berries should be kept in the refrigerator.

CITRUS FRUIT

Oranges originated in China and came to Europe in the 1700s. In addition to the regular oranges, there are blood oranges with red, slightly sour pulp. Peak season is from November to April, and that is when Sweden imports the most oranges mainly from Spain, Israel, and Morocco. Oranges are mostly rich in vitamin C and beta-carotene.

Lemons have been used in folk medicine for detox and cleansing as well as for stimulating digestion. One tablespoon lemon juice in half a glass of water a short while before eating stimulates the hydrochloric acid production. The yellow on the peel is very rich in flavor and works well in flavoring desserts and baked goods. The peel can be dried and used for tasty teas. Lemon juice goes well with most dressings and dishes.

Tip! The lemon stays fresh for longer if you make a small hole in it and squeeze the juice you need for the moment.

Grapefruit contains bitter substances that stimulate both liver and digestion. There are yellow and red grapefruits. Blood grapefruit is primarily rich in the antioxidant lycopene.

Lime is a small green citrus fruit that contains a lot of vitamin C and also is rich in potassium,

phosphorus, and calcium. The flavor, which is both full and mild, is just like the lemon's, mostly found in the peel. Only grate the very outer parts of the peel. The white skin has a bitter flavor. There is also a smaller variant of lime which is a mix between lime and cumquats.

Cumquats look like walnut-size miniature oranges. You eat the whole fruit with the peel. It has a tart, astringent, and very aromatic flavor. It works well natural, sliced in fruit salads, and in desserts. Cumquats are imported from Sicily from November to December.

Pomelo is a pear-shaped, very large citrus fruit, often 8 to 10 inches in diameter. The flavor reminds you of a grapefruit, but it is not as bitter. Slice the fruit in pieces lengthwise and make a few cuts in the pulp so that you can pick the pulp out of the peel.

Mandarins and satsumas are the basic small citrus fruits, which then have been developed further. They are rich in beta-carotene and vitamin C.

Health effects and nutritional value for fruit and berries
- Are very rich in both soluble and insoluble fiber and vitamins. Most fruit and berries are good sources of vitamin C.
- Have an anti-inflammatory effect.
- All fruit and berries are particularly rich in antioxidants and protective substances. See ORAC values, p. 48.
- Reduce the risk of heart and vascular diseases.
- Can reduce the risk of some types of cancer.
- Acids in tart berries like lingonberries, cranberries, and red currants stimulate digestion.
- Many berries, like cranberries and lingonberries, have an antibacterial effect that can lower the risk of urinal infections.

Peruvian cherries

apple pears

pepinos

horned melons

mangosteens

Sweetie is a mix between grapefruit and pomelo. The fruit is similar to grapefruit but has a sweet and full flavor without any bitterness.

Ugli is supposedly a spontaneous cross-breeding between oranges, grapefruit, and clementines that happened on Jamaica in the beginning of the 1900s. It's similar to the grapefruit but larger.

OTHER FRUIT

Pineapple originally comes from South America. Pineapples contain bromeliad, which is a powerful enzyme that can speed up a healing process, has anti-inflammatory abilities, and can improve digestion. The fruit consists of over one hundred berries that grew together into one. That is why the peel is bumpy and the fruit looks like a big cone. In the middle of the fruit is a big stock which should be cut off if it is woody. Choose fruit with a sweet smell. Unripe pineapple shifts in colors of green, and dark spots indicate decay. Unripe fruit will ripen in a few days at room temperature. The fruit is ripe when the peel is yellow-brown.

Apricots come from Armenia and are considered to be very strengthening. Apricots, especially dried, are very rich in beta-carotene and vitamin E. Dried apricots that are light are treated with sulfite. It might cause trouble with some asthmatics but is not considered to be harmful. In health food stores you can find dark, unsulphured apricots. Hunzaa apricots are small, dried apricots with a pit that has a lovely, light, vanilla-like flavor.

pomegranates

guavas

papayas

quinces

Banana plant is not a tree but an herb. It is one of the world's oldest cultural plants and exists in many species. The bananas that are used as food are divided into dessert bananas (fruit bananas) and food bananas (plantains). Food bananas must be cooked before they are eaten as opposed to dessert bananas, which you eat directly.

Aside from regular yellow bananas, there are also yellow or red-brown dessert bananas. Bananas are always harvested green. If they are allowed to ripen on the plant, they turn out starchy and the peel cracks. Bananas ripen while storing; the starch is transformed to sugars, and the flavor turns out rich and sweet.

In folk medicine, bananas are considered to have a healing effect on ulcer and intestinal diseases.

Carambola forms decorative stars when you slice the yellow or green fruit. The flavor is almost like a cucumber's, except more tart. Garnish drinks and dessert with the beautiful "stars."

Cherimoya is sometimes referred to as the fruit of the fruit. It has an intense but mild flavor of wild strawberries, pears, and mangoes. It originated in the tropical areas of Latin America.

In folk medicine, the fruit has been used to cure diarrhea, dysentery, tooth ache, and eye infections.

When the fruit is ripe, a sticky fluid is secreted, particularly on the top. The peel also turns somewhat black and is soft if you press. Cut the fruit lengthwise and scrape off the black seeds.

rambutans

cherimoya

persimmon

tamarillo

passion fruit

pitaya

star fruit

mangoes

pineapple

Dates are the fruit from the date palm. They hang in clusters, with a lot of fruit in each cluster, under the palm crown. From ancient times, they have been the traditional food to bring when traveling in the Orient. We import fresh dates mostly during the winter. Dates are primarily rich in calcium, phosphorus, and iron.

Figs originally came from Anatolia. These days, the figs are cultivated in the Mediterranean as well. The fruit is very rich in calcium, phosphorus, and iron. Figs are usually sold dried. Fresh figs are mostly imported during autumn.

Pomegranates are filled with antioxidants. They are wonderful to eat plain, use as a garnish, or use in drinks and salads.

Tip! Split the fruit in half and knock the seeds out with a wooden spoon or similar.

Guavas grow in tropical countries and are rich in vitamin C.

Indian fig opuntia is found on large cactuses that grow around the Mediterranean and in South America. The beta-carotene rich pulp has a sweet and fresh flavor.

Tip! Take the opportunity to revel in this tasty fruit while on vacation. They grow everywhere in Southern Europe. The fruit has small sharp thorns that you have to be careful with. Use thick gloves and scrape off all thorns with a knife. Split the fruit lengthwise and eat the pulp with a spoon or peel the fruit with a knife.

Horned melon is a cucumber plant that comes from Africa. The spiky fruit has a beautiful green and jelly-like pulp with seed-like stones. The pulp is a little tart, reminiscent of a lime.

Lychee originated in China and has a light, see-through, juicy pulp with a sweet taste. The fruit is best kept in a plastic bag in the refrigerator.

Mango originally came from India and is one of the most cultivated trees in the tropics. The tasty, juicy yellow pulp must be cut off the big core. That is easily accomplished by placing the mango edgeways and cutting on each side of the core. There are many strains of mango and they can be green, yellow, or red. A ripe mango has an intense smell and is very soft if you press your finger into it. Mango is very rich in beta-carotene, vitamin C, E, and folic acid.

Mangosteen comes from Malaysia and is considered to be one of the best tasting fruits in the world. The white pulp is meltingly soft and juicy, and the flavor is similar to peach and pineapple.

Cut a cross in the peel and press the peel toward the bottom of the fruit so the pulp comes out.

Melons are related to cucumber and cultivated in all warmer countries. There are many kinds, like honey, cantaloupe, ogen, and watermelon. Melons with orange pulp contain a lot of carotenoids. Split the melon, remove the core when serving, or cut the pulp in pieces. Peak season is during summer and autumn.

Tip! Choose melons that smell sweet and fast. When they are a little soft at the top, they are ripe.

Papaya grows in all tropical countries and is primarily rich in beta-carotene, vitamin C, and E. The fruit are often pear-shaped. The peel is green, greenish-yellow, or orange with a pulp that reminds you of melon in texture. Ripe fruit should be a little soft. In the middle of the fruit is a cavity with black seeds that is scraped off. Split the fruit lengthwise or cut in pieces. A few drops of lemon or lime juice enhances the flavor. In tropical countries the papaya is often served for breakfast.

Tip! Ripe papaya, and most of all the seeds, contain the enzyme papain which has a strongly antibacterial effect. If you are in a tropical country, you can eat 5 to 6 papaya seeds every day to prevent stomach problems.

Passion fruit has a somewhat leathery peel. When the fruit is ripe, the peel is bumpy and looks wrinkled. The fruit contain plenty of fiber but also beta-carotene, vitamin C, and E. You split the fruit and eat the juicy green-yellow pulp with the seeds directly with a spoon.

Pepino is related to tomato and potato. The fruit comes from Peru, where it grows in the hills of the Andes. The peel turns more yellow when ripening. The pulp has a rich flavor that is similar to pear and melon.

Peaches are imported mostly from the Mediterranean during the months of the summer. Peaches are relatively rich in beta-carotene and vitamin E. Nectarine is a variant of the peach and has a smooth peel.

Persimmon looks like a big orange-red tomato with large leaves. It tastes the best if you let it ripen properly. Split it in the middle and eat with a spoon. Persimmon is rich in fiber and beta-carotene.

Pitaya is a kind of cactus plant, but it has no thorns, unlike the Indian fig optunia. There are yellow and purple fruit that have a sweet, rich, and aromatic flavor.

Peruvian cherry is a beautifully orange, cherry-like fruit that is covered in paper-thin leaves. The flavor is fresh and tart. Peruvian cherries can be cultivated in green houses and will give a fairly large harvest if you let the fruit ripen indoors.

Rambutan is related to the lychee. The light and almost see-through and juicy pulp has a taste of elderberry. Keep the fruit in a plastic bag in the refrigerator.

Tamarillo belongs to the same family as tomato and is sometimes called "tree tomato." It originated in South America. The pulp is juicy and jelly-like, and the flavor is fresh and tart with a little bit of bitterness in the peel. Ripe fruit are a little soft and good to eat plain, in fruit salads, or grilled as a side dish.

Kiwi is also known as Chinese cherry, and unripe fruit can be stored up to 6 months after harvest. The fruit is ripe when it is soft if you press it with a finger. Store ripe fruit in the refrigerator.

Kiwi is most of all rich in fiber, vitamin C, and folic acid. The fruit contains an enzyme that breaks down the protein in cream and that has a bitter flavor. There are several kinds of kiwi—among others, the miniature kiwi that can be grown here.

Grapes are the oldest cultivated fruit. There are many strains of grapes, which can be either green, blue, or red. They are very rich in antioxidants. They are imported all year round, but the autumn is the peak season for grapes from the Mediterranean. Grapes should dry after being rinsed, otherwise they are easily damaged on the top.

Tip! If you are the happy owner of a grapevine, you can use the tart grape leaves for dolmades.

FLOWERS IN THE FOOD

Who can resist a spring cake covered with primroses and wild pansies, or a salad garnished with squash flowers or glowing nasturtium flowers? Beautiful flowers in food is a guaranteed success. There is no nutritional research about flowers, but it is likely that they are rich in vitamins, carotenoids, flavonoids, and other antioxidants since they are so colorful. Throughout history, flowers have enriched food. Even the ancient Greeks ate marigold and carnations. Chinese people have always eaten day lilies and chrysanthemum.

Edible flowers

Common Hollyhock, *Alcea rose*. These beautiful flowers can enhance any meal, dessert, or cake.

Borage, *Borago officinalis*, has lovely small blue flowers. The flowers and the seeds contain plenty of the fatty acid GLA. Oil is extracted from the seeds for commercial use. Garnish drinks, salads, and side dishes with borage. The flowers can be frozen in ice cubes.

Marigold, *Calendula officials*, is used as a medicinal plant in healing creams. Fresh and dried petals give both flavor and color to salads. Marigold petals are also tasty and decorative in tea mixtures.

Chrysanthemum, *Chrysanthemum coronaries*, is often used in Chinese cuisine. Petals and whole young flowers are good to stir-fry, but also works well in salads.

Chicory, *Cichorium intybus*, grows in Gotland, for example. The beautiful light blue flowers are mild and are good for salads and drinks. You can freeze chicory in ice cubes.

Lemons, *Citrus limon*, have deliciously smelling flowers. One lemon tree in a pot can produce a surprisingly large harvest of both flowers and tasty, useful lemons. Both flowers and leaves are used in tea and Oriental cooking.

Squash, *Cucurbit pepo*, cucumber, and pumpkin have large, beautiful yellow flowers. The female flowers have a short stem and a visible fruiting body, while the male flowers only have a long stem. Do not pick all the male flowers; leave a few so that the insects have the possibility of pollinating the female flowers. Squash flowers are especially tasty in salads. When fried, they are a delicacy.

Carnation, *Dianthus*, has been eaten for thousands of years in different cultures. All carnations, both wild and grown in a garden, are edible. Only use the petals since the root is bitter. The petals are tasty in desserts, drinks, or salads.

Meadowsweet, *Filipendula ulmaria*, in general grows on moist grassland throughout the country.

The almond-tasting flowers are good to fry. Garnish salads and desserts with them or make meadowsweet wine. Meadowsweet tea eases pain, like headache.

Daylily, *Hemerocallis*, has been eaten in China throughout time. The beautiful flowers only bloom one single day. Both buds and petals are tasty in salads and soups or in stir-fry. Both flowers and buds can be frozen.

Bitter vetch, *Lathyrus montanus*, usually blooms in pastures during spring and early summer. Eat the tasty flowers when taking a spring walk or pick and mix the flowers in a salad.

Malva, *Malva*, blooms with white, pink to red-purple flowers in grassland. There are different species like *Malva sylvestris* or *Althaea officinalis*. They are all edible, as are those grown in gardens.

Hibiscus is related to Swedish malvas. Malva—or rather hibiscus—tea can be bought in health food stores. Garnish salads and desserts with malva and hibiscus flowers and enjoy.

Pelargonium, is found in about 50 different strains. They have a lovely, refreshing, and somewhat citrusy smell and flavor. Use the leaves in tea, soft cakes, and desserts.

Cowslip, *primula veris*, has sweet flowers that are beautiful in salads and desserts. The leaves can also be used in salads. In some countries, the *primula veris* is endangered. However, many people have them in their garden, where they easily spread out.

Roses, *Rosa*, have been cultivated in big rose gardens in many cultures. From the petals, rose oil, perfumes, and rose water is made. Rose water and rose petals are used for marmalade, desserts, rose vinegar, and fragrance potpourri. Garnish with and enjoy roses in salads, drinks, cakes, and desserts.

Elderflower, *Sambucus nigra*, blooms by the end of June with flat white clusters of flowers. Fry newly bloomed flowers, freeze them in ice cubes,

or dry the flowers and use for a fever-reducing tea. Note! Do not confuse the dibble elder with the toxic red elderberry, which blooms with yellow-green and oval flower clusters during late spring. It has red berries during the summer.

Tangerine Gem, *Tagetes tenuifolia*, has a sharp, citrusy flavor and is well suited as a spice in salads and dishes.

Red clover, *Trifolium pratense*, and all other clover species are edible. The flowers are tasty in salads and rich in plant estrogen.

Indian cress, *Tropaeolum magus*, has a slightly peppery flavor and has been used in the Orient for thousands of years. All salads and dishes will look beautiful with these wonderful flowers in their glowing orange-red and yellow colors. Tender cress seeds can be used as capers or placed in a jar with stock from caper seeds.

Wood violet, *Viola odorata*, has wonderfully scented, blue violet flowers early in the spring. It can easily be confused with heath violet, *Viola canine*, and common dog-violet, *Viola riviniana*, which also are edible. Use violas and pansies as decoration in salads, drinks, cakes, and desserts. The beautiful flowers can also be frozen in ice cubes.

Wild Pansy, *Viola tricolor*, blooms beautifully in the spring. Garnish salads, drinks, cakes, and desserts with pansies. The can also be frozen in ice cubes.

Harvest tips:
- Only pick flowers where there are plenty of them, never any endangered species.
- Only pick one flower here and there so they get a chance to set seeds.
- Only pick flowers that you recognize. There are many toxic species, like buttercups, anemones, belladonna, crocus, common foxglove, and lily-of-the-valley.
- Do not eat a lot of only one flower since it could have unwanted medicinal effects.
- Many flowers close up after harvest. Use them freshly picked or place them in water in order for them to bloom again.

Vegetables, root vegetables, and mushrooms

Is there anything more wonderful than cooking food with good, nutritional, and colorful vegetables? The fact that vegetables, root vegetables, onions, and mushrooms are also the most climate-smart products we can eat is just a bonus.

LETTUCE AND GREEN SHOOTS

There are a variety of different types of lettuce to buy. Many are sold in mixtures of young leaves. The more color the leaves have, the more nutrition and antioxidants they have.

Castel Franco is a very beautiful lettuce that comes in pink and green. It comes from Italy where it is also known as young rosé. It is tasty and flavorful.

Catalogna lettuce, also known as Italian dandelion, has long, dandelion-like leaves with a bitter taste.

Oak leaf lettuce is a variant of butterhead lettuce with oak-like, red brown leaves.

Endive lettuce, which is grown for two years, is compact and tapering with a bitter taste. There is also a red type. It is good in salads as well as boiled, braised, or baked.

Escarole lettuce is related to the endive lettuce and has a somewhat bitter taste.

Frisée lettuce has narrow, curly leaves and a bitter taste. Just like the endive, it stems from chicory.

Butterhead lettuce is rich in beta-carotene and lutein.

Loose leaf is a form of butterhead lettuce that can be harvested during a longer period of time.

Iceberg lettuce is a very sustainable variant of butterhead lettuce. The iceberg lettuce is specially developed for its crisp leaves and does not contain a lot of nutrition.

Lollo rosso is related to the butterhead lettuce and has bitter, red-brown, curly, and thick leaves.

sunflower sprouts

romaine lettuce

celery

lollo rosso

butterhead lettuce

iceberg lettuce

Maché, field lettuce or spring lettuce, is a small, finer type of lettuce with a nutty flavor. It can be bought in small, decorative bunches.

Purslane is an old cultural plant that was grown as early as the Middle Ages. The mildly tart leaves are very nutritious, and especially filled with omega-3 fatty acids, among other EPAs, which otherwise mostly can be found in fatty fish and algae. Purslane is also rich in vitamin E, as well as magnesium, calcium, and iron.

The leaves are easy and fast to grow. You pick the leaf shoots as they grow and use in salads or as spinach in stir-fry, vegetable dips, and soups.

Romaine lettuce has long, big crispy leaves and is an ingredient in the classic Caesar salad.

Radicchio lettuce is similar to red cabbage with decorative and bitter leaves that are good to use in salads.

Arugula lettuce, also known as mustard cabbage, has a wonderful and slightly spicy flavor. It was cultivated as early as the Middle Ages. Arugula is very easy to grow, even in window boxes, and it can handle cold relatively well.

Chard can be found in several different colors and is related to sugar beets and beetroots. This easy-to-grow and nutritious plant is rich in vitamin C and E, beta-carotene, folic acid, magnesium, and iron. Chard is enduring and can be harvested all throughout November. Young leaves are good to use in salads, they can be used the same way as spinach, and the stems can be cooked in stews and soups.

Celery has been cultivated for a long time in the Mediterranean, both as a medicinal plant as well as a spice. It resembles, and is related to, celeriac but has a milder taste. Celery is a diuretic and contains a lot of potassium.

Spinach is related to beetroot. Spinach is full of nutrition, especially beta-carotene, folic acid, vitamin B, C, and E as well as calcium, potassium, magnesium, iron, and lutein. Spinach also contains oxalic acid (see p. 33). Spinach goes well with most things; it can be fried with garlic or go in soups, stews, and sauces. Young leaves are good to use in salads.

arugula

maché lettuce

spinach

endive

loose-leaf lettuce

Chinese cabbage

dicchio

frisée

VEGETABLE FRUIT

Aubergine belongs to the same family as potato and tomato. It is sometimes called eggplant because of its egg-shaped form. The fruit can vary a lot in size, color, and shape. Most common is the violet types. The pulp is white and porous with the texture of a mushroom. Aubergine can be cut in slices, crumbed and fried, or baked in the oven and filled with vegetarian mincemeat.

Do not keep aubergine in the refrigerator. At temperatures below 44.6°F, it turns brown from frostbite.

Tip! Choose firm and shiny aubergine fruit that feels heavy and solid. If the fruit feels soft, it is old and will taste bitter; if it is too firm, it is not ripe. When it gives slightly if you press your finger into it, the ripeness is perfect.

Avocado originated in north South America, where it has been cultivated by the Aztecs. It is grown in most tropical countries as well as the Mediterranean countries.

There are several different kinds with varying shape and color. Avocado is rich in monounsaturated fat (15 percent) and potassium, magnesium, B vitamins, and vitamin E, as well as relatively rich in iron.

Avocado is harvested unripe and has a butter-like texture and a somewhat nutty flavor when ripe. If the fruit feels soft when you carefully press at the root top, it is ripe. Keep ripe fruit in the refrigerator.

Avocado goes well with most dishes and is tasty on bread, and in salads and dips.

Cucumber is related to pumpkin and squash. Cucumber is one of the most water-rich vegetables we have. It should be stored in a cool pantry. The refrigerator is too cold and the cucumber will "sweat," and when it is brought out at room temperature it turns infirm and watery.

Artichoke is a not-yet-bloomed flower basket from a thistle species that has been cultivated for over 5,000 years in the Mediterranean area. It is a nutritional delicacy. Artichoke is also used in many herbal products since it contains bitter substances, which support liver, bile, and digestion, and has a diuretic effect.

How to cook artichokes:
Carefully break off the stem by placing it on a table edge so that the chewy threads in the artichoke bottom comes with it when your break it. Steam or boil artichokes in water and a little salt for 30 to 45 minutes. They are done when the leaves in the middle are easy to break off. Pick up the artichokes and let them drain. Serve with butter or oil, herbed salt, and lemon slices.

How to eat artichokes:
When you eat artichokes, you break off leaf after leaf, dip the inner meaty part of the leaf in butter or dressing, and pull the meat off with your teeth. When all the leaves are gone you tear off the inner leaves and cut off the hairy mass, "the choke" in the middle. Under the choke hides the best part of the vegetable: the artichoke heart.

Corn has been cultivated by the Native Americans for 5,000 years. There are different strains with red, black, blue, yellow, or white kernels. Out of the world's most cultivated grains, corn comes in second place after rice. What people eat in Sweden are the unripe cobs from sweet corn and miniature corn.

Fresh corn has light yellow, firm, and juicy filled kernels. Corn is perishable, and it is the most tasty if you can eat it the same day it is harvested. Newly harvested corn is very good to eat raw. Corn tastes great oven baked, grilled, or boiled, and corn is tasty in salads or stews.

Bell pepper. All bell peppers are green when unripe but as they ripen, depending on their strain they turn red, yellow, orange, or violet. The red pepper is the sweetest and the yellow the most mild. Tomato bell pepper has a somewhat milder taste than the regular one.

Bell peppers are very rich in vitamin C and E. The yellow contains the most vitamin C and the green the most vitamin E. The red bell pepper is very rich in carotene. Yellow bell pepper has the highest amount of protective substances, especially astaxanthin. Bell peppers are good to use in salads, stews, and sauces. Paprika powder has a flavor-enhancing effect.

Pumpkin, also known as winter squash, originated in South America and has been cultivated for 5,000 years. There are many different kinds, and they can be stored for a long time. Pumpkins are very nutritional and have an especially large amount of beta-carotene and lutein.

Many pumpkins are similar to sweet potato in flavor. They are particularly tasty when baked in the oven, but can also be boiled, fried, and used in soups and stews. Roast the seeds and eat for a snack.

Tomatoes go well with most food and are rich in lycopene and vitamin C. Sun-dried tomatoes need to be soaked in water a few hours before using them.

Tip! Let unripe tomatoes sit at room temperature in order for them to develop color as well as antioxidants and aroma. After this, they can be stored in the refrigerator. Room temperature tomatoes have a better aroma than refrigerated cold ones.

Asparagus was cultivated in Egypt as early as 5,000 years ago. It is a lily plant and the same plant can provide a crop for up to 25 years. There are two kinds of asparagus. The white strain is grown at high altitudes and is cut off under the soil when the top shoots come out. White asparagus will become discolored if it is exposed to light and has to be peeled since the skin is bitter. Green asparagus is more nutritional and considerably easier to grow.

Green asparagus is primarily rich in antioxidants and folic acid and quite rich in vitamin C. Asparagus has been used in folk medicine as a diuretic agent and for digestion problems.

Grilled asparagus is very delicious, but when boiled it is a delicacy as well. It is suitable as a starter, in salads, and as a side dish. Eat with a vinaigrette, with butter, herb oil, or dressing. Asparagus is also good for sauces and soups.

How to cook asparagus:
Bend the bottom part of the stems and break it where the stem is still crispy. Tie the stems together in a bundle. Place the asparagus with the top up in a pan with a little more than 2 inches of boiling soy and salted water. Boil for 2 to 10 minutes depending on how fresh the asparagus is. Lift up the asparagus by using tongs. Quickly dip the tops in the boiling water.

Zucchini or squash is related to pumpkin and cucumber. Squash is easy to cultivate and provides a big harvest. In Italy it is called zucchini; in France, courgette; and in the U.S., squash. The smaller the fruit, the finer the texture and the more nutty the flavor. Usually the flavor is very neutral, which makes squash go well with most dishes, especially in dishes with tomatoes and stir-fry.

Health effect and nutritional value for vegetable fruit:
- Vegetable fruit are most of all rich in dietary fiber and vitamins B and C. The nutritional value varies depending on the kind of vegetable, if they are newly harvested and ripe. Handling as well as location and length of storage are important as well.
- Contain antioxidants. See ORAC values, p. 48.
- Have an anti-inflammatory effect.
- Decreases the risk of heart and vascular diseases.
- Can protect you against cancer.

kohlrabi

turnips

fennel

Chinese cabbage

CABBAGE

All kinds of cabbage likely derive from a purple colored strain of cabbage that grows wild on the coasts of southern and western Europe. Cabbage has always been an important vegetable. The Egyptians believed that cabbage was divine and that the overlapping leaves had a symbolic meaning. Cabbage has also been very appreciated within folk medicine. It is considered to cleanse blood and skin as well as work against many problems, anything from headaches to cancer.

In all kinds of cabbage there are goitrogen substances in small amounts. These substances are water-soluble and heating will destroy them. If your diet often contains large amounts of raw cabbage, these substances can result in the appearance of a goiter.

Cauliflower is harvested when the flower bud still has not bloomed. Use tender leaves and the peeled-off petals as well. Cauliflower is most of all rich in vitamin C and B. It is also tasty in salads, gratins, soups, when steamed or boiled, in stir-fry, and stews.

Broccoli is related to cauliflower and is harvested when the flower buds are green and have not yet bloomed. Use both the heads and the peeled stem. Broccoli is rich in antioxidants, vitamin B, C, and E, folic acid, phosphorus, and potassium. Use broccoli in salads, soups, stews, gratins, and in stir-fry.

Brussels sprouts are rich in vitamin C, carotene, and iron. It will taste the best after a cold snap. Use raw in salads. Brussels sprouts are also tasty in soups, stews, and gratins.

red cabbage

kale

romanesco

rutabaga

Fennel has a tasty, tender, and a little spicy flavor, similar to anise. It is very nutritional; primarily, it is rich in antioxidants, folic acid, and iron as well as plant estrogen. Fennel can be used in salads, braised, boiled, or oven baked.

Kale belongs to one of our oldest kitchen plants. It is very nutritional and contains a great amount of antioxidants, iron, calcium, and vitamins B, C, and E. It can be found fresh on the market from September to December. Since it is frost-proof, it can be harvested all the way into the month of March. You can also use the tasty and crispy peeled stem. Kale is great in salads, sauces, and soups.

Kohlrabi is easy to grow and contains a lot of vitamin C. It will turn out the most tasty and crispy if it is harvested young. Small and newly harvested kohlrabi do not need to be peeled and are good when grated raw.

Rutabaga is rich in vitamin C. Botanically it is a kind of cabbage, but it is normally considered to be a root vegetable. Rutabaga is very tasty if grated raw, oven-baked, in mashed root vegetables, stews, and gratins.

Turnip has a mild and nice cabbage flavor. The leaves can be eaten as a salad or used as spinach. Turnips have been considered to be blood-cleansing and-strengthening and have been used in folk medicine.

    The turnip is tasty when grated raw or boiled as a side dish or in stews.

Tip! The marrow of the stem in kale, broccoli, and Brussels sprouts is a crispy delicacy that can be eaten raw or in stir-fry. Peel it first.

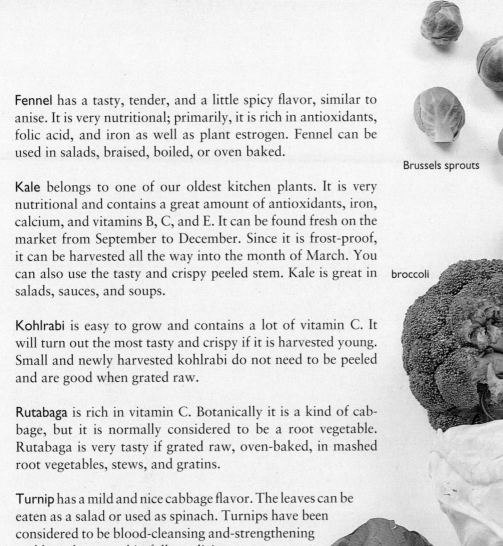

Brussels sprouts

broccoli

pointed cabbage

bok choi

red and green Savoy cabbage

cauliflower

White cabbage is a praised vitamin C-rich leafy vegetable that can be found all year round. During summer and early autumn, a more crispy and tender variant called summer cabbage is sold. Use white cabbage in salads, creamed vegetables, cabbage rolls, and stir-fry.

Tip! Choose heavy and firm cabbage heads.

Romanesco is a cross-breeding of broccoli and cauliflower. It has a mild flavor and is very decorative. The peeled stem can also be used. Romanesco is most of all used in salads and for dipping but is also tasty in soups, gratins, stews, and stir-fry.

Red cabbage can be found fresh during autumn and winter. It has the same nutritional values and is used in the same way as white cabbage.

Chinese cabbage has an aromatic flavor, and the texture is crispy.

It is popular is Asian cuisine, most of all in stir-fry and bundles filled with mincemeat. Chinese cabbage is tasty in salads as well as boiled or creamed. It can also replace white cabbage in cabbage rolls or cabbage pudding.

Savoy cabbage is tender, has a mild flavor, and is very decorative, especially the red variant. The Savoy cabbage is tasty when boiled or braised but can also be used in salads.

Pointed cabbage is a kind of white cabbage with a pointy head and has a milder and finer flavor than white cabbage.

Health effects and nutritional value for cabbage:
- Cabbage contains dietary fiber and is very nutritional, especially in vitamin C and folic acid, and also has the minerals potassium and calcium.
- Rich in antioxidants. See ORAC values, p. 48.
- Has an anti-inflammatory effect.
- Can prevent cancer.
- Can prevent heart and vascular diseases.
- Considered cleansing to the liver.

Asian leafy vegetables have been cultivated in China and Japan for thousands of years. There are several kinds like bok choy, kyona, or tatsoi, and most of them belong to the cabbage family. Bok choy almost looks like chard but is much more tender and crispy. It does not contain a lot of oxalic acid.

The nutritional leaves are very tasty, grow quickly, and provide a good harvest even if the temperature has dropped several degrees below zero. They are sown in cycles starting in very early spring and ending in late summer. Use the delicious leaves in salads, soups, filling, stews, and, above all, in stir-fry.

ROOT VEGETABLES

Our root vegetables can be used for various delicious dishes and are generally not very expensive when they are in season.

How to cook root vegetables:
If you boil potatoes and other root vegetables with the skin on, the nutrients are better preserved. First bring salted water to a boil and then let the root vegetables simmer. If you boil them too vigorously, the skin will crack and the nutrients end up in the boiling water. Potatoes are especially sensitive to vigorous boiling.

Cassava belongs to the base ingredients in African cuisine. There is a sweet and a bitter variant. The root is boiled and eaten on the side with stews and creamed dishes just like when we use boiled potatoes.

Salsify is a very old cultural plant that grows wild in large parts of Europe and also in Sweden. It is related to black salsify and has a sweet flavor. The beautiful plant's leaves are also nice in salads. Salsify is a delicacy in salads, boiled, in gratins, and oven baked.

Jerusalem artichoke is related to the sunflower and belongs in North America. The white or red irregularly shaped lumps have a mild and nutty flavor. Jerusalem artichoke is very rich in soluble fiber and iron; other than this, it has about the same nutritional value as potato. Jerusalem artichokes are a delicacy, especially baked in the oven. They are also tasty when freshly grated or thinly sliced in salads as well as in gratins and soups.

Carrots are popular all over the world. Two-thirds of the vegetables people eat in Sweden are carrots. Carrots are primarily rich in beta-carotene. They can be shredded or used in stews and soups.

Carrot has been a part of many home remedies for most illnesses. From 200 AD, Athenaeus from Naucratis wrote this about the carrot in his work *The Sophists at Dinner*: "It has a fairly strong flavor, very nourishing and quite healthy, has a tendency to turn soft and crooked, is not very easy to digest but very diuretic and is considered to increase the libido, therefore it is known as the love root."

Parsnip was banned in monastery gardens since it was considered to help the love life. It is very rich in fiber and contains a fair amount of vitamin C and minerals. It has a tasty and spicy sweet flavor. Use it grated and raw, cooked, in stews, gratins, and soups.

Potatoes have been cultivated by the natives in South America for thousands of years. The Spaniards brought it to Europe during the 1500s. In the North, potatoes became popular when it was discovered that you could make potato liquor during the 1800s. During war and years of famine, the potato replaced grains, since it is so full of nutrients. It is likely this that has contributed to making potatoes one of our most important basic food. Potatoes contain almost all nutrients we need but in small amounts. Baked potatoes, potato wedges, and hash browns are cheap delicacies. Potatoes are also tasty if you mash them, in gratins, soups, and stews.

Do not use potatoes that are damaged or have green spots. They usually contain too much of the neurotoxin solanin.

Radish is related to daikon and its fresh and somewhat spicy flavor comes from mustard oil. They are very rich in vitamin C and are good for liver and bile production. Radishes are decorative and give a lovely flavor to salads, soups, and stews. Tender leaves are good for salads.

Daikon has thicker skin and sharper taste than radishes. There are several kinds of daikon: white, black, and red. Daikon has been used in folk medicine to cure coughing and hoarseness, and works well as a savory. Daikon is rich in iron and vitamin C. It is tasty to eat shredded or sliced in salads and soups.

Celeriac is a strongly aromatic root vegetable that flavors soups, stews, and gratins. Grate raw celeriac and mix with a tasty dressing. The leaves can also be used. Celeriac is diuretic.

Root parsley is most of all rich in iron and calcium, beta-carotene, and vitamin C. It can be used in the place of parsnip, which it outperforms in both taste and nutritional value. Use both leaves and root in salads, gratins, stews, and soups.

Beetroot is closely related to chard and is just as rich in nitrates. In folk medicine, beetroot has been considered to be blood-strengthening. There are beets with different colors like yellow, white, and red-white. The smaller they are, the better they taste. Beetroot leaves can be used the same way as spinach. Use the beetroot in raw food, bake in the oven, or boil and use in stews and soups.

Tips! Boil beetroots with skin and root tip, otherwise they easily lose their color and turn tasteless. It is easy to rub off the peel if you rinse the hot, newly boiled beetroots with cold water. Use plastic gloves.

Health effects and nutritional value for root vegetables:
- Root vegetables are rich in fiber and also contain B vitamins and minerals like potassium. The vitamin content is at its peak during autumn and is then reduced while storing.
- Contains antioxidants. See ORAC values, p. 48.
- Decreases the risk for heart and vascular diseases.

Black salsify is related to dandelion and rich in fiber and iron. The skin is coarse and sticky but can be peeled after boiling. Black salsify, also known as viper's herb, is tasty both when boiled and oven-baked.

Sweet potato is not related to our potatoes and has a lower GI value. Sweet potatoes are very rich in carotenoids and potassium and fairly rich in iron.

There are several different kinds, and they are called batat or yam and are used in African countries the same way that potatoes are used here. Sweet potatoes have a sweet flavor and are tasty when oven-baked, boiled, or fried as a side dish. It is often used in desserts and cookies.

ONION

As early as 3,000 years ago, onions were cultivated in China. Onions have been an important ingredient in both food and medicine throughout the times. The warmer the climate is, the bigger and milder the onion. The name means "strongly scented" and refers to the characteristic smell, which in turn is caused by several different sulfur compounds in the onion plant. But it is not until you start to cut an onion that the sulfur compounds are released and start to smell.

These sulfur compounds, allyl sulfides, found in all onions, but most of all in garlic, are what have the medicinal attributes. Unheated onion has the best effect. Store all unions, except for leeks, dry and cool, preferably in paper bags.

Tips!
- Peel and chop the onion with good circulation, for example, under the kitchen fan.
- Cut and chop onions on a separate cutting board since the board easily absorbs the onion taste. A wooden cutting board will be good as new after scrubbing or if you rub it with lemon juice.
- The smell of onions on your fingers is reduced by rubbing your fingers with half a lemon.
- Fry onions on a low heat or oven-bake it! This will bring out the sweetness and lovely aroma of the onion.

Health effects and nutritional values for onion:
- Antioxidants. See ORAC values, p. 48.
- Antibacterial effect, especially garlic.
- Anti-inflammatory effect.
- Reduces the risk of heart and vascular diseases.
- Can protect you against cancer.

Yellow onion is the most common kind. During summer season it is sold in bundles with the leaves. If the leaves are fresh and undamaged, they can be used as well.

Leeks are the mildest and most nutritional type of onion, but they do not contain as many sulfur compounds as other onions. They are very rich in beta-carotene, vitamin C, and folic acid.

Tip! Soil and sand are often hidden between the leaves. Therefore cut it lengthwise and rinse the leaves carefully in water.

Pearl onion is small and flat in its shape with a yellow peel and white meat. It is tasty to roast.

Red onion has a milder, richer, and less sweet flavor than yellow onion. It is also very decorative, especially in salads.

Scallion, spring onion, is a tender and mild onion that is tasty in salads and stir-fry.

Shallot has a deliciously rich and fine taste. It is a brown red onion that is divided into smaller cloves. There is also a bigger and oval kind, banana shallot.

Chinese garlic

Silver onion is a large white onion grown in south Europe. It has a mild and fine taste.

Pickled onion is a silver-white miniature onion that is mostly used for pickling.

Garlic has been cultivated for over 6,000 years. It originated in China. There are several different kinds of garlic, like King solo or Super solo, which is somewhat milder and consists of one big clove that is easy to peel. Fresh garlic is a delicacy with a milder taste. Store garlic in a garlic container made of clay.

A proven method to remove the garlic smell is to chew parsley, chervil, peppermint, or ginger.

Growing tips: Garlic is easy to grow. Plant big and healthy cloves in humus-rich and well-fertilized soil in September. As soon as the beginning of May, you can start harvesting the leaves. The onion is harvested in July to August.

leeks

pickled onions

silver onions

yellow onion

garlic

banana shallots

fresh garlic

pearl onions

yellow onions

red onions

MUSHROOM

In Japan, the shiitake mushroom has been cultivated since 200 AD. Europeans started growing and selling mushrooms in the middle of the 1700s. Mushroom is a delicacy that enhances the flavors of most dishes. Mushrooms are good to fry, grill, braise, or boil. Salads with raw mushrooms should be eaten instantly and not be saved for leftovers.

Do not rinse mushrooms unless it is necessary, since many of the flavors are water-soluble. The best thing is if you can brush off eventual traces of soil. Keep mushrooms in a paper bag in the refrigerator. Even if the mushrooms dry a little, you can still use them.

Dried mushrooms are soaked in hot water for at least 10 minutes or at room temperature water for 30 minutes. Then squeeze dry and cook the mushroom in the usual way. Use the water leftover from sauces for soaking.

Do not salt until the dish is done, since salt drives the fluid out of the mushroom.

White button mushroom is the most common mushroom, which can be eaten both raw and cooked. Raw white button mushrooms contain a substance, agaritin, which can be toxic in high doses.

Sheep polypore generally grows in our forests. Cut off the bottom and blanch the tops. It is tasty if marinated and grilled.

Blanched sheep polypore without the stem can be stored in the freezer.

Chanterelles are one of our native delicacies and are more nutritional than other mushrooms. They are rich in beta-carotene as well as vitamin D, which is normally not found in vegetables.

Penny bun or **porcino** is one of the most delicious food mushrooms we have and is especially

Health effects and nutritional value

- Mushrooms contain dietary fiber, small amounts of protein of good quality, as well as B vitamins and some minerals.
- Many mushrooms contain substances with medicinal effects.
- Shiitake is the most studied and has the following health effects: strengthens the immune system, has an antibacterial effect, can lower cholesterol and blood pressure, can protect against cancer.

appreciated in Italian and French cuisine. In central and southern Europe, the mushroom is sold dried in thin slices. The smell of penny bun has a strong resemblance to hazelnuts, and it is a delicacy when fried, cooked, creamed, or in soups.

Baby Bella or **brown mushrooms** are grown in the same way as white, but do not belong to the same family. They have a strong mushroom flavor and are found in different sizes. It is used and cooked the same way as white button mushrooms.

A mushroom that has opened up has more flavor than one that is closed.

Oyster mushroom grows in groups on trees with the hats on top of each other. This protein-rich mushroom has a "meaty" texture and delightful flavor. The foot can sometimes be a little woody and you should then cut off at least the bottom part.

Portabello is really a fully grown Baby Bella, 4 to 5 inches in diameter. It has a rich, aromatic flavor and tastes the best when cooked.

Quorn is an alternative to meat and reminds you of chicken. Quorn is produced from a special mold fungi called *Fusarium veneatum* and is a processed industry product. Mycelium threads create a firm, doughy mycoprotein which is

baby bella mushrooms

funnel chanterelles

white button mushrooms

extracted and treated with heat. Then the substance is dried and egg white is added to bind the product. Lastly, the Quorn mass is given its final structure and texture depending on what kind of meat it is supposed to resemble—for example, mincemeat or chicken.

Quorn is low in fat and very rich in fiber, a complete protein, and a good source of zinc. It can be bought frozen in smaller pieces made for stews, fillets, mincemeat, and pre-made Quorn products. Quorn can be fried, grilled, used in stir-fry, stews, on bread, and in salads. Fillets and smaller pieces of Quorn are tastier if they are marinated before cooked.

Replace the chicken in a recipe with Quorn.

Shiitake is named after the tree shii that it was originally cultivated from in Japan. It has a "meatier" texture than most other mushrooms and a strong, somewhat smoky flavor. Shiitake mushrooms are used as herbal medicine in Japan. The stems are quite chewy and are either cut off or used for flavor in broths and sauces.

Funnel Chanterelles usually grow plentifully in autumn, and they are easy to dry.

chanterelles

oyster mushroom

funnel chanterelles

Portobello

baby bella

shiitake

Noriark, seaweed

Kombu, kelp

Hijiki, seaweed

Dulse, seaweed

Wakame, seaweed

Seaweed and wild plants

In the past, humans had to make use of wild plants and seaweed to survive. The knowledge about wild plants and seaweed that can be used as both food and medicine is inherited from our ancestors.

An interesting finding in Denmark has shown us what humans in the Stone Age ate. A man from that time was found in a bog. Thanks to the bog's preservative effect, an analysis was made of his last meal. It showed that it consisted of seeds and leaves from different wild plants like barley, oats, and flaxseed, as well as smartweed, pondweed, shepherd's purse, field mustard, sorrel, wild turnip, and bindweed.

SEAWEED HAS DEVELOPED in the ocean for millions of years and has been used both as food and medication. As early as 600 BC, the Chinese writer Sze Teu wrote, "Seaweed is a delicacy I serve all of my guests of honor." Seaweed, or algae, as it is also called, is used on a daily basis in Japanese, Chinese, and Korean cuisine.

But seaweed has been eaten in Europe as well. Nordic Vikings are said to have survived their long voyages on the sea thanks to seaweed. Their favorite seaweed is supposed to have been the Irish dulse seaweed, which they preferred to eat raw.

Mineral-rich seaweed. Through constant erosion, nutrients from land have washed down into the oceans for thousands of years. It has depleted our soils of minerals and micronutrients, while the oceans have been fortified. In the oceans we can find all the nutrients that we need. Our blood contains the same salts as the ocean water and in the same proportions, although our blood is five times more diluted.

The ocean's plants, for the majority, are made up of seaweed. In England they are called kelp; in Norway, tare; and in Sweden, tång. There are micro algae, which are unicellular and microscopically small. Together with small animals they form plankton, the nutrient source of the ocean. Macro algae are multicellular and can grow up to 1.3 feet long.

Seaweed has neither leaves nor roots but absorbs the nutrients from the ocean water directly through the cell walls. Larger, leaf-like seaweed are attached to the bottom of the ocean with something that might look like a root. All attached seaweed are called benthic algae. This seaweed is in turn divided into four groups depending on color. There are green, red, brown, and blue-green types of seaweed. Despite having different colors, the seaweed all contain the green pigment chlorophyll.

Spirulina is a blue-green micro seaweed that grows in alkaline lakes in the Mexican highlands. It has been used by the Aztecs as a diet supplement since the 1500s. Spirulina is one of the world's most nutritious plants and is especially rich in complete protein (65 percent) and astaxanthin. It also contains antibiotic and antibacterial substances that strengthens the body's immune system. Spirulina is easier to digest than ocean algae. Use spirulina in smoothies and bread.

FOREIGN SEAWEED

Agar and carrageenan. Agar is the jelly-like product you get from many different red algae that grow in warm oceans. Carrageenan is an agar-like product that is extracted from carrageen seaweed (*Chondrus crispus*) that grows on the west coast of Sweden. In natural food stores, carrageenan is sold dried and bleached as flakes or a white powder that can replace animal gelatin in desserts. The white powder is 10 times more concentrated than usual gelatin.

If you want to extract the jelly substance from carrageenan seaweed, you first rinse the seaweed, soak it, and boil it for 30 minutes. Alternatively, you only soak it, but for one day. Then you strain the fluid, which will harden when cooled. Carrageenan is used in products for constipation and in some cough syrups since it works like an expectorant medicine. Carrageenan is very easy to digest and primarily rich in iodine.

Arame is a thin and narrow red seaweed that can be used after 10 minutes of soaking. It has a mild flavor and is very useful. Soaked arame seaweed is tasty in stir-fry and when marinated. Season with soy, ginger, and sesame oil. Use as a garnish or in soups or stews.

Dulse or dillisk is red seaweed that grows wild along the hilly coast outside of Ireland. It can be eaten just the way it is. The flavor is a little similar to licorice. Dulse is very good in stir-fry, without soaking it, or when marinated.

Iziki, also known as hiziki or hijiki, is a thin red seaweed that needs to be cooked for about 15 minutes. It is good to marinate with garlic and mustard.

Kombu belongs to the *Laminaria* family and is a brown seaweed that grows in large parts of the world. It is very rich in iodine and should not be eaten more than once a month. Seaweed flour is usually produced from the *laminaria* species that often are included in animal feed. Kombu needs to be cooked for about 30 minutes.

Tip! It is easy to make yummy seaweed snacks. Break kombu seaweed into smaller pieces and fry them in coconut fat until they puff up.

Mekabu is a brown seaweed that needs to be cooked for 20 to 25 minutes. Steam it with onions. That will give it a light and sweet taste.

Nori is the most popular and protein-rich seaweed in Japan. It is sold in thin, paper-like sheets and is most of all used for sushi. Nori does not contain a lot of iodine, and you can eat larger amounts of nori than other seaweed.

When you roast nori for a few seconds over a hot stove burner, in the frying pan, or oven grill, it gets a peculiar seafood flavor. When the color changes into gold shimmering green, it is done. Tear or cut in smaller pieces and eat as a snack, or crumble it and use as a spice.

Wakame is a brown seaweed that is an important ingredient in Japanese miso soup. It cooks in 5 to 10 minutes and can be used in salads, soups, and stews. When soaked, it is good to stir-fry flavored with soy and sesame oil.

SWEDISH SEAWEED

Most edible seaweed grows on the west coast. On rocky shores, islets, skerries, and shallow submerged reefs are plenty of seaweed. During the summer, the main growth occurs, and that is the most suitable time to harvest. Choose places where the water circulation is good. Never pick seaweed near ports or next to discharges of industrial waste or sewages.

It is much easier to pick seaweed than mushrooms, since no toxic seaweed that grows on the bottom of the ocean has been discovered along Swedish coastlines. On the other hand, there is seaweed that does not taste very good, is too hard to digest, or has a strongly laxative effect. Seaweed has another advantage. It grows in large populations and is easy to harvest.

▼ THIS IS HOW Swedish seaweed grows.

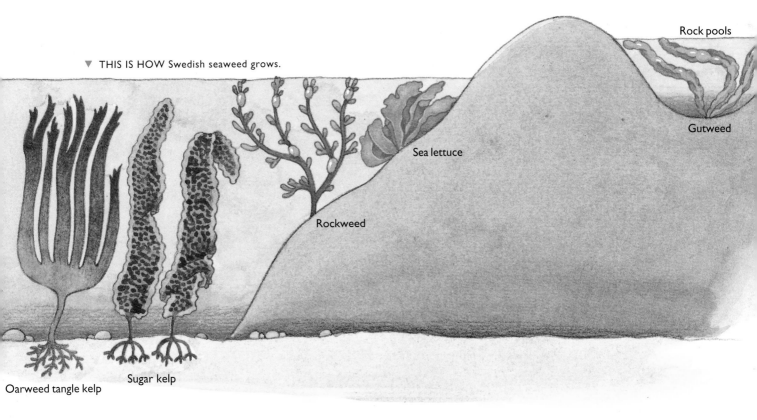

Rock pools

Gutweed

Sea lettuce

Rockweed

Oarweed tangle kelp

Sugar kelp

Rockweed, *Ascophyllum nodosum*. This perennial brown seaweed is olive green. It has sparsely forked branches on a string-like body that periodically curls up in oval-shaped gas-filled sacs. It is easy to recognize and pick. Rockweed grows all along the west coast and in the northern Öresund on rocks in a depth of around 0.6 to 1.6 feet. The rock weed thrives on protected shores.

Only harvest the outer shoots, 4 to 6 inches. That is where the seaweed is the youngest and most tender. The cooking time varies with age; count on 20 to 45 minutes. Rockweed is tasty boiled with squeezed lemon or cooked in soups, stews, or gratins.

Gutweed, *Ulva intestinalis*. This one-year seaweed consists of light green, unbranched, tube-shaped, often gas-filled, intestine-like shoots. Gutweed is very common and grows on shallow gravel and stone shores or in water-filled caves. It grows both on the west coast and in the Baltic Sea. Use it fresh or dried. Roast dried gutweed in a dry frying pan while stirring, and sprinkle over food like a spice.

Oarweed, *Laminaria digital*. This seaweed belongs to the same family as the kombu seaweed and is a perennial, strong, and large brown seaweed. Oarweed is primarily rich in iron and grows all along the west coast as well as in the south Baltic Sea. Usually it grows in a depth of 3 to 23 feet. It thrives in circulating water but still somewhat separate from the larger parts of the lake, like in bed-rock incisions.

Laminaria seaweed grows new leaves that are formed every year in the transition between leaf and stem. The old leaf then falls off. Harvest the lower parts of the seaweed. Let the seaweed cook with soups and stews. It should cook for at least 15 to 20 minutes. Oarweed is good to fry in oil.

Sea belt, *Laminaria saccharina*. Sea belt has a brown, wide, lancet-like leaf with wavy edges and a wrinkled middle section. Often it grows together with oarweed and is used in the same way. Sea belt is rich in iodine and bromine.

rockweed

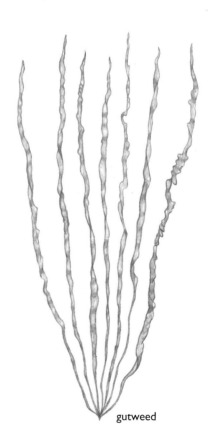

gutweed

Sea lettuce, *Ulva lactuca*. This one-year seaweed has 3 to 6 inches of light-green lettuce-like leaves, that often are branched and folded. Sea lettuce grows along all of the west coast and in the south Baltic Sea. It is primarily rich in ion and iodine. Use it fresh in salads or boil it together with other vegetables.

How to prepare fresh seaweed

Clean all seaweed as soon after harvest as possible. If the seaweed is allowed to sit for too long, it turns slimy and unappetizing. Cut off all the damaged parts. Rinse the seaweed well in fresh water. That will rinse off remaining small animals. Cut them in smaller pieces and store them cold. Dry the rinsed and cleaned seaweed straight on clean rocks in the sun. Store the dried seaweed in a dry place, preferably in a glass jar with a lid.

Nutritional value and health effects

In seaweed, you can find all minerals and micronutrients. They are rich in B vitamins (B12 in very small amounts), vitamin C (only fresh algae), D, E, and K, as well as antioxidants like astaxanthin. Since seaweed contains a large amount of iodine it is important not to eat too much. To eat seaweed with your food once a week is enough.

- Seaweed contains natural antibiotic substances.
- Seaweed strengthens the body's immune system.
- Seaweed can decrease the risk of heart and vascular diseases.
- Seaweed can protect you against cancer.
- Brown seaweed can keep us clean from radioactive decay and possibly also heavy metals. In brown seaweed there is a substance, alginic acid, which has the ability to absorb and concentrate heavy metals and radioactive substances like cesium and strontium-90 in both ocean water and our bodies. But since we cannot digest these substances the seaweed will not release any toxins and instead pass right through the body and come out with waste. It is important to choose seaweed that grows in clean water.

oarweed

sea belt

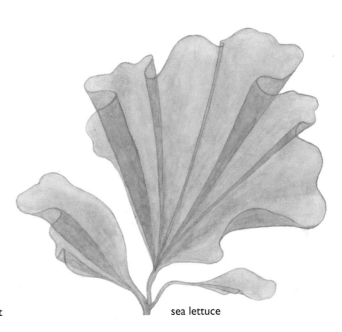

sea lettuce

WILD PLANTS IN FOOD

It is said that more than 230 wild plants that can be used in food exist in Sweden. Take the opportunity to eat fresh herbs when they grow during the summer. Even early in spring it is possible to start harvesting young leaves. Wild plants can be used in the following ways:

- Similar to spinach: Many herbs, like nettle, goosefoot, and ground elderflower, can be used the same way as spinach in stir-fry, soups, and stews.
- In salads: Young leaves from fireweed, goosefoot, bittercress, garlic mustard, wild strawberries, red clovers, and dandelions.
- In dressings and bread: Grind herbs like goosefoot, nettle, and common chickweed in a mixer and mix with dressings and in bread doughs.
- In drinks: Mix nettles, common chickweed, and goosefoot with water and fresh ginger. For a thicker texture, add avocado, cucumbers, pears, or bananas.

Ground elder, *Aegopodium podagraria*, also called herb gerard or goutweed, is a dreaded weed.

It grows in large populations in shady places and quickly spreads out at the expense of other plants. Young ground elder has a tasty and spicy flavor. Use the leaves the same way you use spinach in salads, soups, stews, and gratins.

Yarrow, *Achillea millefolium*, grows wild all over the country. It is an old medicinal plant that primarily has been used for wounds. But it is also considered to be strengthening to the stomach, an anti-convulsant, as well as stimulating for digestion. Yarrow has a sharp and spicy flavor. Use small amounts of young leaves as a spice or use for tea.

Ramson, *Allium ursine*, has leaves that are similar to the poisonous leaves of lily-of-the-valley, but the strong smell of garlic excludes any risk of confusion. From May to June it blooms beautiful white flowers. Ramson was earlier used in folk medicine and was considered to have a disinfecting and blood pressure-reducing effect, like garlic. Finely chopped ramson leaves add a fine garlic flavor in salads, cream cheese, and dressings. The leaves can also be fried and used the same way as garlic.

Bittercress, *Barbarea vulgarism*, is a very common weed that looks like field mustard. It belongs to the very first herbs to be harvested in the spring. The earlier the leaves are picked, the milder the taste will be. Young leaves are tasty in salads. When the stems come up in May to June the leaves turn chewy. Boil the not-yet-bloomed flower buds like "mini broccoli."

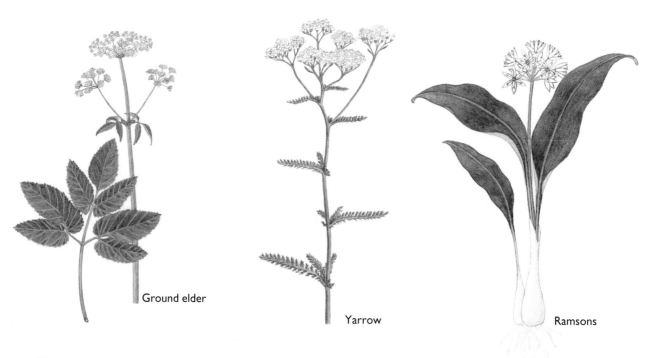

Ground elder

Yarrow

Ramsons

Lamb's quarters, *Chenopodium album*, is a very common weed. The leaves have an irregular shape, and both leaves and stem often look a little mealy. There are many different kinds in the family like grassleaf orache, garden orache and common orache. They are all edible and very nutritional. They are tasty when used as spinach in salads, dressings, soups, stews, and gratins.

Fireweed, *Epilobium angustifolium*, has beautiful pink red flowers that light up clear-cut fields and open spots. Fireweed grows wild in large populations all of the country. Earlier, the whole plant was used, primarily as feed for cows, since it was believed to increase milk production. The leaves were fermented as well as dried and were considered to be the best replacement for Chinese tea. Tender shoots can be used in salads and in the same way as spinach. The root is boiled like a root vegetable.

Field horsetail, *Equisetum ravens*, also known as common horsetail, grows wild all over the country, on the side of roads, in ditches, and in forests. In folk medicine, the field horsetail tea has been used as a universal preparation to help most problems. The herb is rich in silica and is considered to increase the strength of connective tissue and is also diuretic. Boil it and make

tea or mix it in green drinks when it is tender in early summer.

Autumn Joy, *Sedum telephinum*, is a succulent plant that is common on rocky hills and stony ground. It was once used for scurvy and is considered to have a diuretic effect. Use the leaves in salads or boil them.

Common chickweed, *Stellaria media*, is a troublesome weed that often forms entire carpets that suffocate all other vegetation. Use the leaves in energy drinks and salads.

Lamb's quarters   Fireweed

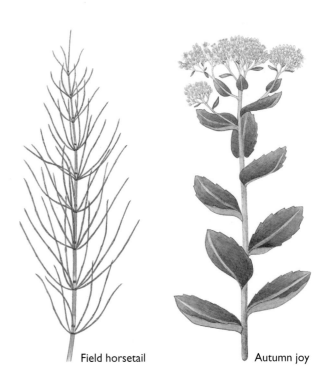

Field horsetail   Autumn joy

Dandelion, *Taraxacum official.* There are many hundreds of different kinds of dandelions. Some species are less bitter. They are often lighter in color and grow in wet spots. If you want light and fine dandelion leaves, you can cover the plant with leaves or an upside-down bucket. Most of the bitterness is found in the leaf's middle vein. If you tear it off and only eat the green of the leaf, the taste will be milder.

The dandelion leaves' bitter substances strengthen the stomach and are good for problems with the liver and bile. The leaves are very nutritional. Use tender leaves in salads and for tea. Tender dandelion buds can be fried with garlic or be pickled like capers. The yellow on the flowers can be used in salads or fried in garlic. If the flowers wilt they can be placed in a bowl of water first. The root is cooked like a root vegetable.

Field penny-cress, *Thlaspi ravens,* is a common weed in fields and meadows. The leaves have an onion-like flavor and the ripe fruit a strong burning spicy flavor. Use the leaves in salads and the fruit in pickling.

Red clover, *Trifolium pratense,* is a well-known feed plant. In earlier days, both flowers and seeds were dried and ground into flour. The flour was used to supplement and enrich regular flour. Both clover flowers and leaves are tasty in salads.

Wych elm fruit, *Ulmus glabra,* are delicious to use in salads. Just-bloomed elm fruit stays fresh in a plastic bag in the refrigerator. Clean and rinse the fruit before serving. Mix it with regular vinegar dressing.

Nettles, *Urtica dioica,* are very nutritional and are believed to increase blood production, act as a diuretic, and mildly reduce blood sugar. You can pick young top shoots almost all summer. If they grow too big, you just cut down the population.

Nettles are used the same way as spinach in stews, soups, and gratins. Fried in garlic, the nettles are a delicacy. If you mix fresh nettles with a hand blender, you can eat them without getting stung, in energy drinks, sauces, and dressings.

Common chickweed

Nutritional and health benefits

- Green leaves contain virtually all of the nutrients we need and are particularly rich in carotenoids, vitamins B, C, E, K, and folic acid, calcium, silicon, iron, and zinc. Additionally, they contain small amounts of fatty acids and protein.
- Reduces the risk of cardiovascular disease. Can protect against cancer.
- Bitter herbs stimulate the liver and digestion.
- Green leaves also contain nitrate and oxalic acid.

Dandelion

Field penny-cress

Red clover

Nettle

Nuts, seeds, and whole grain products

For thousands of years, nutritional nuts, seeds, and grains have been staples. As long as fire has existed in human history, seeds have been used to make porridge. With time, the "porridge" was flattened into loaves of bread that was baked on hot stones.

NUTS AND SEEDS

Nuts and seeds are the most energy-rich food we have. They are filled with nutrients, antioxidants, healthy fatty acids, and protective substances. The more color they have—for example, the brown skin that covers many nuts—the richer they are in antioxidants.

Besides that, they are delicious—perfect as a snack and candy or to sprinkle on salads and dishes. Use them in candy, desserts, cookies, and bread or mix them into pâté, nut butter, vegan milk, or cream.

Nuts and seeds are sensitive to rancidity and mold. They should be kept in a closed container preferably in a cool pantry, refrigerator, or freezer in order for them to not turn rancid. Seeds that have turned rancid increase the production of free radicals. Do not eat nuts or seeds that taste bad.

Cashew nuts are grown in several African countries, India, Brazil, and China. They are rich in vitamins B and E, as well as magnesium, potassium, phosphorus, iron, and zinc. Cashew nuts are sold either raw or roasted.

Chia seeds are tiny seeds that originated in Mexico and were first used by the Aztecs. The seed was not only a staple food but was also sacrificed to the gods. Chia seeds are very nutritional, contain all eight essential amino acids as well as antioxidants, and are one of the best sources of omega-3 in the plant kingdom. Chia seeds are also a fantastic source of calcium; they contain 0.02 oz. per 3.5 oz.

Chia seeds also contain water-soluble fiber that lowers the blood sugar. The fiber also has a bowel regulatory effect. When you soak chia seeds, a "mucous" that is somewhat laxative is formed and helps gastritis. Use chia seeds in oatmeal, bread, cookies, raw food candy, and in smoothies.

Hemp is one of the oldest and most resistant cultural plants. It has been cultivated for several different reasons and has been used as food, medicines, and drugs. There are two different kinds of hemp and the hemp seeds we can buy that are drug-free. The nutritional seeds are, among other things, especially rich in calcium

and omega-3 and 6. Hemp seeds contain all of the eight essential amino acids. Hemp seeds are tasty in salads and breakfast dishes. They can also be used for crumbing.

Hazelnuts contain high levels of monounsaturated fat. The nutritional nut primarily contains a lot of magnesium, potassium, and vitamin E. When the brown inner skin is left, it is rich in antioxidants as well. The delicious flavor comes out when roasting them.

Peanuts originated in South America and are not nuts but legumes. Peanuts, however, contain as much fat as other nuts and can be highly allergenic. They are a better alternative to chips and Cheez Doodles (trademark) since they are rich in protein, vitamins B, and E, as well as antioxidants, magnesium, and zinc.

Chestnuts that are edible only grow by the Mediterranean sea. Fresh chestnuts are available from November to December. Choose chestnuts that feel firm and have a nice shell. Often we eat chestnuts roasted but they can also be blanched, boiled, and mixed to a purée.

How to roast chestnuts:
Cut a cross at the top on each chestnut. Place the chestnuts in a baking pan with a layer of coarse salt. Roast the chestnuts for about 30 minutes in 392 to 437°F or until the shell easily comes off and the chestnut meat is soft. Remove the outer shell and the brown skin that is inside by using a small knife. Serve warm chestnuts with soft butter, gourmet salt, and lemon slices.

Coconuts contain over 90 percent of fat—mostly saturated fat, since 70 percent of the fat is lauric acid, which belongs to medium long saturated fats, and caprylic acid, which belongs to the short saturated fats. These fats are not considered as dangerous to the heart and do not even store like regular fat in the body, but are burned off instantly by the liver and used as energy. This is why many scientists claim that it is easier to maintain weight with coconut fat.

Both of these fatty acids can be found in breast milk and also protects against fungi, viruses, and bacteria. There are scientists that say that lauric acid increases the good cholesterol and protects against heart and vascular diseases and that a high dose of lauric acid in the brain helps mental well-being.

Coconut fat becomes liquid at 77°F and is also called coconut oil. In natural health stores there are two qualities of coconut oil to buy. There is a cold-pressed, virgin coconut oil that has a mild coconut flavor, and there is coconut fat that has been heated up to 212°F to remove flavor and smell. This coconut oil is well suited for cooking. Coconut oil is equally important for external use, mainly to keep connective tissue strong and soft and for the health of your hair.

Coconut milk is the juice you get when you press heated coconut pulp. The first pressing is very thick, looks like cream, and is called coconut cream. Coconut milk is derived from the second batch when pressing the pulp and can be bought in a can or as a powder.

Flaxseeds contain a lot of omega-3 and water-soluble fiber that lowers the blood sugar. The fiber also has a bowel regulatory effect. When you soak the flaxseeds, they form a "mucus" that is somewhat laxative and helps with gastritis. If constipated, the seeds should be swallowed dry with water. They are most effective if you crush or grind them.

Whole flaxseeds practically pass through your body unchanged and the content of the nutrients lack meaning. Whole flaxseeds can be used in drinks, bread, oatmeal, or muesli.

If you want to reach the fatty acids, you have to crush the seeds with a mixer or coffee grinder.

Flaxseeds also contain a preliminary stage of hydrogen cyanide, which blocks the transport of oxygen in the body and is deadly in big doses. Therefore you should not eat more than a maximum of two tablespoons a day of crushed flaxseeds. Crushed and ground flaxseeds easily become rancid because of the high levels of polyunsaturated fatty acids. They should not be kept in the refrigerator for longer than a week and can also be kept in the freezer.

Macadamia nuts are tasty, fairly big, round nuts that grow in tropical countries.

Olives are always green when unripe and turn black when they ripen, with different color changes in red, violet, and brown. They have to be fermented in salty water in order to be palatable. Green olives contain the most antioxidants. There are many kinds of olives with different flavors and appearances. Greek black-purple kalamata olives and French small dark-brown olives are considered to be the best.

Brazil nuts are the best vegetable source of selenium. But the nut is also very sensitive to mold.

Pecan nuts belong in North America and are often used in Native American cuisine. The flavor is similar to that of walnuts but milder, and this nut contains the most antioxidants and is rich in zinc.

Pine nuts are not nuts but seeds from the pine tree. Most people allergic to nuts can eat the pine nut. It is rich in nutrients, especially in protein and the amino acid lysine. Pine nuts are often sold blanched, but the flavor is enhanced if they are roasted.

Pistachios are delightfully green and very tasty as a snack. They are very rich in antioxidants.

Pumpkin seeds are very rich in antioxidants and protein as well as squalene which is a building block for our sex steroids. They also contain phytosterols that is proven to reduce the growth of the prostate in animal testing. The pumpkin seed is tasty as a snack, especially shoyu-roasted. Pumpkin seeds are used as herbal medicine for an enlarged prostate.

Psyllium seeds are used as a bulking agent and are considered to be cholesterol-reducing. The seeds contain water-soluble fiber that lowers the blood sugar. The fiber also has a bowel regulatory effect. When you soak psyllium seeds, they form a "mucus" that is somewhat laxative, greases the bowel, and helps with gastritis.

Walnuts are the fruit of a tree that can grow up to 400 years old. The nuts are tasty and aromatic and contain large amounts of omega-3, folic acid, magnesium, and zinc.

Sesame seeds are very nutritional when unpeeled, especially in vitamins B and E, as well as calcium, potassium, phosphorus, magnesium, zinc, iron, and selenium. Black sesame seeds contain the most antioxidants.

Sesame seeds need to be crushed in order for us to absorb the nutrients. Then we also gain access to a substance called sesamin that has been shown to increase the liver's energy consumption and aids weight loss.

Sunflower seeds are nutritional and tasty seeds that contain high levels of vitamin E and polyunsaturated fatty acids as well as magnesium, iron, and zinc.

Almonds are considered to be easier to digest than other nuts and seeds. It is one of our best sources of vitamin E and also contain a lot of vitamin B, magnesium, calcium, potassium, iron, zinc, and selenium.

Oils

Oils are made from most nuts and seeds. Most oils are refined with the help of heat and chemicals. That causes the level of protective substances to be low and they can contain remnants of chemicals. Choose organic-labeled, cold-pressed oils and extra virgin olive oil.

Eat nuts and seeds
The fat in nuts and seeds is especially good for keeping energy consumption and fat-burning high. Eat nuts and seeds instead of concentrated sources of fat, like oil, butter, and margarine. We absorb less fat from whole or crushed nuts and seeds than from finely ground ones. We absorb the most fat from oils.

Olive oil. The oil that is cold-pressed in the first batch has a very fine flavor and a high level of antioxidants. It is then called virgin olive oil and can be found in three different qualities, depending on how high the content of acid is. The lower the level of acid is, the finer the olive oil. For one quart of olive oil, 11 lbs of olives are used. The finest virgin oil is labeled "natural extra virgin olive oil."

Oils that are hot-pressed have a lower quality, color, flavor, and texture. Oil labeled as olive oil or pure olive oil is a refined olive oil that has been cleaned by using heat or chemicals, and it loses protective nutrients, flavor, and character. The levels of acid can be low because the oil has been refined artificially. Oils are perishable goods and should be consumed as soon as possible. Store oils in a cool and dark place, preferably in a cool pantry.

WHOLE GRAIN PRODUCTS

All grains originally come from different types of grass that have been refined. Wheat, barley, and oats originated in the Mediterranean, rye in Eastern Europe, corn in Mexico, rice and millet from Asia. From South America come many exciting and nutritious seeds, like quinoa and canihua seeds.

People in the Scandinavian countries have primarily been cultivating barley, wheat, rye, and oats, but also buckwheat, to a lesser extent. Most grains can be bought as whole grains, crushed, brans, and flakes, as well as sifted and whole grain flour.

Wheat, regular wheat, is the grain that is most commonly used in Europe and in the U.S. The wheat used today is very refined and it can be the reason that more and more people are becoming allergic to wheat and wheat products.

Conventional wheat fields are often fertilized with sludge, which causes conventional wheat to often contain cadmium. Organically grown wheat is of another quality. Wheat can be replaced with spelt, which works well in all baking.

Cereal wheat germ is especially rich in polyunsaturated fatty acids and vitamin E and B1. The high fat level causes cereal wheat germ to have a limited perishability. Store it in a cool, dry, and dark place. Use cereal wheat germ to enrich bread, oatmeal, and muesli.

Durum flour is produced from durum wheat that is imported from the U.S. and Canada. The core is harder and more protein-rich than regular wheat, is better for baking, and makes pasta more chewy.

Couscous are grains produced from durum wheat with a grind in between regular wheat and whole grain. There is whole grain couscous. Couscous contains gluten. It is tasty in salads and to serve instead of rice or pasta. In whole grain couscous the whole grain with germ, endosperm, and bran are included.

Bulgur is whole wheat grain that is first boiled, dried, and then crushed. Bulgur is similar to couscous but has a higher nutritional value, is rich in fiber, and has more flavor. Bulgur is often used in Turkish and Middle Eastern cuisine. Bulgur contains gluten and can be served in salads and instead of rice, pasta, or potatoes.

Spelt has been cultivated in Sweden since the Stone Age, on Gotland, among other places. Spelt grows well on poor and stony soil. However, the cultivation of wheat took over since it gives a larger crop and is easier to peel.

Spelt is more nutritious, has higher level of protein, and a different amino acid composition than regular wheat. The levels of magnesium, phosphorus, as well as vitamins B1 and B2 are high. Besides this, the grain is very easy to digest. It is believed to strengthen the immune system and is used as diet food.

There are whole grains, flakes, bran, as well as sifted flour and whole grain flour made from spelt. Sifted spelt can replace regular wheat flour in dishes and bread and has excellent baking qualities. Spelt contains gluten.

Kamut is, like spelt, is an old type of wheat that originated in Egypt. Kamut is believed to be the Egyptian word for wheat. The grains have a slightly sweet and nutty flavor and are a little crispy and chewy. Kamut contains gluten but is more nutritious than regular wheat. The grains can replace rice and pasta and are delicious in salads.

Health effects and nutritional value for whole grain products

- All seeds like amaranth, buckwheat, canihua, and quinoa contain fiber and are very nutritional, especially in protein, fatty acids, vitamins B and E, as well as minerals like calcium, magnesium, phosphorus, and iron.
- All grains like wheat, rye, oat, and barley contain plenty of starch and dietary fiber; the protein level varies, and B vitamins, polyunsaturated fatty acids, and vitamin E are present, as well as minerals in varying amounts like magnesium, calcium, sodium, phosphorus, zinc, iron, and silica, depending on type of grain.
- Can reduce the risk of constipation.
- Provides a good sense of satiety when losing weight.
- Can bind bile acids.
- Can lower the levels of cholesterol in the blood.
- Reduce the risk of heart and vascular diseases.
- Can reduce the risk for a certain type of cancer in the stomach, large intestine, breast, and prostate.
- Can help diabetics and others to keep a steady blood sugar level.

Seitan is a gluten-based vegetarian replacement meat product, which Buddhist monks started making in China in the 1000s. You can buy ready-made seitan, but it is easy to make yourself, and homemade versions are more tasty.

Originally seitan was made from wheat flour but sifted spelt flour works just as well. Seitan consists of protein rich gluten and is starch-free. It is tasty to fry, grill, or use in stews and soups.

How to make seitan:
1. Mix one quart flour with 1¼ cup water and work the dough for about 5 minutes. Add more water if the dough seem too hard. The dough should be elastic. Cover the dough with plastic and let sit for 1 to 2 hours.
2. Fill the sink or a bowl with lukewarm water and place the dough in the water. Now is the time to wash off all the starch. Work the dough in the water until the water is cloudy, and then change the water several times. Continue to work the dough until it has transformed into a thready, yellow-like mass. It will take about 10 minutes.
3. Split the dough in two pieces and shape each piece into a patty. Let sit for 10 minutes.
4. Bring 1½ quarts of water to a boil, add a pinch of salt, three tablespoons soy sauce, one tablespoon grated ginger, and chopped garlic. Place the patties in the pan and let them simmer for about one hour. It should only simmer. Let the patties cool in the broth. Take out the patties and cut into strips or pieces. Seitan can be kept in the broth in the refrigerator for several days.

Barley is easy to grow, also in poor soil, and it contains a lot of silica. Barley was the first grain to be cultivated in our country and is our native "rice." Barley is very rich in soluble dietary fiber. Pearl barley is produced from peeled and cut barley. It works well to use instead of rice and potatoes. Barley contains gluten.

Rye is the most fiber-rich grain and is rich in B vitamins, magnesium, zinc, and iron. Rye contains gluten and lignans that can be transformed into plant estrogen.

Oat is the most nutritious native grain. Oat is rich in protein and fat with high levels of

Gluten-free seeds
Buckwheat, corn, quinoa, canihua, rice, millet, and amaranth are gluten-free. Oat is considered gluten-free unless it is contaminated by wheat, rye, and barley.

monounsaturated fatty acids. It is especially rich in vitamin B1, E, and K, as well as minerals, especially iron and calcium but also magnesium, phosphorus, manganese, zinc, copper, and silica.

Oat contains an extra amount of water-soluble fiber that lowers cholesterol and can be added in small amounts to oatmeal and bread. Oat does not contain gluten. It can be boiled like rice, but roast it on low heat before so that the lovely nutty flavor comes out.

Corn is the grain, aside from rice, that is the most cultivated throughout the world. Corn primarily contains plenty of beta-carotene. It does not contain gluten.

Polenta is a cornmeal and the Italian name for corn. Polenta is cooked to a firm porridge that is shaped into a loaf and then fried or grilled. Polenta meal is tasty as porridge, pudding, and in bread.

Millet is an old grain that is believed to originate in Asia. Millet is nutritious and has a relatively high level of fat. It contains a lot of B vitamins and plenty of silica and iron but also magnesium, potassium, phosphorus, silica, and flour in larger amounts.

Millet is easy to digest and used in diet food. Millet does not contain gluten but has a limited perishability since it is rich in fatty acids. Millet contains bitter substances, saponins, which disappear when you rinse the grains in alternating cold and warm water before cooking it.

Rice. The problem with rice and all rice products is that they are one of the worst environmental villains when it comes to emissions of greenhouse gases, since it produces gas while growing. The most climate-smart thing to do is to replace rice with other grains and meals.

Brown rice is nutritious and contains plenty of potassium. Brown rice strengthens the body and is easy to digest. It is often used as special diet food in different diseases. Rice regulates the levels of fluid in the body and is used to help with diseases like high blood pressure, weak kidneys, and water retention in the body. There is both round and oval white refined rice as well as fiber-rich brown rice with the hulls left. Rice does not contain gluten.

Wild rice does not belong to the rice family but is a perennial water plant that grows mostly in North America. It grows wild also in the south of Sweden, but it is rare. Wild rice, just like regular rice, produces methane gas during growth. Wild rice is used in raw food, then soaked for about three days with change of water morning and night.

Buckwheat is not a grain but an herb that originated in Asia and grows in light, poor soils. We have cultivated buckwheat here in Sweden since the 1600s. Buckwheat is neither fertilized nor sprayed and does not contain gluten. Buckwheat is rich in protein and contains a lot of calcium, but also other mineral substances like iron, potassium, magnesium, zinc, selenium, silica, and the antioxidant rutin.

Buckwheat is easy to digest and used as special diet food in stomach and intestinal diseases and contains D-chiro-inositol, which is a substance that increases insulin sensitivity. The outer husk of buckwheat contains a red substance, fagopyrin, which can cause an allergic reaction in some people. This substance is removed when rinsing the buckwheat in varying hot and cold water or pouring out the boiling water and adding new. Buckwheat is more tasty and will get a better texture if you roast it before boiling.

Quinoa is a very easily digestible and nutritious herb, especially rich in protein, fatty acids, vitamins B and E as well as magnesium, zinc, and iron. South American natives have cultivated quinoa throughout the ages. There is white, red, and black quinoa. The more color, the more antioxidants.

The grains look and taste a little like couscous and can replace it in meals. Quinoa does not contain gluten. It contains bitter substances that are removed if you rinse quinoa in hot water. Quinoa can be used in salads or to replace rice and pasta.

Amaranth is a family of herbs. In Asia and South America species have been refined and cultivated for food. It is easy to digest and very nutritious. It originated in tropical countries, but can also be grown here. The levels of protein, calcium, and iron are unusually high. Amaranth is use for oatmeal, bread, or as an alternative to rice, pasta, and potatoes. Amaranth is often used as diet food especially to help problems with stomach and bowels.

Canihua seed is a very nutritious small seed that comes from Peru. The grains contain a lot of protein as well as omega-3, 6, and 9, calcium, phosphorus, and iron. They do not contain gluten. Canihua seeds are smaller than quinoa and are tasty in salads or as a side dish instead of rice, pasta, or potatoes.

Beans and lentils

Legumes are plants that have been cultivated all over the world for thousands of years. They are divided into three main groups: beans, peas, and lentils. Legumes are very nutritious and contain more protein than other vegetables. By combining them with grains, rice, bread, or pasta, you will acquire a complete protein.

Throughout the ages, a complete protein has been achieved by eating lentils and rice in India, while beans and corn have been combined in South America. In China and Japan, a lot of tofu and other soy products are eaten with rice.

FRESH GREEN BEANS AND PEAS

Fava beans are nutritious. You do not use the pods, only the unripe, light green beans inside them. Fava beans are tasty in salads, soups, and stews.

Green beans have round, full pods. They are harvested before the seeds are fully developed. One sign of good quality is when the bean is so crispy that it snaps when you break it apart. Green beans do not have a chewy plant string. They are eaten boiled, marinated, in salads, as a side dish, or in stews and soups.

Edamame beans are green crispy Japanese soybeans that are found fresh or frozen. There are both peeled and unpeeled beans. They are popular as snacks and tasty in salads, as a side dish, or in stews and have been used for thousands of years in Asia.

Haricots verts are green beans of particular quality that are harvested at an early stage. The name comes from French and means "green beans."

Okra is also known as gumbo or lady's finger. The green fruit looks like an oval capsule and has a mild tasty flavor. There are also red, yellow, and green variants. Okra is very popular in African and Asian cuisine. It is especially tasty in stews together with onion, chili, tomatoes, and curry. Okra has a juice that is secreted when cooking and thickens soups and stews. When you fry okra, the sticky substance is not secreted.

Snow peas are somewhat coarser than green beans. They have a chewy membrane and chewy plant threads and must be cut in pieces before cooking. Snow peas are tasty in soups, stews, and with creamed vegetables.

Wax beans are yellow-white or wax-yellow. They are used the same way as green beans.

Sugar peas are crispy and tasty just the way-they are, in salads and stews as well as in stir-fry or boiled as a side dish. Pull off strings from the stem end and break of the top before cooking it.

Green peas are peas that have been removed from their pods. Peas are very nutritious and tasty in salads, stews, and soups.

How to cook beans:
The secret of tasty beans is to use enough salt in both soaking and boiling water. The salt causes the beans to swell more and prevents them from cracking.

Soak dried peas and beans in plenty of water. Add ½ teaspoon salt per quart of water. Let them soak for 8 to 10 hours.

Pour off the soaking water and rinse the beans. Let the beans boil in new water with 1 teaspoon of salt per quart of water. Remove the foam! The cooking time varies; see recommendations on the package. Taste the beans. They should be soft but not mushy.

Beans contain lectins, which is a substance that can inhibit decomposition of proteins and minerals. This substance disappears if you cook the beans long enough.

DRIED BEANS; PEAS AND LENTILS

Aduki beans are small red beans that are popular mostly in Chinese and Japanese cuisine. They are considered very easy to digest and are good to use in mincemeat, stews, soups, and as sprouts.

Borlotti beans are brown with red dots. They have a creamy texture and chestnut-like flavor. They can be found both dried and fresh.

Brown beans are cultivated in Sweden and resemble kidney beans. They are tasty in salads, stews, and soups.

Black-eyed peas are small white beans with one black dot on one side. The bean is light and tasty and cooks faster than other beans. They can be used in salads, stews, and soups.

Yellow peas have been grown for a long time in the country and pea soup is still a popular dish.

Green peas can also be found dried and are good for stews and soups.

Kidney beans are tasty in salads, stews, and soups and as side dishes.

Chickpeas look like large, slightly bumpy peas. They have a nutty flavor and do not mash during cooking. They are good in salads, stews, soups, and hummus.

Lima beans has been cultivated in Central America since the beginning of time. They are similar to fava beans in both color and shape. They are tasty in salads, soups, and stews.

Lentils are rich in antioxidants, B vitamins, magnesium, iron, and zinc. Imported lentils are also good sources of selenium.

There are brown, green, red, yellow, and black lentils. Brown are the largest and cook in half an hour. Dark brownish green small Puy lentils are considered to be the tastiest. They do not mash as easily and has a somewhat shorter cooking time than the brown lentils. Both brown and green lentils are tasty in salads, soups, and stews.

Small red or yellow lentils are split and have a shorter cooking time. They easily mash and are perfect for soups and sauces.

Mung beans are old cultural plants from India that now are grown in all of Asia. Mung beans are often sprouted. Sprouted mung beans are also called Chinese bean sprouts.

White beans have been cultivated by Native Americans. They are found in many different sizes. The larger they are, the longer the cooking time. White beans are good in salads, stews, and soups.

Black beans are related to white beans. They are also very popular in Latin America and go well with salads, stews, and soups.

Soybeans have been cultivated for 5,000 years in China. In Asian countries, you rarely eat cooked soybeans in their original form. They are considered to be too heavy and difficult to digest. Instead, fermented soybean products are eaten, like tempeh, tofu, and miso. Soybeans contain phytic acid like other legumes, which inhibits the absorption of minerals. If you ferment the soybeans most of the phytic acid disappears.

Soybeans are extremely nutritious and contain more protein (34.2 percent) and fat (17.7 percent) than other legumes. The soybean has complete protein and is equivalent to meat protein. The fat is mainly polyunsaturated and contains a large amount of lecithin. The soybean is also rich in vitamin K, E, and the B-group vitamins except B12, as well as minerals, primarily calcium, magnesium, potassium, zinc, phosphorus, and iron. The soybean's iron is easier to absorb than iron in other vegetables.

Soybeans are currently one of the most grown crops and have been GMO-refined to withstand strong chemical pesticides. Organically grown soybeans are not GMO-refined.

Health effects and nutritional values for beans and lentils

- Legumes are rich in protein, most B-vitamins, and many minerals like magnesium, calcium, phosphorus, iron, and zinc. Most legumes also contain selenium. The levels vary depending on what country they come from. Beans have a low GI value and contain plenty of fiber, especially water-soluble fiber, which stimulates the intestinal bacteria. Green beans and peas are also rich in beta-carotene and vitamin C.
- Contain protective substances, including plant estrogen and antioxidants (see ORAC values, p. 48).
- Can reduce a heightened cholesterol value.
- Reduce the risk of heart and vascular diseases.
- Can protect against cancer in breast, prostate, and large intestine.

SOY PRODUCTS

There are several different kinds of soy products that are produced from de-oiled soy items like mincemeat, strips, balls, sausage, fillets, patties, and tzay skewers. They are very processed industrial products and they are expensive. Most soy products are found frozen in the store.

There is also lactose-free soy milk, soy cream, soy ice cream, soy desserts, and soy cheese. It is best to first choose calcium-enriched milk since soy milk does not contain a lot of calcium.

Soy flour is produced by de-oiling peeled soybeans that are treated with hot steam. Use soy flour as enrichment in vegetarian mincemeat, bread, and pancakes. Keep soy flour dry and cool.

Soy sauce. Real soy sauce, or shoyu, is made from spring water, soy beans, lactic acid culture, and sea salt, and often roasted barley grains and mushroom extract. The mixture is then fermented in cedar wood barrels for 18 to 24 months. Cheap soy mostly contains colored sugar water.

Miso is a lactic acid-fermented paste made from soybeans, water, salt, bacterial culture, and, in most cases, an additive of some kind of grain—for example, barley. Miso is mainly used for flavoring miso soups.

Miso is stored in a wood barrel for 1 to 3 years depending on what strength the final product should have. The white miso has the shortest storage time and is the mildest. Miso is rich in enzymes, lactic acid bacteria, complete protein, and many minerals like iron, limestone, phosphorus, and B vitamins including B12, although in very small amounts.

Miso contains plenty of heat-sensitive enzymes and lactic acid bacteria. Stir miso with some cold water first and do not add the paste until the soup has cooled off somewhat.

Tempeh is an amazing meat-like product that is produced from soybeans. You could describe tempeh as a cake of soybeans that has been woven together with mushroom mycelium. Originally the technique came from Indonesia, where it is still used daily by the population. It is said that about 40,000 small family-based tempeh producers are located on Java.

Tempeh has many benefits. The product is very rich in nutrients and fiber, is cheap, climate-smart, and easy to digest and easy to make at home. The protein content is as high as in beef. Depending on the level of bacterial culture, tempeh can contain high amounts of B12. About 3.5 oz of tempeh provides the daily need of B12 if you use the bacteria *Klebsiella* when producing it. Tempeh is also low in carbohydrates, for those who want to eat fewer carbohydrates.

Tempeh has a nutty flavor, lovely texture, and can be fried, deep-fried, used in stir-fry, boiled, baked in the oven, or be used as an alternative to meat in burgers, stews, or salads. It is tasty to flavor it with chili sauce and soy, preferably together with garlic and ginger.

If you want to make tempeh yourself, there are instructions and a start-kit you can buy online (see p.339). A simplified explanation is that you soak soybeans and boil them for 10 to 15 minutes and let them cool for a few hours. Then you rub off most of the peel and rinse.

Then you mix the soybeans with a bacterial culture. Place a cake, 0.8 to 1.2 inches, in a plastic bag. Close the bag and poke holes with a sterilized toothpick on both sides. A good distance between the holes is 0.4 to 0.8 inches. Then it will take about 36 hours in a warm place, optimally 86 to 89.6°F, for the tempeh to cook. If you have the oven turned off and leave only the lamp on, you can usually keep the right temperature if the oven door is slightly ajar.

Tofu is a cream cheese made from soy milk. During production you strain off most of the fiber-rich soybean. Tofu has a natural flavor and has been made in Asia for 2,000 years. Tofu will have a firmer texture if you fry it. Soy sauce, grated ginger, and garlic add nice flavor to it. Tofu can be used on sandwiches, in stir-fry, and in stews and salads.

How to make soy milk and tofu:
1. Soak 2 cups of soybeans for 10–12 hours.
2. Rinse the beans. Mix them well in a food processor. Add 1 cup of water a little at a time while mixing.

3. Bring 2 quarts of water to a boil in a large pan. Pour the soy purée in the boiling water. Constantly stir from the bottom while the fluid starts to boil again. Set the pan aside when the foam starts to rise. Place a lid on the pan and let it sit for 5–10 minutes.

4. Place a cloth over a large drainer that is placed on top of another pan. Strain the soy milk through the cloth. Wring the rest of the soy milk from the cloth by using your hands. Use plastic gloves.

5. Bring the soy milk to a boil and let it simmer on low heat for about five minutes. Be careful to not let the milk boil over. After that the soy milk is ready to use. It stays fresh in the refrigerator for 4–5 days.

6. If you want to make tofu, you let the soy milk stay in the pan. Mix ⅓ cup vinegar with 2 cups hot water. Take the pan with the hot soy milk off the stove. Quickly stir with a wooden spoon all the way from the bottom, five times one way and then stop the movement with the spoon. Pour a third of the vinegar in.

   Stir with the wooden spoon in the opposite direction five more times and then stop the movement with the spoon. Pour another third of the vinegar all over the surface. Put the lid back on the pan and let the milk rest for 5 minutes. Carefully stir the cheese mass that now floats in a yellow whey. Pour the rest of the vinegar over the parts that have not curdled. Put the lid on again and let rest for some more time.

7. Place a new cloth in a clean strainer. Pick up the cheese mass by using a slotted spoon and place in the strainer. When all cheese mass is in the cloth, wring and press the cheese mass together. Put a small plate on top and add a weight. Let the tofu sit under pressure for about 5 minutes.

   Open the cloth again and press the cheese mass again. Put the weight back on and let the tofu press for 20–60 minutes. The longer time the cheese is pressed, the firmer the cheese/tofu will turn out.

8. Then put the tofu in a bowl of cold water and let it stay there for 10 minutes. Then separate the cloth from the tofu. Keep the tofu in a jar of water in the refrigerator. It stays fresh for 7–10 days.

Tip! Use 3 ½ quarts pre-made store-bought soy milk and start with step 5. If the cheese is made from regular cow milk, it is called paneer, which is common in Indian cuisine.

Milk, cheese, and eggs

Regular milk or milk from seeds and nuts? Here are recipes as well as nutritional and other comparisons between regular milk and milk products with more ethical and eco-friendly vegan alternatives like sesame milk and cashew cream, as well as cream cheese made from vegan yogurt.

MILK AND MILK PRODUCTS

Cow milk. Swedes grow up drinking plenty of milk, while other countries use it sparingly or not at all. Swedes belong to the exception among the earth's population, and more and more people have trouble digesting milk sugar (lactose).

The Swedish National Food Agency recommends ½ quart milk for a grown person a day. That amount includes sour milk, yogurt, and the milk that is used in cooking. Milk gives you a complete protein, plenty of calcium and vitamin A, D, and all B-vitamins, also B12, as well as iodine and traces of selenium.

There is a big difference between today's refined and compound-fed cows which produce a considerably larger amount of milk compared to other breeds. One single cow produces about 11,440 lbs of milk each year. In order for a cow to be able to give milk, she has to calve once a year. Half of all the calves that are born are bulls and most of them are sent to slaughter. Because of this the milk production contributes to an inevitable meat production.

Today, milk is a processed product in which you first separate the cream from the skim milk. Then follows a standardizing that mixes different milk products to create a guaranteed fat content. Thereafter, the milk is heated to 167°F for a total of 15 seconds (flash pasteurizing). During this process, homogenization also occurs, which means that the fat is dispersed under pressure. After a cooling process the milk is packaged and reaches the consumer several days later.

Fermented milk biologically activates the milk, which has turned sterile through the pasteurizing process. Pasteurized milk is easier to digest than fresh milk. The acid and the lactic acid bacteria are good for digestion.

Ten percent of lactic acid bacteria from regular sour milk survives all the way through our digestive system to the large intestine. All special kinds of sour milk contain another kind of lactic acid bacteria, like A-fil and dophilus, where almost all lactic acid bacteria survives all the way to the large intestine.

Butter is not only tasty but also healthy. Since butter consists of only milk fat (the cream), it is a good source of fat-soluble vitamins like A, D, and E as well as beta-carotene.

Milk fat has a complex composition of 400 different fatty acids. Recent research has shown that several of these fatty acids have positive effects on health; for instance, butyric acid, which is anti-inflammatory, provides the cells of the intestinal mucosa with nutrients and has virus-and cancer-protective attributes.

Ghee (clarified butter). In traditional Chinese medicine and within ayurvedic medicine, ghee is considered to be both healthy and strengthening. In Asia, ghee is used for flavor when cooking, but not when baking. When the butter is clarified, proteins that can be difficult to digest or are allergenic are removed. Ghee can also be used if you are intolerant to milk protein.

How to make ghee:
- Melt 1.1 lbs organic butter in a saucepan on low heat.
- Bring the butter to a boil and remove all foam.
- Reduce the heat and let the butter simmer on low heat for 10 minutes in order to let the water steam off.
- Remove the pan from the stove and pour ghee in a glass jar with a lid. Leave whatever is left in the bottom of the pan. Ghee can be kept for an unlimited amount of time in the refrigerator and can also be kept for weeks at room temperature.

Cheese. About 22 lbs of milk makes 2.2 lbs of cheese. In all cheese production, the milk is heated to a temperature of about 86°F, and then a lactic acid culture and rennet is added. This causes the milk to solidify. It is possible to produce rennet synthetically, but usually rennet is taken from the calf stomach. But more and more cheese producers use synthetic rennet; the ingredients list reads vegetarian rennet, vegetable curdle enzyme, or microbial rennet.

The mass of cheese is processed in different ways. Through different maturation and storing times, each cheese gets its own characteristics characters. Most cheeses also have different additives like potassium or sodium nitrate, sodium, hypochlorite, or potassium sorbate, and as stabilizer, calcium chloride or sodium phosphate. There are types of cheese with fewer or no additives at all, like quark, cottage cheese, Parmesan, Emmental, feta, or goat cheese.

Chèvre is a goat cheese with a distinct, sharp flavor. Depending on age, it can be fresh and soft or crumbly and dry. When it is very young is it soft enough to be used as a spread, but it obtains a firmer texture with age. Chèvre is suitable for many things, like salads, stews, and gratins as well as oven-baked dishes.

Feta cheese was originally made from sheep cheese by shepherds in the Greek mountain regions. Fresh feta cheese is crumbly and drips with the whey it matures in. As it grows older, it dries and has more salinity. Feta cheese usually does not contain any additives other than salt.

Many so-called feta cheeses today are produced from cow milk and lack the characteristic, somewhat tart flavor that sheep's-milk feta cheese has.

Parmesan is an Italian grainy aromatic hard cheese without additives that is only made from unpasteurized cow milk. Real Parmesan cheese is called Parmigiano Reggiano and is stamped with the name. It is stored for at least two years and if it is stored more than three years it is called "stravecchio" and is extra fine. The fat content in Parmesan is 30 percent.

Parmazano is a vegan option in a jar for anyone who wants the flavor of Parmesan.

Pecorino includees different types of Italian cheeses made from sheep's milk. The matured ones often have a resemblance to Parmesan but are more salty and often used in pesto.

Cream cheese *Lacto or vegan*

Homemade cream cheese is tasty and simple to make. Use the whey for lactic acid or as a fluid when baking bread.

ABOUT 1¼ CUP
1 quart yogurt
herb salt and pepper

■ Let the yogurt sit at room temperature for about 8 hours. Then pour the yogurt into a cloth or a coffee filter. Let the whey drip off for 8–10 hours or longer depending on how firm you want the cheese mass to be.

Flavor the cheese with salt and pepper as well as one or more of the following alternatives:
• pressed garlic or finely grated horseradish
• finely chopped basil, coriander, dill, chives, parsley, leek, or chervil
• saffron, lemon zest, and finely chopped coriander or dill
• finely chopped chili and paprika powder
• roasted cumin
• finely chopped paprika and walnuts

Herb cheese balls
1 batch cream cheese, according to above basic recipe.

Flavor the cheese mass with 1–2 pressed garlic cloves, herb salt and pepper, finely chopped dill, parsley, and chives. Make small balls from the cheese mass and roll them in the green chopped herbs.

Saffron mousse *Lacto or vegan*
*PHOTO P. 145

■ Follow the above basic recipe but make double the amount of cream cheese.
■ Mix 0.02 oz saffron with 1 tbsp boiling hot water and let sit. Flavor the cream cheese with a couple of tbsp honey, grated lemon peel, and saffron.
■ Beat the dessert until fluffy, preferably with an electric mixer. Serve with fresh fruit or berries.

Marinated goat cheese *Lacto*
Place layers of goat and sheep's-milk cheese cut in cubes with sliced garlic and chili as well as a few rosemary sprigs in a glass jar. Pour nice olive oil over it until the cheese is covered. Let sit for at least one day and then store at a cool place.

VEGAN MILK AND CREAM

Today there are many good vegan alternatives to milk and dairy products, made from soy, oats, quinoa, almond, or coconut. There is also vegan yogurt, cream cheese, vegan cheese, and vegan mayonnaise. If you want to, your own milk or cream can be made from seeds or nuts. You can read about soy and soy products on page 110.

Sesame milk *Raw*

Sesame milk is very nutritious but does not contain complete protein and is fatter than cow milk. The fat mostly contains polyunsaturated fatty acids but also monounsaturated fatty acids.

Sesame milk made from unpeeled sesame seeds contains 0.007 oz calcium per 3.5 oz sesame milk, while peeled sesame seeds only contain 0.0005 oz compared with the cow milk's 0.004 oz. Sesame milk stays fresh for several days in a refrigerator.

ABOUT 2 CUPS
1⅓ cup sesame seeds
2½ cup water

■ First grind the dry sesame seeds in a mixer or food processor into a fine flour. Add the fluid a little at a time and continue to mix until the drink is very fine. If you want to you can strain the coarse mass, which can be used in bread or mincemeat.
■ The milk can be drunk like it is or be sweetened with agave syrup, honey, dates, banana, or pear.

Tip! Unpeeled sesame seeds have the best nutritional value but the taste is somewhat astringent. Use half peeled and half unpeeled sesame seeds or use half unpeeled sesame seeds and half sunflower seeds.

Almond milk *Raw*

The milk comes out better if you soak the almonds.
ABOUT 2 CUPS
1⅓ cups soaked almonds
2 cups water

Vegan milk

It is easy to make your own milk and it turns out tasty and nutritious. Strain the milk through a fine cloth after mixing it. Optionally, sweeten with banana, dates, honey, agave syrup, or vanilla. The milk stays fresh for a couple of days in the refrigerator.

The mass that is left you can use in a few different ways:

- Herb cheese. Mix the leftovers with coconut oil and season with lemon juice, garlic, fresh herbs, chili, and salt.
- Seed hummus. Mix the rest with tahini and coconut oil. Season with lemon juice, garlic, cumin, chili, and salt.
- Pie crusts. Mix almond leftovers with mashed dates, coconut oil, honey, and chopped nuts.

■ Soak the almonds overnight.
■ Rinse the almonds and mix with water. Strain the milk.

Almond cream *Raw*

Wonderfully tasty and creamy cream. Optionally sweeten with some agave syrup or honey.
ABOUT ¾ CUPS
1⅓ cup soaked almonds
⅓ cup water

■ Soak the almonds during night.
■ Rinse the almonds and mix with water until the texture is creamy.

Almond ice cream

Follow the recipe above but stir another ¼ cup of water into the mixture and season with 1 tbsp honey and vanilla. Leave the cream in the freezer for one hour. Stir and let the ice cream stand in the freezer for another hour.

Cashew milk *Raw*

If you have a good mixer, it is not necessary to strain the milk.

ABOUT 1⅔ CUPS
1⅓ cup cashew pieces
1½–1⅔ cup water

■ First mix the cashew pieces to a fine powder. Add water and mix the cream.

Cashew ice cream

Follow the recipe above, but stir another ¼ cup of water into the mixture and season with 1 tablespoon honey and vanilla. Leave the cream in the freezer for one hour. Stir and let the ice cream stand in the freezer for another hour.

Mung bean milk *Raw*

Tasty and protein-rich vegan milk that can replace soy milk. Young and tender sprouts are the best to use (0.4 inches) and the milk is best if you drink it immediately after mixing it.

ABOUT ⅔–1¼ CUP
1⅓ cup mung bean sprouts
⅔–1¼ cup water

■ Mix mung bean sprouts and water. Strain the drink.

EGGS

Eggs are a rich source of complete protein, vitamins A, D, and E, folic acid, riboflavin, choline, B2, B6, B12, calcium, iron, zinc, phosphorus, and selenium. Missing in eggs are vitamin C and carbohydrates. A normal-size egg gives more than a third of our daily need of selenium, vitamin E, and B12.

The yolk contains most of the fat in the egg and the white mostly contains water and protein. The yolk also contains several different carotenoids, among them lutein and zeaxanthin. Research shows that we absorb more carotenoids from egg than from carotenoid-rich vegetables.

Recent research shows that eggs do not cause high cholesterol, as previously thought. You can eat 1 to 2 eggs a day without any problems. There are also some scientists who believe eggs can prevent heart and vascular diseases.

Organically raised chickens live a better life than conventionally raised. The eggs taste better and have a different and better fatty acid composition. There are also special omega-3 eggs to buy, and the chickens have been fed with a special feed containing a lot of omega-3. If you have chickens of your own, you can feed them purslane, which will increase the levels of omega-3 in the eggs.

Tips! Eggs at room temperature are fluffier when they have been whipped. It is easier to separate cold eggs, since the yolk is less liable to break. If you place boiled eggs in cold water it will be easier to peel them.

Herbs and spices

It is so inspiring to cook food today when we can buy aromatic herbs from all over the world in most grocery stores. Any simple and everyday dish is boosted with fragrant fresh herbs. Fresh herbs are also beautiful to decorate with.

To have your own "herb garden" in the window or, even better, outside is worth its weight in gold. If you had to choose one single herb to grow, it should be parsley. You can harvest it all the way until frost comes. Finely chopped parsley goes perfectly with almost all dishes.

THROUGHOUT THE TIMES, herbs have been highly valued. For centuries they had the same value as noble metals. Spices and herbs have been used in both food and as medicine. During the Middle Ages, the habit of using herbs spread from the Mediterranean to Scandinavia through the herb gardens of monks. The monks themselves mostly used herbs for medication. Today our scientists are starting to confirm the herbs' fantastic healing abilities, especially cinnamon, turmeric, ginger, and garlic.

HERBS

Chives, *Allium schoenoprasum*, grow wild on rocks and dry meadows all over the country.

Garlic chives, *Allium tuberous*, have a nice flavor of garlic. Both plants are perennial and are easy to grow both outside and on the windowsill.

Chives together with parsley, chervil, and tarragon make the classic spice fines herbes. A mix of finely chopped chives, parsley, and dill is a delight to sprinkle on a "summer" sandwich together with tomato slices and herb salt.

Dill, *Anethum graveolens*, is an ancient cultivated plant that belongs to the same family as parsley, fennel, and carrots. Both seeds and leaves are used. The seeds are considered to be good for digestion problems and gas. Dill contains a lot of antioxidants.

You can store dill leaves tightly packed in jars in the freezer. All you have to do then is to scrape off as much as you need. Dill is tasty in oil, salads, sauces, warm dishes, stews, soups, and pickles.

Chervil, *Anthriscus cerefolium*, is very easy to grow and easily spread. There is also a bush-like variant, cicely, *Myrrhis odorata*, which is also easy to grow yourself.

The herb is considered to be appetizing and blood-cleansing. It has an aromatic smell, almost a little sweet, and the taste is spicy and similar to anise. Chervil enhances the good flavor of all vegetables and other herbs. Chervil is a part of fines herbes together with parsley, tarragon, and chives.

The aroma easily disappears and the herb should be used fresh, deep frozen, or pickled in vinegar. Tender leaves are tasty and decorative in salads. Finely cut chervil can be used instead of or together with parsley. The harshness in nettle soup disappears with some chervil.

Lemon Balm

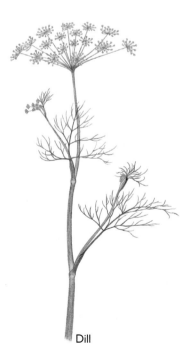

Dill

Tarragon

Tarragon, *Artemesia dracunculus*, is related to absinthium. The herb is considered to be appetizing and stimulates digestion. It is the young tender leaves of the French tarragon that give the nice aromatic but somewhat bitter flavor. Russian tarragon, which is common in our gardens, has a different flavor.

Since tarragon contains very volatile essential oils, it should be used fresh or kept in the freezer. Among French spices, tarragon is a natural choice. Tarragon is a classic spice in vinegar and mustard. Tarragon is also tasty to use in salads, mushroom dishes, stews, soups, sauces, and with pickled cucumber.

Lime leaves, *Citrus x hystrix, Rutaceae*, are the lovely aromatic leaves from the tropical kefir lime tree. The leaves are used in Asian cuisine, in the same way we use bay leaves.

Coriander, *Coriandrum sativum*, is one of our oldest, most well-known spices. In Asian cuisine fresh coriander is used as often as parsley is in Sweden. To us coriander lovers, it enhances the flavor of most dishes, especially sauces and dressings.

Coriander seeds are a part of curry. They have a mild and nice aroma that resembles bitter orange peel. The flavor is best enhanced when you grind the seeds. The seeds are anticonvulsant and help with gases and digestion.

Lemongrass, *Cymbopogon citrates*, is a tropical herb that is often used in Asian cuisine, especially in Thailand. Both flavor and smell are similar to lemon. Lemongrass can be replaced by lemon peel. Peel off the outer chewy layers of the lemongrass. Slice or chop the soft part at the bottom, and let it fry or cook together with the dish. Make a tasty tea from the leftovers of the stem.

Growing tips: It is easy to grow lemongrass on the windowsill. If you place several lemon grass stems in a glass with a little water to cover the bottom, roots will grow. Then plant the cuttings in soil. In the summer when it is warm, the pot can be kept outside.

Bay leaf, *Laurua nobles*, comes from the constantly green bay laurel trees that grow in the Mediterranean. The ancient Greeks gave laurel wreaths to winners in the Olympic Games and to heroes. The aromatic leaves are a part of the French *bouquet garni*. Fresh or dried bay laurel will give marinades and stews a lovely flavor.

Lovage, *Levisticum official*, is easy to grow and considered to be soothing, stomach-strengthening, and helps with gases. The herb has a strongly aromatic yeast flavor that resembles celery.

Savory

Chervil

Lovage

Only a small piece of a big leaf is enough to give flavor to soups and stews. The herb also has an ability to enhance other flavors. The really small and tender leaves are very tasty and can be used as parsley.

Lemon balm, *Melissa officials*, is made into a tea that is considered to be soothing and strengthen your nerves. It is rich in antioxidants. Lemon balm is easy to grow and gives off a lovely lemon fragrance when you touch it. The aroma is volatile and the herb should preferably be used fresh. Finely chopped leaves are tasty in salads and desserts. Whole leaves and stems are decorative and give a fresh flavor to drinks and punch. Whole leaves can be frozen in ice cubes for winter storage.

Mint, *Mentha*, has an enormous growing power and the different species like to cross-breed. There are many different kinds of mint—for example, peppermint, *Mentha x piperita*, spearmint, *Mentha spicata*, and *Mentha citrata*, which has a lemon and orange flower-like fragrance. They contain plenty of antioxidants.

Mint makes a lovely tea and is beautiful to decorate with. Place a twig of mint in a jug of water. It will both taste and look beautiful.

Basil, *Ocimum basilicum*, is a delightful herb that is best to eat when it is fresh. It is related to mint and contains plenty of antioxidants. Basil is considered to be anticonvulsant and soothing as well as able to stimulate digestion. There are many kinds of basil to buy today. Basil goes well with most dishes but is especially good with pasta and all tomato dishes. In Asian cuisine, sweet basil is used, with a somewhat spicy flavor similar to cloves.

Growing tips: For those who wants to grow basil, there are at least 20 different kinds of seeds to buy. You can also cut down and plant a pot of basil, and then replant in a bigger pot during the warm part of the year. Basil likes it best in temperatures around 68°F and wants quite a lot of water and fertilizer. Thai basil or Siam Queen is considered to be one of the finest kinds with its somewhat licorice-like flavor. The more top shoots you cut off, the more the plant itself will grow.

Marjoram, *Origanum majorana*, is related to oregano. It has a fine, slightly sweet, fresh aroma.

The herb is considered to be anticonvulsant and analgesic and contains plenty of antioxidants.

Marjoram is a classic spice in pea soup and can also be used in place of oregano in salads, tomato dishes, and pizza.

Marjoram

Rosemary

Oregano, *Origanum vulgar*, has a lovely, strong, spicy, somewhat bittersweet flavor. It grows wild in all of Europe and is very easy to cultivate. The herb, which contains high levels of protective substances, is considered to be anticonvulsant and analgesic. Oregano goes well with basil. It goes well with salads, especially Greek salad, tomato dishes, and pizza.

Parsley, *Petroselinum crispum*, is very nutritious and contains high levels of the flavonoid apigenin. The herb is considered slightly diuretic and anti-inflammatory. Flat-leaved parsley, *Petroselinum crispum* var. *neapolitanum*, has more flavor than the curly-leaved kind. Finely chopped parsley enhances the flavor in most dishes, salads, and soups.

Watercress, *Rorippa nasturtium-aquaticum*, usually grew in water in the old days. The nutritious leaves, with their spicy and bitter flavor, are good in salads.

Growing tips: Watercress is very easy to grow and spreads like weed. Place watercress stems in a glass of water so that roots grow out. Then plant them in soil. Watercress needs soil that is constantly moist. Place the cress in half-shade.

Rosemary, *Rosmarinus officinalis*, means "the ocean's dew" in Latin and has a fresh, spicy pine needle-like flavor. The herb is considered to be good for the heart and to increase circulation in the body. It is rich in antioxidants and protective substances. Rosemary is a wonderful spice that is especially tasty in tomato dishes. It goes well with garlic and parsley. But do not use too much of it, since the strong flavor easily kills other flavors.

Place a few rosemary twigs on the warm coal in the barbecue and the air will be filled with lovely Mediterranean aromas.

Sorrel, *Rumex acetone*, grows in wet meadows. With its tart and fresh flavor, it is good in salads, sauces, and soups.

Growing tips: Sorrel is easy to cultivate and grows quickly. Sow the seeds about 0.4 inches apart and keep the soil constantly moist. Sorrel likes half-shade.

Salvia, *Salvia officinalis*, has beautiful blue gray-green leaves. It is an easy-to-grow perennial and ancient medicinal plant. The leaves have an intense spice flavor and make a wonderful tea. Salvia tea is considered to be mildly energy-stimulating and is especially good to use for sore throats and for bothersome sweating. Salvia contains extra amounts of protective substances.

Savory, *Satureja hortensis*, belongs to the mint family and has a somewhat peppery and rich flavor. In the past it was often used in food. Savory is easy to combine with other herbs. Since it is believed to help gas and ease digestion, it is perfect for any dish with beans, lentils, or cabbage.

Thyme, *Thymus vulgaris*, grows wild in the Mediterranean and has a wonderfully aromatic and spicy flavor. There are several different kinds. Thyme is considered to be antibacterial and anticonvulsant and is rich in protective substances.

Thyme is a part of classic French cuisine with parsley, chives, and bay leaves. Thyme goes well with onion, bean, and mushroom dishes and enhances the flavors of all tomato dishes.

ROOT AND BARK SPICES

Horseradish, *Armoracia rusticate*, has been cultivated in Sweden since the 1200s. It easily spreads and therefore grows wild almost everywhere in the country. The root contains a sharp essential oil, which makes a nice spice and is considered to increase circulation as well as stimulate stomach and bowel movements.

Horseradish is especially tasty with beetroot, but also goes well in sauces and dressings. The root also has a preservative effect in pickles.

Use leaves and flowers from the horseradish. They only have a mild horseradish flavor and are tasty in finely chopped salads, sauces, and dressings.

If you do not want to eat garlic, it works fine to replace it with horseradish in any dish.

fenugreek seed

bitter orange

caraway

coriander

juniper

turmeric root

star anise

star aniseed

tamarind fruit

bay lea[f]

sweet basil

chervil

horseradish

galangal root

Cinnamon, *Cinnamomum zeylandicum*, is the dried and rolled-up inner bark from the cinnamon tree. Cinnamon exudes a rich and full fragrance, adds a rich flavor to dishes, and goes well with anything from apple compote to stews.

Cinnamon can inhibit the growth of bacteria, help with digestion problems and gases, strengthen the insulin effect, and reduce high blood sugar and high blood fats. You should not use more than one teaspoon a day.

Turmeric, *Curcuma long*, is related to ginger and has been used in both Chinese and Indian ayurveda for its anti-inflammatory abilities and to help digestion problems and liver diseases. The active substances in turmeric is the yellow-colored substance curcumin, which is a very powerful antioxidant.

A lot of research has been done on the medicinal abilities of turmeric. Animal testing has shown that turmeric has an effect on many diseases and problems like some types of cancer, diseases in lungs and liver, rheumatoid arthritis, diabetes, obesity, as well as heart and vascular diseases.

According to many scientists, turmeric also protects the brain cells from damage and stimulates the growth of new brain cells and can prevent Alzheimer's disease and dementia as well as damages after a stroke. In Indian cuisine the turmeric is a must and is used primarily in curry. An average Indian eats 80 to 200 mg per day. In large amounts, turmeric can have a bitter taste and somewhat of a bile-stimulating effect.

mustard seed

Use turmeric when cooking! Preferably freshly grated, since the difference in flavor is just as big as between dried and fresh ginger. A tablespoon of finely grated turmeric is equivalent to one teaspoon dried.

Ginger, *Zingiber official*, has been cultivated in Asia for thousands of years and is considered a panacea and helps most complaints. Ginger is believed to prevent digestion problems and ease and prevents nausea and motion sickness. It is also thought to reduce the risks of thrombus, act as an anti-inflammatory, and ease aches and stiffness. There are also studies that show that ginger can have a cancer-preventive effect.

It is not the root of this tropical plant that we use, but the underground stem (rhizome), which is peeled and can be pressed in a garlic press, grated, finely chopped, or cut in small thin sticks. Dried ginger can also be bought. Fresh ginger should be kept cool, but not in a plastic bag. Peeled ginger can also be deep frozen and grated while still not yet defrosted.

Ginger is used daily in Asian cuisine and often in tea. There is no other spice that is as universal as ginger. Ginger goes well in drinks, salads, stews, stir-fry, dessert, cookies, candy, and bread.

FLOWER SPICES

Caper, *Capparis spinosa*, is a perennial bush that grows in the Mediterranean. The mature flower buds are pickled in vinegar and salt, which bring out the caper acid that gives the buds the piquant spice flavor.

Giant capers are large capers with milder flavors than the small. Capers are traditionally used on pizza and in sauces.

nutmeg flower

coriander seed

sorrel

flat-leaf parsley

cinnamon

nutmeg

ginger

watercress

Saffron, *Crocus sativus*, consists of the dried threads of the pistil of a lily flower, which is similar to crocus. Since 175,000 handpicked flowers are used per 2.2 pounds of saffron, it is not hard to understand why the price is so high. But fortunately not much of the spice is needed to provide a dish with color and flavor. Saffron is used a lot in Asian cuisine and is used primarily in Asian dishes, fish soup, and risotto.

Cloves, *Eugenia aromatica*, are the dried fully grown buds from a tree in the myrtle family.

They have an aromatic, sharp, almost burning spicy flavor. Cloves are tasty in tea, drinks, gingerbread dough, and marinades, as well as in marmalade and jam.

FRUIT AND SEED SPICES

Celery, *Apium graveolens*, in small amounts has the ability to enhance other flavors. The aromatic leaves and seeds are believed to have a blood-cleansing effect. Celery is tasty in salads, onion dishes, soups, gratins, stews, and sauces.

Caraway, *Carum carvi*, grows wild on dry meadows all over the country. In the past the whole plant would be used. The root was boiled, the leaves used in salads and soups, and the seeds used as a spice in cabbage dishes, breads, and sauerkraut. It is the cumin oil in the cumin seeds that are appetizing, and the oil strengthens the stomach and helps digestion. The further north the herb grows, the higher the level of cumin oil in the seeds.

Bitter orange, *Citrus aurantium*, is the dried peel of a citrus fruit with a flavor of bitter orange. The peel should be boiled until soft before it is used in bread and desserts.

Cumin, *Cuminum cyminum*, with its wonderful aromatic, earthy, and warm flavor, is often used in Asian and Moroccan cuisine. Cumin is an important ingredient in curry. You can use whole seeds or grind them. In Indian cuisine you usually roast the seeds first or fry them in oil.

Cardamom, *Elettaria cardamomum*, is the fruit of an Indian lily plant related to ginger. The spice has a strong, aromatic flavor and is the most important ingredient in garam masala. In India it is often used in curry and rice dishes.

Fennel, *Foeniculum vulgare*, is a perennial herb with aromatic, somewhat sweet seeds. There is a annual variant with swollen stems that we eat as a vegetable. Fennel seeds are good for digestion and prevent gas. Fennel seeds make a good tea and are usually used for bread seasoning.

Star anise, *Illicium velum*, are the fruit on a small, evergreen Chinese tree. The strongly aromatic oil in star anise resembles anise but is not as subtle and slightly more bitter. Star anise is tasty in tea, drinks, and desserts.

Juniper, *Juniperis communis*, has a fresh aromatic forest flavor. The juniper blooms in the spring, but it takes the berries 3 years to ripen. Juniper is appetizing and a diuretic as well as stimulatant for digestion.

Pick and eat the ripe blue junipers when walking in nature. But you should not eat more than five berries at once. If you have kidney problems, you should not eat juniper at all, since they irritate the kidneys even in small dosages. Juniper berries are used in sauerkraut, marinades, stews, and juniper juice.

Nutritional value and health effects
- Spices are very rich in antioxidants and contain protective substances, many with medicinal effects.
- Herbs are especially rich in vitamin C and E and minerals.
- Spices can protect you from cancer.
- Spices can protect you from heart and vascular diseases.
- Herbs stimulate digestion.
- Bitter herbs stimulate liver function.

Nutmeg, *Myristica fragrans*, is harvested from an up to 33-foot-high tree. The nutmeg is the seed of a peach-like fruit. Surrounding the nut is a skin consisting of a fine bright red membrane that is called nutmeg flower. Both nut and flower contain the same essential oil, but the flower has a softer and less hot flavor. Nutmeg will in small amounts give a nice contrast in sauces, mashed potatoes, spinach, macaroni, and stews.

Poppyseed, *Papaver somniferum*, comes from the opium poppy. The fragrance-free seeds have a strong nutty flavor when roasted. They are primarily used as garnish and filling in different kinds of bread.

Aniseeds, *Pimpinella anisum*, have a sweet, aromatic, somewhat licorice-like flavor. They are believed to be anticonvulsant and help digestion. Usually anise is used in breads alone or together with fennel and caraway. Anise is good in tea, cabbage, and onion soup.

Mustard seed, *Sinapis alba*, *Brassica nigra*, is believed to increase circulation and comes from an annual plant that is grown in Sweden. There are three kinds: yellow, green, and black seeds. Black mustard seeds have the strongest flavors.

Whole yellow mustard seeds are often used in different kinds of pickles since they have a strongly preservative effect. The sharp, burning flavor does not come out until the seeds are crushed. Mustard is made from ground seeds. Black mustard is common in Indian cuisine.

Tamarind, *Tamarindus indica*, is the fruit in a tropical tree and grows in capsules.

The fruit is an important flavor in Indian cuisine and can be bought as tamarind purée or as whole dried fruit.

Tamarind juice: Soak 2.6 oz dried tamarind in 1 cup of hot water for about 30 minutes. Wring the fruit thoroughly so all of the pulp is used. Strain and use for seasoning dishes. (Vary the texture by adding a different amount of water.)

Fenugreek seed, *Trigonella foenum-graecum*, comes from a legume. The seeds have a spicy, somewhat bitter flavor and is often a part of curry mixtures. Fenugreek seed stimulates metabolism and is especially rich in iron, phosphorus, and lecithin.

Vanilla, *Vanilla planifolia*, is harvested as unripe fruit of an orchid plant. The fruit goes through a process of fermentation which gives it that well-known aroma. They are dried into brown-black beans.

To get the spice vanillin, the small white crystals inside, you split the bean lengthwise. The aroma is released when you mix or place the beans in warm liquid. Vanilla makes a nice contrast in most desserts. Vanilla sugar consists of synthetically produced vanillin and sugar.

PEPPER SPICES

We call many spices pepper, but they are not necessarily related.

Pepper, *Piper nigra*, is the fruit on the pepper vine that is grown in tropical countries. The unripe fruit is first green, then turns white, and finally black when ripe. In today's cuisine, black pepper is used most, while white pepper is the more common in traditional Swedish cuisine. The best aroma is achieved if grinding with a pepper mill right over the cooked food.

Green pepper is the fresh fruit that consist of both skin and core. It has a mild flavor and aroma. White pepper is the unripe, peeled grayish white fruit. White pepper has a stinging, sharp flavor but is milder than the black. Black pepper is the ripe seeds consisting of both peel and core. The flavor is hot and burning but still aromatic and rich.

Peruvian pepper does not belong to the pepper family but is a fruit of a tropical tree. The sweet, mildly peppery flavor goes well with pickles, sauces, and desserts.

Cloves, *Pimenta officinalis*, are the dried fruit from a tropical tree that belong to the myrtle family. The flavor is mild, somewhat carnation-like, with a hint of both nutmeg and cinnamon. It goes especially well with mashed root vegetables and in soups with beetroots, peas, and cabbage.

Chili pepper, *Capsicum*, is a very vitamin C-rich fruit that grows on a bush and is related to tomato, tobacco, and potato. Archaeological findings show that chili has been cultivated for at least 8,000 years and originated in South America. The Aztec name "chil" turned into "chile" in Spanish and "chilipeppar" in Swedish. In the heyday of the Mayan people, over 30 different kinds were cultivated. Today there are 150 to 200 different types of chilis with varying strength.

The chili fruit did not come to Asia until after Columbus discovered it in America. He thought that the strong chili pepper was related to the black pepper in India. The Spaniards and Portuguese also brought chili to their African colonies, where it is called piri piri.

Chili fruit has many health effects. They are considered to prevent blood clots and stimulate circulation as well as cleanse the airways if you have a cough or cold. Chili is also believed to aid digestion and increase energy consumption. Chili enhances the flavors of most dishes, from salads to deserts. Keep chilis in a plastic bag in the refrigerator or freezer.

Growing tips: Chili is perennial and can survive over winter in a cool place. It is easy to grow in a warm and sunny place. You can also scrape off the seeds from ripe (red) chili fruit and sow in moist soil.

A few common species of chili pepper:
Anaheim cubano is a fruit about 6 inches long and is harvested both when green and red. The red fruit are mild, and the green ones can be very hot. Anaheim has a tough skin and should be roasted and peeled before used in cooking. It works as an excellent filling but is also good in stews and sauces.

Jalapeño is one of the world's most common and popular types of chili. The medium spicy green fruit, 2 to 2.7 inches long, are tasty to fill with goat cheese, for example. Jalapeño can also be found as snacks or pickled in vinegar and sauces. Smoked and dried jalapeño is known as chipotle, which is tasty in marinades, sauces, soups, and bread.

Piri piri are very small, red, and spicy fruit.

Habanero is one of the hottest chili fruit and can be found in green, orange, and red.

It has a wonderful flavor of tropical fruit and tomato. Habanero is very easy to grow.

Hungarian wax can be found in yellow, green, and red. The green and yellow are medium strong. The red is considerably milder and is tasty when roasted and marinated. You can also fill it with goat cheese.

Serrano is one of the most popular chili fruit. It can be found in green and red and has a fresh flavor and heat that increases with ripeness. It is especially popular in sauces and pickles.

Chili pepper, or Dutch chile, is one of the most common types and is usually available all year round. It is medium strong and is found in green, orange, and red. The green fruit is somewhat astringent with an unripe flavor, while the red has a fuller flavor and sweetness. It goes well with most food, like sauces, chutney, soups, stews, and desserts.

Thai chilis are small and pointy fruit that are very spicy. They are often used in Thai cuisine. Thai chili is harvested both when green and red.

Poblano is a medium strong, very aromatic and tasty chili fruit that comes from Mexico. When it is dried, it is called "ancho." The fruit goes well with sauces and desserts.

Cascabel is a mild chili fruit from Mexico, with a slightly tart and smoky flavor. It is wonderful in sauces, soups, and stews.

Pasilla is generally sold as dried fruit. It has a mild and aromatic flavor and is commonly used in sauces.

New Mexican is a medium spicy green chili fruit from Mexico. Traditionally, it is baked in the oven and then used in sauces, soups, and stews.

cascabel

rose pepper

chipotle

chili
pepper

green pepper

cloves

serrano

piri piri

ancho chile

jalapeño

pasilla

New Mexican chili

Thai chili

habanero

Anaheim cubano

Hungarian wax

Spanish
pepper

ancho chile

129

Preparation and seasoning

There are many different ways of cooking vegetables. Different methods of preparation have their pros and cons and leave their mark on the vegetables, as well as spices and seasoning.

Avoid keeping the vegetables warm for any long period of time after cooking them, since flavor, color, texture, and vitamin content deteriorate.

KITCHEN TOOLS SAVE TIME and facilitate in many steps of the cooking process. It pays off to invest in kitchen tools of good quality. See the advice of a consumer report group's tests.

A blender, preferably of glass, is the most effective when used for raw material with liquids or completely dry. It mixes dressings, sauces, sesame milk, drinks, and soups and also finely chops nuts and almonds.

Hand blender. There are many advantages with a hand blender. It is quick to use and is easy to clean. The hand blender does almost the same thing as the mixer, except being able to mix sesame milk and smoothies fine enough. The biggest advantage is that you can mix right in a pan of soup, for example. You can usually buy a smaller chopping and mixing device to attach it to.

A KitchenAid stand mixer whips, mixes, and kneads large dough as well as shreds, grates, and slices vegetables. A mixer is usually included in the standard equipment. Accessories like a purée tool, meat grinder, and grain mill are usually found as accessories.

Food processor is something in between a mixer and a KitchenAid. It works the most effectively when it has to process something of a somewhat firm texture. Besides being able to do the same things as the mixer, it also grates, shreds, and slices vegetables. It is ideal when you want to make a pasta dough, pie crust, shortcut pastry, and patty or different kinds of mincemeat. Most food processors also knead smaller bread doughs.

Tips!

- If you use the food processor several times during the same meal preparation, you do not have to clean it in between.
- Start with all dry ingredients that need to be ground, chopped, or blended. This means that you will have to work backward in some recipes. First read through the whole recipe and then plan in what order to do each step.

PREPARATION

Boil vegetables like this: Bring water and ½ to 1 tsp salt per 1 quart of water to a boil. Place the vegetables in the pan and let them simmer under a lid for as short amount of time as possible. The ideal heat for all boiling is around 203°F, when it only simmers. When it starts bubbling, the heat has reached 212°F. But after that, the temperature cannot get higher not matter how much it bubbles.

The vegetables are the tastiest when they still have their vitality and crispiness left. If the vegetables have a long cooking time, you first place these in the water. Then add other vegetables in the order of their cooking time.

While boiling some mineral substances, vitamin C and B as well as some flavors are extracted into the boiling water. Save the broth and use in cooking—for example in soups and sauces. Avoid keeping the vegetables warm for any long period of time after cooking them, since flavor, color, texture, and vitamin content deteriorates.

Approximate cooking time in minutes

Type	Whole	I piece
artichoke	30–50	
asparagus	10–45	
beans, fresh	5–10	
broccoli, fresh	10–15	5–10
brussels sprouts	5–10	
carrots	10–15	5–10
cauliflower	10–15	5–10
celery	8–10	
Chinese cabbage	5–10	
corn	5–10	
endive	15–20	5–10
fennel	20–25	10
kohlrabi	10–20	5–10
leek	10–20	5–10
red cabbage	20–30	
spinach, leaves	5–7	
sugar peas	2–6	
white cabbage	10–20	
yellow onion	10–15	5–10

How to braise: Pour 0.4 to 0.8 inches of water or broth in a pan as well as one tablespoon of butter, oil, or coconut fat. Place vegetables like Chinese cabbage, endive, fennel, broccoli, or kohlrabi in the pan and simmer on low heat until they are soft enough.

Both taste and nutrition will be better when you cook vegetables this way compared to regular boiling in water. The disadvantage is that you need to supervise it so it does not boil dry.

How to steam: There are several types of steamer tools to buy. Place the steamer tool in the pan and fill with water until it is right under the steamer. Bring water to a boil and place the vegetables in the steamer and let them cook until they are just soft.

Steaming makes the vegetables richer in flavor, since the flavor substances do not disappear in the boiling water. The hot steam will destroy some of the vitamin C and B, but all the minerals will be there.

How to pressure cook: Place all vegetables like artichokes, beetroots, or rutabagas in the pressure cooker and pour ⅔ cup water in the cooker. Beans and grains are cooked with water directly in the cooker. Put the heat on maximum. When the red ring is visible, the heat is reduced to medium or low. Use the prescribed time. When cooking is done you remove the pressure cooker from the stove, and when the pressure gauge is lowered completely the cooker will open. You can speed up the opening by flushing it with cold water on the lid and slowly pulling the regulator to open.

Pressure cookers can be found in different brands and models and can work in different ways. Follow the instructions. Pressure cooking halves the cooking time. You will save both time and energy. The steam that is formed from the water is held in the pressure cooker, and after a few minutes, high pressure is formed in the cooker. This makes it possible for the temperature to reach 248°F. The high temperature reduces some of the C and B vitamins.

Spelt, oats, beans, and vegetables cook in half the time. White beans are cooked soft in half an hour and dry, hard beans need 80 to 90 minutes. Winter potatoes cook in 10 to 15 minutes and artichokes in 12 to 18 minutes.

How to fry: The ideal frying temperature is around 302°F. If the fat is warmer than 365°F, it quickly oxidizes and will also create changes in flavor. The hotter the fat becomes, the bigger is the risk that carcinogenic substances and trans fat are produced. To fry in butter is the easiest since the butter starts bubbling when it is time to reduce the temperature. Coconut, canola, and olive oil will not change color but start to smoke at 482°F. Then the oil is already ruined and should not be used at all. Coconut oil has the highest heat resistance, then butter.

You can fry in olive and canola oil if you are careful with heat. You can add a little bit of butter to the oil or a piece of bread to get a color signal. Other oils should not be used at all since they oxidize quickly in heat.

Tip! Fry vegetarian patties in the oven. Place them on a greased baking sheet and brush with 1 tablespoon oil mixed with 1 tablespoon soy sauce. Bake in the oven for 15 to 20 minutes in 356°F.

How to fry: Vegetables, patties, snacks, or fruit are good to fry. Heat coconut oil to 338–356°F. Measure the temperature with a cooking thermometer. Be careful when frying and keep the kitchen fan on. Always keep a lid close to smother possible burning oil.

SEASONING

In Indian cuisine, people usually say that a meal needs to contain sweet, sour, salty, spicy, astringent, and bitter to be balanced.

- **Sweet** is found in honey, root vegetables, cauliflower, spinach, peas, pumpkin, in most grains, fruit, and in some nuts. Sweet spices are anise, fennel, cardamom, or saffron.
- **Salty** is found in sea and rock salt.
- **Sour** is found in lemon, lime, vinegar, tomato, green apples, and sourdough rye bread.
- **Spicy** is found in most spices like chili, ginger, black pepper, mustard seeds, mint, oregano, parsley, marjoram, basil, and fresh and dried coriander.
- **Astringent** flavor stimulates digestion and is found in lentils, beans, turmeric, rosemary,

celery, zucchini, buckwheat, rye, walnuts, and sunflower seeds.
- **Bitter** flavors stimulate digestion and are found in bitter types of lettuce, dandelion leaves, turmeric, and fenugreek.
- **Umami** is called the "fifth taste" and has a very rich taste that works like a flavor enhancer. In the food industry (particularly in Chinese cuisine) as well as in different spices, umami is used as a flavor enhancer in the form of the questionable additive, glutamate. Umami is formed naturally when protein in food is broken down during storing. Dried algae, Parmesan, and green tea contain the most umami. Other good sources are vegetables, capers, miso, shoyu, and soy sauce as well as dried mushrooms and dried tomatoes. An additive of one or many of the abovementioned food enhances both flavor and aroma in all food. Fresh food like onions, tomatoes, and celery also have some umami flavor.

SPICE MIXES

There are many exciting spice mixes of varying strength from different countries.

Curry is an Indian spice mix that consists of at least eight spices, usually turmeric, ginger, cloves, nutmeg, cayenne pepper, cinnamon, coriander, and cardamom. Curry comes into its own if it is first fried in some fat when cooking.

Mix your own curry:
1 tsp ground cumin
1 tsp ground coriander
1 tsp ground turmeric
¼ tsp ground black pepper
¼ tsp ground cardamom
¼ tsp ground ginger
¼ tsp ground cinnamon
⅛ tsp ground cayenne pepper

Garam masala is an Indian spice mix that often consists of cinnamon, black pepper, coriander, cumin, cardamom, cloves, and nutmeg or nutmeg flower. In India, almost every family has its own garam masala mix. The aroma of the spice is enhanced if you fry it in some fat when cooking.

Four Spices can consist of eight spices despite the name, including ginger, tarragon, basil, rosemary, cloves, cumin, and bay leaf. The rich flavor goes well with vegetable dishes.

Five Spices is a fragrant mix that is often used in Chinese cuisine. It consists of Sichuan pepper, star anise, fennel, cloves, and cinnamon.

Gomasio
1¼ CUP
1–2 tbsp sea salt or Himalayan salt (12.5–25 g)
1–2 tbsp unpeeled sesame seeds (10–20 g)

- Roast the salt carefully in a frying pan while stirring on low heat. Place the salt in a mortar. Then roast the sesame seeds carefully while stirring on low heat. If it starts to "pop," the heat is too high. Taste the seeds to see if the flavor is good. The seeds should not change color in any significant way.
- Grind the seeds together with the salt until two-thirds of the sesame seeds are finely ground. Keep the spice in a jar with an airtight lid.

Tip! If you do not have a mortar you can use a food processor but the result will turn out best in a mortar.

Roasted seaweed spice
ABOUT 2¼ CUPS
¾ cup pumpkin seeds (110 g)
1 cup, 2 tbsp black sesame seeds (170 g)
6 dried nori sheets
gourmet salt (gives a more interesting texture)

- Roast the pumpkin seeds in a frying pan while stirring for a while. Add the sesame seeds and continue to stir the seeds until they smell good. Place in a bowl.
- Roast the nori sheets, one at a time, on high heat until they shimmer in gold. Turn them many times.
- Mix 5 of the nori sheets in a food processor until they are finely chopped but not a powder. Coarsely crumble the last sheet and mix algae and roasted seeds. Add salt to taste.

SALT AND HERB SALT

We descend from the ocean and our blood contains the same salt concentration and the same levels of other minerals and micronutrients as ocean water. Our ancestors valued salt highly and also used it to cure different illnesses. Salt regulates the fluid and electrolyte balance in all cells of our body.

The daily requirement is about 0.2 oz a day, but generally most people eat almost double that amount of salt each day. Many people have a craving for salt even if they have normal salt intake, caused by the fact that our regular table salt is refined and does not contains the minerals and micronutrients found in ocean water.

High consumption of table salt strains your kidneys and is considered to be a contributing factor to high blood pressure as well as heart and vascular diseases for those who have a predisposition to it. Ten percent of the salt we eat is found naturally in vegetables, 60 percent comes from restaurant food and the food industry, and 30 percent is added ourselves when salting food.

Table salt is a refined product in which all the minerals and micronutrients except for sodium chloride are removed. Often iodine, anti-caking agents, and other additives are added.

Sea salt contains all the minerals and micronutrients found in the ocean, but the iodine level is naturally low. It is produced by letting ocean water evaporate in pools. Since our oceans have become the dump of the world's waste, sea salt does not have the same positive effect on our health that it used to.

Rock salt is a salt found in mountains after the disappearance of earlier oceans. It contains all minerals and micronutrients found in the sea, but the iodine level is naturally low.

Crystal salt, Himalayan salt. It is the finest salt which is found in special veins in salt layers in some mountains where the salt has been exposed to an enormous pressure during a long time. That makes crystal salt the most expensive salt.

Some scientists consider crystal salt to be a pure light energy, saying that it works as an information carrier in the cells which gives our bodies the right frequency pattern. It also contains all the minerals and micronutrients found in the sea, but the iodine level is naturally low.

Herb and spice salt is found in a variety of brands. All these products are based on sea salt in varying amounts (70 to 95.5 percent, depending on product) as well as herbs.

The best herb salt. Mix your favorite spices— for instance, cleaned and sliced chili fruit as well as basil and/or parsley in a food processor.

Stir pressed garlic and ground crystal salt into the mixture by hand. The salt will absorb the aromatic juice. Spread out the salt on a plate and let it dry in a warm place. After drying, keep the salt in a jar with a lid. Other tasty things to put in a herb salt are celery leaves or very young and tender leaves from lovage.

SUGAR AND SWEETENERS

Sugar. In recent years, we have become increasingly aware of how harmful sugar is. Sugar creates large blood sugar swings and is very addictive. Sugar stimulates the body's reward system and causes us to want more and more.

Agave syrup is similar to honey in taste and is extracted from a cactus plant. It is rich in iron, calcium, and potassium and has a low GI. Agave syrup is 25 percent sweeter than sugar.

Avoid sugar!
Avoid all white sugar, fructose, raw sugar, brown sugar, syrup, and maple syrup! Dried fruit, malt, agave syrup, honey, and stevia are fine in small amounts. Fruit and berries in reasonable amounts spread out during the day are a good addition of antioxidants, fibers, and other nutrients.

Fructose syrup consists of fructose and is twice as sweet as regular sugar. Fructose has a low GI since fructose is transformed into glucose in the liver. Glucose works as the body's backup and is used when the blood sugar is too low.

Normally there are 1.7 to 2.6 oz of stored backup nutrition (glucose) in the liver. The larger the intake of fructose, the larger the risk that the glucose storage in the liver is filled and that the liver will transform the excess to fat.

Fruit and berries contain relatively small amounts of fructose. If the liver's glucose storage is empty (see above), you would need to eat, for example, more than seven apples at once in order for the liver to start transforming the fructose to fat.

Malt is similar to dark syrup but the taste is not as sweet. Malt is produced by whole, sprouted grains and has a decent nutritional value.

Stevia rebaudiana, or sweet leaf, is a herb that originally comes from Paraguay, where it has been used by the Guarani people for 1,500 years. Stevia is considerably sweeter than sugar and can be grown at home on the windowsill or be bought dried as a green powder. The green powder has somewhat of a licorice flavor. There are also more refined and concentrated products to buy, like syrup and white powder.

Stevia can be used in cooking, desserts, and baking but has a too distinctive taste to use in mild dishes like vanilla sauce. Baked goods will also not have the same brown color as regular sugar gives them when they are baked.

In Japan, China, and Brazil, the herb is recommended for diabetics, since it regulates the blood sugar levels and has a positive effect on the pancreas. Stevia also reduces the craving for sweets, is thought to help caries, sore lips, candida, and the flu. It contains none or few calories.

Tip! A few sprinkles of stevia is perfect when you want to add some sweetness to the food—for example, a tomato sauce.

Honey contains about 75 percent sugar—mostly glucose and fructose. It contains small amounts of vitamins and minerals as well as antibacterial substances like inhibin as well as acetylcholine, which has a calming and soothing effect. These substances are very sensitive to heat and are destroyed at temperatures over 113°F.

There are also pollen grains in honey, which add a certain cloudiness. Honey that is liquid and clear has generally been heated. Foreign honey has usually been heated.

Research shows that honey in small amounts lowers the blood sugar and strengthens the immune system and production of the powerful antioxidant glutathione by 7 percent. In ayurveda, honey in small amounts is considered to heighten life energy.

Garlic honey is good to keep at home for dressings and sauces and to mix with lukewarm water and drink when you have a cold. Stir crushed garlic cloves into honey. The honey will eventually turn to liquid and has a long perishability.

Aromatic honey. Honey can also be seasoned with essential oils like eucalyptus, peppermint, lavender, and lemon balm. First heat the honey to 107.6°F while stirring and then add the essential oil. Instead of essential oils, you can season the honey with fresh herb flowers like lavender. The flowers can stay in the honey but the perishability will not be as long.

Summer buffet

Here is a simple, good, and delicious summer buffet in which most dishes can be prepared in advance. On the buffet table, we find Raspberry Drink with Lime; Romaine Salad with Walnuts; three snacks: Crostini with Tapenade, Feta and Watermelon, as well as Blue Cheese and Melon; Potato Salad with Asparagus and Tomatoes as well as Grilled Tzay Skewers; Marinated Artichoke Hearts, Olives and Marinated Tomatoes on a Bed of Arugula and Other Tender Leaves; as well as Chanterelle Pie.

A few days before: Marinate the artichoke hearts and make tapenade, alternatively buy ready-made. Make the dressing for the salad.

The day before: Potato Salad and Chanterelle Pie. Grill the Tzay skewers. Strain frozen raspberries for the drink but add the fruit soda just before serving.

The same day: Salad and snacks.

Just before serving: Warm chanterelle pie and skewers in the oven and pour the drinks.

Recipes are found on the following pages:
Raspberry Drink (321), Snacks (194), Tapenade (175), Marinated Artichoke Hearts (179), Salad (150), Potato Salad (163), Chanterelle Pie (227). (The Tzay Skewers can be bought frozen.) Garnish the buffet table with beautiful and edible flowers.

Autumn buffet

A colorful Mediterranean-inspired autumn buffet is easy to prepare. On the buffet table, we find Herb Gratin Mushrooms, Delicious Salad Dish, Dolmades, Tzatziki, Olives, Spinach Pie with Chèvre, and Honey Marinated Strawberries.

A few days before: Make the Dolmades.
The day before: Make Tzatziki, Spinach Pie, and blanch all the vegetables for the salad dish.
The same day: Marinate the strawberries and herb gratin the mushrooms.
Just before serving: Heat the pie and place all the dishes on generous trays.

Recipes can be found on the following pages: Herb Gratin Mushrooms (188), Salad Dish (155), Dolmades (189), Tzatziki (170), Spinach Pie (228), Honey Marinated Strawberries (279). Garnish the buffet table with beautiful and edible flowers, autumn leaves, or Rowan berries.

Winter buffet

A lovely winter buffet with rich flavors is easy to prepare. The buffet is perfect as an alternative Christmas buffet. On the buffet table, we find three snacks: Chèvre Bundles with Gingerbread Crumbles, Persimmon with Blue Cheese, and Pumpernickel with Herb Pâté and Cucumber. There is also Hummus, Mustard Marinated Aubergine, Beetroot Salad, Mushroom Salad with Sesame, Orange Marinated Kale Salad with Pomegranate, Chèvre Gratin Sweet Potato and Fried Vegetarian Soy Sausage as well as Soy or Quorn Balls (frozen section).

A few days before: Hummus, Beetroot Salad, Mustard Marinated Aubergine.

The day before: Prepare the sweet potatoes for the gratin and make the chèvre batter for the Chèvre Bundles.

The same day: Snacks, Kale Salad, and slice the mushrooms for the salad.

Just before serving: Gratin sweet potatoes with chevré and fry the sausage and soy or Quorn balls. Finish the Mushroom Salad.

Recipes are found on the following pages:
Snacks (194), Hummus (176), Mustard Marinated Aubergine (187), Beetroot Salad (156), Mushroom Salad with Sesame (186), Kale Salad (155), Chevré Gratin Sweet Potato (246).

Indian buffet

Surprise your friends with an Indian buffet or cook the food together. On the buffet, we find Strawberry Lassi, Samosa, Papadam, Bengali Flower Rice, Green Beans, Paneer and Badi in Tomato Sauce, Tomato Raita, and Apple Chutney, Indian Nut and Fruit Balls, and Saffron Mousse with Strawberry Sauce. This meal is composed by Rosemarie Geiss and the recipe comes from her book *Vediska Läckerheter*.

A few days before: Apple Chutney and Indian Nut and Fruit Balls.
A few days before: Prepare the Saffron Mousse.
The day before: Saffron Mousse, Tomato Raita and Green Beans, Paneer and Badi in Tomato Sauce (except for frying the badi), and prepare the Samosas.
The same day: Strawberry Sauce and frying Samosas, Papadam and Badi.

Just before serving: Bengali Flower Rice and heat the Green Beans, Paneer and Badi in Tomato Sauce.
The recipes can be found on the following pages: Samosa (192), Strawberry Lassi (319), Papadam (196), Bengali Flower Rice (220), Green Beans, Paneer and Badi in Tomato Sauce (241), Tomato Raita (170), Apple Chutney (199), as well as Saffron Mousse (115) with Strawberry Sauce (281), and Indian Nut and Fruit Balls (293).

Asian buffet

A delicious buffet with an Asian touch! It is nice to cook food together with friends. On the buffet table, we can find Papaya Salad with Coconut Dressing, both Boiled and Fried Dumplings, Grilled Marinated Mushroom Skewers, Vegetable Stir-Fry, as well as Mango Ice Cream with Coconut and Lime. Serve with Cooked Rice, Couscous, or Naked Oat.

The day before: Grill the Mushroom Skewers.
The same day: Make the Mango Ice Cream, Dumplings, Salad, and prepare vegetables as well as sauce for the stir-fry.
Just before serving: Cook the rice, couscous, or naked oats, stir-fry the vegetables, and heat the Mushroom Skewers.

Recipes can be found on the following pages: Papaya Salad (161), Dumpling (187), Grilled, Marinated Mushroom Skewers (267), Vegetable Stir-Fry (262), Mango Ice Cream (277).

Salads

The old Greeks cultivated several types of green leaves that they used in their food. But the Romans were the first ones to eat a whole dish with different vegetables that they called a salad.

There are hundreds of different kinds of salads. A salad can be varied in endless ways. Take advantage of seasonal vegetables, herbs, and berries as well as wild plants and vary with exciting dressings. Here are many suggestions of salads both as sides and as a main meal.

Basic Salad with Variations
Vegan or raw

Estimate one shredded romaine lettuce head for four servings or feel free to mix different types of lettuce and/or green leaves. Mix the leaves with some of the following dressings or serve the dressing separately.

Vary the salad with one or more ingredients:
- grated red onion
- nuts and seeds
- avocado
- tomato
- radish
- chopped herbs, like parsley
- sprouted sunflower seeds and sprouts
- shaved carrots and celery
- shredded cabbage
- grated fennel
- finely chopped or mixed broccoli
- Garlic Roasted Chickpeas, p. 197
- sliced Parmigiano or soy Parmigiano

Basic Dressing

The dressing will turn out the most tasty if you let it rest for a while and mature. Balsamic vinegar can be replaced completely or partly with lemon or lime juice.

4 SERVINGS
1 tbsp balsamic vinegar (15 ml)
3–4 tbsp olive or canola oil (45–60 ml)
herb salt (salad spices) and black pepper

Dressing with Mustard
Follow the recipe above but add one or two teaspoons of Dijon mustard.

Dressing with Mustard and Garlic
Follow the basic recipe but add two teaspoons of Dijon mustard and one half pressed clove of garlic.

Dressing with Mustard, Garlic, and Honey
Follow the basic recipe above but add one or two teaspoons of Dijon mustard, one half pressed clove of garlic as well as a pinch of honey.

Make Your Own Salad Mix
The traditional Italian salad mix misticanza includes about 30 different types of leaves. Create your own salad mix by mixing different types of leaves and lettuce like arugula, spinach, and tender beetroot greens. Other tasty things to mix in your salad are crispy purslane and fig marigold as well as wild plants like lamb's quarters. Shred the leaves in big pieces.

Add small amounts of basil, parsley, lemon balm, and mint in small pieces, berries, and beautiful tasty flowers. Rinse everything and press out the water in a salad dryer. That way, the salad will be perfect and stays fresh in the fridge for days.

Strawberry Salad with Blue Cheese *Lactose*

Simple, good, and fresh! Romaine lettuce can be replaced with other green leaves.

4 SERVINGS
2.1 pints of strawberries (1 liter)
1 small romaine lettuce head
7 oz blue cheese (200 g)
½ to ¾ cups basil leaves (75–110 g)
¼ cup coarsely chopped walnuts (40 g)

Dressing:
1 tbsp balsamic vinegar (15 ml)
3–4 tbsp canola or olive oil (45–60 ml)
herb salt and black pepper

■ Wash and cut the strawberries and lettuce in pieces. Cut the cheese in cubes. Mix strawberries, lettuce, cheese, basil, and walnuts with the dressing.

Apple Salad with Blue Cheese and Nuts
Follow the recipe above but change strawberries to apples and walnuts to hazelnuts.

▶ STRAWBERRY SALAD with blue cheese, basil, and walnuts

Pear Salad with Blue Cheese and Walnuts

Follow the above recipe but replace strawberries with sliced pears.

Pear Salad with Celery and Nuts

Follow the basic recipe above but use strawberries and basil instead of sliced pears as well as grated celery.

Apple Salad with Celery and Blue Cheese

Follow the basic recipe above but replace strawberries and basil with pieces of apple and grated celery as well as hazelnuts instead of walnuts.

Vegetable Dip *Vegan*

Dip with vegetables is something that both adults and children appreciate. Serve pieces of vegetables with one or many dips like Guacamole, p.176, Tapenade, p.175, and Tzatziki, p. 170.

Choose some of the following vegetables:

- carrot sticks
- cucumber sticks
- fennel sticks
- bell pepper sticks
- cauliflower florets
- broccoli florets
- radish

Eco-friendly tips!

The selection of vegetables is best during summer and autumn, and we can indulge in almost all vegetables and root vegetables. Coarsely grated kohlrabi, radishes, and turnips are simple to make, juicy, and surprisingly tasty. Colorful berries like strawberries, blueberries, and raspberries are delicious in salads.

Apples can be used to make a lot of tasty things, everything from desserts and baked goods to appetizing salads. They also go well with stir-fry and stews, and especially with curry.

Fennel Salad with Apples *Raw*

4 SERVINGS
1 fennel bulb
1 apple
¾ cup green leaves (110 g)
¼ cup chopped walnuts (40 ml)

Dressing:

1 tbsp balsamic vinegar (15 ml)
3–4 tbsp olive or canola oil (45–60 ml)
½ to 1 tsp Dijon mustard (2.5–5 ml)
herb salt and black pepper

■ Grate the fennel finely. Cut an unpeeled apple in four pieces. Core and cut in smaller pieces. Mix fennel, green leaves, and apple with the dressing. Sprinkle with walnuts.

Fennel Salad with Pomegranate Apple

Follow the recipe above but add pomegranate seeds.

Fennel Salad with Oranges

Follow the recipe above but use a sliced orange instead of an apple.

Endive Salad with Oranges

Follow the recipe above but replace fennel and apple with endive and oranges.

Waldorf Salad

Lactose or vegan

4 SERVINGS
2 apples
about 2 cups coarsely grated celeriac (300 g)
3–4 tbsp chopped walnuts (60–80 g)

Dressing:

1–2 tbsp mayonnaise (15–30 ml)
¾ cup yogurt (200 ml)
1–2 tsp mustard (5–10 ml)
1 tsp lemon juice (5 ml)
herb salt and pepper

■ Cut unpeeled apples in four pieces. Core and cut in small cubes. Mix celery and apples with dressing. Sprinkle with walnuts.

▲ TOMATO and mozzarella salad

Tomato and Mozzarella Salad

Lactose

A true classic. The salad will turn out the most successful if the onion sits for a while in the dressing.

4 SERVINGS
1 red onion
12–16 cherry tomatoes
7.05 oz mozzarella (200 g)
basil leaves
olives (optional)

Dressing:
1 tbsp vinegar (15 ml)
3 tbsp canola or olive oil (45 ml)
1 crushed garlic clove
salt and pepper

■ Peel and finely chop the onion and mix with the dressing. Cut some of the tomatoes as well as the cheese into cubes. Mix the tomatoes, cheese, basil, and olives (optional) in the dressing.

Tomato and Onion Salad *Vegan*
Follow the recipe above but do not use cheese and increase the amount of onions.

Tomato Salad with Corn and Olives *Raw*
Follow the basic recipe above but replace cheese and basil with corn and olives.

Avocado Salad with Tomatoes and Arugula *Raw*

Avocado is available all year round, but is more eco-friendly to buy from October to April when avocado is imported from the Mediterranean.

4 SERVINGS
1 red onion
2 avocados
12–16 cherry tomatoes
1 small package of arugula

Dressing:
1 tbsp vinegar (15 ml)
3 tbsp canola or olive oil (45 ml)
1 crushed garlic clove
herb salt and pepper

■ Peel and finely chop the onion. Let it sit in the dressing for a few minutes. Cut avocados and tomatoes in cubes. Mix the dressing with the arugula, avocado, and tomato. Add herb salt and pepper to taste.

Avocado Salad with Tomato and Walnuts
Follow the recipe above but add chopped walnuts.

Delicious Salad Dish *Vegan* * PHOTO P. 140

A colorful salad dish with many different types of fresh and parboiled vegetables is fresh and tasty. It is perfect for the buffet table and is easy to prepare. The vegetables that need to be parboiled can be prepared the day before. Place the vegetables in separate plastic bags when they have cooled off.

Choose different kinds of vegetables like asparagus, carrot sticks, small florets of broccoli and cauliflower, miniature corn, zucchini half moons, sugar peas, and scallions. Bring water and salt to a boil in a large pan (1 tsp salt per 1 quart water). Boil each type of vegetable separately for about one minute. Pick up the vegetables with a slotted spoon and place them in a colander and then rinse them in cold water.

Place the vegetables in groups together with cherry tomatoes, radishes, cucumber sticks, carrot sticks, sliced mushrooms, and bell peppers. Serve with Tapenade, p. 175, Tzatziki, p. 170, and Hummus, p. 176.

Orange Marinated Kale Salad with Pomegranate *Raw*

Tasty and climate-smart salad for autumn and winter that goes just as well on the Christmas table. Pomegranate can be bought all year round, but it is more eco-friendly to buy from August to March when they are imported from Mediterranean countries.

4–5 SERVINGS

1 orange
1 sweet apple, preferably red
⅓ cup walnuts (50 g)
3⅓ cups finely chopped kale or Savoy cabbage (500 g)
2 tbsp dried cranberries (20 g)
juice from ½ orange
1 tbsp canola oil (15 ml)
pomegranate seeds

■ Cut off both peel and the white part of the orange and slice it. Keep the peel on the apple and first cut it in pieces and then in thin slices. Chop the walnuts coarsely.
■ Mix orange slices, apple, walnuts, kale, and cranberries with orange juice and canola oil. Place the salad on a dish and sprinkle with pomegranate seeds.

◀ ORANGE Marinated Kale Salad With Pomegranate

Kale Is the Best Vegetable in the World

It is tasty and useful, extremely nutritious, and has the highest ORAC value of all vegetables (see p. 48). It is also very easy to grow.

Growing tips! Fill a flower pot with sand (0.3 inches) or soil. Plant five plants (can be bought in the plant shop in spring). Plant each with plenty of compost soil or other high-quality soil. Then all you have to do is place cut grass on the surface of the soil during summer and water it sometimes.

If there is a risk for cabbage butterflies, which also love kale, you have to cover the kale with a row cover. You can start to harvest in August; the biggest leaves are picked from the bottom and then up. If the kale thrives, each plant can grow to be over 3.2 feet high, and the plant continues to grow until frost hits if you just save the top. Usually you can harvest fresh leaves for 3 to 4 months.

Salad with Carrot, Beetroots, Apple, and Capers *Raw*

4 SERVINGS

2 carrots
3 small beetroots
1 apple
1 green bell pepper
1 piece of leek
2–3 tbsp capers (20–30 g)

Dressing:

1 tbsp balsamic vinegar (15 ml)
3–4 tbsp olive or canola oil (45–60 ml)
herb salt and black pepper

■ Peel carrots and beetroots as well as core apple and bell pepper. Cut all the vegetables in very small cubes. Shred the leek. Mix vegetables with capers and dressing.

Kale Salad *Raw*

1–2 SERVINGS
1–2 large kale leaves
½ apple
1 tbsp dried cranberries (10 g)
1 tbsp pumpkin seeds (10 g)

Dressing:
1 tbsp olive or canola oil (15 ml)
½ tsp vinegar or lemon juice (2.5 ml)
½ tsp shoyu (2.5 ml)
½ tsp sesame oil (2.5 ml)

■ Remove the coarse leaf nerve on the kale leaves and shred them in smaller pieces. Finely mix with a hand blender. Use a fork to make the chopped kale fluffy.

■ Cut the unpeeled apple half into pieces. Remove the core and slice each piece thinly. Mix apple, kale, and cranberries with the dressing and sprinkle with pumpkin seeds.

Kale Salad with Variation *Raw*

Follow the recipe above but replace and create other combinations according to the following alternatives:

- Apple pieces and corn kernels from fresh corn as well as chopped walnuts
- Parsley, chopped cucumber, and chopped walnuts
- Thinly shaved kohlrabi and pumpkin seeds
- Thinly shaved carrots and chopped hazelnuts
- Thinly shaved daikon and chopped hazelnuts

Beetroot Salad

Lacto or vegan

4 SERVINGS *PHOTO P. 143
½ cup finely chopped red onion (75 g)
1⅓–2 cup boiled, finely chopped beetroots (200–300 g)
⅔–1⅓ cup finely chopped sour, salt, or pickled cucumber (100–200 g)
1–2 finely chopped apples
2–3 tbsp mayonnaise (30–45 ml)
¾-1¼ cup yogurt (200–300 ml)
herb salt

■ Mix red onion, beetroots, cucumber, and apple. Stir mayonnaise together with yogurt. Mix the dressing with the vegetables and add herb salt to taste.

Beetroot Carpaccio *Lacto or Vegan*

A different and tasty way to serve root vegetables. Goes well with the buffet table! If the beetroots are not juicy enough, you can boil or bake them in the oven before serving. Beetroots can be replaced with turnip, kohlrabi, or daikon.

4 SERVINGS
3 large tender beetroots, preferably candy tripod beetroots
½–1 tbsp lemon or lime juice (7.5–15 ml)
2 tbsp canola or olive oil (30 ml)
black pepper
salt flakes
young arugula or other leaves
Parmesan cheese
pine nuts
regular capers or large capers

■ Peel the beetroots and slice very thin slices with a knife or a cheese slicer. Mix with lemon juice and oil and let sit for a while.

■ Spread the beetroots on plates. Sprinkle with pepper and some salt. Add green leaves, thinly sliced Parmesan, and pine nuts. Top with capers.

Beetroot Carpaccio with Feta Cheese and Roasted Hazelnuts *Lacto*

Follow the recipe above but replace Parmesan, capers, and pine nuts with crumbled feta cheese or chevré and roasted hazelnuts.

Kohlrabi Carpaccio with Walnuts *Raw*

Follow the basic recipe above but exclude the cheese. Replace pine nuts and capers with 4 tbsp chopped walnuts that first are seasoned with ½ tsp shoyu or tamari and ½ tsp sesame oil.

Raw Grated Kohlrabi
Kohlrabi has a crispy, mild, and sweet pulp. If coarsely grated it will turn out extra juicy and tasty. It can be served coarsely grated or thinly sliced, with or without dressing. The smaller the kohlrabi, the more tender. To coarsely grate or thinly slice Jerusalem artichoke, turnip, and radish with a cheese slicer is also very tasty.

▲ BEETROOT CARPACCIO

Pizza Salad with Variations *Raw*

White cabbage, red cabbage, and pointed cabbage can be bought almost all year round. It is tasty together with a dressing (see p. 150) or mixed with other vegetables. Make a big batch of cabbage salad since it stays fresh for almost a week without taste or nutrients deteriorating. (If you want to use a grated apple, see underneath; the perishability is somewhat shorter.)

Finely shred the cabbage in a processor or with a cheese slicer. In the winter, when the cabbage is a little drier, you can "juice it up." Place shredded cabbage in a bowl and press the cabbage down with your fist until it starts becoming more juicy.

Vary the salad with some of the following:
- shredded bell pepper
- chopped parsley
- coarsely grated apple
- thinly shaved carrot
- shaved carrot and celery
- thinly sliced celery
- finely shredded leek

Ginger Carrots *Raw*

Simple and delicious with most things.

4 SERVINGS
4–5⅓ cup finely grated carrots (600–800 g)

Dressing:
2 tsp honey (10 ml)
1 tsp grated ginger (3 g)
1 tbsp apple cider vinegar (15 ml)

■ Mix the finely grated carrots with the dressing and stir.

Carrot Salad with Sesame Marinated Algae *Vegan*

4 SERVINGS
⅔–1⅓ cup arame algae (100–200 g)
3 carrots

Marinade:
1 tbsp oil (15 ml)
1 tbsp lemon juice (15 ml)
1 tbsp shoyu (15 ml)
1 tbsp sesame seeds (10 g)
1 tbsp pumpkin seeds (10 g)
½–1 tbsp grated ginger (5–10 g)
1 pressed garlic clove

■ Boil the algae in water for about 20 minutes. Let it drain in a colander. Mix the warm algae with the marinade and let cool. Grate the carrots finely and top with algae.

Salad with Orange, Red Onion, and Pomegranate *Raw*

Maché lettuce is a wonderful lettuce with a nutty character. It is also very resistant to cold and stays fresh even under the snow. Maché lettuce can be replaced with Chinese cabbage, white cabbage, kale, or other green leaves.

4 SERVINGS
1 red onion
1 large orange
5⅓ cup maché lettuce (800 g)
½ pomegranate

Dressing:
1 tbsp vinegar (15 ml)
3 tbsp canola or olive oil (45 ml)
1 crushed garlic clove
herb salt and pepper

■ Peel and thinly slice the onion. Let the onion sit in the dressing for a few minutes. Peel and slice the orange. Remove the seeds from the pomegranate. Stir lettuce leaves and orange into the dressing. Sprinkle with pomegranate seeds.

Salad with orange, kiwi, and pomegranate

Follow the recipe above but add peeled and sliced kiwi.

Coleslaw with Apple

Lacto or Vegan

A tasty salad that stays fresh several days in the refrigerator. The salad is also good to use as a filling in bread and wraps.

4–5 SERVINGS
2⅔–3⅓ cup finely sliced pointed cabbage/white cabbage (400–500 g)
2 cups coarsely grated carrot (300 g)
1 large grated apple

Dressing:
2–3 tbsp mayonnaise (30–45 ml)
¾ cup yogurt (200 ml)
a few dashes of curry
lemon pepper

■ Slice the cabbage with a cheese slicer. Mix cabbage, carrots, and apple with the dressing. Add lemon pepper to taste.

◀ SALAD with Orange, Red Onion, and Pomegranate

Rabbislaw

Follow the recipe above but replace cabbage with kohlrabi.

Coleslaw with Parsley *Lacto or vegan*

Replace white cabbage with red cabbage, pointed cabbage, fennel, or kohlrabi if you want to.

4 SERVINGS
2⅔ cup sliced white cabbage, red cabbage, or pointed cabbage—alternatively, kohlrabi (400 g)
2 cups coarsely grated carrot (300 g)
⅔ cup finely chopped parsley (100 g)

Dressing:
2–3 tbsp mayonnaise (30–45 ml)
¾ cup yogurt (200 ml)
2–3 tsp Dijon mustard (10–15 ml)
salt and pepper

■ Slice the cabbage with a cheese slicer. Mix cabbage, carrots, and parsley with the dressing. Add salt and pepper to taste.

> **Eco-friendly tips!**
> During winter and early spring it is the season for lovely oranges, which will go very well with salads. There are still Swedish apples for a few months. Besides that, it is mostly white cabbage and root vegetables that are still available. If the root vegetables are turning a little bit dry, it is tasty to marinate them.
>
> Complement with fresh sprouts and green shoots. Later during spring, nettles and other green leaves start to sprout in nature. Fresh spring vegetables like daikon and asparagus can be found in May. If you grow your own vegetables you can start harvesting cold-resistant Asian lettuce plants, winter lettuce, and radishes as early as April.

▲ MARINATED Sugar Peas and Asparagus

Marinated Sugar Peas and Asparagus *Vegan*

4 SERVINGS
5.3 oz sugar peas (150 g)
6–7 radishes
1 bunch green asparagus
⅓ cup chopped parsley (50 g)

Dressing:
1 tbsp light balsamic vinegar (15 ml)
3–4 tbsp canola or olive oil (45–60 ml)
½–1 tsp mustard (2.5–5 ml)
salt and pepper

■ Clean sugar peas and radishes. Break off the bottom, chewy part of the asparagus. Quickly parboil the vegetables separately in boiling water with salt. Cut the asparagus in pieces and mix with radishes, sugar peas, parsley, and dressing.

Parsnip Salad with Parsley and Nuts *Raw*

Make something new and exciting with our wonderful root vegetables. The salad is quick to make and turns out juicy and good. Parsnip can be replaced with kohlrabi, turnip, rutabaga, and celeriac.

4 SERVINGS
1–2 parsnips
⅔ cup chopped parsley (100 g)
⅓ cup chopped hazelnuts or walnuts (50 g)

Dressing:
1 tbsp vinegar (15 ml)
3–4 tbsp canola and olive oil (45–60 ml)
herb salt and pepper

■ Peel and slice the parsnips. Mix them in a food processor to a texture that is similar to a fluffy couscous. Mix with parsley, nuts, and dressing by hand.

Jerusalem Artichoke Salad with Parsley and nuts

Follow the recipe above but replace parsnip with Jerusalem artichokes, which has somewhat of a nutty taste.

Papaya Salad with Coconut Dressing *Vegan*

4 SERVINGS *PHOTO P. 146
1 avocado
1 papaya
different kinds of lettuce leaves
coriander leaves
2–3 tbsp roasted and salted cashew nuts (20–30 g)

Dressing:
2–3 tsp soy sauce (10–15 ml)
½ tbsp lime juice (7.5 ml)
¼ cup coconut milk (50 ml)
½–1 tsp grated ginger (1–3 g)
1 pinch of sambal oelek

■ Peel, clean, and slice the avocado. Peel, clean, and slice the papaya in pieces lengthwise.
■ Place the pieces of papaya like rays of sun on the outer edge of the plate. Shred lettuce leaves and mix with coriander and avocado. Place the lettuce in the middle of the plate. Pour the dressing over the salad and sprinkle with cashew nuts.

Lemon Marinated Haricot Verts *Vegan*

Delicious salad that goes well with most food. Perfect when you need to increase the protein intake in a meal. The salad stays fresh in the refrigerator for several days. Replace half of the haricots verts with kidney brand and chickpeas if you want to.

4–6 SERVINGS
1–2 red onions
1 lemon
1 big package frozen green beans (25.5 oz/750 g)
⅔ cup finely chopped parsley (100 g)

Marinade:
1 tbsp light balsamic vinegar (15 ml)
1–2 tbsp lemon juice (15–30 ml)
2 tsp broth (10 ml)
1–2 tsp Dijon mustard (5–10 ml)
1 pressed garlic clove
3–4 tbsp canola or olive oil (45–60 ml)
salt and pepper

■ Peel and slice the onion. Grate the lemon zest finely. Boil the beans according to instructions on the package and drain. Mix the onion, lemon zest, and beans with the marinade. Add salt and pepper to taste. Let cool off and then stir the parsley into the salad.

Lemon Marinated Haricots Verts with Walnuts

Follow the above recipes but sprinkle with chopped walnuts.

Lemon Marinated Haricots Verts with Cheese *Lacto*

Follow the basic recipe above but stir grated cheese into the warm salad.

Lemon Marinated Haricots Verts with Potatoes and Capers *Vegan*

Follow the basic recipe above but replace lemon zest with sliced cold-boiled potatoes and capers.

▲ TOMATO MARINATED Bean Salad

Tomato Marinated Bean Salad
Vegan

The salad stays fresh for 5–6 days in the refrigerator. It is convenient to have a prepared salad at home, and the taste of the salad can be varied by adding one or several vegetables like chopped fresh tomatoes, bell peppers, avocado, arugula, tender green shoots, and sprouts when serving.

6 SERVINGS
1 red onion
2 cups kidney beans (1 can)
2 cups borlotti beans (1 can)
⅓ cup sliced marinated tomatoes (50 g)
⅔ cup finely chopped parsley (100 g)
a few drops lemon juice

Dressing:
2 tbsp balsamic vinegar (30 ml)
3–4 tbsp olive oil (45–60 ml)
1–2 tsp Dijon mustard (5–10 ml)
1 pressed garlic clove
2 tsp broth (10 ml)
4–5 drops Tabasco
salt, pepper

■ Peel and slice the onion. Mix the warm and drained beans with marinated tomatoes and parsley as well as dressing. Add a few drops of lemon juice to taste, right before serving.

Bean Salsa *Vegan*

A delicious and colorful bean salad.

4 SERVINGS
2–3 tomatoes
½ bell pepper
½ red onion
½ mild chili fruit
2 cups drained large white beans (1 can)

Dressing:
2 tbsp canola and olive oil (30 ml)
½–1 tbsp lemon juice (7.5–15 ml)
1 pressed garlic clove
⅔ cups finely chopped basil, parsley, or
   coriander (100 g)
salt and pepper

■ Finely chop all vegetables. Rinse the beans and drain. Mix beans with vegetables and dressing. Add salt and pepper to taste.

Bean Salsa with Avocado
Follow the recipe above, but add a chopped avocado.

Parsnip Salad with Almond *Vegan*

Delicious, filling, and fresh salad. When you use boiled parsnip that has been in the refrigerator for half a day, the starch has time to transform and the GI value will be low.

4 SERVINGS
28.2 oz boiled, cold parsnip (800 g)
1 cup almonds (150 g)
3 tbsp olive or canola oil (45 ml)
2 tbsp water (30 ml)
2 tsp broth (10 ml)
1 tbsp vinegar (15 ml)
1–1½ tbsp Dijon mustard (15–22.5 ml)
1⅓ cup chopped parsley (200 g)
½ tbsp lemon juice (7.5 ml)
salt and pepper

■ Cut the parsnip in pieces. Mix the almonds. Stir almonds together with oil, water, broth, vinegar, and mustard. Mix with parsnip and parsley. Add lemon juice, salt, and pepper to taste.

Potato Salad with Almonds and Herbs
Follow the recipe above but replace parsnip with boiled potatoes.

Rutabaga Salad with Almonds and Herbs
Follow the recipe above but replace the parsnip with boiled rutabaga.

Pesto Beans *Lacto or Vegan*

6 SERVINGS
⅔ cup pine nuts, sunflower seeds, or almonds (100 g)
2–2⅔ cups coarsely chopped parsley (300–400 g)
1 cup grated Parmesan or Västerbotten cheese (100 g)
1–2 pressed garlic cloves
⅓–¾ cup olive and canola oil (100–200 ml)
4 cups large white beans (2 cans) (600 g)
salt and pepper

■ First mix nuts, seeds, and almonds in a food processor or with a hand blender. Add basil, cheese, and garlic. Continue to mix and add oil until the texture is good. Rinse beans and drain. Mix the pesto with the beans. Add salt and pepper to taste.

Beans are Superfood!
Beans, lentils, and peas all have advantages. They are tasty, affordable, climate-smart, nutritional, and have a low GI. Make a big batch of bean salad since it stays fresh for long in the refrigerator. Bean salad is good to have ready to eat at home, primarily because it is tasty, but also because beans increases the nutritional value and protein quality of all meals. The bean salad is the most tasty when it is room temperature or slightly heated.

The secret with juicy and tasty bean salads is that you mix warm boiled beans with the dressing to make the beans juicy. If you use beans from a can you heat the beans.

Potato Salad *Lacto or Vegan*

The secret with this tasty potato salad is a lot of finely chopped apples and capers that should only be sensed in the finished salad.

4 SERVINGS
8–10 boiled, cold potatoes (28.2 oz/800 g)
1 sweet apple
2–3 tbsp capers, chopped with a little broth (20–30 g)
2–3 tbsp mayonnaise (30–45 ml)
¾-1¼ cup yogurt (200–300 ml)
2 tsp mustard (10 ml)
herb salt and pepper
⅔ cup chopped chives, parsley, or scallions (100 g)

■ Peel and cut potatoes into small cubes. Clean and chop unpeeled apple very finely. Chop the capers very finely.
■ Mix mayonnaise, capers, and yogurt. Add mustard, caper broth, salt, and pepper to taste. Stir apple, chives, or scallions and potatoes into the mixture.

Potato Salad with Asparagus and Cherry Tomatoes
Follow the recipe above and garnish with lightly boiled asparagus and cherry tomatoes.

MEAL SALADS

Salad with Sesame Marinated Tofu *Vegan*

Sesame marinated tofu is practical and good to keep at home. It stays fresh for several days in the refrigerator. It is as good at room temperature as when slightly heated.

Goes well with most things, on bread (tofu burger) or served with Spelt with Avocado and Tomato, p. 222, Tabbouleh, p. 219, Oat with Apple and Ginger, p. 219, Quinoa with Beans, p. 222 or with Potato Gratin, p. 258.

3 SERVINGS (18 SLICES)

1 package tofu (7 oz/200 g), preferably almond sesame
2⅔ cups mache lettuce (400 g)
1⅓ cup finely sliced white cabbage (200 g)
1 carrot
1 red onion
1 avocado
1–2 oranges
sunflower seed shoots, sprouts
3–3⅓ cup cooked quinoa, naked oats, bulgur, couscous or pasta (400–600 g)

Marinade:

1–2 tbsp mango chutney (mild chili) (15–30 g)
4 tbsp canola or olive oil (60 ml)
1 tbsp soy (15 ml)
2 tsp grated ginger (6 g)
1–2 pressed garlic cloves
2 tsp sesame oil (10 ml)

■ Cut the tofu in thin slices (0.1–0.15 inches) and mix with the marinade. Make sure all slices are covered by the marinade.

■ Shred the lettuce leaves. Finely slice white cabbage, onion, and carrot. Slice the avocado and orange. Take cooked whole grain or pasta of choice and spread in the bottom of a bowl. Place the vegetables on top, and top with tofu and marinade as well as sunflower seed shoots and sprouts.

Salad with Sesame Marinated Tempeh

Follow the basic recipe above but replace tofu with tempeh or seitan. (Can be found in the health food store.)

Salad with Tomato Marinated Tofu

Follow the basic recipe above but replace ginger and sesame oil with 1–2 tbsp tomato purée as well as ½–1 tsp crumbled oregano. Another tasty ingredient to add to this marinade is 1–2 tbsp finely chopped dill.

Salad with Tomato Marinated Tempeh

Follow the basic recipe above but replace tofu with tempeh or seitan. (Can be bought in the health food store.)

Salad with Tandoori Marinated Tofu *Vegan*

Tandoori marinated tofu is tasty and stays fresh for many days. Good to have prepared in the refrigerator and is an easy and quick meal by topping the filling salad with marinated tofu.

It is also tasty to serve together with Spelt with Avocado and Tomato, p. 222, Tabbouleh, p. 219, Oat with Apple and Ginger, p. 219, as well as Quinoa with Beans, p. 222.

3 SERVINGS

1 package tofu (7 oz/200 g) preferably almond sesame
1 romaine lettuce head
1 avocado
2 scallions
1 red onion
10 cherry tomatoes
sunflower shoots
3–3⅓ cup cooked quinoa, naked oats, bulgur, couscous or pasta (400–600 g)

Marinade:

2–3 tbsp tandoori paste (30–45 g)
1 tbsp sesame seeds (10 g)
½–1 tsp shoyu or tamari (2.5–5 ml)
½ cup canola or olive oil (100 ml)

■ Cut the tofu in thin slices (0.1–0.15 inches) and mix with the marinade. Make sure that all slices are covered in marinade.

■ Shred the lettuce leaves. Slice the avocado and thinly slice the scallions and red onion. Split the tomatoes. Place cooked whole grain or pasta of choice at the bottom of a bowl. Place the vegetables on top, and top with tofu with marinade.

▶ SALAD with tandoori marinated tofu

▲ PASTA SALAD with feta and marinated tomatoes

Pasta Salad with Feta *Lacto or vegan*

A filling and tasty salad that can be varied in many ways.

4 SERVINGS

7.9 oz pasta (225 g)
½ orange
½ orange bell pepper
3–4 tomatoes
3–4 handfuls of arugula
1 red onion
⅔ cup shredded marinated tomatoes (100 g)
⅔ cups olives (100 g)
7 oz feta cheese or todo (200 g)
⅓ cup chopped walnuts (50 g)

Dressings:

1 tbsp balsamic vinegar (15 ml)
3 tbsp oil (45 ml)
1 pressed garlic clove
salt and pepper

▪ Boil the pasta until it is al dente and rinse it in a colander. Mix with the dressing.

▪ Cut bell pepper, tomatoes, and arugula in pieces. Thinly slice the onion. Mix the pasta with the vegetables, marinated tomatoes, and olives. Cut the cheese in cubes and stir into the salad. Sprinkle with nuts.

Spelt Salad with Feta

Follow the recipe above but replace pasta with cooked spelt or other grains.

Pasta Salad with Roasted Chickpeas

Follow the basic recipe but replace cheese with Garlic Roasted Chickpeas, p. 197. The chickpeas are the tastiest when somewhat heated.

Greek Salad *Lacto or Vegan*

A colorful classic. Vegans can replace the feta with marinated tofu.

4 SERVINGS

6 tomatoes
½ cucumber
1 yellow or red bell pepper
1 romaine lettuce
1–2 red onions
3–3⅓ cup cooked quinoa, naked oats, bulgur, couscous or pasta (400–600 g)
⅔ chopped parsley (100 g)
7 oz feta cheese or marinated tofu (200 g)
12 black olives
basil leaves

Dressing:
1 tbsp vinegar (15 ml)
3 tbsp oil (45 ml)
1 pressed garlic clove
salt and pepper

■ Clean and slice tomatoes and cucumber. Clean and cut bell pepper and lettuce. Peel and finely slice the onion. First, place cooked whole grain or pasta of choice on a plate, and then lettuce, onion, and parsley. Top with tomato, cucumber, bell pepper, and crumbled feta cheese. Pour the dressing over the salad. Garnish with olives and basil.

Greek Salad with Garlic Roasted Chickpeas Vegan

Follow the recipe above but replace cheese with Garlic Roasted Chickpeas, p. 197, and sprinkle over the finished salad. The chickpeas are the most tasty if they are slightly heated.

Salad with Grilled Quorn Lacto

Marinated Quorn fillets are tasty and stay fresh for several days in the refrigerator. Perfect to keep in the house for simple, quick, and tasty meals. Garnish a filling salad with vegetables of the season and marinated Quorn or serve with Spelt with Avocado and Tomatoes, p. 222, Tabbouleh, p. 219, Oat with Apple and Ginger, p. 219, or to Quinoa with Beans, p. 222.

6 SERVINGS. PHOTO P. 148
1 package of Quorn fillets
½ zucchini
1 carrots
1 red onion
3.5 oz sugar peas (100 g)
1⅓ cup blueberries (200 g)
3–3⅓ cup cooked quinoa, naked oats, bulgur, couscous, or pasta (400–600 g)

Marinade:
2–3 tbsp mango chutney (mild chili) (30–45 g)
½ cup canola or olive oil (100 ml)
1 tbsp soy (15 ml)
2 tsp grated ginger (6 g)
2 pressed garlic cloves

■ Bring water and salt to a boil. Place the Quorn fillets in the pan and boil them quickly until they defrost. Stir the marinade together and place the Quorn fillets in the marinade. Let sit in the refrigerator for an hour.
■ Grill the Quorn fillets. Place cooked whole grains or pasta of choice at the bottom of a bowl. Cut the zucchini in half moons, and thinly slice the carrot, onion, and sugar peas. Mix the vegetables with lettuce leaves and spread on top. Sprinkle with blueberries. Top with Quorn fillets and marinade.

Quinoa Salad with Roasted Vegetables Vegan

Quinoa can be replaced with cooked oats or spelt. Sesame Marinated Tofu, p. 164, also goes well with the salad.

4 SERVINGS
1 onion
1 fennel
1 red bell pepper
1 yellow bell pepper
2 tomatoes
½–1 zucchini
2 tbsp olive oil (30 ml)
3–3⅓ cup cooked quinoa (400–600 g)

Dressing:
2 tbsp canola or olive oil (30 ml)
2 pressed garlic cloves
⅓ cup chopped parsley (50 g)
1 tbsp lemon juice (15 ml)
salt and pepper
Oven temperature: 437°F

■ Clean and cut onion, fennel, bell pepper, and tomato in big pieces. Slice the zucchini. Place the vegetables in a oven dish and mix with the oil. Roast the vegetables in the middle of the oven for about 25 minutes.
■ Mix the ingredients for the dressing and add salt and pepper to taste. Spread the cooked quinoa on a dish. Place the roasted vegetables on top and pour the dressing over it.

Quinoa Salad with Roasted Root Vegetables

Follow the recipe above but replace fennel, bell pepper, tomato, and zucchini with Jerusalem artichoke, carrot, and parsnip.

Sauces, Dips, and Marinades

Marinated vegetables give any dish or salad that little extra. Here are suggestions of different dips to use as sides, dip sauces, or sandwich spreads.

Something else you can never have too many of are delicious sauces. They can improve any dish. You can make it even more exciting by combining a couple or more sauces. Serve sauces as dips, dressings, sides, or with pasta.

SAUCES AND DIPS

Basil yogurt *Lacto or Vegan*

A wonderful and useful sauce that can be varied in many ways. You can use a herb or mix many different kinds. The herb sauce can be rounded off by using crème fraiche, regular mayonnaise, or soy mayonnaise.

4 SERVINGS
1⅓–2 cups coarsely chopped basil (200–300 g)
¾ cup Greek yogurt or soy yogurt (200 ml)
1–2 crushed garlic cloves
herb salt and pepper

■ Mix basil, yogurt, and garlic into a green sauce. Add herb salt and pepper to taste.

Tip! Herbs and garlic lose a little of the flavor and yogurt can turn thin in the texture if you mix the sauce for too long. The best aroma is achieved by mixing yogurt, very finely chopped herbs, and pressed garlic by hand.

Mint Yogurt *Vegan*
Follow the recipe above but replace basil with mint leaves.

Lemon Balm Yogurt *Vegan*
Follow the basic recipe above but replace basil with lemon balm leaves.

Chili Yogurt *Lacto or Vegan*

4 SERVINGS
¾ cup Greek yogurt or soy yogurt (200 ml)
1–2 tbsp chili sauce (15–30 ml)

■ Mix yogurt and chili sauce.

Ginger Yogurt
Follow the recipe above but replace chili sauce with grated ginger.

Tzatziki *Lacto or Vegan*

4 SERVINGS
⅓ cucumber
¾ cup Greek yogurt or soy yogurt (200 ml)
2 tbsp finely chopped mint (20 g)
1 pressed garlic clove
herb salt

■ Grate the cucumber coarsely and press out the liquid with a wooden spoon or with the fist in a strainer. Mix the grated cucumber with yogurt, mint, and garlic. Add salt to taste.

Apple Tzatziki
Follow the recipe above but replace cucumber and mint with coarsely grated apple. (The liquid does not need to be pressed out of the apple.)

Carrot Tzatziki
Follow the basic recipe above but replace cucumber and mint with coarsely grated carrot and lemon peel. (The liquid does not need to be pressed out.)

Tomato Raita *Lacto or Vegan*

Raita is a common side dish in Indian cuisine. Goes well with all Indian food, stews, and whole grain dishes.

4–5 SERVINGS
1 tsp brown mustard seeds (3 g)
1 tbsp coconut oil (15 ml)
⅔ cup Greek yogurt or soy yogurt (200 ml)
2–3 chopped tomatoes
2 pinches hint (found in Asian stores)
2 tbsp finely chopped parsley, dill, or coriander (20 g)
salt and pepper

■ Fry mustard seeds in coconut oil while stirring until they stopped popping. Mix yogurt, chopped tomatoes, mustard seeds, hint, herbs, and add salt and pepper to taste.

Coco Raita
Follow the recipe above but replace tomatoes with ⅔ cup coconut flakes that is mixed with the yogurt.

▶ AVOCADO SAUCE, Tomato Salsa, and Tzatziki

Beetroot Salsa *Lacto or Vegan*

1¼ CUP (300 ML)

⅔ cup Greek yogurt or soy yogurt (200 ml)
2–3 tbsp fermented or regular beetroots (20–30 g)
herb salt and pepper

■ Mix yogurt with fermented beetroots and add salt and pepper to taste.

Caviar Sauce *Lacto or Vegan*

Simple to make and tasty, especially with avocado or baked potatoes. Vary the taste with finely chopped dill and/or chives.

1¼ CUP (300 ML)

1 very finely chopped red onion
1 can red alga caviar (vegetarian caviar)
⅔ cup Greek yogurt or soy yogurt (200 ml)

■ Mix finely chopped onion, alga caviar, and yogurt.

Mayonnaise *Lacto-Ovo*

1¼ CUP (300 ML)

2 egg yolks
1–2 tsp lemon juice (5–10 ml)
1 tsp mustard (5 ml)
¼ tsp salt (1 ml)
½ pinch honey (0.5 ml)
⅔ cup canola oil or mild olive oil (200 ml)
salt and white pepper

■ Mix egg yolks, lemon juice, mustard, salt, and honey in a food processor. Drip down the oil while continuing to mix. Add salt and pepper to taste.

Tip! If all the ingredients have the same temperature, the risk of the mayonnaise curdling is decreased.

> **Herb Sauces and Yogurt**
> Poke around in the herb garden and pick one or many herbs—for instance, lemon balm, dill, and parsley. Mix the herbs with yogurt and garlic. Add herb salt and pepper to taste. Easy and fresh!

Mild Garlic Aioli *Lacto or Vegan*

1 CUP (150 ML)

2–3 tbsp regular mayonnaise or soy mayonnaise (30–45 ml)
⅔ cup Greek yogurt or soy yogurt (200 ml)
1–2 pressed garlic cloves
salt and pepper

■ Mix mayonnaise, yogurt, and garlic. Add salt and pepper to taste.

Avocado Sauce *Raw*

The vegetarians' equivalent to Béarnaise sauce, but much fresher! Delightfully light green and filled with good fatty acids and other things that are good for you. Goes well with almost anything—salads, grilled and fried food, as well as whole grain dishes. Combine with Peanut Sauce, p. 175, and/or Tomato Salsa, p. 174.

4 SERVINGS

2 ripe avocados
2–3 tbsp lemon juice (30–45 ml)
¼ cup water (50 ml)
1 pressed garlic clove
½–1 tsp tarragon (1–3 g)
herb salt

■ Scoop the avocado meat out of the peel and mix with lemon juice and water until the sauce is smooth. Add garlic, crumbled tarragon, and herb salt to taste.

Dill Dressing *Raw*

A wonderful and fresh summer dressing that goes just as well with salads as sprinkled over cooked potatoes, boiled or grilled vegetables, and soups.

⅔ CUP (200 ML)

⅔–1⅓ cup coarsely chopped dill (100–200 g)
⅔ cup olive or canola oil (150 ml)
2–3 tbsp vinegar, preferably balsamic vinegar (30–45 ml)
1 tsp lemon juice (5 ml)
1 tbsp ground coriander (7.5 g)
1–2 pressed garlic cloves
½ tsp salt (1 g)

■ Mix dill, oil, vinegar, lemon juice, coriander, and garlic. Add salt to taste. Let sit for a couple of hours.

▲ GRILLED TZAY SKEWERS, Cooked Naked Oats, Salad, Peanut Sauce, and Avocado Sauce.

Sweet and Sour Dill Dressing *Raw*

A lovely and creamy dressing that goes well with salads, fried, grilled, and whole grain dishes.

1¼ CUP (300 ML)
⅔ cup soaked sunflower seeds (100 g)
¾-1 cup water (200–250 ml)
¼ cup canola or olive oil (50 ml)
⅔–1⅓ cup dill leaves (100–200 g)
1–1½ tbsp vinegar (15–22.5 ml)
1–1½ tbsp Dijon mustard (15–22.5 ml)
1–2 tbsp agave syrup or honey (15–30 ml)
herb salt and pepper

■ First mix soaked and drained sunflower seeds with some of the water in a food processor. Add the rest of the water, oil, and dill and continue to mix. Add vinegar, mustard, honey, herb salt, and pepper to taste.

Sweet and Sour Dressing with Avocado *Raw*

Follow the recipe above but add avocado and possibly some more water.

Tomato Dressing With Basil *Raw*

A salad dressing that is smooth and the most tasty when freshly made. It achieves the best flavors when the tomatoes are really ripe.

4–6 SERVINGS
4 tomatoes
⅓ cup coarsely chopped basil (50 g)
¼ cup canola or olive oil (50 ml)
1 tbsp vinegar (15 ml)
1 tsp shoyu or soy (5 ml)
1 tsp honey (5 ml)
2 pressed garlic cloves
herb salt

■ Clean and cut the tomatoes in pieces. Mix tomatoes, basil, oil, vinegar, shoyu, honey, and garlic to a sauce. Add herb salt to taste.

Cashew Dressing *Raw*

A creamy salad dressing with the wonderful flavor of bell peppers.

ABOUT 1¼ CUP (300 ML)
1⅓ cup cashew nuts (200 g)
1 small red bell pepper
⅔ cup basil leaves (100 g)
½–¾ cup water (100–200 ml)
2 pressed garlic cloves
½–1 tbsp lemon juice (7.5–15 ml)
a couple of drops smoked Tabasco
herb salt and pepper

▪ First mix the nuts to a fine powder in a food processor. Add pieces of bell pepper, basil, water, and garlic and mix until the dressing is smooth. Add lemon juice, Tabasco, salt, and pepper to taste.

Mango Salsa *Vegan*

4 SERVINGS
1 ripe avocado
½ red onion
2 tomatoes
1–2 tbsp sweet and sour chili sauce (15–30 g)
⅓ cup chopped coriander (50 g)
salt and pepper

▪ Peel and chop the mango. Finely chop the red onion and tomatoes. Mix mango, onion, and tomatoes with chili sauce and coriander. Add salt and pepper to taste.

Tomato Salsa *Raw*

A fresh salsa is always nice as a side dish, especially with grilled and tacos. Combine with Avocado Sauce, p. 172.

1¼ CUP (300 ML)
2 tomatoes, ripen
½ red bell pepper
½ red onion
½ mild chili fruit
1 pressed garlic clove
1 tbsp olive or canola oil (15 ml)
½ 1 tbsp lemon or lime juice (7.5–15 ml)
2 tbsp finely chopped basil, parsley, or coriander (20 g)
salt and pepper

▪ Finely chop all vegetables. Mix everything and add salt and pepper to taste.

Tomato and Avocado Salsa
Follow the recipe above but add a ripe, chopped avocado.

Pesto *Lacto*

Homemade pesto has a completely different taste than that which is store-bought. Make a double batch. The sauce stays fresh for about a week in the refrigerator. Pesto is great with pasta and as a side with most meals. In the classic pesto you roast the pine nuts first. Then you grind all the ingredients into a sauce in a mortar.

4–6 SERVINGS
⅔ cup pine nuts, sunflower seeds, or almonds (100 g)
2–2⅔ cups coarsely chopped basil (300–400 g)
1 cup grated Parmesan or Västerbotten cheese (100 g)
1–2 pressed garlic cloves
½-¾ cup olive or canola oil (100–200 ml)
salt and pepper

▪ First mix nuts or almonds in a food processor or with a hand blender. Add basil, cheese, and garlic. Continue to mix and dilute with oil until the texture is good. Add salt and pepper to taste.

Arugula Pesto
Follow the recipe above, but replace basil with arugula.

Parsley Pesto with Lemon *Lacto*

4–6 SERVINGS
⅔ cup pine nuts, sunflower seeds, or almonds (100 g)
2–2⅔ cups coarsely chopped parsley (300–400 g)
1 cup grated Parmesan or Västerbotten cheese (100 g)
1–2 pressed garlic cloves
½-¾ cup olive or canola oil (100–200 ml)
zest and juice from ½ lemon
salt and pepper

▪ First mix nuts or almonds in a food processor or with a hand blender. Add parsley, cheese, garlic, lemon zest, and juice. Continue to mix and dilute with oil until the texture is good. Add salt and pepper to taste.

Mint Pesto

Follow the recipe above but replace parsley with mint.

Nettle Pesto

Follow the recipe above but replace parsley with young nettles.

Lemon Balm Pesto

Follow the recipe above but replace half of the parsley with lemon balm.

Green Pea Pesto

Follow the recipe above, but replace the parsley with defrosted green peas.

Peanut Sauce Vegan

4 SERVINGS

1 yellow onion
1 tbsp coconut fat (15 ml)
¼ cup peanut butter (crunchy) (50 g)
1 cup coconut milk (250 ml)
2 tbsp sweet chili sauce (30 g)
2 tbsp soy (30 ml)

■ Chop the onion and fry until soft on low heat in coconut fat. Stir peanut butter, coconut milk, and chili sauce into the pan. Add soy to taste. Let simmer for a few minutes.

Spinach Sauce Lacto or Vegan

Delicious sauce that goes well with any meal and is quick to make.

2 SERVINGS

about 5.3 oz whole spinach leaves, possibly frozen (150 g)
1–2 tbsp olive or canola oil (15–30 ml)
3–4 tbsp Greek or soy yogurt (45–60 ml)
1 tsp vegetable broth (5 ml)
1 pressed garlic clove
1–2 pinches sambal oelek
salt and pepper

■ Cut the spinach leaves in coarse pieces. Fry them in the oil while stirring until most of the fluid is gone. Take the pan off the stove and stir yogurt and garlic into it. Add broth, sambal oelek, salt, and pepper to taste.

Broccoli Sauce Lacto or Vegan

The world's most tasty and simple broccoli sauce!

2–3 SERVINGS

8.8 oz broccoli (250 g)
2–3 tbsp water (30–45 ml)
½ tbsp olive or canola oil (7.5 ml)
¾-1¼ cup Greek yogurt or soy yogurt (200–300 ml)
1–2 tsp vegetable broth (5–10 ml)
1 pressed garlic clove
1–2 pinches sambal oelek (1–2 ml)
a few drops lemon juice
salt and pepper

■ Clean and cut the broccoli in pieces. Place it in a pot together with water and oil. Let the broccoli simmer under a lid until it is just soft. Be careful to not burn.

■ Remove the pot from the stove and pour yogurt, broth, garlic, and sambal oelek in it. Mix the sauce smooth with a hand blender. Add lemon juice, salt, and pepper to taste.

Nettle Sauce

Follow the recipe above but replace broccoli with boiled and drained nettles.

Tapenade Vegan

Delicious together with bread, bruschetta, or as a side dish or dip sauce.

¾ CUP (200 ML)

1⅓ cup black olives, preferably Kalamata olives (200 g)
1 tbsp capers (10 g)
2 tbsp olive oil (30 ml)
2 pressed garlic cloves
1 tsp Dijon mustard (5 ml)

■ Pit the olives. Mix olives, capers, oil, garlic, and mustard into a creamy dip.

Green Tapenade

Follow the recipe above but replace black olives with green. Finish by stirring finely chopped parsley into the dip.

Guacamole _Raw_

Wonderful dip that works well with most dishes. Guacamole turns out best of you crush the avocados by hand.

4–6 SERVINGS

3 ripe avocados
1 tbsp lemon juice (15 ml)
3 tbsp finely chopped shallots (30 g)
1 finely chopped tomato
½ finely chopped red bell pepper
1 pressed garlic clove
a few drops of Tabasco
herb salt

■ Take the avocados out of the peel and crush it together with the lemon juice by using a fork. Stir onion, bell pepper, tomato, and garlic into the mixture. Add Tabasco and herb salt to taste.

Chèvre Cream _Lacto_

4–5 SERVINGS

7.5 oz chèvre (200 g)
⅔ cup yogurt (150 ml)
2–3 crushed garlic cloves
herb salt and pepper

■ Mix the cheese with yogurt and garlic. Add herb salt and pepper to taste.

Hummus with Sesame Oil

Vegan

Imagine all the delicious things you can make with chickpeas. Perfect for dip sauces, bread, and salads. This hummus is seasoned the classic way, with an extra sting of sesame oil.

4–6 SERVINGS

2⅔ cups cooked or canned chickpeas (400 g)
3 tbsp tahini, sesame paste (45 g)
juice from 1 lemon
2 garlic cloves
1 tbsp ground cumin (15 g)
1–2 pinches sambal oelek (1–2 ml)
2 tbsp olive oil (30 ml)
½ tsp sesame oil (2.5 ml)
1–2 tbsp water (15–30 ml)
salt and black pepper

■ Rinse the chickpeas and mix them in the food processor for a few seconds. Add tahini, lemon juice, pressed garlic, ground cumin, sambal oelek, olive and sesame oils and continue to mix. Drip the water into the mixture while the machine is running, until the hummus feels "fluffy" in texture. Add salt and pepper to taste.

Tip! The secret behind good hummus is to mix it long enough for the texture to become "fluffy."

Hummus _Vegan_

Here is a tasty alternative with only garlic, lemon, and chili, which has a more neutral taste.

4–6 SERVINGS

2⅔ cups cooked or canned chickpeas (400 g)
juice from 1 lemon
2 pressed garlic cloves
1–2 pinches sambal oelek
¼ cup olive oil (50 ml)
1–2 tbsp water (15–30 ml)
salt and black pepper

■ Rinse the chickpeas and mix them in the food processor for a few seconds. Add lemon juice, garlic, sambal oelek, and olive oil and continue to mix. Drip the water into the mixture while the machine is running, until the hummus feels "fluffy" in texture. Add salt and pepper to taste.

Hummus with Roasted Bell Pepper

Follow the recipe above but add 7.5 oz (200 g) roasted red bell pepper without broth and ½ tsp (1 g) paprika powder. Replace the sambal oelek with chipotle chili if you want to.

Hummus with Curry and Herbs

Follow the basic recipe above but add 1½ tsp (4 g) grated fresh ginger and 1 tsp (3 g) curry. Finally, stir ⅔–1⅓ cup (100–200 g) finely chopped dill and coriander.

▶ HUMMUS with Roasted Bell Pepper and Hummus with Curry and Herbs

Aubergine Dip *Vegan*

Tasty both as a spread and dip.

4 SERVINGS
2 aubergines
¼ cup olive oil (50 ml)
2–3 tbsp lemon juice (30–45 ml)
2 pressed garlic cloves
1–2 chili flakes (1–2 ml)
a pinch of ground cumin
salt and pepper
⅔ cup chopped parsley or coriander
Oven temperature: 392°F

■ Place the aubergine fruit on a oven rack and bake for about 40 minutes. Split them and scrape off the fruit meat.

■ Crush the fruit meat with a fork. Stir oil, lemon juice, garlic, chili, and ground cumin into the mixture. Add salt and pepper to taste. Finish by adding the chopped herbs.

Tip! Do not crush the aubergine meat for too long. The dip will turn out the best if it has a little coarser texture.

Herb Pâté *Raw*

Easy-to-make and tasty pâté with a lovely dill flavor that goes just as well with bread and crackers as with dip sauce.

1⅔ CUP (400 ML)
1⅓ cup sunflower seed (200 g)
⅓ cup sesame seed (50 g)
⅓ almonds (50 g)
1–2 bunches of dill
½ red onion
1 pressed garlic clove
½–1 tsp chili flakes (2.5–5 ml)
2–3 tbsp tomato purée (30–45 g)
1 tbsp lemon juice (15 ml)
¼ cup oil (50 ml)
¼ cup water (50 ml)
1 tsp thyme (3 g)
herb salt

■ First mix the seeds and almonds in a food processor. Pour the mix into a bowl. Chop dill and red onion finely.

■ Stir dill, onion, chili, tomato purée, lemon juice, oil, and water. Add crumbled thyme and herb salt to taste.

Tip! This pâté can be varied with many different types of seeds, nuts, and herbs. Water and lemon juice can be replaced with fermented vegetables and broth.

Cashew Sour Cream with Curry and Dill *Raw*

A great and different flavor combination that has the potential of becoming your new favorite. And the cream has a neat yellow color!

1 CUP (200 ML)
1⅓ cup cashew nuts (200 g)
¼ cup water (50 ml)
1 tbsp lemon juice (15 ml)
⅓–⅔ cup finely chopped dill (50–100 g)
1–2 pressed garlic cloves
1 tsp broth (5 ml)
1–2 pinches turmeric (1–2 ml)
1–2 pinches curry (1–2 ml)
herb salt

■ First mix the nuts to a fine powder in a food processor. Add water, lemon juice, dill, garlic, broth, turmeric, and curry. Add herb salt to taste.

Cashew Sour Cream with Curry and Coriander

Follow the recipe above but replace dill with finely chopped coriander.

Cashew Sour Cream with Chives and Garlic *Raw*

A more neutral taste with the classic combination of garlic and chives.

1 CUP (200 ML)
1⅓ cup cashew nuts (200 g)
¼ cup water (50 ml)
1 tbsp lemon juice (15 ml)
⅔ cup coarsely chopped chives (100 g)
1–2 pressed garlic cloves
1 tsp broth (5 ml)
herb salt

■ First mix the nuts to a fine powder in a food processor. Add water, lemon juice, chives, garlic, and broth. Add herb salt to taste.

Cashew Sour Cream with Dill and Horseradish

Follow the recipe above but replace chives and garlic with dill and grated horseradish.

Cashew Sour Cream with Avocado

Follow the basic recipe above but use less liquid and instead mix with a avocado.

MARINATED VEGETABLES

Marinated Beetroots *Vegan*

Marinated beetroots is a delicacy, especially together with Chèvre Cream, p. 176.

4 SERVINGS
17.6 oz beetroots (500 g)
finely chopped parsley

Marinade:
1 tbsp vinegar, preferably balsamic vinegar (15 ml)
3 tbsp olive or canola oil (45 ml)
1 tsp Dijon mustard (5 ml)
1 pressed garlic clove
herb salt and pepper

■ Steam or boil the beetroots with peel in water until they are soft. Rinse them in cold water. Rub off the peel by using your hands. (Use plastic gloves.)
■ Cut the beetroots into cubes and mix with the marinade. Let cool and then stir chopped parsley into the mix.

Marinated Rutabaga

Follow the recipe above but replace beetroots with boiled, peeled rutabaga cut into cubes.

Marinated Kohlrabi

Follow the recipe above but replace beetroots with boiled, peeled kohlrabi cut into cubes.

Marinated Fennel

Follow the recipe above but replace beetroot and mustard with sliced boiled fennel and the juice from half a orange.

Marinated Artichoke Hearts *Vegan*

6 SERVINGS
2 cans artichoke hearts
1 red onion
1 tbsp capers (10 g)

Marinade:
1 tbsp vinegar (15 ml)
2 pressed garlic cloves
1 tbsp mustard (15 ml)
⅓–⅔ cup olive oil (100–150 ml)
salt and pepper

■ Drain the artichoke hearts. Then cut them in large pieces. Peel and thinly slice the onion. Make layers of artichoke pieces, onion, and capers. Mix all the ingredients for the marinade and pour on top. Add salt and pepper to taste.

Lemon Marinated Olives *Vegan*

A wonderful marinade that is as great on the buffet table as a gift. And it is quick to make.

ABOUT 1 QUART (1 LITER)
1 quart olives, preferably of mixed sort
1 chili fruit
3–4 garlic cloves
fresh rosemary
juice from 1 lemon
olive oil

■ Let the olives drain in a colander. Clean and slice the chili and rosemary. Pour lemon juice and oil over the olives until they are covered. Let sit for at least one day.

> **Marinated Vegetables**
> Marinated vegetables, like fennel, beetroots, kohlrabi, and rutabaga are easy to make and tasty. Goes well as a side dish with most meals. Make a double batch since marinated vegetables stay fresh in the refrigerator for 4 to 5 days.

Marinated, Grilled Bell Pepper

Vegan

6 SERVINGS
4–5 orange and red bell peppers

Marinade:
1 tbsp balsamic vinegar (15 ml)
3 tbsp olive or canola oil (45 ml)
salt and pepper
Oven temperature: 482°F

■ Split the bell peppers lengthwise and remove the seeds. Place them on the oven rack with the peel facing up. Grill them in the top of the oven for about 5 minutes until the peel starts to get black spots.
■ Rinse the peppers in cold water and peel them. Stir the peeled bell peppers into the marinade and let sit for at least half a day. Stir occasionally.

Bell Pepper Salad with Pine Nuts
*PHOTO P. 168
Roast a couple of tablespoons of pine nuts in a frying pan while stirring. Spread out marinated bell peppers according to above recipe, olives, capers, and pine nuts, as well as arugula and other green leaves on a plate.

Tip! Garnish the salad with shaved Parmesan.

VINEGAR

Vinegar comes from the French "vinaigre" which means sour wine. If fruit and berry wine is left to sit at room temperature and ferment, vinegar is produced. Vinegar has a preservative and flavor-enchanting effect.

Balsamic vinegar is full and rich in flavors and made from fresh grape must that is boiled until the liquid is reduced by 30 to 70 percent. When the grape concentrate has cooled off, it is poured in a wooden barrel where it ferments and matures for a year. Every year the vinegar is moved to another smaller barrel of different types of wood. The procedure takes at least 12 years. From the first barrel of 16 gallons, about 5 gallons of high-quality balsamic vinegar remain at the end of the process.

Old remedy
There is an old remedy that has a cleansing effect and is good for bowel problems as well as stimulating both digestion and metabolism: Drink a glass of water with 2 tsp apple cider vinegar and 1 tsp unheated honey every morning.

The finest traditional balsamic vinegar's full aroma disappears when heated, and it is best when sprinkled over a cooked meal. Today it is possible to buy affordable balsamic vinegar that is made in a faster process but still has a nice flavor.

Herb vinegar is milder and has a lovely aroma of herbs and berries. It is easy to make and good for dressings and drinks. Fill a glass jar or a bottle with some of the following alternatives and pour vinegar over it until it is covered. French canning jars are the best to use.

Choose one of the following alternatives and let the jar stand in sunlight for 2 to 3 weeks. Strain the herbs and pour the vinegar in bottles. Squeeze the vinegar from the herbs and use that vinegar first. Other vinegar stays fresh for a year if it is kept cool.

Basil Vinegar. Red basil leaves are the most beautiful. You can use regular basil leaves and a couple of handfuls of raspberries or strawberries.

Blueberry Vinegar. Freshly picked blueberries give the vinegar an aromatic flavor and a ruby red color.

Citrus Vinegar. Sliced oranges, lemons, and lime.

Tarragon Vinegar. Whole stems of tarragon as well as whole peeled garlic cloves.

Raspberry Vinegar. Freshly picked raspberries, preferably wild. This vinegar is done in a week.

Strawberry Vinegar. Freshly picked strawberries. This vinegar is done in a week.

Saffron and Citrus Vinegar. Dissolve saffron by boiling the spice with a couple of tablespoons of vinegar for a while. Pour saffron vinegar and regular vinegar on orange and lime slices.

Health Effects:
- Vinegar contributes to lowering blood sugar levels after a meal.
- Can contribute to lowering blood fats and blood pressure.
- Vinegar is antibacterial and can have an anti-inflammatory effect.
- Apple cider vinegar has been used in folk medicine to increase cleansing and blood circulation and stimulate digestion and metabolism, and also fights against bowel problems.

HERB OILS

Season oils with whole garlic cloves, chili fruit, and/or rosemary that is left to soak in the oil for a couple of days before they are removed. Poke several holes in the garlic, chili, and rosemary leaves in order to give the oil more flavor and let sit in the oil for a few days before you strain it.

Green Herb Oil

The oil turns a lovely green and enhances the flavor in almost everything like sauces, dressings, soups, and many dishes. Decoratively sprinkle with oil over the food.

ABOUT ¾ CUP (200 ML)

1⅓–2 cups herbs, for example basil, dill, parsley, or chervil (200–300 g)

1–2 pressed garlic cloves

¾ cup olive or canola oil (200 ml)

■ Mix the herbs together with garlic and oil. Strain the oil. Herb oil stays fresh for about a week in the refrigerator.

Tip! Use a small plastic bottle with a pipe, the kind you find in artist shops, to use for sprinkling oil over food.

Chili Oil

Chili oil turns a lovely orange red and enhances most flavors.

ABOUT ¾ CUP (200 ML)

4–5 red, Spanish pepper fruit

1 tsp paprika powder (3 g)

1–2 pressed garlic cloves

¾ cup olive or canola oil (200 ml)

■ Clean and cut the pepper fruit in coarse pieces. Mix the pepper fruit, paprika powder, and garlic with the oil. Strain the oil. Chili oil stays fresh for about a week in the refrigerator.

Small Dishes, Snacks, and Sides

Finger food and snacks are easy to prepare ahead of time and are always welcoming and nice. Add a few bowls of shoyu, roasted pumpkin seeds, almonds, and popcorn, as well as olives. Complement with one or a few small dishes, and the meal is perfect for a mingle party.

SMALL DISHES

Vegetable Cocktail *Vegan*

Delicious entrée

4 SERVINGS

1 blood grapefruit
2 avocados
8 cherry tomatoes
8 green asparagus stems
1 tbsp olive or canola oil (15 ml)
½ lime (juice)
gourmet salt and pepper
cocktail capers
1 can black alga caviar

■ Cut off all peel and white parts of the grapefruit. Make a cut on each side of every grapefruit wedge and pick out the wedges. Peel and slice the avocado; cut the tomatoes in halves.
■ Break off the chewy part of the asparagus and then place the stems in boiling water. Let the asparagus boil for a few minutes with the top facing up until they are just soft. Cut the asparagus in pieces but save eight asparagus tops for decoration.
■ Mix all the vegetables with grapefruit and oil. Add lime juice, salt, and pepper to taste. Place the mixture in glasses. Garnish with asparagus shoots and capers as well as a little bit of alga caveat. Drip some lime juice over the caviar.

Thin Flakes With Avocado Mousse *Raw*

A colorful vegetable flake has its given place on a buffet table. Both flakes and filling can be made ahead and kept in the refrigerator. Do not garnish until right before serving.

6–8 SERVING * PHOTO P. 182

Pie Crust:

1 cup cashew nut pieces (150 g)
5–6 sun dried tomatoes in oil
2–3 tbsp water (30–45 ml)
1½ tsp shoyu or soy (10 ml)
1–2 pinches chili flakes (1–2 ml)
⅔ chopped walnuts (100 g)
⅓ sesame seeds (50 g)
⅓ pumpkin seeds (50 g)
herb salt

Avocado Filling:

2 ripe avocados
2–3 tbsp lemon juice (30–45 ml)
2–3 water (30–45 ml)
⅓–⅔ chopped parsley (50–100 g)
1 pressed garlic clove
½–1 tsp tarragon (1–3 g)
herb salt

Garnish:

fresh vegetables—for example, radishes, cherry
    tomatoes, scallions, broccoli, asparagus,
    cucumber, zucchini, olives,
fruit—for example, figs
flowers—for example, squash and cress flowers

■ First mix cashew pieces finely. Add tomatoes, water, shoyu, and chili flakes and continue to mix the dough until smooth. Stir walnuts and seeds by hand and add herb salt to taste. Spread the batter on a oiled plate.
■ Take the avocado meat out of the peel and mix with lemon juice and water. Add parsley and garlic, crumbled tarragon, and herb salt to taste. Spread the avocado cream on top and garnish with vegetables, fruit, and flowers.

White Button Mushroom Salad

Raw

The salad turns out best if it is not left to sit for too long. If you want to prepare it ahead, the mushrooms can be cleaned and sliced a few hours ahead and mixed with the dressing right before serving.

4 SERVINGS *PHOTO P. 143

10.6 fresh mushrooms (preferably baby bella
    mushrooms)
⅔ cups chopped parsley (100 g)

Dressing:

1–2 tbsp balsamic vinegar (15–30 ml)
3–4 tbsp canola and olive oil (45–60 ml)
1 crushed garlic clove
salt and pepper

■ Clean and slice the mushrooms. Mix with parsley and dressing.

▶ VEGETABLE COCKTAIL

▲ CHANTERELLE SALAD With Croutons, Blueberries, and Chèvre

White Button Mushroom Salad With Parmesan Lacto or vegan

Follow previous recipe but add finely sliced celery and shaved Parmesan.

White Button Mushroom Salad with Sesame Raw

Follow previous recipe but replace parsley with 3–4 tsp sesame oil, 2–3 tsp shoyu or tamari, as well as 1 tbsp sesame seeds, preferably black.

Chanterelle Salad Lacto

Perfect as an appetizer or on the buffet table.

4 SERVINGS

10.6–14–1 oz mushrooms like chanterelles (300–400 g)
2–3 tbsp olive or canola oil (30–45 ml)
a pinch of curry
salt and white pepper
4 slices of bread
1 romaine lettuce
⅓ cup chopped parsley (50 g)

½–1 cup finely sliced red onion
⅓–⅔ cup blueberries (50–100 g)

Chèvre Cream:
7.05 oz chèvre (200 g)
⅔ cup yogurt (150 ml)
2–3 crushed garlic cloves
herb salt and pepper

■ Clean and cut the mushrooms in big pieces. Fry the mushrooms first without any fat in order to reduce most of the fluid. Continue to fry the mushrooms together with curry in half of the oil. Add salt and pepper to taste. Place the mushrooms on a dish.

■ Cut the bread in cubes and fry while stirring in the rest of the oil. Mix the cheese for the chèvre cream with yogurt and garlic. Add herb salt and pepper to taste.

■ Break the lettuce in pieces and place on plates. Sprinkle with parsley, red onion, and berries. Garnish with mushroom, croutons, and chèvre cream.

Mushroom Salad *Lacto or Vegan*

Here is a version of a Finnish mushroom salad. You can use any mushrooms you like, but we recommend Wood Hedgehog and Sheep polypore.

It is delicious on dark sourdough bread as canapés, filling in baguettes, or with avocado as well as side dishes on the buffet table. Vary the seasoning with mustard and chopped dill.

4 SERVINGS
1⅓ cup parboiled, finely chopped mushrooms
½–1 tsp balsamic vinegar (2.5–5 ml)
½–1 tsp salt (1–3 g)
1–2 pinches ground allspice
pepper mix
1 large red onion
1 sweet apple
1 can crème fraiche (8.8 oz/250 g) or soy yogurt

■ Fry the parboiled mushroom while stirring to remove all fluid. Add balsamic vinegar, salt, allspice, and pepper mix to taste.
■ Peel, clean, and chop onion and apple very finely. Mix onion, apple, and mushroom with crème fraîche. Add more of the spices if needed. The better mushroom you use, the less spices are needed.

Dumplings *Lacto or Vegan*

30 PIECES *PHOTO P. 147
30 dumpling wrappers

Filling:
1 small onion
1 garlic clove
½ carrot
1 tbsp canola or coconut oil (15 ml)
5.3 oz Quorn mincemeat or soy mincemeat (150 g)
1 tbsp soy (15 ml)
1 tbsp mango chutney (15 g)
½ tsp finely grated ginger (1 g)
a pinch sambal oelek (1 ml)
1 pinch cinnamon (1 ml)
salt
2 tbsp finely chopped coriander (20 g)
2 tbsp sesame oil (30 ml)

Dip Sauce:
¼ cup shoyu or soy (50 ml)
2 tsp sesame oil (10 ml)
1–2 tbsp vinegar (15–30 ml)

1–2 pinches sambal oelek (1–2 ml)
2 tsp roasted sesame seeds (6 g)

■ Peel and chop the onion and garlic. Peel and grate the carrot. Fry onion and carrot in the oil. Stir Quorn mincemeat into the mixture and continue to fry on low heat while stirring.
■ Season with shoyu, mango chutney, ginger, sambal oelek, cinnamon, and salt. Stir the herb spices and sesame oil into the mixture.
■ Use a couple of dumpling wrappers at a time and let the other stay in the package. Place about one teaspoon of filling on each wrapper. Moisten the edges with a little water and pinch together until they form a bag or a miniature pierogie.
■ Place the bundles in a steamer tool, but make sure they are not placed against each other. Steam the bundles for 10 minutes or fry them for 4–5 minutes in coconut oil. Stir all the ingredients for the dip sauce into a mix and serve with the dumplings.

Mustard Marinated Aubergine
Lacto or vegan

Similar to pickled herring and tasty on the Christmas buffet or other buffets. Aubergine can be replaced by zucchini.

4 SERVINGS *PHOTO P. 142
1 large firm aubergine
2 tbsp Skånsk coarse grained mustard (30 ml)
1½–2 tsp raw sugar (4–6 g)
½ tbsp vinegar (7.5 ml)
3 tbsp oil (45 ml)
½ cup cooking cream or oat cream (100 ml)
1 red onion
1 sweet apple
1 pickled cucumber
1 bunch chives

■ Cut the aubergine in thin strips, about 3 by 0.8 inches. Boil the aubergine strips for about 20 minutes in salted water. Rinse in cold water.
■ Mix mustard, sugar, and vinegar together. Slowly add oil while stirring. Add the cream to the mixture. Pour the sauce over the aubergine.
■ Finely chop onion, apple, cucumber, and chives. Garnish the aubergine with the chopped vegetables.

▲ HONEY GRATED Chèvre with Apple

Honey Grated Chèvre *Lacto*

Goat cheese, fruit, and honey is an unbeatable combination. Apples can be replaced with pears, figs, and apricots.

4 SERVINGS

2 tbsp pine nuts and walnuts (20 g)

2 large apples

4 slices chèvre

different lettuce leaves, preferably arugula

sunflower shoots

2–3 tbsp honey, preferably seasoned with saffron
   or lavender flowers (30–45 ml)

1 tbsp butter or olive oil (15 ml)

½ tbsp balsamic vinegar (7.5 ml)

Oven temperature: 437°F

■ Roast the pine nuts in a dry frying pan while stirring. Cut the apples in four large pieces, about 0.6 inches thick. Remove the core.

■ Place apple slices with a cheese slice on top in a greased baking pan. Grate for about 20 minutes until the cheese has a nice color.

■ Place lettuce leaves and sunflower shoots on small plates. Place the grated cheese on top of the salad. Sprinkle with pine nuts. Place a spoon of honey, butter or oil and balsamic vinegar in the warm baking pan. Pour sauce over the cheese.

Herb Grated White Button Mushrooms *Lacto or Vegan*

4 SERVINGS *PHOTO P. 140

8 large white button mushrooms

⅔ bread crumbs from a day-old whole grain bread
   (100 g)

⅔ cups finely chopped parsley (100 g)

2 pressed garlic cloves

1.75 oz butter, canola or olive oil (50 g)

salt and pepper

Oven temperature: 437°F

■ Break the stems off the mushroom. Mix bread crumbles and parsley. Add garlic, butter, or oil and season with salt and pepper. Spread the herb butter in the mushroom hats. Grate for 5–10 minutes.

Sesame Balls with Mushrooms and Walnuts *Raw*

10.6 oz white button mushrooms (300 g)
1 shallot
1 small carrot
2 cups walnuts (300 g)
⅔ cup chopped parsley (100 g)
1.2 pressed garlic cloves
2 tsp shoyu or soy (10 ml)
1 tsp tarragon (3 g)
herb salt
a couple of drops lemon juice
sesame seeds

■ Clean and slice mushroom, onion, and carrot coarsely. Mix nuts. Then add mushroom, onion, carrot, parsley, garlic, shoyu, as well as tarragon and continue to mix the batter. Add herb salt to taste. Let the batter sit in the refrigerator for an hour before shaping into balls. Roll the balls in sesame seeds. If the batter feels to loose, add sesame seeds.

Dolmades *Lacto or Vegan*

Dolmades with mushrooms and oats. Tasty as an appetizer or on the buffet table with Tzatziki, p. 170.

Oats can be replaced with spelt and/or quinoa. Grape leaves can be replaced with chard or Savoy cabbage.

12 PIECES *PHOTO P. 141
12 large grape leaves (fresh or canned)

Filling:
1 onion
2 garlic cloves
7.05 oz parboiled mushroom (200 g)
⅔ cup coarsely grated carrot (100 g)
1 tbsp olive and canola oil (15 ml)
½ vegetable stock cube
½ cup crème fraîche or soy cream (100 ml)
⅓ cup finely chopped parsley (50 g)
1 cup cooked naked oats (200 g)
1 tsp oregano (3 g)
salt

Boiling:
¾ cup vegetable stock (200 ml)
1 tbsp lemon juice (15 ml)

■ Cut off the stems on the grape leaves and parboil them for just a minute if they are fresh.

Peel and chop onion and garlic. Fry onion, garlic, mushroom, and carrot in the oil. Crumble the stock cube and stir with crème fraîche or soy cream as well as parsley and oats. Add oregano and salt to taste.

■ Spread about one tablespoon of filling on each leaf. Fold the sides together and roll up the leaf. If the leaves are small you can put several together. Place the dolmades with the seam facing down in a pot. Place a couple of grape leaves on top. Pour stock and lemon juice and let simmer under a lid for about 10 minutes.

Carrot Pâté with Herbs *Raw*

A classic raw food pâté that can be varied in many ways.

4 SERVINGS
⅔ cup sunflower seeds (100 g)
⅔ cup hazelnuts (100 g)
⅔ cup almonds (100 g)
1–2 celeries
2–3 carrots
1–2 tbsp water (15–30 ml)
⅔ cup chopped parsley (100 g)
1 chopped shallot
1 pressed garlic clove
1 tsp crumbled rosemary, thyme, and basil (3 g)
2–3 tsp shoyu or soy (10–15 ml)
½–1 tbsp lemon juice (7.5–15 ml)
spinach leaves

Garnish:
Sherry tomatoes, zucchini, cucumber, sprouts, and/or broccoli florets

■ Soak seeds, nuts, and almonds for a half-day. Drain.
■ Slice celery and carrot. Mix seeds, nuts, almonds, celery, and carrot. Dilute with water until the mixture reaches a good texture. Add parsley, onion, garlic, and herbs. Add shoyu and lemon juice to taste. Shape into a pâté and place on spinach leaves on a dish. Garnish the pâté with vegetables.

Cauliflower Pâté with Herbs
Follow the basic recipe above but replace carrot with cauliflower.

Bell Pepper Pâté with Tomato and Chili

Follow the basic recipe on the previous page but replace carrots with red and yellow bell peppers as well as dried tomatoes. Season the pâté with chili instead of herbs.

Vego Sushi *Vegan*

It might look advanced, but is easy to make and is always appreciated on a potluck or on the buffet table. The sushi is best when it is freshly made, but can be done a couple of hours before the meal.

4 SERVINGS
¾ cup short grain rice (150 g)
¾ cup water (175 ml)
4 nori sheets

Sushi Vinegar:
1 tbsp rice vinegar (15 ml)
½ tbsp palm sugar (12.5 g)
1 pinch salt (1 ml)

Filling:
2 large carrots
1–2 avocados
½ cucumber

Sides:
⅓ cup shoyu or other mild soy sauce (75 ml)
1–2 tsp finely grated ginger (3–6 g)
wasabi
pickled ginger

■ Rinse the rice five times until the water becomes clear. Drain. Pour water over and let the rice soak for about 30 minutes.
■ Bring rice and water to a boil and let boil for a few seconds. Reduce the heat and then let the rice simmer on low heat for about 20 minutes. Remove the pan from the stove and let sit for about 10 minutes. Then allow the rice to stand without lid for a while.
■ Heat vinegar, sugar, and salt for the sushi vinegar and stir rice into it.
■ Peel the carrots for the filling and cut them in about 0.4 inches thick sticks lengthwise. Boil the carrot sticks in water until just soft. Peel the avocado and cut into sticks. Cut the cucumber in sticks.
■ Place the nori sheets with the shiny side facing down and the stripes toward you.

You can use a bamboo stick sushi pad, but it works fine without it. Spread a layer of lukewarm rice, about 0.4 inches thick, on half of the nori sheet closest to you, but leave the edge empty. Then place vegetables on the rice so the filling goes in the middle of the rice.
■ Roll up the nori sheet, like a jelly roll, by using the bamboo pad. Moist the edge with water and attach to the roll. Let the rolls sit about 10 minutes before they are cut into about 0.8 inches thick slices with a sharp knife.
■ Mix shoyu with ginger. Serve with the sushi together with pickled ginger as well as wasabi.

Sushi with Mango Salsa

Follow the recipe above but garnish every slice with a dot of Mango Salsa, p. 174.

Sushi with Egg *Lacto-Ovo*

Follow the recipe above but only use a couple of nori sheets for garnish. The filling is rolled up in an omelet instead of a nori sheet. Beat 6 eggs with 1 batch of sushi vinegar. Pour the batter into a greased baking pan and bake in the middle of the oven for about 8 minutes in 392°F. Let the omelet cool off.

Cut the omelet in four pieces and turn them. Spread a thin layer of sushi rice according to the basic recipe on half of the omelet and add a carrot stick and roll up like a jelly roll. Cut each roll in three pieces.

Cut a couple of nori sheets into 12 strips. Roll a nori strip around each piece and attach the edge with some water (see picture).

Raw Sushi with Parsnip Rice *Raw*

Follow the basic recipe above but replace cooked rice with mixed raw parsnip and palm sugar in the sushi vinegar with agave syrup. Use sticks of fresh carrot, cucumber, and avocado or daikon in the filling.

Raw Sushi with Cashew Sour Cream *Raw*

Follow the recipe above but replace parsnip rice with Herb Pâté, p. 178, or one of the versions of Cashew Sour Cream, p. 178.

▶ VEGO SUSHI and Sushi with Egg, Grated Ginger, and Miso Soup.

Soy Fried Oyster Mushroom *Vegan*

Tasty both warm and cold. A great side dish that goes well with most food—salads, sandwich spreads, on the buffet table, and as stir-fry vegetables. Place the mushroom on a bed of spinach.

4 SERVINGS *PHOTO P. 144
14.1 oz oyster mushrooms (400 g)
1 tbsp oil (15 ml)
1½ tsp cumin (4 g)
3–4 tsp soy sauce (15–20 ml)

■ Slice the mushroom and fry it in oil for a few minutes. Add the cumin to fry in the pan for the last couple of minutes. Stir soy sauce into the pan.

Chili Marinated Oyster Mushroom

Follow the recipe above and stir 2–3 tbsp sweet and sour chili sauce when the mushroom is done frying.

Samosa *Vegan*

These small vegetable pierogies are very popular in India. They are excellent for a picnic and can also be frozen. If you want to, you can bake the pierogies in 437°F for 20–30 minutes instead of frying them.

10 PIECES *PHOTO P. 144

Dough:
3⅓ cup sifted spelt flour (385 g)
½ tsp salt (1 g)
2 tsp coconut oil (10 ml)
1½ tbsp yogurt (22.5 ml)
½-⅔ cup water (125–150 ml)

Filling:
1 tbsp coconut oil (15 ml)
1 tsp cumin (3 g)
1 tsp grated ginger (3 g)
1 tsp ground coriander (3 g)
5.3 oz small cauliflower florets (150 g)
5.3 small potato cubes (150 g)
⅔ cup green peas (100)
1 pinch cinnamon (1 ml)
1 pinch hing (1 ml)
1 pinch turmeric (1 ml)
1–2 finely chopped chili fruit
1 tsp finely chopped coriander or parsley (3 g)
1–2 pinches lemon juice (1–2 ml)
½ tsp salt (1 g)

Frying:
coconut oil

■ Mix flour and salt in a food processor. Add coconut oil and yogurt. Continue to mix the dough and add water. Work the dough until a ball is shaped. Let the dough rest covered for at least 20 minutes.

■ Heat the oil. Add cumin and fry while stirring until the seeds are lightly brown. Add ginger and coriander, fry for another few seconds. Add cauliflower, potatoes, green peas, cinnamon, hing, turmeric, and chili. Fry everything on low heat while stirring until the vegetables are soft. Stir coriander, lemon juice, and salt into the mix.

■ Split the dough into 5 balls and cover with a moist kitchen towel. Take a ball and flatten it into a circle of about 6 inches in diameter. Split each circle in half. Moisten the straight edge of the half-moon with water. Place it in your hands and press the edges together so a cone is formed.

■ Fill the cone with the vegetable filling. Leave a 0.2 inch-wide edge on the top of the cone. Wet the inside of the cone edge, press both edges together, and fold a braid by using your thumb and index finger. The pierogies will be triangle-shaped. It also works to close it by using a fork: press the edges together.

■ Fry the pierogies in oil until they are crispy and golden brown. Let them drain on household paper.

Asparagus with Parmesan
Lacto or Vegan

4 SERVINGS
⅔ cup walnuts (100 g)
24 stems green asparagus
green leaves like spinach and arugula
shaved Parmesan cheese or soy Parmesan

Dressing:
1½ tbsp balsamic vinegar (22.5 ml)
¼ cup olive oil (50 ml)
1 finely chopped garlic clove
gourmet salt and black pepper

■ Chop the nuts coarsely and roast them while stirring in a frying pan on low heat. Steam the asparagus with the top up, until they are just hardly soft, for 1–3 minutes, or grill them.

■ Mix the dressing with the asparagus. Place the leaves on plates and add the asparagus. Garnish with Parmesan cheese and sprinkle with walnuts.

SNACKS

Flax Seed Crackers with Raw Topping
Raw
Flax Seed Crackers, p. 312, topped with Gua-camole, p. 176, Herb Pâté, p. 178, or any of the variants of Cashew Sour Cream, p. 178–179. Garnish with bell peppers or cucumber and herbs.

Pumpernickel with Herb Pâté and Cucumber *Vegan*
Garnish a small round pumpernickel with herb pâté in tube and decorate with a thin half-slice of pickled cucumber.

Crostini with Tapenade *Vegan*
Garnish the crostini with Tapenade with black olives or green, p. 175.

Chèvre Balls with Gingerbread Crumble *Lacto*
Mix two parts chèvre with one part quark and season with salt and pepper. Shape balls that are rolled in crushed ginger bread.

Feta and Watermelon *Lacto*
Cut small balls with a melon baller or cut cubes of watermelon as well as small cubes of feta cheese. Stick a toothpick through a basil leaf, watermelon, and feta cheese.

Cherry Tomato with Feta *Lacto*
Stick a toothpick through a basil leaf, feta cheese cube, and cherry tomato.

Persimmon with Blue Cheese *Lacto*
Cut small cubes of blue cheese and cut persimmon in pieces. Stick a toothpick through the persimmon and cheese.

Blue Cheese and Melon *Lacto*

Cut small cubes of booth melon and blue cheese. Stick a toothpick through both cheese and melon.

Blue Cheese and Grape *Lacto*

Cut the cheese in cubes. Stick a toothpick through grape and cheese.

Roasted Almonds and Nuts *Vegan*

Place cashew, pecan, walnuts, and/or almonds in a heatproof pan or on a baking sheet. Lightly moisten them with a spray can or wet hands. Add salt flakes. Roast the nuts in the oven at 347°F for 5–10 minutes until they have a golden brown color. Be careful to not burn them. Almond and seeds are ready when they start to smell and have a golden color.

Roasted Hazelnuts *Vegan*

Spread hazelnuts on a baking sheet. Roast the nuts at 347°F for about 4–6 minutes. Be careful to not burn them. Let the nuts cool off and then rub them with your hands until most of the brown peel falls off.

Spicy Nuts *Vegan*

Tasty spicy snacks. Almond and cashew nuts can be replaced with boiled and drained chickpeas.

1⅔ CUPS (250 ML)
1–3 pressed garlic cloves
½–1 pinch sambal oelek (1 ml)
2–3 tbsp canola or olive oil (30–45 ml)
7.9 oz almonds and/or cashew nuts (225 g)
gourmet salt

■ Fry garlic and sambal oelek in oil for a while. Add nuts while stirring. Reduce the heat and shake the nuts until they are crispy and golden brown for 3–5 minutes. Salt the nuts and serve them fresh.

Shoyu Roasted Pumpkinseeds

Vegan

Tasty snacks that are low in fat and great to sprinkle over most dishes.

2 CUPS (300 ML)
2 cups pumpkin seeds (300 g)

2 tbsp shoyu or tamari (30 ml)

■ Roast the pumpkin seeds while stirring in a dry frying pan until the seeds "pop up." Be careful to not burn them. Set the pan aside and stir shoyu or tamari into the seeds.

Shoyu Roasted Almonds

Follow the recipe above but replace pumpkin seeds with almonds.

Popcorn with Peanut Butter

Lacto or vegan

Pop popcorn yourself in coconut oil since microwave popcorn contains trans fat.

2 QUARTS (2 LITERS)
1–2 tbsp coconut oil (15–30 ml)
⅔ cup popcorn kernels (100 g)

Seasoning:
1–2 tbsp butter or coconut oil (15–30 ml)
2 tbsp peanut butter (30 g)
½ tsp chili powder (2.5 ml)
salt

■ Heat coconut oil with a couple of popcorn kernels under a lid. When they pop, it is time to add the rest of the popcorn. Let the pan remain on the hot stove, but shake the pan until the kernels are done.

■ Heat butter or coconut oil as well as peanut butter and chili powder for the seasoning. Place popcorns in a bowl and mix with the seasoning and salt.

Popcorn Barbecue

Follow the recipe above but replace peanut butter and chili powder with 1 tsp garlic powder, 1 tsp paprika powder, 1 tsp thyme, 1 tsp oregano, or a few drops of Tabasco chipotle.

Popcorn With Sesame Seeds

Follow the basic recipe above but replace peanut butter with 2 tbsp sesame oil and 3 tbsp sesame seeds, preferably mixed colors.

Phyllo Pierogies With Chèvre and Marinated Tomatoes Lacto

Phyllo dough can be found in the shape of deep frozen thin sheets in foreign stores and some grocery stores.

20 PIECES
3.5 oz chèvre (100 g)
3.5 oz quark (100 g)
4–5 chopped, marinated, dried tomatoes
1 pressed garlic clove
1–2 pinches sambal oelek (1–2 ml)
2 tbsp chopped parsley (20 g)
16 sheets phyllo dough (8.8 oz/250 g)
about 1.75 oz melted butter (50 g)
1 beaten egg, sour milk or soy cream
Oven temperature: 392°F

■ Crush the cheese and mix with quark and tomatoes. Season with garlic, sambal oelek, and parsley.
■ Use a couple of dough sheets at a time. Let the rest sit under a wet kitchen towel. Brush one of the sheets with butter and place the other one on top. Then cut about 3-inch-long strips from the double dough. Place about one tablespoon of filling at the bottom of each strip.
■ Take one of the bottom corners and fold over the filling, to form a triangle. Continue to fold triangles until the whole dough is used. Place the pierogi with the seam facing down on a baking sheet with parchment baking paper. Place a wet kitchen towel over the pierogies until they are baked in the oven. Brush with alternative of choice. Bake in the middle of the oven for 15–20 minutes.

Papadam Vegan

Papadam is a thin, crispy sun-dried flatbread that is usually made of bean flour. The bread is often fried, but can also be placed on a oven rack over a very hot stove and then be turned from one side to another, until crispy.

4 SERVINGS *PHOTO P. 145
coconut oil for frying
5 papadam (Asian stores)

■ Heat the oil for frying. Fry the bread with the help of tongs until it turns golden and starts to wrinkle at the edges. It only takes a few seconds. You can fry several papadams at once. Let them drain on paper towels.

Tip! Leftover papadams can turn fresh and crispy again if they are heated in the oven for a few minutes at 301°F.

Miniature Pierogies with Feta and Spinach Lacto

30 PIECES
1 package cold puff pastry
3.5 oz parboiled, whole spinach leaves (100 g)
2.6 oz feta cheese (75 g)
3 tbsp crème fraiche or quark (45 ml)
1–2 crushed garlic cloves
black pepper
1 beaten egg or sour milk
Oven temperature: 392°F

■ Defrost the frozen puff pastry under a towel. Wring the spinach dry. Chop it coarsely. Crush the cheese and mix with crème fraîche or quark as well as spinach. Season with garlic and pepper.
■ Roll out one sheet of dough at a time to make it twice its length. Let the rest of the dough sit under a towel. Make circles of about 8 inches in diameters in the dough. Place a little bit of filling on each circle. Brush with egg or any of the alternatives and carefully squeeze the edges together. Fold the edges towards the middle.
■ Place on a baking sheet with parchment baking paper. Brush with egg or sour milk. Bake in the middle of the oven for 8–10 minutes.

Avocado Canapés *Lacto or Vegan*

16 CANAPÈS

1 red onion
2 cans red alga caviar (vegetarian caviar)
1 can crème fraîche or soy yogurt
1 ripe avocado
½ lemon
16 small triangles from a thin and dark bread,
    for example, pumpernickel
dill

■ Peel and finely chop the onion. Mix onion and one can of alga caviar with crème fraîche or soy yogurt. Peel and slice the avocado.

■ Place a little caviar mixture on each piece of bread. Garnish with avocado, caviar, and dill. Drip lemon juice over.

SIDES

Creamed Parsley Wax Beans

Lacto or Vegan

Replace the wax beans with green beans or runner beans if you want to.

4 SERVINGS

21–24 oz wax beans (600–700 g)
⅔ cup water (150 ml)
1 tsp stock powder (3 g)

Cream:

2 tbsp butter or coconut oil (30 ml)
3 tbsp sifted spelt flour (20 g)
1¼ cup milk, soy, or oat milk (300 ml)
salt and white pepper
⅓–⅔ cup finely chopped parsley (50–100 g)

■ Clean and cut the wax beans in pieces. Boil the beans in water and stock until they are just soft. Pour off the stock and save it.

■ Melt the fat in a pan. Stir flour into it and dilute with stock and milk. Let the cream simmer for a couple of minutes. Add salt and pepper to taste. Stir beans into the cream and then parsley.

Quick and Simple Sides!
- Fried Finely Sliced White Cabbage.
- Fried Finely Sliced White Cabbage with Curry.
- Fried Finely Sliced White Cabbage and Spinach Leaves.
- Zucchini Sticks Stir-Fry. Season with chili sauce.
- Broccoli Mousse—mix lightly boiled broccoli with finely mixed almonds and oil.
- Cauliflower Mousse—mix lightly boiled cauliflower with finely mixed almonds and oil.

Creamed Parsley Cabbage
Follow the recipe above but replace wax beans with white or pointed cabbage.

Garlic Roasted Chickpeas

These chickpeas are delicious both as snacks and in salads as well as stir-fry.

4–6 SERVINGS

2⅔ cups cooked or canned chickpeas (400 g)
2 garlic cloves
2 tbsp olive, coconut, or canola oil (30 ml)
1 tsp curry (3 g)
1 tsp paprika powder (3 g)
salt and pepper

■ Rinse the chickpeas. Peel and finely chop the garlic. Fry the chickpeas in oil for a while. Add garlic and curry and continue to fry while stirring. Add paprika powder, salt, and pepper to taste.

Lemon Fried Chickpeas with Spinach
Follow the recipe above but replace curry and paprika powder with baby spinach. Add herb salt, pepper, and lemon zest and juice to taste.

▲ APRICOT MARMALADE

Apricot Marmalade with Chili and Lemon *Raw*

Delicious and easy-to-make sugar-free marmalade. The chili adds that little extra and has somewhat of a preserving effect. The marmalade stays fresh for 3–4 days in the refrigerator.

I CUP (250 ML)
½–I tsp chili flakes (1–3 g)
¾ cup water (200 ml)
½–I tsp lemon zest (1–3)
a few drops lemon juice

■ Stir chili flakes into the water and mix with the apricots. Let soak for a few hours. Then mix apricots and lemon zest with the soaking water. Add lemon juice to taste.

Red Apricot and Currant Marmalade *Raw*

Great summer fresh marmalade that is mixed in no time. Replace red currants with black currants, blueberries, raspberries, blackberries, pitted plums, or cherries if you want to. You can use frozen berries. Marmalade stays fresh for 3–4 days in the refrigerator.

I CUP (250 ML)
½ cup water (100 ml)
8.8 oz dried apricots (250 g)
1⅓ cup red currants (200 g)
I tsp vanilla (3 g)

■ Let the apricots sit in the water until all liquid is soaked up. Mix currants, soaked apricots, and vanilla.

Raw lingonberries *Raw*

Lingonberries can be replaced with berries like currants, blueberries, and raspberries.

¾ C.UP (200 ML)
1⅓ cup lingonberries (200 g)
1 tsp honey or agave syrup (5 ml)
½ banana

■ Mix lingonberries with honey or agave syrup for a few seconds. The lingonberries are the most tasty if they are not too finely mixed. Then coarsely crush the banana with a fork and stir into the lingonberry mixture by hand.

Raw Strawberries *Raw*

⅔ CUP (200 ML)
½ banana
1⅓ cup sliced strawberries (200 g)
½–1 tsp lemon juice (2.5–5 ml)

■ Mash the banana coarsely and mix with the strawberries. Season with lemon juice.

Raw Raspberries

Follow the previous recipe but omit the lemon juice and replace the strawberries with raspberries.

Marinated Seaweed with Almonds *Vegan*

Marinated Seaweed is great as a side dish.

4 SERVINGS
1⅓ cup almonds (200 g)
0.9 oz iziki or arame seaweed (25 g)

Marinade:
½ tbsp balsamic vinegar (15–30 ml)
½ tbsp agave syrup (15–30 ml)
½–1 tbsp shoyu or tamari (7.5–15 ml)
½ cup oil (50 ml)
Oven temperature: 347°F

■ Roast the almonds 5–10 minutes. Boil the seaweed for 10–20 minutes and pour off the water. Mix seaweed and almonds with the marinade.

Marinated Seaweed with Sesame Seeds

Follow the recipe above but replace almonds with sesame seeds and season the marinade with ½–1 tsp sesame oil.

Apple Sauce with Almonds *Raw*

Incredibly tasty apple sauce that should be eaten instantly or else the color will darken.

1⅔ CUP (400 ML)
3–4 sweet apples
1 tbsp coconut oil (15 ml)
2 tbsp ground almonds (mixer) (20 g)
½–1 tsp vanilla (1–3 g)
½–1 tbsp honey (7.5–15 ml)

■ Cut the apple in pitted slices but keep the peel. Cut the slices in smaller pieces. Mix the apples and coconut oil into a firm sauce. Do not mix too long as it will make the sauce too watery. Stir the almonds into the apple sauce and then add vanilla and honey to taste.

Apple Chutney *Lacto or vegan*

2 CUPS (450 ML)
3 large apples
1–2 chili fruit
1 tbsp ghee or oil (15 ml)
1½ tsp anise seeds (4 g)
1 tbsp grated ginger (20 g)
½ tsp turmeric (1 g)
2 tbsp orange juice (30 ml)
1 cup raw sugar (200 g)
½ tsp grated orange or lemon zest (1 g)
1 pinch ground cardamom (1 ml)
2 pinches ground cinnamon (2 ml)
2 pinches ground nutmeg flower (2 ml)

■ Peel and cut the apples in small pieces. Clean and finely chop the chili fruit.
■ Heat the ghee or oil and fry chili and anise while stirring. Add ginger, turmeric, and apple pieces. Pour orange juice, sugar, orange zest, and spices into the mixture. Let simmer on low heat for 30 minutes or until the apples fall apart. Stir often. The apples may be crushed by the end of the cooking time. Let the chutney cool off and then store in the refrigerator.

Soups

Soups are easy to make and can become a culinary delicacy with cheap and climate-smart raw material. There are soups for all occasions.

A warming and filling soup in winter darkness or a cooling and refreshing soup on a hot summer day. To quote Molière: "You cannot live on beautiful words, good thing we have soups."

Avocado Soup *Raw*

The soup that has it all! Delicious flavor with a smooth and creamy texture. Freshly light green, full of antioxidants, and easy to make in just a few minutes.

1–2 SERVINGS
1 avocado
One small piece of fresh or dried chili
¼ cucumber
1⅓ cup coarsely parsley
½ tbsp lemon juice (7.5 ml)
½–1 tsp tarragon, dried or fresh (1–3 g)
1¼-1⅔ cup water (300–400 ml)
1–2 tsp stock (1–2 ml)
1 pressed garlic clove
herb salt
pumpkinseeds

■ Peel and clean the avocado. Cut the fruit meat in smaller pieces. Mix avocado, cucumber, parsley, lemon juice, and tarragon with half of the water. Add stock, garlic, and herb salt to taste. Dilute with water until the texture is good. Sprinkle with pumpkin seeds.

Avocado Soup with Celery
Follow the recipe above but replace tarragon with 1–2 sticks of celery.

Kale Soup with Avocado
Follow the basic recipe above but replace cucumber, parsley, and tarragon with 2 large kale leaves. Remove the coarse stem on the leaves.

Broccoli Soup with Avocado
Follow the basic recipe above but replace cucumber, parsley, and tarragon with broccoli.

Gazpacho *Raw*

4 SERVINGS *PHOTO P. 200
½ cucumber
5–6 tomatoes
2 bell peppers, red and yellow
3 cups vegetable stock (300 ml)
1–2 tbsp lemon juice (15–30 ml)
1–2 pinches sambal oelek (1–2 ml)
basil leaves

■ Clean and cut the cucumber and other vegetables in small pieces. Mix the vegetables in a food processor. Add the stock. Continue to mix the soup until smooth and add lemon juice, garlic, and sambal oelek to taste. Sprinkle with basil leaves.

Gazpacho with Celery
Follow the recipe above but add a few celery stems that is mixed with other vegetables.

Creamy Gazpacho
Follow the recipes above but add one avocado.

Saffron Soup with Asparagus
Lacto or Vegan

4 SERVINGS
3–4 potatoes
1 large carrot
3 tomatoes
½ celery
2 pressed garlic cloves
1 tbsp olive or canola oil (15 ml)
2½ cup vegetable stock (600 ml)
1 pinch saffron (0.5 ml)
1 tsp thyme (3 g)
1 tsp fennel (3 g)
1–2 pinches sambal oelek (1–2 ml)
½–1 package halloumi or tofu
4.2 oz green asparagus, optionally deep frozen (120 g)
¾ cup white wine or lemon water (200 ml)
salt and pepper
chopped dill

■ Peel and slice the potatoes. Peel and cut the carrot in long sticks. Chop the tomatoes. Clean and slice the celery. Fry celery together with garlic in the oil for a while. Pour the stock over and bring to a boil.

■ Add potatoes, carrot, chopped tomatoes, saffron, thyme, fennel, and sambal oelek. Let boil for about 15 minutes or until the vegetables are soft. Add asparagus and wine or lemon juice to boil with the vegetables for a few minutes at the end.

■ Cut halloumi or tofu into cubes and add the cubes to the soup. Add salt, pepper, and dill to taste. Serve with Mild Garlic Aioli, p. 172.

▲ SAFFRON SOUP with asparagus

Vegetable Broth *Vegan*

Many of the coarse leaves and stems that you clear off the vegetables are great for flavoring broth, such as cauliflower leaves, cabbage leaves, leek leaves, tops of beets, carrots, celery, parsnips, kale, Brussels sprouts, and broccoli stalks.

2 LITER

2 parsnips

2 carrots

a piece of celery root

1 beetroot

1 leek

5 parsley stems

2½ liters of water

5 white peppercorns

5 allspice cloves

3 bay leaves

3 star anise

1½ teaspoons salt

■ Peel and cut root vegetables and leeks into pieces. Also use the tops of root vegetables. Boil vegetables and root vegetables in water with spices and salt. Let the broth simmer 1½ to 2 hours on low heat.

■ Strain the vegetables and let the broth cool.

Pumpkin Soup *Vegan*

The soup is lovely and creamy with mild and delicate flavor, and the pumpkin seeds can be roasted. Scrape off all seeds and clean off the fruit meat. Roast the seeds in a dry frying pan. Stir and make sure they do not burn. Sprinkle the soup with seeds or eat as snack.

4 SERVINGS

1–2 shallots
2½–3 cups vegetable stock (600–700 ml)
1 quart peeled orange pumpkin cut in cubes (21 oz/600 g)
⅓ cup oat or soy cream (100 ml)
2 pressed garlic cloves
1–2 pinches sambal oelek (1–2 ml)
1–2 tbsp lemon juice (15–30 ml)
salt and pepper
⅓–⅔ finely chopped parsley, basil or dill (50–100 g)

■ Peel and chop the onion coarsely. Bring the stock to a boil and let pumpkin and onion simmer for 5–10 minutes. Stir cream into the pan and season with garlic, sambal oelek, lemon juice, salt, and pepper. Mix the soup until smooth and optionally dilute with more stock. Sprinkle with herbs.

Sweet Potato Soup

Follow the recipe above but replace pumpkin with sweet potatoes.

Chèvre Grated Sweet Potato Soup

Lacto

Follow the basic recipe above but replace pumpkin with sweet potato and exclude the cream. Pour the soup in four bowls and garnish with a slice of chèvre. Grate at 437°F in the oven for about 1 minute until the cheese has a nice color.

Potato and Broccoli Soup *Vegan*

4 SERVINGS

4 potatoes
4 garlic cloves
14 oz broccoli (400 g)
3½ cup vegetable stock (800 ml)
½ tsp thyme (1 g)
1 tbsp olive or canola oil (15 ml)
½–1 pinch sambal oelek (0.5–1 ml)
salt and pepper

■ Peel and cut potatoes and garlic coarsely. Clean and cut the broccoli in pieces. Let potatoes, garlic, broccoli, and thyme cook in the stock for about 10 minutes.
■ Mix potatoes and broccoli. Stir the oil into the soup and add sambal oelek, salt, and pepper to taste.

Potato and Onion Soup

Follow the recipe above but replace broccoli with leeks and yellow onion.

Borscht *Vegan*

This wonderful Russian beetroot soup is said to have as many variations as there are chefs. In Eastern Europe fermented beetroots or a pieces of sourdough are used when the soup is done.

4 SERVINGS

1 yellow onion
2 garlic cloves
7 medium sized beetroots
1 carrot
1 small piece white cabbage (7 oz/200 g)
1–2 tbsp vegetable stock (15–30 ml)
1 bay leaf
5 allspice corns
2–3 tsp vinegar (10–15 ml)
salt and pepper

Horseradish Yogurt

¾ cup yogurt (200 ml)
finely grated horseradish
herb salt

■ Peel and chop onion and garlic. Clean, peel, and coarsely grate the beetroots, carrot, and white cabbage. Grate one beetroot separately and set aside.
■ Fry all vegetables and root vegetables in the oil. Add stock, bay leaf, and allspice. Let the soup simmer for about 20 minutes. Add the grated beetroot. Add vinegar, salt, and pepper to taste.
■ Season yogurt with horseradish and herb salt. Serve the soup with a little horseradish yogurt.

▲ POTATO AND BROCCOLI SOUP with thyme.

Pea Soup with Halloumi *Lacto*

We have been eating pea soup since the Middle Ages. Filling and tasty! Make a large batch and store in the freezer.

4 SERVINGS
4 cups yellow peas (600 g)
1½ quart water (1½ liter)
1–2 chopped onions
1–2 vegetable stock cubes
2 bay leaves
3 allspice corns
½ tsp grated ginger (1 g)
1–2 sliced carrots
½ package halloumi cheese
salt
2 pinches marjoram (2 ml)
2 pinches thyme (2 ml)
mustard

- Soak the peas for 6–8 hours in water.
- Pour off the water and add new water. Bring peas and water to a boil and remove foam. Add onion, stock, bay leaves, allspice, and ginger. Let the soup boil for about 1½ hour. Add the carrots to boil with the soup for the last half-hour.
- Cut the cheese in small cubes and add it while stirring. Add stock, salt, and crumbled marjoram to taste. Sprinkle with fresh thyme. Serve with mustard.

Pea Soup with Tofu *Vegan*
Follow the basic recipe but replace the halloumi cheese with tofu.

Chanterelle Soup *Vegan*

4 SERVINGS
1 shallot
about 1 quart parboiled chanterelles (1 liter)
2 tbsp olive oil (30 ml)
1 pinch curry (1 ml)
1 quart vegetable stock (1 liter)
2 pressed garlic cloves
½ tbsp tomato purée (7.5 g)
4 tbsp flour (30 g)
¾ cup oat or soy cream (200 ml)
1–2 tsp balsamic vinegar (5–10 ml)
salt and pepper
⅓ cup finely chopped parsley (50 g)

■ Peel and slice the onion. Mix onion and a third of the mushrooms into a smooth mix. Fry the mix and whole chanterelles in oil together with curry while stirring for about 10 minutes.
■ Pour stock over and add garlic and tomato purée. Let the soup boil for a few minutes. Stir the flour into the cream and add to the soup while whipping. Bring the soup to a boil and let simmer for a few minutes. Add vinegar, salt, and pepper to taste. Sprinkle with parsley.

Chanterelle Soup with Blue Cheese
Lacto

Blue cheese rounds off the mushrooms flavor in a nice way. Follow the recipe above but finish by adding 1.4 oz (40 g) crushed blue cheese to the soup.

Tomato Soup *Vegan*

4 SERVINGS
1 yellow onion
1–2 garlic cloves
1 pinch curry (1 ml)
1 tbsp olive oil (15 ml)
3½ cup vegetable stock (800 ml)
2 packages whole tomatoes, about 28.2 oz (800 g)
1 tbsp tomato purée (15 g)
1–2 pinches sambal oelek (1–2 ml)
1 bay leaf
2 tbsp sifted spelt flour (13 g)
1–2 tbsp lemon juice (15–30 ml)
salt and pepper
⅓ cup chopped basil (50 g)

■ Peel and chop onion and garlic. Fry onion, garlic, and curry for a few minutes in the oil.

Add stock, tomatoes, tomato purée, sambal oelek, and bay leaf. Let the soup simmer for about 10 minutes.
■ Stir the flour into some of the stock and add to soup while whipping. Bring to a boil and add lemon juice, salt, and pepper to taste. Sprinkle with basil.

Chickpea Soup with Basil *Vegan*

4 SERVINGS
1 chopped yellow onion
3–4 garlic cloves
1 bunch basil
3 tbsp peeled sesame seeds (30 g)
1 tsp whole cumin (3 g)
2 tbsp olive or canola oil (30 ml)
1 can crushed tomatoes
1¼-1⅔ cup water (300–400 ml)
4 chopped tomatoes
2–3 tbsp tomato purée (30–45 g)
2–3 tsp vegetable broth (10–15 ml)
2 cans chickpeas (5⅓ cup or 800 g)
1–2 tbsp lemon juice (15–30 ml)
salt and pepper

■ Peel and chop onion and garlic. Chop the basil. Save half of the basil. Fry onion, garlic, half of the basil leaves, sesame seeds, and cumin in the oil. Add crushed tomatoes, water, fresh tomatoes, tomato purée, and stock. Let boil for about 20 minutes.
■ Rinse the chickpeas and drain. Mix the soup with half of the chickpeas. Stir whole chickpeas and basil into the soup. Add lemon juice, salt, and pepper to taste.

Indian Lentil Soup with Coconut *Vegan*

4 SERVINGS
2 yellow onions
1–2 garlic cloves
1 tbsp oil (15 ml)
½–1 tsp curry (1–3 g)
1 quart vegetable broth (1 liter)
2⅔ cup red lentils (250 g)
2 bay leaves
1–2 tbsp lemon juice (15–30 ml)
finely chopped parsley

When serving: Sprinkle with raisins and coconut flakes.

■ Peel and chop onion and garlic. Fry the onion in the oil at low heat together with curry. Pour stock over and add lentils and bay leaves. Let boil until the lentils are soft for about 15 minutes. Add lemon juice to taste. Sprinkle with parsley and serve the soup with raisins and coconut flakes.

Dhal, Indian Lentil Soup Stew
Vegan

4–5 SERVINGS
2 yellow onions
1 tbsp coconut oil (15 ml)
2 pressed garlic cloves
1–2 tsp garam masala or curry (3–6 g)
1 tsp cumin (3 g)
½ tsp turmeric (1 g)
3½–3 ¾ cup vegetable broth (800–900 ml)
2 cups red lentils (200 g)
1–2 tsp grated ginger (3–6 g)
1–2 pinches sambal oelek (1–2 ml)
4 chopped tomatoes
⅓–⅔ chopped coriander or parsley (50–100 g)

■ Peel and chop the onion. Fry it until soft in the oil at low heat. Add garlic, garam masala, cumin, and turmeric and fry in the pan at the very end.

■ Add stock, lentils, ginger, sambal oelek, and tomatoes. Let the soup boil for about 15 minutes or until the lentils are done. Sprinkle with chopped coriander. Garnish with Ginger Yogurt, p. 170.

Green Pea Soup with Horse Radish Yogurt *Vegan*

4 SERVINGS
3½ cup vegetable stock (800 ml)
10.6 oz green peas (frozen or fresh) (300 g)
1 small onion
2–3 tsp broth (10–15 ml)
1½ tbsp sifted spelt flour (20 g)
⅓ cup soy cream (100 ml)
herb salt and white pepper

Horseradish Yogurt
¾ cup yogurt (200 ml)
finely grated horseradish
herb salt

■ Bring half of the stock to a boil. Place peas and onion in the pan. Let boil for a couple of minutes. Mix the soup with a hand blender. Add the rest of the vegetable stock as well as broth and bring the soup to a boil.

■ Stir the flour into the cream and add to soup while whipping. Let the soup boil for an additional few minutes. Add salt and pepper to taste.

■ Flavor with horseradish and herb salt. Serve the soup with a bit of horseradish yogurt.

Zucchini Soup *Lacto or Vegan*

A great soup that is even more nutritional and filling thanks to the lentils.

4 SERVINGS
1 cup lentils (100 g)
2½ cup water (600 ml)
1 yellow onion
1 quart coarsely chopped zucchini (1 liter)
1 tbsp olive or canola oil (15 ml)
1 pinch curry (1 ml)
3–4 tsp broth (15–20 ml)
1 pressed garlic
1–2 pinches sambal oelek (1–2 ml)
¼ cup yogurt or soy cream (50 ml)
2–3 tbsp grated Parmesan or vegan Parmesan (30–45 g)
1 tbsp lemon juice (15 ml)
sake and white pepper
⅓–⅔ finely chopped parsley (50–100 g)

■ Rinse the lentils and boil them in the water for about 10 minutes.

■ Chop onion and zucchini. Fry the vegetables in the oil together with curry for a few minutes while stirring.

■ Add vegetable fry, broth, garlic, and sambal oelek to the cooked lentils. Let boil for a few minutes. Remove the pan from the stove and add yogurt or cream as well as Parmesan. Mix the soup smooth and dilute with more water if necessary. Add lemon juice, salt, and white pepper to taste. Sprinkle with basil.

You Take What You Have-Soup
Follow the recipe above but replace half of the zucchini with white cabbage, kale, or other vegetables you have at home. Basil can be replaced with parsley.

Miso Soup with Tofu *Vegan*

In Japan, miso soup is often served for breakfast or as an appetizer. The soup will turn out the best if you cook it for several hours and then strain the vegetables.

4 SERVINGS
4 inches wakame seaweed (10 cm)
3 cups water (700 ml)
1 large onion
1 carrot
2–4 tsp miso (10–20 ml)
1–2 tsp vinegar (5–10 ml)
½–1 tsp grated ginger (1–3 g)
finely sliced leek
tofu cubes

■ Rinse the seaweed and let soak in water for about 5 minutes. Peel and slice the onion. Peel and slice the carrot. Bring soaking water, algae, onion, and carrot to a boil. Let simmer for at least 15 minutes.

■ Stir miso into some of the broth. Remove the soup from the stove and stir miso into it. Add vinegar and ginger to taste. Sprinkle with garlic and tofu.

Lentil Soup *Vegan*

A tasty and warming lentil soup—perfect for a bleak day.

4 SERVINGS
1 yellow onion
1 garlic clove
1 tbsp olive or canola oil (15 ml)
1 pinch curry (1 ml)
1 carrot
1⅔ cup red lentils (150 g)
1 can crushed tomatoes
3 cups water (700 ml)
1 vegetable stock cube
1 tsp paprika powder (3 g)
1–2 pinches sambal oelek (1–2 ml)
1–2 tbsp lemon juice (15–30 ml)
salt and pepper
⅓–⅔ finely chopped parsley, basil, or coriander
   (50–100 g)

■ Peel and chop onion and garlic. Fry onion and garlic until soft on low heat in the oil. Add the curry to fry in the pan at the end.

◄ SPELT MINESTRONE

■ Peel and grate the carrot coarsely. Rinse the lentils in a colander. Add carrot, lentils, water, stock, paprika powder, and sambal oelek. Let the soup boil for about 15 minutes or until the lentils are soft. Add lemon juice, salt, and pepper to taste. Sprinkle with herbs.

Spelt Minestrone *Lacto or Vegan*

4 SERVINGS
1 onion
2 garlic cloves
½–1 chili fruit
4 tomatoes
2 celery stems
2 potatoes
1 tbsp olive oil (15 ml)
1 quart vegetable stock (1 liter)
½ cup spelt grains (100 g)
1 red bell pepper
½ zucchini
1 cup cooked borlotti beans (can) (150 g)
½–1 cup grated Parmesan or vegan Parmesan
   (50–100 g)
salt and pepper
⅓–⅔ chopped parsley (50–100 g)

■ Peel and chop onion and garlic. Clean and chop chili, tomatoes, and celery. Peel and slice the potatoes.

■ Fry onion, garlic, and celery in the oil at low heat for a while. Pour stock and spelt grains into the pan and bring to a boil. Add chili, tomatoes, and potatoes and let simmer on low heat for about 20 minutes.

■ Clean and cut bell pepper and zucchini in small pieces. Add bell pepper, zucchini, and rinsed beans and let the soup simmer for an additional 10 minutes. Stir Parmesan into the soup and add salt and pepper to taste. Sprinkle with parsley and serve with Mild Garlic Aioli, p. 172.

Spelt Minestrone with Pesto
Follow the recipe above and season with Pesto, p. 174.

Spelt Minestrone with Root Vegetables
Follow the basic recipe above but replace bell pepper and zucchini with chopped parsnip, carrot, and rutabaga.

Onion Soup *Vegan*

Onion soup is an affordable delicacy, especially when grated with cheese.

4 SERVINGS
5–7 onions
2–3 garlic cloves
½ tsp curry (1 g)
1 tbsp olive oil (15 ml)
1 quart vegetable stock (1 liter)
½ tsp paprika powder (1 g)
1 tsp thyme (3 g)
2 bay leaves

■ Peel and slice the onion and garlic thinly.
■ Fry the onion together with the curry on low heat until it is soft and golden yellow. Dilute with stock and add spices. Let the soup simmer for about 10 minutes.

Chèvre Grated Onion Soup *Lacto*

Follow the recipe above and make the soup. Cut 4 to 6 slices of one-day-old bread into cubes. Roast for a few minutes at 482°F in the oven. Place the soup in four oven-safe soup bowls. Place the bread cube on top and add a slice of chèvre. Grate at 482°F in the oven for about 10 minutes.

Jerusalem Artichoke Soup *Vegan*

4 SERVINGS
1 leek
2 garlic cloves
1 tbsp olive or canola oil
17.6 oz Jerusalem artichokes (500 g)
7 oz potatoes (200 g)
3½ cup vegetable stock (800 ml)
¼-½ cup soy or oat cream
salt and pepper

■ Peel and slice onion and garlic. Fry the onion in the oil at low heat.
■ Peel and cut Jerusalem artichoke and potato into smaller pieces. Pour the stock over the fried onion and bring to a boil. Add Jerusalem artichokes and potatoes and let simmer for about 15 minutes. Mix the soup until smooth. Bring to a boil and add cream, salt, and pepper to taste.

■ Clean and slice leek and garlic. Cut the broccoli in pieces. Fry the onion in oil until soft. Pour water, stock, and thyme into the pan. Bring to a boil. Add the broccoli and let the soup boil for about 5 minutes.
■ Add the cream and mix the soup. Add lemon juice, salt, and pepper to taste. Serve with some yogurt, algae caviar, and fresh thyme.

Cauliflower Soup

Follow the basic recipe above but replace broccoli with cauliflower.

Celery Soup

Follow the basic recipe above but replace broccoli with celery.

▶ BROCCOLI SOUP

Pasta, Noodles, and Whole Grain Dishes

These days, it is fun to search through the shelves of whole grain products. There is a variety of different exciting whole grain pasta and noodles, like, for example, quinoa, amaranth, and buckwheat.

Many whole grain products with whole grains like oat, spelt, and buckwheat are steamed or processed to make cooking time shorter. Whole grain products have a low GI value and are full of fibers and other nutrients.

Zucchini Pasta with Tomato and Avocado Salsa *Raw*

PER SERVING

1 zucchini

2 tomatoes

½ avocado

1 piece red bell pepper

1 tbsp finely chopped red onion (15 ml)

2 tbsp finely chopped basil, parsley, or coriander (20 g)

Marinade:

½–1 pressed garlic clove

1 tbsp olive or canola oil (15 ml)

½–1 tbsp lemon juice (2.5–5 ml)

salt and pepper

■ Make wide strips of zucchini with a potato peeler. Chop tomatoes, avocado, and bell pepper. Mix all the vegetables with the marinade and add salt and pepper to taste.

Zucchini Pasta with Seaweed *Raw*

PER SERVING

1–2 tbsp arame seaweed (10–20 g)

¼ cup water (50 ml)

1 carrot

1 zucchini

⅓ broccoli

1 tomato

2 tbsp finely chopped parsley (20 g)

salt and pepper

Marinade:

1 tbsp olive oil (15 ml)

½–1 tsp shoyu (2.5–5 ml)

½–1 tsp sesame oil (2.5–5 ml)

½ pressed garlic clove

■ Let the seaweed soak in water for about 30 minutes.

■ Make wide strips of zucchini and carrot by using a potato peeler. Knead the broccoli a little with your hand and then divide it into small florets. Chop the tomatoes. Mix all vegetables with parsley.

■ Let the seaweed drain. Mix the seaweed with the marinade. Garnish the pasta with the algae and sesame mixture.

Zucchini Pasta with Marinated White Button Mushrooms

PER SERVING

4 sliced white button mushrooms

1 zucchini

1 carrot

1 tomato

2 tbsp finely chopped parsley (20 g)

Marinade:

1 tbsp sesame seeds (15 ml)

1 tbsp olive oil (15 ml)

½ tbsp shoyu (7.5 ml)

½ pressed garlic

1 tsp sesame oil (5 ml)

■ First marinate the mushrooms in the marinade. Make wide strips of zucchini and carrot with a potato peeler. Chop the tomato. Mix zucchini, carrot, tomato, and parsley. Garnish with marinated mushrooms.

Zucchini Pasta with Broccoli *Raw*

PER SERVING

1 carrot

1 zucchini

⅓ broccoli

4–5 cherry tomatoes

3–5 olives

½–1 tbsp pumpkin seeds (5–10 g)

2–3 tbsp finely chopped basil (20–30 g)

Marinade:

1 tbsp olive oil (15 ml)

½ tbsp lemon juice (7.5 ml)

½ tsp shoyu (2.5 ml)

½ pressed garlic clove

½ tsp sesame oil (2.5 ml)

herb salt and pepper

■ Make wide strips of zucchini and carrot with a potato peeler. Knead the broccoli a little with your hand and then divide it into small florets. Split the tomatoes in half. Mix vegetables, pumpkin seeds, and basil with the marinade. Add salt and pepper to taste.

▶ ZUCCHINI PASTA with Broccoli

Pasta Sauce with Tomato *Lacto or Vegan*

If you want the pasta sauce to have a rounder taste, you can add ½ cup crème fraîche or soy cream to the finished sauce.

4 SERVINGS

1 onion
2 garlic cloves
½–1 mild Spanish pepper fruit
1 large carrot
1 tbsp olive or canola oil (15 ml)
2 cans crushed tomatoes
1–2 tbsp tomato purée (15–30 g)
1 vegetable stock cube
1 tsp paprika powder (3 g)
1 tsp basil (3 g)
1 tsp thyme (3 g)
½ tsp oregano (1 g)
salt and pepper
optionally ½ cup crème fraîche or soy cream
  (100 ml)

■ Peel and chop onion, garlic, and pepper fruit. Peel and grate the carrot coarsely. Fry the vegetables until soft on low heat in the oil.
■ Add crushed tomatoes, stock, and paprika powder and let boil under lid for about 20 minutes. Optionally add crème fraîche or soy cream. Add herb spices, salt and pepper to taste.

Tomato Sauce with Mincemeat

Fry 10.6 oz (300 g) soy or Quorn mincemeat in oil. Then let the mincemeat boil with the recipe of tomato sauce found above.

Greek Pasta Sauce *Lacto*

4 SERVINGS

1 onion
8 tomatoes
1 tbsp olive or canola oil (15 ml)
2 pressed garlic cloves
1 stock cube
½–1 tbsp thyme (5–10 g)
⅔–1⅓ cup Kalamata olives (100–200 g)
1½ package feta cheese

■ Chop onion and tomatoes. Fry onion in the oil on low heat until shiny. Add garlic, stock, thyme, olives, and tomatoes. Bring to a boil and let simmer for 20–30 minutes. Crumble the cheese into the sauce and bring to a boil.

Cheese and Spinach-Filled Pasta Rolls *Lacto*

4 SERVINGS

10 lasagna sheets
2 yellow onions
2 garlic cloves
1 tbsp olive and canola oil (15 ml)
18.6 oz coarsely chopped spinach leaves (300 g)
½–1 pinch sambal oelek (1 ml)
salt and pepper
8.8 oz chèvre or cream cheese (250 g)
grated Parmesan
grated gratin cheese
Oven temperature: 482°F

■ Cook the lasagna sheets al dente in a big pot with water and a few drops of oil.
■ Peel and chop onion and garlic. Fry the onion on low heat in the oil until soft. Add the spinach and sambal oelek and fry everything while stirring. Add salt and pepper to taste.
■ Place a spoon of spinach filling and a spoon of cheese on the lasagna sheets and roll up. Place the rolls tightly together in a greased baking pan with the seam facing down. Sprinkle with Parmesan and gratin cheese. Grate in the upper part of the oven for 10–15 minutes. Serve with Tomato Salsa, p. 174, or chili sauce.

Pasta Buffet

Simple and tasty for both young and old. Serve freshly cooked pasta with some of the following alternatives in small bowls. That way everyone can make their own combination of pasta.

• Tomato Sauce with Mincemeat, to the left
• Grated Parmesan Cheese
• Marinated Feta Cheese
• Marinated, Sun Dried Tomatoes
• Garlic Fried Mushrooms
• Crumbed Zucchini, p. 269
• Crumbed Aubergine, p. 269
• basil leaves
• olives

Root Vegetable Lasagna *Lacto*

4 SERVINGS

8–10 lasagna sheets
2 yellow onions
1 tbsp olive and canola oil (15 ml)
2 carrots, 7 oz (200 g)
1 piece celeriac, 7 oz (200 g)
1 piece rutabaga, 7 oz (200 g)
2 pressed garlic cloves
1 package crushed tomatoes, 17.6 oz (500 g)
1–2 tbsp tomato purée (15–30 g)
1–2 pinches sambal oelek (1–2 ml)
2–3 tsp broth (10–15 ml)
1 tsp basil (1 g)
salt and white pepper

White Sauce:
2½ cup soy or oat milk (600 ml)
3 tbsp sifted spelt flour (20 g)
2 cups grated cheese (200 g)
salt and white pepper
Oven temperature: 437°F

■ Peel and chop the onion. Fry the onion in oil on low heat until soft. Peel and grate the root vegetables coarsely. Stir root vegetables, pressed garlic, crushed tomatoes, tomato purée, sambal oelek, and broth into the pan. Let the sauce simmer under a lid for 10–15 minutes.

■ Whip milk and spelt flour into a mixture. Let boil while stirring continuously for a few minutes. Stir most of the cheese into the pan and add salt and pepper to taste. Make four layers of root vegetable mixture, sauce, and lasagna sheets. Finish with plenty of sauce at the top. Sprinkle with grated cheese. Bake in the lowest part of the oven for 25–30 minutes.

How to Cook Pasta:
Use 3.5–4.4 oz (100–125 g) dried pasta per serving. Bring plenty of water to a boil in a large pot. Add salt as well as a few drops of oil, which prevents the water from boiling over. Let the pasta boil without a lid until it is al dente.

A few drops of truffle oil when serving enhances the flavor even further.

Spinach Lasagna *Lacto*

4 SERVINGS

1 package deep frozen, whole spinach leaves (8.8 oz/250 g)
1–2 pinches grated nutmeg (1–2 ml)
1 can quark (not the liquids)
1 cup grated Parmesan (100 g)

Tomato Sauce:
2 yellow onions
2 garlic cloves
7 oz white button mushrooms (200 g)
1 tbsp oil or butter
1 package crushed tomatoes (13 oz/370 g)
1 vegetable stock cube
8–10 sliced green olives
1–2 pinches sambal oelek (1–2 ml)
1 tsp basil (3 g)
1 tsp thyme (3 g)
½ tsp oregano (1 g)
salt and pepper

8–10 whole grain lasagna sheets
¾–1 cup milk (200–250 ml)
2 cups grated cheese (200 g)
Oven temperature: 437°F

■ Defrost the spinach according to instructions on the package. Wring dry and cut the leaves coarsely. Season with nutmeg. Remove the pot from the heat and add quark and Parmesan cheese.

■ Peel and cut the onion and garlic. Clean and slice the mushroom. Fry onion, garlic, and mushrooms in the fat on low heat for a while. Add tomatoes, vegetable stock, and olives. Season with sambal oelek, herbs, salt, and pepper. Let the sauce simmer on low heat for about 10 minutes without a lid.

■ Place layers of spinach, lasagna sheets, and tomato sauce in a greased baking pan. The spinach filling should go underneath and the tomato sauce on top. Pour the milk over the lasagna and sprinkle with grated cheese. Bake in the lowest part of the oven for about 30 minutes.

Spinach Lasagna with Chèvre
Follow the recipe above but replace the cheese with sliced chèvre.

▲ OAT with Apple and Ginger

WHOLE GRAIN DISHES

Oat with Apple and Ginger
Vegan
4–5 SERVINGS
1½ cup naked oats (300 g)
2½ cup water (600 ml)
1 tsp broth (5 ml)
1 apple
1 scallion
2 tbsp olive or canola oil (30 ml)
1–2 tsp grated ginger (3–6 g)
salt and pepper

■ Boil the oats in water and broth for about 50 minutes until the oat is soft.
■ First cut the apple in slices and then remove the core. Slice the apple pieces and scallion thinly. Remove the pot from the stove and add oil and scallions. Add ginger, salt, and pepper to taste. Carefully stir the apple pieces into the mixture.

Tabbouleh *Vegan*
4 SERVINGS
1 cup bulgur (200 g)
1 cup water (200 ml)
½ stock cube
1 red onion
2–3 tomatoes
1 lemon, juice and grated zest
¼ cup canola or olive oil (50 ml)
1⅓–2 cups finely chopped parsley and/or mint
  (200–300 g)
2 tsp paprika powder (6 g)
salt and pepper

■ Boil bulgur in water with stock for about 10 minutes. Let cool off.
■ Chop onion and tomatoes. Grate the lemon zest and squeeze the juice. Mix bulgur, onion, tomatoes, and lemon peel. Stir oil and herbs into the mixture. Add salt, pepper, and lemon juice to taste.

Tabbouleh with Almonds *Raw*
Follow the recipe above but replace bulgur with 1⅔ cup (200 g) well mixed almonds.

Oatsotto with Spinach
Lacto or Vegan

4–5 SERVINGS

1 yellow onion
2 garlic cloves
1 tbsp butter or coconut oil (15 ml)
1½ cup naked oats (300 g)
2½ cup vegetable stock (600 ml)
5 star anise
1–2 pinches chili flakes (1–2 ml)
1–2 cups Parmesan, Västerbotten cheese, or vegan
    Parmesan (100–200 g)
1 bag baby spinach
1 tbsp butter or coconut oil (15 ml)
1–2 tbsp lemon juice
salt and pepper

■ Peel and chop onion and garlic. Fry it in oil until soft. Add naked oats, stock, star anise, and chili. Let boil until the oats are soft, according to instructions on package.

■ Stir Parmesan cheese, spinach, and butter or oil. Add lemon juice, salt, and pepper to taste. Serve with oven-baked sweet potatoes and beetroots, p. 254, as well as Lemon-Marinated Haricots Verts, p. 161.

Saffronotto with Spinach
Follow the recipe above but add a pinch (0.5 ml) saffron in the stock.

Grilled Polenta *Lacto or Vegan*

4 SERVINGS *PHOTO P. 237

1 quart mild vegetable stock (1 liter)
1–2 tbsp olive or canola oil (15–30 ml)
7.9 oz polenta grains (225 g)
1 cup grated Parmesan cheese or vegan Parmesan
    (100 g)
3–4 tbsp finely chopped parsley and basil (30–40 g)
salt and pepper

■ Bring stock and oil to a boil. Slowly stir the polenta into the pot. Let simmer on low heat for about 10 minutes and stir often. When the porridge is firm it is done. Stir cheese and herbs into the polenta. Add salt and pepper to taste. Let the porridge cool off, preferably during night.

■ Cut it in pieces. Grill or fry it a couple of minutes on each side in a little oil.

■ Serve with Greek Aubergine Stew, p. 237.

Bengali Flower Rice
Vegan or Lacto

4–6 SERVINGS *PHOTO P. 144

2 cups basmati rice (400 g)
2½ cup water (600 ml)
1 pinch saffron (0.5 ml)
2 tsp salt (6 g)
¼ cup coconut oil or Ghee, p. 114 (50 ml)
⅓ cup raw cashew nuts (50 g)
⅓ cup raw pistachios (50 g)
1 tsp fennel (6 g)
2 cinnamon sticks
6 cloves
⅓ cup coconut flakes (50 g)
1 tsp ground cardamom (3 g)
1 pinch hing (Asian stores) (1 ml)
½ tsp cayenne pepper (1 g)
2 tbsp raisins (20 g)
⅔ cup deep frozen green peas (100 g)
⅔ cups dried pineapple cubes (100 g)
⅔ cups dried papaya cubes (100 g)

■ Wash and rinse the rice until the water is clear. Let the rice soak in lukewarm water for about 10 minutes. Drain the rice in a strainer. Bring water with saffron and salt to a boil.

■ Heat the oil and roast the cashew nuts and pistachios while stirring. Add fennel, cumin, cinnamon, and cloves. Fry while stirring and finally add coconut flakes, cardamom, hint, cayenne pepper, as well as raisins and rice. Fry everything while stirring for another minute.

■ Add the hot saffron water and bring everything to a boil. Add peas, cover with a thigh-fitting lid and let rise on low heat for 15–20 minutes. Finally add pineapple and papaya with a fork. Serve with Green Beans, Paneer and Badi in Tomato Sauce, p. 241.

▶ OATSOTTO WITH SPINACH, beetroots, and sweet potatoes baked in oven as well as lemon-marinated haricots verts

▲ QUINOA with beans

Quinoa with Beans *Vegan*

A delicious side that goes well with most other food. Just as tasty when warm as when room temperature. Stays fresh for a couple of days in the refrigerator. Perfect for the lunchbox.

4 SERVINGS

1⅔ cup quinoa, preferably red (300 g)
1 cup edamame beans (green soy beans) (150 g)
1 lemon
1 scallion
2–3 tbsp olive or canola oil (30–45 ml)
1–2 tsp broth (5–10 ml)
⅔ cup finely chopped coriander or parsley (100 g)

■ Boil the quinoa according to the instructions on the package. Add the beans to boil in the pan by the end of the cooking time. Grate the lemon zest and squeeze the juice. Chop the onion.

■ Remove the pan from the stove and stir oil and lemon zest into the mixture. Add broth and lemon juice to taste. Add onion and herbs.

Spelt with Avocado and Tomato *Vegan*

Simple and tasty! Goes well as a side dish to almost anything.

4 SERVINGS

1½ cup spelt grains (300 g)
1 avocado
2 tomatoes
1 scallion
2 tbsp olive or canola oil (30 ml)
salt and pepper

■ Cook the spelt according to the instructions on the package. Cut avocado and tomato in pieces. Slice the scallion. Mix vegetables and oil with drained spelt grains. Add salt and pepper to taste. Serve with Kidney Burger, p. 268.

▲ SPELT with avocado and tomato

Spelt Pancakes *Vegan or Lacto*

10 PIECES
1⅔ cup sifted spelt flour (180 g)
1⅔ cup spelt flour whole grain (180 g)
1 cup soy flour (100 g)
½ cup buckwheat flour (60 g)
½ tsp herb salt (1 g)
3½ cup soy or oat milk (800 ml)
coconut oil or butter for frying

■ Mix all flour with herb salt. Add the milk a little at a time and whip everything into a smooth batter. Let the batter sit for about half an hour. Fry pancakes or crepes in oil or butter.

Corn Crepes

Follow the recipe above but add 1⅓-2 cups (200–300 g) drained whole kernel corns and fry crepes.

Grated Crepes with Spinach

Fry crepes according to the basic recipe above. Place a few tablespoons of Spinach Sauce, p. 175, on each crepe and roll up. Place the crepes in a greased baking pan. Sprinkle with grated vegan Parmesan or Parmesan or gratin cheese. Grate in 482°F in the upper part of the oven for 10–15 minutes.

Grated Crepes with Mushroom

Fry crepes according to the basic recipe above. Place a few tablespoons creamed mushrooms on each crepe and roll up. Place the crepes in a greased baking pan. Sprinkle with grated vegan Parmesan or Parmesan and gratin cheese. Grate in 482°F in the upper part of the oven for 10–15 minutes.

Tasty Leftovers!

Leftovers of cooked bulgur, quinoa, oats, and spelt are good to keep at home when you want to quickly throw a meal together. Start by frying chopped onion and garlic in oil with curry and/or cumin on low heat.

Then add vegetables like sliced carrot and zucchini and finely sliced cabbage as well as something rich in proteins like haricots verts, tofu, halloumi, or soy sausage. Finally add whole grain leftovers like quinoa and oats. Other good things for this mixture is mushrooms, spinach leaves, fennel, cauliflower, bell pepper, and tomato.

Pizza, Pies, and Sandwiches

In the past, all bread was made with sourdough, including baguettes and pizza.

In Italy, the meal is often started with a bruschetta or smaller-variant crostini.

It is usually a piece of yesterday's bread that has been grilled on both sides and

rubbed with a garlic clove, brushed with oil, and optionally some salt flakes.

Pizza *Lacto*

Originally pizza was made from sourdough. The easiest way to do it is just like the Italians: to use a piece of the dough when baking bread—for example, the basic recipe of Spelt Bread, p. 308.

4 PIECES

Pizza Dough:
¾ cup water (200 ml)
0.9 oz yeast (25 g)
optionally 1 tbsp Sourdough, p. 302 (15 ml)
1½ tbsp oil (22.5 ml)
½ tsp herb salt (2.5 ml)
1⅔ cup spelt flour whole grain (180 g)
about 2¾ cup sifted spelt flour (300 g)

Tomato Sauce:
2–3 yellow onions
1 tsp oil (5 ml)
1 package crushed tomatoes
1 tbsp tomato purée (15 g)
½ crumbled bay leaf
1–2 pressed garlic cloves
1–2 pinches sambal oelek (1–2 ml)
½ tsp oregano (1 g)
½ tsp basil (1 g)
salt and pepper

Gratin:
5–6 cups grated cheese, preferably mozzarella
  (500–600 g)
1–2 tbsp olive oil (15–30 ml)
Oven temperature: 482–527°F

■ Heat the water to 98.6°F and dissolve the yeast. Add sourdough (optional), oil, and salt. Work spelt whole grain into the dough and most of the sifted spelt flour. Place the dough on a table with flour. Work the rest of the flour into the dough, until smooth. Let the dough sit and rise, covered with a kitchen towel for about 30 minutes.

■ Make the tomato sauce while waiting for the bread: Peel and chop the onion and fry it in the oil on low heat until soft. Add crushed tomatoes, tomato purée, garlic, and sambal oelek. Let the sauce simmer. Add crushed herbs, salt, and pepper to taste and let the sauce cool off.

■ Roll the dough into two large thin crusts which cover two greased baking sheets. Or roll the dough into four round crusts about 9.5 inches in diameter. Place the pizza crusts on two baking sheets with parchment baking paper. Spread the tomato sauce over the pizzas but save a thin line around it. Sprinkle with about half of the cheese. Place the ingredients of some of the following options and sprinkle with remaining cheese. Brush the edges with the oil. Bake the pizzas in the middle of the oven for about 12–15 minutes.

Pizza with Bell Pepper, Capers, and Olives
Pieces of marinated grilled bell pepper as well as capers and olives.

Pizza Vegetariana
Sliced mushrooms, strips of red bell pepper, pineapple pieces, olives, as well as pieces of artichoke hearts.

Pizza with Mozzarella and Arugula
Follow the basic recipe above and use mozzarella for the pizzas. Place arugula over the pizza when it is baked and optionally salt flakes.

Pizza with Mushroom and Arugula
Sliced fresh white button mushrooms or portobello on top of the tomato sauce. Then place arugula over the baked pizza and optionally salt flakes.

PIES

Spelt and Sesame Seed Pie Crust *Vegan or Lacto*

1 PIE CRUST
1¼ cup spelt flour whole grain (140 g)
1 cup sifted spelt flour (110 g)
½ cup sesame seeds, preferably black (75 g)
1 pinch salt (1 ml)
3.5 oz butter or coconut oil (100 g)
Oven temperature: 392°F

■ Quickly work flour, sesame seeds, salt, and fat, cut in smaller pieces, together in a food processor. Let the dough sit for 30 minutes in the refrigerator.

■ Press out the dough into a greased pie pan. Bake it in the bottom of the oven for 10 minutes.

Tip! It does not take much longer to make an additional pie crust while you are still at it. A pie crust wrapped in plastic can last for three months in the freezer.

Chanterelle Pie *Lacto*

6 SERVINGS

1 pre-baked Pie Crust, p. 226

Filling:

1 large shallot

about 11.6 oz parboiled chanterelles

2 tbsp butter (30 g)

1 pinch curry (1 ml)

salt and white pepper

3 eggs

½ cup cream (100 ml)

¾ cup milk (200 ml)

2 cups grated sharp cheese (200 g)

2 pinches salt (2 ml)

1 pinch white pepper (1 ml)

thyme

Oven temperature: 392°F

■ Peel and chop the onion. Cut the mushrooms in large pieces. Fry the mushrooms in butter and curry on low heat for about 10–15 minutes while stirring. Add the onion and let it fry with the mixture by the end of the cooking time. Add salt and pepper to taste.

■ Beat egg, cream, milk, cheese, salt, and pepper together. Place the mushrooms in the pie crust and pour the egg and milk mixture over it. Bake in the middle of the oven for about 20 minutes.

■ Sprinkle with crumbled thyme when the pie is done.

Tomato and Onion Pie *Lacto*

6 SERVINGS

2–3 red onions

1 tbsp olive or canola oil (15 ml)

2 pressed garlic cloves

⅔ coarsely chopped basil leaves (100 g)

1–2 pinches chili flakes (1–2 ml)

salt and black pepper

4–5 tomatoes

8–10 olives

3 eggs

¾ cup milk (200 ml)

2 cups grated sharp cheese (200 g)

2 pinches salt (2 ml)

1 pinch black pepper (1 ml)

Oven temperature: 392°F

■ Peel and chop the onion. Fry in the oil on low heat until soft while stirring. Add garlic and basil and add chili, salt, and pepper to taste. Place the onion-fry in the pie crust. Slice the tomatoes and place in the crust together with olives.

■ Beat eggs, milk, cheese, salt, and pepper. Pour the egg and milk mixture in the crust. Bake in the middle of the oven for about 20 minutes.

Broccoli and Blue Cheese Pie *Lacto*

6 SERVINGS

1 pre-baked Pie Crust, p. 226

Filling:

8.8 oz deep-frozen broccoli (250 g)

1 pressed garlic clove

3 eggs

¾ cup milk (200 ml)

2 pinches salt (2 ml)

1 pinch black pepper (1 ml)

3.5 oz blue cheese (100 g)

Oven temperature: 392°F

■ Parboil the broccoli florets. Drain and place in the pie crust. Press the garlic over.

■ Beat egg, milk, salt, and pepper. Pour the egg and milk mixture over the pie crust. Crumble the blue cheese over. Bake in the middle of the oven for about 20 minutes.

Spinach Pie with Chèvre *Lacto-Ovo*

Replace the spinach with nettles if you want to.

6 SERVINGS

1 pre-baked Pie Crust, p. 226

Filling:

2 packages frozen spinach leaves (8.8 oz/250 g)

3 eggs

¾ cups half-and-half (200 ml)

1 pressed garlic clove

1–2 pinches sambal oelek (1–2 ml)

salt and pepper

5 slices chèvre

10–12 black olives

Oven temperature: 392°F

■ Cut the deep-frozen spinach packages into 3 pieces. Defrost the spinach according to the instructions on the package. Wring the spinach dry.

■ Beat eggs and milk. Stir spinach into the mixture and add garlic, sambal oelek, salt, and pepper to taste. Place the filling in the pie crust and place cheese slices and olives in top. Bake in the middle of the oven for about 20 minutes.

Seaweed Pie with Corn and Olives *Lacto*

6 SERVINGS

1 pre-baked Pie Crust, p. 226

Filling:

about 0.35 oz wakame seaweed (10 g)

¼ cup water (100 ml)

2 yellow onions

2 pressed garlic cloves

1 tbsp olive or canola oil (15 ml)

8.8 oz drained cottage cheese (250 g)

2 tbsp tomato purée (30 g)

½ tsp cinnamon (1 g)

1 pinch ground allspice (1 ml)

1 pinch ground cloves (1 ml)

½–1 tsp ground thyme (1–3 g)

½–1 vegetable stock cube

salt and pepper

8.8 oz whole corn kernels (250 g)

4 tomatoes

8–10 black olives

2 cups grated cheese (200 g)

Oven temperature: 392°F

■ Crumble the seaweed and let them soak in the water for about 10 minutes. Pour off the water and chop the seaweed. (0.35 oz seaweed is about ⅓ cup chopped and soaked seaweed.)

■ Peel and chop the onion. Fry onion and garlic until soft in the oil on low heat while stirring. Add seaweed, cottage cheese, tomato purée, spices, and stock. Add salt and pepper to taste.

■ Place the onion-fry in the pie crust and then add the drained corn kernels. Slice the tomatoes and add them on top as well as olives. Sprinkle with cheese. Bake in the middle of the oven for about 20 minutes.

Seaweed Pie with Corn and Olives *Vegan*

Follow the recipe above but replace cottage cheese with cream cheese made from soy milk and exclude the cheese.

Pie with Mincemeat, Tomato, and Olives *Lacto*

6 SERVINGS

1 pre-baked Pie Crust, p. 226

Filling:

1 large onion

2 garlic cloves

1 small carrot

1 tbsp canola oil (15 ml)

10.6 oz deep frozen Quorn or soy mincemeat (300 g)

2 tbsp soy (30 ml)

1–2 tbsp mango chutney (15–30 g)

1 tsp finely grated ginger (3 g)

1–2 pinches sambal oelek (1–2 ml)

salt and pepper

4–5 sliced tomatoes

8–10 olives

2 cups grated cheese (200 g)

Oven temperature: 392°F

■ Peel and chop onion and garlic. Peel and grate the carrot coarsely. Fry onion, garlic, and carrot on low heat. Stir Quorn mincemeat into the pan and continue to fry while stirring.

■ Season the mincemeat with soy, mango chutney, ginger, sambal oelek, salt, and pepper. Fill the pre-baked pie crust with the mincemeat and place tomato slices and olives on top. Bake in the middle of the oven for about 20 minutes.

▶ SPINACH PIE with chèvre

SANDWICHES

Bruschetta with White Button Mushrooms _Vegan_

4 SERVINGS
7 oz white button mushrooms
2–3 tbsp chopped parsley (30–45 g)
4 slices bread
olive oil

Marinade:
3 tbsp oil (45 ml)
1 tbsp vinegar (15 ml)
1 crushed garlic clove
1 tsp French mustard (5 ml)
salt and pepper

■ Clean and thinly slice the mushrooms. Mix with parsley and marinade.
■ Grill the bread on both sides. Brush with olive oil all the way to the crust. Place the mushrooms on the bread.

Bruschetta with Avocado _Vegan_

4 SERVINGS
1 ripe avocado
1–2 tsp lemon juice (5–10 ml)
½–1 pressed garlic clove
½–1 tbsp water (7.5–15 ml)
½–1 tsp tarragon (1–3 g)
4 slices bread
olive oil

■ Peel and scoop up the meat from the avocado. Mix avocado, lemon juice, and garlic in a food processor. Dilute with water until the texture is good and add tarragon, salt, and pepper to taste.
■ Grill the bread on both sides. Brush with oil all the way to the crust. Place the avocado mixture on the bread.

Bruschetta with Tomato and Feta _Lacto_

4 SERVINGS
3–4 tomatoes
basil leaves
1.75–3.5 oz feta cheese (50–100 g)
4 slices bread
½–1 garlic
olive oil

■ Clean and remove the seeds from the tomatoes. Chop the tomato meat and let drain in a drainer. Chop the basil and cut feta cheese into cubes.
■ Grill the bread on both sides. Rub the bread on one side with garlic. Brush with oil all the way to the crust. Mix tomatoes, feta cheese, and basil and spread on the bread.

Bruschetta with Mushroom _Vegan_
Follow the recipe above but replace tomatoes, feta cheese, and basil with garlic-fried mushroom that is seasoned with soy, salt, and pepper.

Bruschetta with Grilled Bell Pepper _Vegan_
Follow the recipe above but replace tomatoes and feta cheese with Marinated Grilled Bell Pepper, see p. 180, as well as olives.

◀ BRUSCHETTA with different types of spread according to recipes above

▲ PITA BREAD with Falafel and Hummus

Filled Wraps

Wrap means to fold around and cover something. To wrap the spread or filling in tortilla bread or in a large lettuce leaf makes the sandwich easy to eat and easy to bring with you. Wraps are simple and tasty for lunch or dinner. Place out different sides so everyone can make their own favorite wrap.

First heat whole grain tortillas on both sides in a fairly hot frying pan with a couple of drops of canola oil. Then place the filling in the middle of the bread, fold one side up as a bottom, and fold the tortilla together like a roll. Place some greaseproof paper around the wraps. Here are some suggestions of fillings:

• **Avocado and Marinated Tomatoes:** Strips of Romaine lettuce, sliced avocado, sliced and marinated tomatoes, sprouts, red bell pepper, and basil.

• **Avocado and Mushroom:** Strips of Romaine lettuce, tomato pieces, garlic, fried mushrooms, sliced avocado, and tzatziki.

• **Aubergine Dip and Feta:** Aubergine Dip, p. 178, and strips of Romaine lettuce, sunflower shoots, cucumber, and bell pepper pieces as well as crumbled feta cheese.

• **Tandoori marinated tofu and avocado:** Tandoori Marinated Tofu, p. 164, as well as tomato and crushed avocado.

• **Hummus, carrot, and olives:** Hummus of choice, p. 176, strips of Romaine lettuce, coarsely grated carrots, sunflower shoots, tomato pieces, and olives.

• **Falafel and Hummus:** Falafel, p. 271, Hummus of choice, p. 176, young lettuce shoots, tomato pieces, sunflower shoots, and pepperoni.

• **Hummus Mexicans:** Hummus of choice, p. 176, strips of Romaine lettuce, sliced avocado, tomato pieces, whole corn kernels, thinly sliced red onion, crème fraîche, and tomato salsa.

• **Coleslaw Filling:** Coleslaw, p. 159, strips of Romaine lettuce, tomato pieces, and sunflower shoots.

• **Cottage Cheese and Olives:** Strips of Romaine lettuce, arugula, cottage cheese or soy cream cheese, alfalfa sprouts, tomato pieces, cucumber slices, and thinly sliced red onion as well as olives.

▲ WRAPS with Tandoori Marinated Tofu as well as Tomato, Basil, and Crushed Avocado

Sandwich Cake *Lacto or Vegan*

A delicious Swedish sandwich cake that needs to sit overnight in order to become really juicy and tasty. It is important to chop both the pickled cucumber and onion very finely to make the fillings tasty.

8–10 PIECES *PHOTO P. 224
2 white pan breads

Filling 1:
⅔ tube vegetarian herb pâté—for example, Tartex
⅓ cup finely chopped pickled cucumber (50 g)

Filling 2:
½–1 cup finely chopped red onion (75–150 g)
1 can red alga caviar (vegetarian caviar)
1 can quark or soy cream cheese
1–2 tsp lemon juice (5–10 ml)

Filling 3:
1.75 oz butter or margarine (50 g)
1 pressed garlic clove
1–2 tsp lemon juice (5–10 ml)
⅔ cup chopped dill (100 g)

Garnish:
⅔ cup (150 g) regular or soy mayonnaise
⅔ cup quark or soy cream cheese (150 g)
1⅓ cup finely chopped parsley (200 g)
1 large ripe mango

1 ripe papaya
½–1 can black algae caviar
½–1 can red algae caviar
basil

■ Cut off the bread crust so that two slices form a square. Cut off the bottom. Slice the bread lengthwise in four slices.
■ For filling 1: Mix pâté and cucumber.
■ For filling 2: Mix onion, caviar, quark, or cream cheese and season with lemon juice.
■ For filling 3: Mix butter with dill and season with garlic and lemon juice.
■ Spread filling 1 on two slices of bread. Place another two slices in the opposite direction and spread filling 2 on them.
■ Place the last two slices in the opposite direction again and spread filling 3 on them. Wrap the cake in plastic and let sit in the refrigerator during night.
■ When serving: Mix mayonnaise with quark or cream cheese. Spread the mixture around the edges of the cake and on top. Cover the edges with parsley.
■ Peel and cut mango and papaya in pieces. Garnish with fruit, caviar, and basil leaves.

Stews

Filling, aromatic stews and slow-cooked dishes are warming foods for chilly days. You can almost say that they take care of themselves on the stove.

While you are still at it, make a larger batch and eat the stew a couple of days later grated with cheese or—why not?—as a soup. Simple, since all you have to do is make the stew thinner with vegetable stock.

Sweet and sour soup with tomato and dill *Vegan*

4 PORTIONS
2 yellow onions
3–4 potatoes
½ cauliflower head
4 tomatoes
1 tablespoon canola or olive oil
½–1 teaspoon curry powder
1 teaspoon turmeric
4 cups vegetable stock
1–2 tsp grated ginger
7–10 oz (200–300 g) sugar peas or green beans
¼–½ cup (½–1 dl) soy cream
1 cup finely chopped dill
½–1 tbsp lemon juice
herbal salt and pepper

■ Peel and cut onions into wedges. Peel and slice the potatoes. Break the cauliflower into florets and chop the tomatoes. Sauté the onion in the olive oil along with curry powder and turmeric.
■ Add the broth, chopped tomatoes, and potatoes. Bring to a boil and season with ginger. Let the pot simmer until the potatoes are soft, about 15 minutes. Add the cauliflower and peas or green beans to boiling pot near the end of cooking time.
■ Stir in cream and dill. Add lemon juice, herbal salt and pepper.

Ratatouille *Vegan*

A classic accessory that tastes great with everything.

5–6 PORTIONS
2 yellow onions
1 eggplant
1 small zucchini
1 green bell pepper
1 red bell pepper
½–1 chopped chilies
1 tablespoon olive or canola oil
1 can chopped tomatoes (about 500 g)
1–2 tsp rural broth
1 teaspoon thyme and / or rosemary
2 pressed garlic cloves
salt

■ Peel and cut onions into wedges. Clean and cut eggplant, zucchini, and peppers into pieces. Fry onions and chillies in the oil a few minutes on low heat. Stir in the eggplant, zucchini and peppers and continue to stir while cooking.
■ Add tomatoes, broth, herbs, and garlic. Let the pot simmer for 10–15 minutes uncovered. Season with salt.

Ratatouille with chipotle
Follow the above basic recipe but replace peppers with roasted peppers in a jar, and regular chili with chipotle, smoked chili.

Ratatouille with Beans
Follow the above basic recipe but add a couple ounces of rinsed and drained chickpeas and/ or large white beans and let a large handful of green beans to boil with the end of cooking time.

Thai soup with coconut *Ovo*

A wonderful stew with aromatic spices that as good as the soup if you increase the amount of broth.

4 SERVINGS
2–3 cloves of garlic
2 lemon grass stalks
1–2 tsp grated ginger
1 tablespoon coconut oil
1 tbsp Thai curry paste
2 cups coconut milk
10.5 oz (300 g) of frozen quorn pieces
2–3 tbsp soy bean or vegetable broth
3 lime leaves
1 carrot
1 piece of broccoli
1 red bell pepper
2 tomatoes
4–5 spring onions
1 lime
salt
chopped cilantro

■ Peel and chop garlic. Chop the soft insides of the lemon grass stalks. Fry the garlic, lemon grass, and ginger in oil. Stir in curry paste. Add the coconut milk, Quorn, soy bean or vegetable broth, and lime leaves. Bring to a boil.
■ Peel and shred carrot. Cut broccoli, peppers, tomatoes and onions into pieces. Stir in the vegetables to the pan and simmer until they are almost soft. Season with lime juice and salt. Sprinkle with cilantro.

▲ GREEK EGGPLANT CASSEROLE with olives and feta and grilled polenta

Greek Eggplant Casserole *Vegan*

SERVES 4

2 large eggplants
3 celery stalks
2 onions
4 cloves of garlic
2–3 tbsp olive or canola oil
28 oz. peeled tomatoes
1–2 tsp sambal oelek (chili-based condiment)
1 cup raisins
½ tsp rosemary
3 tbsp chopped parsley
salt and black pepper

■ Clean the eggplant and cut them into chunks. Dice the celery. Peel and slice the onion. Peel and slice the garlic. Fry the onions, eggplant, and celery in the oil for a few minutes.

■ Add tomatoes, sambal oelek, raisins, rosemary, and parsley. Season with salt and pepper. Add a little water if necessary. Let the pot simmer 20–55 minutes. Serve with Roasted Polenta, p. 220, and Tzatziki sauce (Greek cucumber sauce), p. 170.

Greek Eggplant Casserole with Olives *Lacto*

Follow the previous recipe but replace the raisins with a cup of kalamata olives. Boil the olives together with the vegetables, and add a package of crumbled feta cheese near the end.

Greek casserole with soy balls *Lacto*

Follow the above recipe with olives and feta. Let 10–12 frozen soy balls or quorn balls (meat-free meatballs) come to a boil by the end of cooking time.

▲ SAFFRON COUSCOUS with Vegetables

Saffron Couscous with Vegetables *Vegan*

Couscous is the national dish of Morocco and it is said that the stew should have seven different vegetables to bring luck.

5–6 SERVINGS
1 small leek
6–8 small onions
4 garlic cloves
½–1 red chili fruit
1 carrot
1 parsnip
1 piece white cabbage
1 young zucchini
1 piece pumpkin
1 can chickpeas
3 tbsp olive or canola oil (45 ml)
⅔ cup sultanas (100 ml)
1 tsp ground cumin (3 g)
1 tsp ground paprika powder (3 g)
2 pinches cinnamon (2 ml)
salt and pepper
Oven temperature: 392°F

Saffron Couscous:
1⅔ cup couscous (300 g)
1¼ cup vegetable stock (300 ml)
1 pinch saffron (0.5 ml)

■ Clean and cut the leek in pieces. Peel and cut the onion in pieces and slice the garlic. Chop the chili. Peel, clean, and cut other root vegetables and vegetables in coarse pieces. Rinse the chickpeas and drain. Mix vegetables and chickpeas with oil and place in a greased baking pan. Bake in the middle of the oven for 20–30 minutes. Stir occasionally.

■ Take out the pan with vegetables and add raisins and season with cumin, paprika powder, cinnamon as well as salt and pepper.

■ Boil couscous in stock and saffron according to instructions on the package. Place cooked couscous on a plate and garnish with vegetables.

238

Inger's Quorn Stew with Banana and Curry Lacto

4 SERVINGS

1 yellow onion
2–3 tsp curry (6–9 g)
butter
1 package defrosted Quorn fillets
1–2 tbsp sifted spelt flour (7.5–13 g)
¼ cup cream or oat cream (50 ml)
3–4 tbsp water (45–60 ml)
2 tbsp chili sauce (30 ml)
2 garlic cloves
1 tsp thyme (3 g)
salt and pepper
2 bananas (not too ripe)
finely chopped parsley

■ Chop the onion and fry it in half of the curry in some butter in a sauté pan or a pot.

■ Cut the fillets in slices on the diagonal. Place flour and Quorn slices in a plastic bag. Shake it to cover the slices in flour. Then fry them lightly in butter. Dilute with cream and water until the sauce just covers the Quorn fillets. Mix chili sauce, garlic, and crumbled thyme into the pan. Add salt, pepper, and optionally curry to taste.

■ Slice the bananas and sprinkle with curry. Fry them briefly in fat and place on top of the Quorn fillets. Let simmer for a little while. Sprinkle with parsley. Serve with bulgur, couscous, or quinoa.

Chili con Quorn Vegan or Lacto

6–8 SERVINGS

1 large onion
2 garlic cloves
1 tbsp olive or canola oil (15 ml)
1 package crushed tomatoes, about 14 oz (400 g)
10.6 oz Quorn or soy mincemeat (300 g)
1 vegetable stock cube
1 bay leaf
½–1 tsp sambal oelek (1–3 g)
1 tsp ground cumin (3 g)
½–1 pinch cinnamon (0.5–1 ml)
1 can kidney beans
salt and pepper

■ Peel and thinly slice onion and garlic. Fry the onion in the oil on low heat until shiny. Add crushed tomatoes, tomato purée, Quorn or soy mincemeat, stock, spices, as well as rinsed and drained kidney beans. Let simmer for about 15 minutes. Add salt and pepper to taste.

■ Serve with couscous or naked oats.

Chickpea Stew with Seaweed

Vegan

5–6 SERVINGS

1½ cup chickpeas (3⅓ cups cooked, 200/500 g)
2–4 inches kombu seaweed (5–10 cm)
2 yellow onions
2 garlic cloves
8.8–12.3 oz mushrooms (250–300 g)
2 bell peppers, red and yellow
1 tbsp olive or canola oil (15 ml)
⅓ cup arame seaweed (50 g)
1 can crushed tomatoes
1 tbsp tomato purée (15 g)
1 tsp paprika powder (3 g)
1–2 tsp sambal oelek (5–10 ml)
1 vegetable stock cub
½ cup soy cream (100 ml)
1 sliced banana
3–4 tsp soy sauce (15–20 ml)
salt
chopped parsley

■ Soak the chickpeas during night. Boil then together with the kombu seaweed for about one hour.

■ Peel and chop onion and garlic. Clean and cut the mushroom in pieces. Rinse, clean, and cut the bell peppers in pieces. Fry onion, garlic, and mushroom on low heat for about 15 minutes.

■ Drain the chickpeas. Cut the kombu seaweed into thin strips. Add the seaweed as well as the arame seaweed, drained chickpeas, bell pepper, crushed tomatoes, tomato purée, paprika powder, sambal oelek, and stock to the mushroom fry. Let simmer for 10–15 minutes. Add the soy cream and banana. Add soy sauce and salt to taste. Sprinkle with parsley.

▲ BEETROOT STEW with Horseradish Yogurt

Beetroot Stew *Vegan*

4 SERVINGS
2 onions
2 garlic cloves
6–7 beetroots
1 small piece white cabbage (7 oz/200 g)
1 carrot
1 tbsp oil (15 ml)
2 bay leaves
4 allspice corns
1 tbsp sifted spelt flour (7.5 g)
salt and pepper
2–3 tsp vinegar (10–15 ml)
⅔ cup finely chopped parsley (50 g)

■ Peel and chop onion and garlic. Peel and cut beetroots, white cabbage, and carrot in fairly big pieces. Fry the onion and garlic on low heat in the oil for a while.

■ Add stock, bay leaves, and allspice and bring to a boil. Stir beetroots, white cabbage, and carrot into the pan and let simmer for 20 minutes or until the beetroots are soft.

■ Stir around the flour in some water and then whip into the stock. Let the stew simmer for a few minutes on low heat. Set the stew aside and add salt, pepper, and vinegar to taste. Sprinkle with parsley.

■ Serve beetroots stew with Horseradish Yogurt, p. 204.

240

Green Beans, Paneer, and Badi in Tomato Sauce *Lacto or Vegan*

If you want to, you can replace badi with frozen soy or Quorn balls or cauliflower florets that are added to the stew at the end of the cooking time.

4 SERVINGS *PHOTO P. 145

Badi:

1 cup chickpea flour (Govinda or Asian stores) (160 g)
1 pinch baking powder (1 ml)
1 pinch salt (1 ml)
1 pinch paprika powder (1 ml)
½ cup cold water (100 ml)
coconut oil for frying

Tomato Sauce:

2 tbsp coconut oil or Ghee, p. 114 (30 ml)
2–3 finely chopped fresh chili fruit
1 tbsp fennel (10 g)
1 tsp black cumin (3 g)
1 tsp brown mustard seeds (Asian stores) (3 g)
2 pinches hing (Asian stores) (2 ml)
1 pinch turmeric (1 ml)
1 tbsp raw sugar (12.5 g)
2 packages crushed tomatoes (13 oz/370 g)
salt
7 oz Paneer (p. 111) or tofu in cubes (200 g)
12.3 oz haricots verts (350 g)
1–2 tbsp chopped coriander (10–20 g)

■ Badi: Mix the chickpea flour, baking powder, and spices. Add the water and beat into a smooth batter. Heat the oil. Fry teaspoon-size balls for 3–5 minutes until they are golden brown. Let drip on paper towels.

■ Tomato Sauce: Heat oil/ghee and add chili, fennel, cumin, as well as mustard seeds. Fry while stirring until the mustard seeds start to pop. Add hing, turmeric, sugar, and tomatoes. Add salt to taste and add paneer and haricots verts to the sauce. Let simmer on low heat for a few minutes.

■ Add badi. Let the pot sit for about 15–20 minutes. Sprinkle with chopped coriander. Serve with Coconut Raita, p. 170, or Ginger Yogurt, p. 170.

Indian Chickpea Stew with Spinach

4 SERVINGS

1 onion
2 garlic cloves
1 carrot
2 tbsp coconut oil (30 ml)
½–1 tsp ground cumin (1–3 g)
1 tsp paprika powder (1 g)
1 package crushed tomatoes (about 17.6 oz/500 g)
2 cups cooked chickpeas (can, 300 g)
1–2 tsp broth (5–10 ml)
1–2 pinches chili powder (1–2 ml)
1–2 tsp grated ginger (3–6 g)
1 bag whole spinach leaves (5.3 oz/150 g)
salt and pepper

■ Peel and chop onion and garlic. Clean and cut the carrot in sticks. Fry the onion on low heat in the oil until shiny. Add cumin and paprika powder by the end of the frying.

■ Add crushed tomatoes, carrot, chickpeas, broth, and chili. Let simmer for about 15 minutes.

■ Add the spinach leaves and add salt and pepper to taste. Serve with Coconut Raita, p. 170 or Ginger Yogurt, p. 170.

When love is the spice, everyone enjoys the food.
—*Plautus*

Oven Dishes

All vegetables and root vegetables get a wonderful aroma and sweetness when baked in the oven or grated. Furthermore, the dish almost takes care of itself in the oven. Crumbling thyme over a baked dish will produce a lovely fragrance.

> **Roasted Vegetables**
> Roasted vegetables will get a wonderful aroma and sweetness. The coarser the vegetables are, the better the taste will be. Most vegetables are great to roast, like onion, fennel, pumpkin, zucchini, and corn.
> Tomatoes, aubergine, and bell pepper give off a tasty flavor, but causes more fluids to be produced. Mix vegetables with root vegetables like sweet potatoes and potatoes.

Roasted Vegetables *Vegan*

Classic side dish that goes well with almost anything.

4 SERVINGS
½ aubergine
1 small zucchini
2–3 tomatoes
1 orange bell pepper
1 red bell pepper
2 onions
2 garlic cloves
1 tsp crumbled rosemary (3 g)
2 tbsp olive or canola oil (30 ml)
pepper and salt
Oven temperature: 392°F

■ Cut all the vegetables and onions in quite big pieces. Peel and slice the garlic. Mix vegetables, onion, garlic, and oil in a greased pan. Sprinkle with pepper and salt. Bake in the middle of the oven for about 30 minutes. Stir a few times.

Roasted Vegetables with White Beans
Follow the recipe above but add one can of rinsed and drained large white beans. Bake in the oven together with the vegetables.

Roasted Vegetables with Chèvre *Lacto*
Follow the basic recipe above but take the vegetables out of the oven after 15 minutes. Stir and place chèvre slices on top and continue to bake until the cheese has a nice color, about 15 minutes.

Roasted Aubergine Wedges *Vegan*

Roasted aubergine wedges are a common side dish in the Middle East.

4 SERVINGS
2 firm aubergines
1–1½ tbsp olive oil (15–22.5 ml)
salt flakes
Oven temperature: 437°F

■ Split every fruit lengthwise in four wedges (including the stem). Make a few cuts on crosswise on each wedge. Brush the fruit with oil.
■ Place the pieces in a greased pan. Sprinkle with flake salt. Bake in the oven for about 30 minutes. Turn the wedges after half of the time so that the peel is facing upwards.

Roasted Pumpkin *Vegan*

4 SERVINGS
2.2 pounds pumpkin (1 kg)
2 tbsp olive oil (30 ml)
salt flakes and pepper
Oven temperature: 392°F

■ Remove the seeds and cut the pumpkin in about 1-inch-thick slices or pieces. Brush with oil and place in a greased baking pan. Sprinkle with salt and pepper. Bake in the oven for 25–30 minutes or until the pumpkin is soft. Stir occasionally.

Roasted Corncobs
Follow the recipe above but replace the pumpkin with whole corncobs or corncobs in pieces. Bake in the oven for 10–15 minutes. Flip the corn a few times.

Oven-Baked Red Onion *Vegan*

4 SERVINGS
2 red onions
coarse salt
olive oil
Oven temperature: 347°F

■ Place an unpeeled red onion on a bed of coarse salt in a frying pan. Bake in the middle of the oven for 30–40 minutes.

▶ ROASTED VEGETABLES With Chèvre

Climate-Smart Delicacy

Pumpkins or winter squash are perfect if you live in the north and want to eat climate-smart food. You would think that it is a new vegetable, but different kinds of pumpkins were found in stores as early as the 1800s. The best thing is that most types can be stored for up to a year.

Pumpkins are a forgotten and nutritious delicacy, with a far different flavor than the large pumpkin we use for Halloween. Most pumpkins have a sweet and tasty orange-colored pulp that is rich in antioxidants and can be baked in the oven, fried, grated, creamed, and used in soups, pies, and desserts. On top of all this, you can roast the seeds or eat them as they are.

Chèvre Grated Sweet Potatoes Lacto

A tasty side dish that goes well on the buffet table. The long time in the oven makes the sweet potato turn into "butter" and melt in your mouth.

4–5 SERVINGS *PHOTO P. 242
1–2 sweet potatoes (about 28 oz/800 g)
1 onion
3 tbsp olive or canola oil (45 ml)
½ tbsp balsamic vinegar (7.5 ml)
salt and black pepper
3 slices chèvre
Oven temperature: 437°F

■ Peel and cut sweet potatoes in cubes. Peel and chop the onion. Mix sweet potatoes and onion with oil and vinegar. Add salt and pepper.
■ Bake in the middle of the oven Stir occasionally. Take out the baking pan after 25 minutes and lightly mush the mixture. Add the slices of chèvre. Continue to bake in the oven for an another 20 minutes or until the cheese has color.

Tip! If you parboil the sweet potatoes first, you can add the cheese right away and oven-bake for about 20 minutes.

Oven-Baked Garlic Vegan

A delicacy that is easy to make. The coarse salt can be used many times.

4 SERVINGS
4 large cloves of fresh garlic
coarse salt
olive oil
black pepper
thyme or rosemary
Oven temperature: 347°F

■ Cut the top of each whole garlic. Place the cloves of garlic with the cut facing on top of the coarse salt in a frying pan. Brush with oil and sprinkle with black pepper. Bake in the middle of the oven for 30–40 minutes. Garnish with some crumbled thyme or rosemary when serving.

Grated Cheese Fennel with Nuts Lacto

An easy-to-make and tasty vegetable gratin with crispy cheese on top. Fennel can be replaced with broccoli, cauliflower, and/or brussels sprouts.

4 SERVINGS
21 oz fennel (600 g)
½ cup soy or oat cream (100 ml)
1–2 tsp Dijon mustard (5–10 ml)
2 pinches salt (2 ml)
½ pinch white pepper (0.5 ml)
3–4 tbsp chopped walnuts (30–40 g)
2 cups grated cheese (200 g)
Oven temperature: 392°F

■ Cut the fennel in pieces. Bring cream, mustard, salt, and pepper to a boil. Place fennel in the pan and let simmer for a couple of minutes. Make sure it does not boil dry.
■ Place the vegetable mixture in a greased baking pan. Sprinkle with nuts and the grated cheese on top. Grate in the middle of the oven for about 15 minutes.

Grated Chèvre Broccoli with Nuts

Follow the recipe above but replace fennel with broccoli as well as grated cheese with crumbled chèvre.

▶ OVEN BAKED Garlic

▲ MOZZARELLA GRATED Aubergine

Zucchini Gratin with Parmesan
Lacto or Vegan

4–5 SERVINGS

7–8 tomatoes

2 zucchini, (about 21 oz/600 g)

⅓ cup chopped parsley (50 g)

salt and pepper

¾ cup grated Parmesan or vegan Parmesan (75 g)

2 pressed garlic cloves

I tsp oregano (3 g)

I tsp basil (3 g)

tbsp olive oil (60 ml)

Oven temperature: 392°F

■ Clean and slice the tomatoes. Clean and slice the zucchini in about 0.2-inch-thick slices. Make layers of zucchini and parsley. Add salt and pepper.

■ Mix Parmesan and garlic as well as crumbled oregano and basil with 3 tbsp of the oil. Place the cheese mixture on top of the vegetables. Sprinkle with the remaining oil. Bake in the bottom of the oven for about 35 minutes.

Zucchini and Tomato Gratin à la Provencale
Follow the recipes above but replace the parmesan with 3–4 slices crumbled bread. Sprinkle with grated Parmesan cheese on top.

Zucchini and Tomato Gratin with Feta Cheese *Lacto*
Follow the recipes above but replace the Parmesan cheese with crumbled feta cheese.

Mozzarella Covered Aubergine
Lacto

4 SERVINGS

3 firm aubergines

6 tomatoes

2 small mozzarella

3 tbsp olive oil (45 ml)

basil leaves

salt and pepper

Oven temperature: 392°F

■ Slice aubergines, tomatoes, and mozzarella in 0.2-inch-thick slices. Heat a grill pan. Brush the aubergine slices on one side with half of the oil. Grill the aubergines first with the brushed side facing down and then turn them around.

▲ MOUSSAKA

■ Place layers of aubergine and tomato slices as well as basil in a greased pan. Finish with tomatoes. Add salt and pepper to each layer. Drizzle the rest of the oil and place the cheese on top. Grate in the middle of the oven for about 20 minutes.

Moussaka with Parmesan *Lacto or Vegan*

4 SERVINGS
2 aubergines (21 oz/600 g)
1 tbsp olive oil (15 ml)
1 cup grated Parmesan or vegan Parmesan (100 g)

Tomato sauce:
2 yellow onions
1 yellow pepper
1 package crushed tomatoes (17.6/500 g)
2 pressed cloves of garlic
2 tsp broth (10 ml)
½–1 tsp rosemary (1–3 g)
½–1 tsp thyme (1–3 g)
1 package soy or Quorn mincemeat (10.6/300 g)
2–3 tbsp tomato purée (30–45 g)
salt and pepper
⅓ cup chopped parsley (50 g)
Oven temperature: 392°F

■ Begin with the tomato sauce. Cut the onion and bell pepper in pieces. Place bell pepper and onion in a pot and add crushed tomatoes, garlic, broth, rosemary, and thyme and bring to a boil. Let simmer under a lid for about half an hour. Add the mincemeat and let the sauce boil for about 5 minutes without a lid. Add tomato purée, salt, and pepper to taste. Add parsley to the sauce.
■ Cut the aubergines in 0.2-inch-thick slices. Brush one of the sides with oil. Grill the sides with the oiled side facing down and then turn them. Make layers of aubergine and tomato sauce in a greased baking pan. Sprinkle with Parmesan or garnish with thin slices in a check pattern. Bake in the oven for about 20 minutes.

Moussaka with Zucchini
Follow the recipe above but replace aubergine with zucchini.

Moussaka with Mint and Feta *Lacto*
Follow the basic recipe above but season the tomato sauce with 1–2 tbsp crumbled mint and replace the Parmesan with 1¼ cup Greek yogurt which is whipped together with 3 eggs. Add pepper to taste. Place the batter over the moussaka and sprinkle with 5.3 oz (150 g) feta cheese.

Mushroom Pâté with Lingonberry Sauce *Lacto-Ovo*

Tasty on the buffet table or as an appetizer with lingonberry sauce and gherkins.

4–6 SERVINGS

17.6 oz fresh mixed mushrooms, chanterelles, or white button mushrooms
1 shallot
1 pinch curry (1 ml)
2 tbsp butter or coconut oil (30 ml)
⅓ cup chopped walnuts (50 g)
½–1 tbsp shoyu or soy (7.5–15 ml)
1–2 pinches thyme (1–2 ml)
1 pressed garlic clove
salt and white pepper
3 eggs
⅔ cup cream or soy cream (150 ml)
Oven temperature: 347°F

Lingonberry Sauce:

1⅓ cup lingonberries (200 g)
2 tbsp water (30 ml)
1–2 tbsp honey or agave syrup (15–30 ml)
½ tsp grated ginger (1 g)

■ Clean the mushrooms and cut in pieces. Chop the onion. First fry the mushrooms without fat in order to remove all fluid. Then fry mushroom and onion with curry in butter or oil on low heat for about 15 minutes. Add walnuts and parsley. Season with shoyu, thyme, garlic, as well as salt and pepper.

■ Mix the ingredients in a food processor. Add one egg at a time as well as cream. Place the batter in a small greased ceramic baking pan that has room for 2–2½ cups (500–600 ml). Bake in the middle of the oven for 35–40 minutes. Let the pâté cool off.

■ Mix lingonberries and water and season with honey and ginger. Serve the pâté with lingonberry sauce.

Filled Grated Bell Pepper *Lacto or Vegan*

4–6 SERVINGS

4 bell peppers

Filling:

1 large onion
2 garlic cloves
¾ tbsp whole cumin (7.5 g)
2 tbsp oil (30 ml)
10.6 oz frozen Quorn or soy mincemeat (300 g)
2–3 tbsp tomato purée (30–45 g)
½ tbsp soy (7.5 g)
2 tbsp chili sauce (30 ml)
1 tsp basil (3 g)
½ tsp rosemary (1 g)
½ tsp thyme (1 g)
salt and pepper
⅓–⅔ cups chopped parsley (50–100 g)
1½ cup grated spicy cheese or pumpkin seeds (200 g)
Oven temperature: 392°F

■ Split the bell peppers lengthwise and remove the seeds. Peel and chop onion and garlic. Fry the cumin as well as onion and garlic on low heat in the oil. Stir the Quorn mincemeat and fry on low heat while stirring. Add tomato purée, soy, crumbled basil, rosemary, and thyme as well as salt and pepper to taste.

■ Add parsley and place the mincemeat mixture in the bell pepper halves. Sprinkle with cheese or pumpkin seeds. Grate for about 20 minutes. Serve with cooked oats, salad, and Mint Yogurt, p. 170.

Grated Filled Zucchini

Follow the recipe above but replace bell peppers with 3–4 zucchini. Scoop out the inside of the zucchini and cut in pieces. Let the zucchini pulp fry together with the onion.

Grated Filled Aubergine

Follow the basic recipe above but replace bell peppers with aubergine. Scoop out the pulp of two aubergines and cut in pieces. Let the pulp fry together with the onion.

◄ FILLED Grated Bell Pepper with Cooked Oat and Mint Yogurt

Root Vegetables and Potato Dishes

Root vegetables are delicacies that are rich in fiber as well as climate-smart and affordable.

You can cook so many delicious dishes with root vegetables. Some root vegetables like kohlrabi, daikon, and turnips are incredibly fresh, crisp, and have a little sweeter flavor that goes just as well with salads as warm dishes.

Roasted Root Vegetables *Vegan*

All root vegetables like parsnip, beetroots, carrot, rutabaga, kohlrabi, turnip, Jerusalem artichoke, sweet potato, black salsify, and potatoes will acquire a wonderful aroma and sweetness when they are baked in the oven. You can use one type or mix several kinds of root vegetables.

4 SERVINGS
6 Jerusalem artichokes
4 potatoes
1 parsnip
2 onions
2 tbsp olive oil (30 ml)
1 pressed garlic clove
salt flakes and pepper
Oven temperature: 437°F

■ Scrub potatoes and Jerusalem artichokes, but leave the peel. Peel parsnip and onion. Cut the potatoes into quite big wedges, split the Jerusalem artichokes in halves, and cut the parsnip in smaller pieces. Cut the onion in coarse pieces.
■ Mix root vegetables and onion with oil and garlic. Place in a greased baking dish and sprinkle with salt and pepper. Bake in the middle of the oven for 20–25 minutes. Stir a few times.

Roasted Vegetables with Beetroots *Vegan*

Follow the recipe above but replace potatoes with beetroots.

Roasted Potato Wedges *Vegan*

Potato wedges will turn out the most crispy and tasty if you leave the peel and add salt after they have been in the oven for a while, since salt absorbs the liquid in potatoes.

4 SERVINGS
10–12 potatoes
2 tbsp olive oil (30 ml)
2 garlic cloves
salt and pepper
Oven temperature: 437°F

■ Scrub the potatoes and cut in even wedges. Mix with oil and garlic. Place the potatoes in a greased baking pan. Place the pan in the middle of the oven and bake for about 10 minutes. Bring out the pan, stir, and add salt and pepper. Then leave the potatoes in the oven for about 10 minutes or until the wedges have a nice color.

Baked Potatoes

Scrub big potatoes. They will turn out the best if you leave the peel on. Place the potato in a greased pan and make acute lengthwise on each potato. Bake in the middle of the oven at 392°F for 40–50 minutes.

Serve with salad, Caviar Sauce, p. 172, and garnish with a finely chopped red onion, dill, and a lemon slice.

Oven Baked Beetroots

Place brushed small beetroots with peel on a bed of salt in a baking pan and bake for 40–50 minutes at 392°F. (The salt can be used again.)

Braised Black Salsify *Vegan*

A simple and tasty way to prepare root vegetables. Black salsify can be replaced with sweet potatoes, kohlrabi, turnips, or other root vegetables.

4 SERVINGS
2–3 black salsify
1–2 tbsp olive or canola oil (15–30 ml)
¼ cup water (50 ml)
salt flakes

■ Peel the roots and cut them in long pieces. Bring water and oil to a boil. Place the root vegetables in the water and let them simmer on low heat for 10 minutes or until they are soft enough but a little chewy. Sprinkle with salt flakes.

Potato Cake *Lacto*

4 SERVINGS
10 potatoes
1 onion
½ cup grated cheese, preferably Västerbotten cheese (50 g)
⅓ cup coarsely chopped, flat-leaf parsley (50 g)
2 tbsp oil, butter, or margarine (30 g)
salt and pepper
Oven temperature: 392°F

■ Peel and slice the potatoes and onion thinly. Make layers of potatoes, onion, cheese, and parsley in a greased baking pan. Add salt and pepper and drizzle with oil. Bake in the middle of the oven for 20–25 minutes.

▶ ROASTED Root Vegetables

Algae-Jansson *Vegan*

4 SERVINGS

about 0.35 oz dulse seaweed (red seaweed) or
   wakame seaweed (10 g)
½ cup water (100 ml)
2–3 yellow onions
1 tbsp olive oil (15 ml)
1 tbsp vinegar (15 ml)
1 tbsp tomato purée (15 g)
1 tbsp dark syrup (15 ml)
½ tsp cinnamon (1 g)
1 pinch ground allspice (1 ml)
1 pinch ground cloves (1 ml)
1 pinch ground ginger (1 ml)
½–1 vegetable stock cube
salt
10–12 potatoes
1¼–1⅔ cup soy or oat milk (300–400 ml)
sesame seeds
1 tbsp coconut oil (15 ml)
Oven temperature: 392°F

■ Break the seaweed into smaller pieces. Let
the seaweed soak in the water for about
10 minutes. (0.35 oz seaweed turns into about
⅔ cup chopped, soaked seaweed.) Drain the
seaweed and then chop it.
■ Peel and chop the onion. Fry it on low heat
in the oil until soft. Stir algae, vinegar, tomato
purée, syrup, and spices into the onion fry. Add
stock and salt to taste.
■ Peel and thinly slice the potatoes. Make layers of potatoes and onion-fry with potatoes on
top in a greased baking pan. Pour the milk over.
Sprinkle with sesame seeds and add spoonfuls
of the coconut oil. Bake in the middle of the
oven for about 50 minutes.

Root Vegetable Mix with Tofu

Vegan

4 SERVINGS

1 package tofu
2 onions
2 garlic cloves
4 potatoes
1 carrot
1 piece rutabaga
1 piece celeriac
1 parsnip

2–3 tbsp coconut fat (30–45 ml)
salt and white pepper
chopped parsley

To serve with:
Beetroot Salsa with Fermented Beetroots, p. 172,
Grated Horseradish.

■ Cut the tofu in cubes. Peel and chop onion
and garlic. Peel and cut the root vegetables in
small cubes.
■ Fry tofu, onion, and root vegetables in the
fat on low heat while stirring, until they are
soft. Add salt and pepper to taste. Serve with
Beetroot Salsa with Fermented Beetroots as well
as Grated Horseradish.

Root Vegetable Mix with Chanterelles
Follow the recipe above but replace the
tofu with parboiled chanterelles that is fried
together with the onion.

Pink Root Vegetable Mix
Follow the recipe above but replace half of the
root vegetables with beetroots.

Root Vegetable Mix with Halloumi
Lacto
Follow the basic recipe above but replace tofu
with halloumi cheese cut in cubes, which is
fried separately until tcrispy and then mixed
with the fried root vegetables.

Hash Browns *Lacto or Vegan*

4 SERVINGS

10 potatoes
1 tsp salt (3 g)
butter or coconut oil

■ Peel and grate the potatoes coarsely. Add salt.
Heat the fat in a frying pan and portion out
in small piles into the frying pan. Fry the hash
browns a few minutes on each side until crispy.
■ Serve them right away with Raw Lingonberries, p. 199, and fried mushroom, or as an
appetizer with a spoon of yogurt as well as
algae caviar and finely chopped red onion.

▶ ROOT VEGETABLE MIX with Halloumi

Potato Gratin *Lacto or Vegan*

If you do not want to use cheese, you can sprinkle with sesame seeds and add a few small spoons of coconut oil over the gratin instead of cheese.

4 SERVINGS
10–12 potatoes
1 leek
1¼ cup soy or oat milk (300 ml)
¾ cup soy or oat cream (200 ml)
2 pressed garlic cloves
1½ tsp salt (4 g)
1 pinch white pepper (1 ml)
1–2 cups grated cheese, preferably Västerbotten cheese (100–200 g)
Oven temperature: 392°F

■ Peel and slice the potatoes. Rinse, clean, and finely slice the leek. Bring milk and cream to a boil together with garlic, salt, and pepper. Add the potatoes and let them boil for about 10 minutes or until the potatoes are just soft.
■ Add the leek to the potatoes and place the mixture in a greased baking pan. Sprinkle with cheese. Put in the middle of the oven for about 20–25 minutes.

Potato and Jerusalem Artichoke Gratin
Follow the recipe above but replace half of the potatoes with Jerusalem artichokes.

Potato and Parsnip Gratin
Follow the basic recipe above but replace half of the potatoes with Jerusalem artichokes.

Beetroot Hash Browns *Lacto-Ovo*

4 SERVINGS
4–5 beetroots (17.6 oz/500 g)
½ yellow onion
2 eggs
1 tbsp corn starch (20 g)
½ tsp salt (1 g)
1 pinch white pepper (1 ml)
butter or coconut oil

■ Peel and grate beetroots and onion coarsely. Mix with eggs, cornstarch, salt, and pepper. Fry the hash browns in butter or coconut oil for a couple of minutes on each side. Serve with Greek yogurt which has been seasoned with finely grated horseradish and herb salt.

Beetroot Hash Browns with Halloumi
*PHOTO P. 252
Follow the basic recipe above but add half a package of very finely chopped halloumi as well as 2–3 tbsp capers.

Mashed Root Vegetables *Vegan*

4 SERVINGS
1 large rutabaga (about 2.2 pounds/1 kg)
5–6 potatoes
1 carrot
1¼ cup vegetable stock (300 ml)
3 allspice corns
1 tbsp oil (15 ml)
salt and white pepper
finely chopped parsley

■ Peel and slice rutabaga, potatoes, and carrot. Bring stock to a boil with allspice corns and let the root vegetables cook for about 20 minutes or until soft.
■ Remove the allspice corns and strain the stock. Then mash the root vegetables with a masher and dilute with the stock. Stir oil into the mash and add salt and pepper to taste. Sprinkle with parsley.

Tips for all root vegetable lovers!
The easiest and fastest way to scrub a potato is to roll all potatoes at the same time under running water in the sink. After that you can cut off eventual damages.

The beetroots turn out best if you cook the with the peel and root left. Cut off the stem an inch above the actual beetroot. Steam or boil in salted water until they are soft. Place in the sink and rinse with cold water. Cut off the stem and then rub off peel and root with the hands. Use plastic gloves to avoid getting the color red on your hands.

Mashed Potatoes *Lacto or Vegan*

Mashed potatoes will be extra tasty with finely chopped parsley, pressed garlic, and/or grated Parmesan cheese.

4 SERVINGS
8–10 potatoes of a starchy kind, preferably almond potatoes
¼-½ cup hot milk (50–100 ml)
2 tbsp butter or oil (30 ml)
salt and white pepper

■ Peel and cut the potatoes in cubes. Boil in water until soft. Pour off the water and mash the potatoes with a masher. Dilute with some hot milk, a little at a time, and work until the mash is fluffy. Add butter or oil as well as salt and pepper to taste. Serve with Kidney Burger, p. 268.

Green Mashed Potatoes
Follow the recipe above but mix 1⅓ cup coarsely chopped parsley with the hot milk.

Mashed Celeriac
Follow the recipe above but replace half of the potatoes with celeriac.

Mashed Sweet Potatoes
Follow the recipe above but replace regular potatoes with sweet potatoes.

Swedish Potato Dumplings *Vegan*

Make a large batch and fry leftover chopped potato dumplings a few days later. Tasty and the GI level is considerably lower.

4 SERVINGS
10–12 potatoes
2 ¾ cup sifted spelt flour (300 g)
salt and pepper

Filling:
3 onions
1 tbsp olive oil (15 ml)
2 tbsp chopped parsley (20 g)
½–1 tsp ground allspice (1–3 g)
salt and pepper

Serve with:
Green Herb Oil, p. 181, Raw Lingonberries, p. 199, Garlic Fried Oyster Mushroom with Soy

Tasty Leftovers!
Leftovers from cooked root vegetables are good to keep in the house, when you want to throw a tasty meal together. The starch in cooked root vegetables is transformed when they are kept in the refrigerator for half a day and that makes the GI value low.

Leftover mix: Start by frying chopped onion and garlic in oil. Then add chopped root vegetables, like, for example, potatoes, chopped fennel, and bell pepper as well as soy sausage. Season with paprika powder, salt, and white pepper. Other tasty things for the mix is mushrooms, spinach leaves, cauliflower, haricots verts, and tomato as well as tofu or halloumi.

■ Boil the potatoes and peel them. Press the potatoes with a potato ricer and let the mash cool off.

■ Peel and chop the onion for the filling. Fry it in the oil until soft. Stir parsley into the pan. Add allspice, salt, and pepper to taste.

■ Mix the potato purée with the flour. Add salt and pepper to taste. Form the dough into a thick roll on a floured cutting board. Cut the roll in 10–12 even pieces. Make a little hole in each piece and place some of the filling in it. Form into round buns so that the filling is covered. Flatten the potato dumplings somewhat.

■ Bring a couple of quarts of water with 2 tsp salt to a boil in a large pot. Place a few potato dumplings at a time in the pot. Let them simmer for about 5 minutes after they have risen to the surface.

■ Serve the potato dumplings with Green Herb Oil, Lingonberry Jam, and Garlic Fried Oyster Mushroom with Soy.

Potato Dumplings with Halloumi *Lacto*
Follow the recipe above but add ½–1 package chopped halloumi, which is fried separately and then mixed with the fried onion.

Stir-Fry, Grill, Fry, and Deep-Fry

Stir-fry is an unbeatable way of cooking vegetables. It is quick, looks delicious, and the vegetables turn out crispy and tasty. That most nutrients are kept during the gentle preparation makes it even better. Vegetable patties, fried or grilled, can be that "little extra thing" that lifts a meal.

STIR-FRY

Stir-Fry Vegetables with Sweet and Sour Sauce *Vegan*

The Asian way of making stir-fry vegetables is great. It is quick, looks delicious, and the vegetables turn out crispy and tasty. Most of the nutrients are kept during the gentle preparation.

Do not mix too many vegetables at the same time in the stir-fry. Only red onion, pointed cabbage, carrot, sugar peas or haricots verts, and tomatoes will turn out delicious in both color and taste. If you would like a more simple version of sauce, you can use chili sauce mixed with sesame oil.

PER SERVING
3⅓–4 cups vegetable pieces (500–600 g):
one kind of onion: yellow, red, leek, or scallion
one kind of cabbage: broccoli, white, pointed,
   cauliflower, Chinese, or fennel
something orange/red: carrot or orange
   bell pepper
another tasty vegetable: zucchini, sugar peas,
   haricots verts, spinach leaves, mushrooms
   (preferably shiitake), green asparagus, miniature
   corn, bell peppers, bean sprouts, or pea shoots.
½–1 chopped tomato
½ tbsp coconut oil (7.5 ml)

Sauce:
1 tbsp mango chutney (15 ml)
½ tbsp coconut oil (7.5 ml)
½–1 tsp shoyu or soy sauce (2.5–5 ml)
½ pressed garlic clove
½ tsp sesame oil (2.5 ml)
½–1 tsp grated ginger (1–3 g)
1 pinch ground coriander (1 ml)

■ Mix all the ingredients to the sauce. Cut the onions in wedges and the vegetables in pieces. Heat the wok pan and add coconut oil as well as all the vegetables except for the tomato. Fry the vegetables quickly while stirring until they are soft but still crispy.

■ Turn off the heat and stir chopped tomato as well as sauce into the pan and quickly heat up. Serve right away with cooked quinoa, oats, bulgur, rice, couscous, or noodles.

How to Stir-Fry:
The secret with stir-fry is to prepare sauce and all ingredients to the sauce as well as all the vegetables beforehand to make the frying time as short as possible. Cut yellow or red bell pepper in wedges and other vegetables in coarse pieces. Use coconut oil (not virgin) since coconut is the fat that can handle the most heat.

Stir-Fry Vegetables with Roasted Cashew Nuts

Follow the basic recipe above. Sprinkle with roasted cashew nuts when the vegetables are done.

Stir-Fry Vegetables with Tofu

Follow the basic recipe above but first fry the tofu cubes in coconut oil. Place the cubes in a bowl and continue to stir-fry the vegetables in the pan according to the above basic recipe. Add the tofu at the very end.

Stir-Fry Vegetables with Halloumi
Lacto

First fry halloumi cut into cubes in some butter or coconut fat until it turns crispy. Then place the cheese cubes in a bowl and continue to stir-fry the vegetables according to the recipe above. Add the cheese at the very end.

Stir-Fry Vegetables with Eggs
Lacto-Ovo

Start by beating one or two eggs that are fried on both sides. Cut the eggs in strips. Stir-fry the vegetables according to the basic recipe above and add the egg strips at the end.

▶ STIR-FRY VEGETABLES WITH HALLOUMI and Sweet and Sour Sauce

▲ STIR-FRY VEGETABLES WITH HALLOUMI and Sweet and Sour Sauce

Stir-Fry Vegetables with Coconut Sauce *Vegan*

Boil noodles or couscous in water, salt, as well as a pinch of saffron and serve with the stir-fry vegetables. The combination of sweet and sour sauce, coconut, and saffron is delicious!

4 SERVINGS

1–2 carrots
½–1 broccoli
½–1 zucchini
1 red bell pepper
1 bunch scallions
2 garlic cloves
1 tbsp coconut oil (15 ml)

Sauce:

1 lemongrass stem
3 tbsp chili sauce (45 ml)
2–3 tsp shoyu or soy (10–15 ml)
¾ cup coconut milk (200 ml)

■ Peel and cut the carrots in sticks. Cut the broccoli in small florets. Slice the zucchini. Clean and cut bell pepper and scallions in pieces. Peel and slice garlic. Clean and thinly slice the soft inner parts of the lemongrass stem. Mix the ingredients for the sauce.

■ Heat a wok pan. Stir oil, carrots, broccoli, bell pepper, and onion into the pan. Quickly fry while stirring. Add the sauce.

■ Serve with noodles, quinoa, couscous, or bulgur.

Cabbage Stir-Fry *Vegan or Lacto*

4 SERVINGS

2 tomatoes
1⅓ cup small broccoli florets (200 g)
1 red onion
2 garlic cloves
1 can black beans
1 tsp whole cumin (3 g)
2 tbsp coconut oil (30 ml)
2⅔ cups strips red or white cabbage (400g)
10.6 oz soy or Quorn mincemeat (300 g)

Sauce:

1–2 tbsp soy sauce (15–30 ml)
2–3 tsp grated ginger (6–9 g)
2–3 tbsp chili sauce (30–45 ml)

■ Cut the vegetables in pieces. Peel and chop onion, garlic, and ginger. Rinse the beans and drain.

■ Fry onion, garlic, and cumin on low heat in the oil. Add cabbage and continue to fry while stirring. Add mincemeat, broccoli, and tomatoes and continue to fry while stirring. Add the beans as well as soy, ginger, and chili sauce to taste.

Noodle Stir-Fry with Seaweed *Vegan*

4 SERVINGS

⅓–⅔ cup arame seaweed (50–100 g)
½ cup water (100 ml)
1–2 carrots
1 broccoli
1 bunch scallions
2–3 garlic cloves
3–4 tbsp sesame seeds, preferably black (30–40 g)
2 tbsp coconut oil (30 ml)
7 oz cooked buckwheat noodles (200 g)

Sauce:

3 tbsp chili sauce (45 ml)
2–3 tsp soy or shoyu (10–15 ml)
2–3 tsp grated ginger (6–9 g)
2–3 tsp sesame oil (10–15 ml)

■ Soak the seaweed in the water for a while. Peel and cut the carrots in sticks. Cut the broccoli in small florets. Thinly slice the scallions and garlic.

■ Heat a wok pan and roast the sesame seeds while stirring. Place them in a bowl. Place oil, carrots, broccoli, scallions, and garlic in the wok pan. Fry quickly while stirring. Add noodles, sesame seeds, and seaweed without the water for soaking. Add chili sauce, soy, ginger, and sesame oil to taste.

GRILL

Grilled Vegetable Skewers *Vegan*

Grilled vegetable skewers are always appreciated and can be varied in many ways—only vegetables or combined with pieces of halloumi, mozzarella, tofu, or vegetarian sausage.

4–6 SERVINGS

2 bell peppers
8–12 portobello mushrooms
1 zucchini
½–1 sliced aubergine
4–6 green fresh asparagus stems
2–3 red onions in coarse pieces

Marinade:

½ cup coconut or olive oil (100 ml)
2–3 tbsp mango chutney (30–45 ml)
½–1 tbsp soy (7.5–15 ml)
1 pressed garlic clove
½–1 tsp sambal oelek (2.5–5 ml)

■ Clean and cut all vegetables in pieces. Cut the onion in coarse wedges and parboil them for a few minutes in lightly salted water. Mix the marinade in a large bowl and marinate the vegetables for about half an hour before draining them.

■ Place the vegetables on soaked wood skewers and grill them in a grill pan, the oven, or on the barbecue grill. Turn them occasionally.

Grilled Mozzarella Skewers *Lacto*

Place baby mozzarella on soaked wooden skewers and brush with oil. Sprinkle with salt flakes and pepper. Grill the skewers for about a ½ minute. Continuously flip the skewers.

▲ GRILLED Marinated Quorn Fillets and Zucchini

Grilled Marinated Quorn Fillets and Zucchini *Lacto*

4 SERVINGS
¾ cup water (200 ml)
1 pinch salt (1 ml)
1 package Quorn fillets
1 zucchini

Marinade:

¼ cup mango chutney (50 ml)
½ cup olive or canola oil (100 ml)
1–2 tbsp shoyu or soy (15–30 ml)
2 pressed garlic cloves
1–2 tsp grated ginger (3–6 g)
½–1 tsp sambal oelek (2.5–5 ml)
½ pinch ground coriander (0.5 ml)

■ Bring water and salt to a boil. Place the Quorn fillets in the pot and quickly boil until they defrost. Slice the zucchini in thin slices. Mix the marinade and place it in a large plastic bag together with Quorn and zucchini. Make sure the marinade covers everything. Let sit in the refrigerator for an hour.

■ Grill the Quorn fillets and the zucchini in a hot grill pan or on the grill. Serve with cooked couscous, quinoa, or Bulgur with Caviar Sauce, p. 172, or Mint Yogurt, p. 170, as well as a tomato and onion salad.

266

Grilled Marinated Mushroom Skewers *Vegan*

4 SERVINGS *PHOTO P. 146

28 oz large portobello mushroom or sheep polypore (800 g)

Marinade:

½ cup coconut or olive oil (100 ml)
3 tbsp mango chutney (45 ml)
½–1 tbsp grated ginger (1–3 g)
2 tsp sesame oil (10 ml)
sesame seeds, preferably black

■ Clean and cut off the stem of the mushrooms. Cut the mushrooms in about 1-inch-thick strips.
■ Parboil the mushrooms in salted water for a few minutes. Mix the marinade and marinate the mushrooms for about half an hour.
■ Place the mushrooms strips on the skewers so that they are a little bit folded. Grill the skewers in a grill pan or on the barbecue grill. Turn them occasionally. Sprinkle with sesame seeds.

Grilled Halloumi *Lacto*

Simple and amazingly tasty! Perfect for a salad.

4 SERVINGS

2 packages of halloumi
black pepper

■ Split the halloumi lengthwise and sprinkle with some black pepper. Grill in a grill pan or on the barbecue grill. Turn the cheese occasionally and make sure the heat is not too strong, since the cheese should become soft all the way through.

Grilled Fresh Vegetables Vegan

Fresh vegetables like green asparagus and carrot are brushed with olive oil and grilled right away.

Grilled Corncobs

Peel off the coarse leaves, but save a thin layer of leaves around the corncob. Grill the corncob for about 10–15 minutes, but turn it a few times.

Grilled Onion

Wrap peeled red onion or fresh garlic in a couple of layers of folio. Place the onion directly on the live coal. It needs to be barbecued for 20–25 minutes.

Grill Tips

Zucchini, bell pepper, aubergine, scallions, mushrooms, and fresh green asparagus are fine to grill as they are. Other vegetables and root vegetables should be parboiled in lightly salted water first.

• Wooden skewers should be soaked for at least half an hour before the grilling.
• Use an environmentally friendly electrical coal lighter. Fire starters or lighting paper made of stearic acid or lighting blocks of wood are climate-friendly alternatives to lighter fluid.
• Wait until the bed of coal is hot.
• If you place a few twigs of rosemary or salvia on the grill rack, it will let off a wonderful fragrance.

FRY

Mushroom Burger *Lacto or Vegan*

8 PIECES

1 cup whole grain bread crumbs (100 g)
¼ cup regular cream or soy cream (50 ml)
1 yellow onion
14 oz parboiled white button mushrooms (400 g)
1 tbsp coconut oil or butter (15 ml)
½–1 vegetable stock cube
1⅓ cup cooked and mashed cold potatoes (200 g)
2 tbsp buckwheat flour (15 g)
1 tsp basil (3 g)
whole grain bread crumbs
coconut oil or buyer for frying

■ Let the bread crumbs soak in the cream for about 5 minutes. Peel and finely chop the onion. Rinse and clean the mushrooms and slice them. Fry mushrooms and onion in the fat on low heat. Add the stock cube after a few minutes.
■ Mash the potatoes and mix with the bread crumbs, mushroom-fry, buckwheat flour and crumbled basil. Form round patties from the batter and roll them in bread crumbs. Fry on low heat.

Kidney Burgers *Lacto or Vegan*

12 PIECES *PHOTO P. 260

2 cans kidney beans (4 cups/600 g)
1⅓ cup cooked oats, spelt, or other grains (250 g)
½ cup sliced olives (75 g)
⅓ cup whole grain bread crumbs (50 g)
¼ cup cream or oat cream (50 ml)
3–4 tbsp tomato purée (45–60 g)
2–3 tsp broth (10–15 ml)
2 pressed garlic cloves
2 tsp basil (6 g)
1 tsp ground cumin (3 g)
1 tsp paprika powder (3 g)
½–1 tsp sambal oelek (2.5–5 ml)
1 tbsp potato starch (10 g)
salt and pepper
sesame seeds or bread crumbs
coconut oil for frying

■ Mix the beans coarsely in a food processor. Add cooked grains, olives, cream, and bread crumbs by hand. Add tomato purée, broth, garlic, basil, cumin, paprika powder, sambal oelek, salt, and pepper to taste. Add the potato starch at the end.

■ Form into patties and roll them in sesame seeds or bread crumbs. Fry in coconut oil.

Tip! Replace the kidney beans with chickpeas or other peas or beans.

How to fry:

The best temperature for frying is around 302°F. If the fat is hotter than 365°F, it will oxidize. When you fry in butter this will not be a problem since the butter changes color when it is time to lower the temperature.

Oils do not change color but start to smoke at 482°F. By then it is already too late and the oil is destroyed. Coconut oil and butter can stand higher temperatures than other oils.

Kidney Burgers with Jalapeño

Follow the recipe above but replace sambal oelek and olives with ⅓ cup chopped pickled jalapeño.

Sesame Breaded Chickpea Nuggets

Lacto-Ovo

28 PIECES

⅓ cups whole grain bread crumbs (50 g)
1 egg
2 can chickpeas (4 cups/600 g)
1 tsp sesame oil (5 ml)
1–2 tbsp lemon juice (15–30 ml)
2 pressed garlic cloves
2 tsp ground cumin (6 g)
½–1 tsp sambal oelek (2.5–5 ml)
1 coarsely grated carrot
1 tbsp potato starch (10 g)
salt and pepper
about 1 cup sesame seeds (200 g)
butter or coconut oil for frying

■ Let the bread crumbs soak in the whipped egg. Rinse the beans if they are from a can and drain. Mix the chickpeas coarsely with olive oil, sesame oil, lemon juice, garlic, cumin, and sambal oelek in a food processor. Add carrot and potato starch by hand. Add salt and pepper to taste.

■ Pour the sesame seeds over a plate. Make small piles of the batter and form into small balls that are flattened out into patties. Turn them in sesame seeds. Fry the patties in butter or coconut oil on low heat. Serve with Spinach Sauce, p. 175, and Ginger Carrots, p. 157.

Breaded Halloumi *Lacto*

4 SERVINGS

1 package halloumi cheese
½ cup sifted spelt flour (55 g)
1 whipped egg
⅔ cup whole grain bread crumbs (100 g)
coconut oil or butter for frying

■ Cut the cheese in thin slices. First turn the slices in the flour and then in the whipped egg. Finally dip the slices in bread crumbs and fry or deep-fry them in oil or butter. Serve with Mint Yogurt, p. 170, olives, and salad.

▲ SESAME BREADED CHICKPEA NUGGETS with Spinach Sauce and Ginger Carrots

Breaded Celeriac Patties *Vegan or Lacto*

4 SERVINGS
1 celeriac
1¼ cup coarse rye flour (150 g)
½–1 tsp paprika powder (1–3 g)
½–1 tsp herb salt (1–3 g)
coconut oil or butter for frying

■ Peel and cut the celery in about 0.4-inches-thick slices. Boil until just soft for 5–10 minutes.
■ Mix rye flour, paprika powder, and herb salt and turn the slices in the mixture. Fry the patties in coconut oil or butter on low heat. Beetroot Salsa, p. 172, goes well with the patties.

Tip! Extra tasty is to place a slice of cheese between two slices of celeriac and then bread it.

Breaded Beetroots Patties

Replace celeriac with beetroots. Serve with Creamed Parsley Cabbage or Creamed Parsley Wax Beans, p. 197.

Breaded Aubergine

Cut the aubergine in 0.2-inches-thick slices. Layer the slices with salt in a colander and let sit for half an hour. Rinse and dry them. Bread, fry, or grill according to the instructions above.

Breaded Zucchini

Cut the zucchini in 0.2-inches-thick slices. Layer the slices with salt in a colander and let sit for half an hour. Rinse and dry them. The slices can either be fried or grilled the way they are or breaded according to recipes above.

Potato Patties *Lacto-Ovo*

4 SERVINGS
10–12 potatoes
⅔ cup finely chopped dill or parsley (100 g)
2 eggs
1–2 tbsp oil (15–10 ml)
⅔ cup bread crumbs (100 g)
coconut oil or butter for frying

■ Boil and peel the potatoes. Press or mash the potatoes and mix with other ingredients.
■ Mix mashed potatoes, herbs, eggs, oil, and salt. Form into patties and turn in bread crumbs. Fry them on low heat in coconut oil or butter. Serve with Bean Salsa, p. 162.

Zucchini Pancakes with Feta

Lacto-Ovo

4 SERVINGS
1 quart coarsely grated zucchini (1 liter)
2–3 scallions
1 ¾ cup sifted spelt flour (190 g)
1 tsp baking powder (3 g)
2 tbsp chopped mint (20 g)
1 tsp paprika powder (3 g)
½ tsp salt (1 g)
2 pinches black pepper (2 ml)
1 package feta cheese (6.3 oz/180 g)
2 eggs
butter or coconut oil for frying

■ Chop the scallions finely. Place in a bowl with flour, baking powder, mint, paprika powder, salt, and pepper. Crumble feta cheese over. Stir the eggs and zucchini into the mixture. The batter will turn juicy when mixing it.

■ Place a full tablespoon of the batter in a warm frying pan with butter. Flatten the batter a little and fry a couple of minutes on each side until the pancakes turn golden brown. Serve with pomegranate seeds or lingonberries, tzatziki, and salad.

Corn Pancakes with Feta

Follow the recipe above but replace the grated zucchini with whole corn kernels.

DEEP-FRY

Deep-Fried Vegetables *Lacto-Ovo*

Thin slices of different vegetables, like onion, whole garlic, carrot, mushroom, bell pepper, small broccoli or cauliflower florets, zucchini, aubergine, pumpkin, potatoes, and split and seeded chili fruit, are tasty to deep-fry.

4–6 SERVINGS
about 1 quart vegetables (1 liter)
about 1 cup sifted spelt flour (110 g)
coconut oil for frying

Fry-Batter:

2 cups whole grain spelt flour (220 g)
1 cup ice-cold mineral water or water (250 ml)
1 egg yolk

◄ ZUCCHINI PANCAKES WITH FETA and Pomegranate Seeds

> **How to Deep-Fry:**
> Vegetables, falafel, and vegetarian patties are tasty to deep-fry. Heat coconut oil (not virgin) to 338–356°F. Measure the temperature with a household thermometer. Be careful when deep-frying and turn off the hood fan. Always keep a lid nearby to smother eventual burning oil since it cannot be extinguished with water.

Dip Sauce:

¼ cup shoyu or soy (50 ml)
¼ cup mirin, rice wine (50 ml)
1–2 tsp finely grated ginger (1–3 g)
1–2 pinches chili flakes (1–2 ml)
2 tbsp sesame seeds (20 g)

■ First roll the vegetables in the flour. Mix the ingredients for the fry-batter.

■ Heat the oil. Dip the vegetables in the fry-batter and fry them until golden. Let them drain on kitchen towels. Serve with dip sauce.

Falafel *Vegan*

Make a large batch and store in the freezer.

5–6 SERVINGS
2 cups chickpeas (300 g)
2 yellow onions
½ tube vegetable herb pâté, like Tartex
1 vegetable stock cube
3–4 pressed garlic cloves
½–1 tsp sambal oelek (2.5–5 ml)
⅔ cup finely chopped parsley (100 g)
coconut oil for frying

■ Soak the chickpeas for about 10 hours. Pour away the water.

■ Peel and chop the onion. Mix onion and chickpeas in a food processor. Add remaining ingredients and continue to mix until the batter is smooth.

■ Heat the oil and form balls with wet hands and fry the balls until golden brown.

Desserts
and Pastries

The most simple dessert is fresh fruit and berries. Ripe and at room temperature, they are the very best.

But there are so many other fresh, tasty, and exciting things to try, like avocado panna cotta, chocolate mousse with mint, and pear Carpaccio with walnuts, as well as delicious raw food tortes.

Pear Carpaccio with Mint and Walnuts *Raw*

A decorative dessert that is easy to make! Serve with ice cream, Almond Cream, p. 116, or Cashew Cream, p. 117. Walnuts can be replaced with almonds or hazelnuts.

3–4 SERVINGS
3–4 pears
1–2 tbsp lemon or lime juice (15–30 ml)
1–2 tbsp honey (15–30 ml)
1–2 tsp lemon or lime zest (3–6 g)
⅓ cup small mint leaves (50 g)
⅓ cup chopped walnuts (50 g)

- Make very thin slices of the pears. Place the slices on a large dish. Mix the lemon or lime juice with honey and spread over the pear slices. Sprinkle with lemon or lime peel, mint, and walnuts.

Pear Carpaccio with Walnuts and Chocolate
Follow the recipe above but also sprinkle with raw dark chocolate.

Mango Carpaccio with Walnuts
Follow the recipe above but replace pears with mango.

Fruit Salad with Coconut Cream
Lacto or Vegan

4 SERVINGS
1 mango
1 papaya
½ pineapple
1 banana

Coconut Cream
1⅔ cup very finely chopped pineapple (250 g)
1⅔ cup coconut flakes (150 g)
1 can quark or soy cream cheese
½ tsp vanilla sugar (1 g)
2 tbsp honey (30 ml)

- Peel and cut all the fruit in small pieces. Mix the fruit and let stand for an hour until it creates juice.
- Mix pineapple, coconut, quark, or cream cheese as well as vanilla for the coconut cream. Add vanilla and honey to taste. Place the fruit salad in glasses and garnish with coconut cream.

Fruit Salad with Raspberries *Raw*

A fruit salad can be varied in so many ways and is always tasty. Vary with peaches, nectarines, and melon. The most important thing is that the fruit be ripe enough.

Serve the fruit salad with ice cream or Almond Cream, p. 116, or Cashew Cream, p. 117.

4 SERVINGS
1–2 bananas
2 oranges
2 pears
1⅓ cup sweet seeded grapes (200 g)
1⅓ cup raspberries (200 g)

Dressing:
¼ cup squeezed orange juice (50 ml)
1 tbsp honey (15 ml)

- Peel the fruit and cut in small pieces.
- Mix orange juice and honey. Mix with the fruit. Raspberries are added just before serving.

Fruit Salad with Mint
Follow the above recipe but add a few tablespoons finely chopped mint.

Fruit Salad with Lemon Balm
Follow the basic recipe above but add a few tablespoons of finely chopped lemon balm.

▶ FRUIT SALAD with coconut cream

▲ AVOCADO PANNA COTTA

Citrus Fruit Salad with Avocado and Pomegranate *Raw*

Pomegranate seeds can be replaced with chopped mint or lemon balm leaves.

3–4 SERVINGS
2 blood grapefruit
2 oranges
1 avocado
½ pomegranate

Marinade:
½ orange (juice)
1–2 tbsp honey or agave syrup (15–30 ml)

■ Peel off the white of the blood grapefruit and oranges. Then cut skin-free wedges. Peel and cut the avocado in pieces. Squeeze the pomegranate to soften the fruit. Then bang on top of it with a wooden spoon in order to make the seeds fall out.

■ Mix orange and blood grapefruit wedges with avocado and marinade. Sprinkle with pomegranate seeds.

Avocado Panna Cotta *Raw*

3–4 SERVINGS
⅔ cup cashew nuts (100 g)
1 large ripe avocado (7 oz/200 g)
1 lemon or lime
2–3 tbsp honey (30–45 ml)
2–3 tbsp water (30–45 ml)
½ tsp vanilla (1 g)

Garnish:
Peruvian cherry
strawberries
seeded blue grapes

■ First mix the cashew nuts very finely. Split the avocado and scoop out the fruit meat. Grate the zest of a lemon or lime and save. Add avocado, honey and water, vanilla, as well as a few drops of lemon or lime juice and continue to mix until the cream is smooth.

■ Place the cream in glasses and garnish with fruit and berries as well as lemon or lime zest.

Strawberry Ice Cream with Coconut *Raw*

A delicious soft ice cream that can be eaten directly or stand in the freezer a couple of hours before serving. If the ice cream is left for too long in the freezer without stirring, it will end up being hard as a rock.

The ice cream can also be made in an ice cream machine. Strawberries can also be replaced with other berries like raspberries, buckthorn, blueberries, or black currants.

2–3 SERVINGS
14–17.5 oz frozen strawberries (400–500 g)
¾ cup coconut milk (200 ml)
1–2 tbsp honey (15–30 ml)
½–1 tsp grated ginger (1–3 g)
½ lemon, peel and juice

■ Mix the frozen strawberries with coconut milk, honey, ginger, and lemon peel in a food processor. Add lemon juice to taste.

Mango Ice Cream with Coconut and Lime

Follow the recipe above but replace strawberries with frozen mango pieces as well as lemon with lime fruit.

Raspberry Sorbet *Raw*

A refreshing sorbet! Raspberries can be replaced with other frozen berries like black currants, strawberries, blueberries, or red currants.

4 SERVINGS
7.9 oz frozen raspberries (225 g)
1 banana
1 tbsp honey (15 ml)
½ tsp vanilla (1 g)
1 tbsp lemon juice (15 ml)
2 tbsp water (30 ml)

■ Mix berries, banana, honey, vanilla, lemon juice, and water. The sorbet can be eaten directly or sit a couple of hours in the freezer before serving. If the sorbet is left for too long in the freezer, it will end up being hard as a rock.

Lingonberry Sorbet with Cinnamon

Follow the recipe above but replace raspberries with lingonberries and season the sorbet with cinnamon.

Chocolate Mousse *Raw*

2 SERVINGS
4 pitted fresh dates
2 tbsp cacao, preferably raw (20 g)
1 tbsp coconut oil, virgin (15 ml)
¼ cup water (50 ml)
1 avocado
1 pinch salt (1 ml)
1–2 tbsp honey (15–30 ml)
1 pinch chili powder (1 ml)

■ First mix dates, cacao, coconut oil, and water. Add avocado as well as honey and chili to taste. Serve with fruit and berries as well as Cashew Cream, p. 117.

Mint Chocolate Mousse

Follow the recipe above but add finely chopped mint leaves.

Chocolate Mousse with Orange

Follow the recipe above but season the mousse with finely grated orange zest.

Hot Bananas *Vegan*

4 SERVINGS
4–6 bananas
1 orange
½–1 tsp finely chopped chili fruit (1–3 g)
1 tbsp lemon zest (20 g)
½–1 tsp grated ginger (2.5–5 ml)
⅓ cup chopped nuts (50 g)
1–2 tbsp maple syrup or agave syrup (15–30 ml)
1 tbsp coconut oil, virgin (15 ml)
Oven temperature: 347°F

■ Peel the bananas and split them lengthwise. Place them in a greased baking pan.
■ Squeeze the orange and add chili, lemon zest, and ginger. Pour the orange juice over the bananas and sprinkle with chopped nuts. Drizzle with maple syrup and place small piles of coconut oil over the bananas. Bake in the oven for about 15 minutes. Scoop up and pour the juice over the bananas a few times during the baking. Serve with ice cream.

Apple Stir-Fry with Cinnamon

Lacto or Vegan

4 SERVINGS

½ cup yogurt (100 ml)
1 tsp vanilla sugar (3 g)
⅔ cup walnuts (100 g)
2–3 apples
2 tbsp butter or coconut oil (30 ml)
1 tsp cinnamon (3 g)
½ tsp grated ginger (1 g)
⅓ cup raisins (50 g)
juice from 1 sweet orange

■ Mix yogurt and vanilla sugar.

■ Chop the walnuts coarsely and roast on low heat while stirring. Core and slice the unpeeled apples. Stir-fry the apple pieces in butter or coconut oil. Sprinkle with cinnamon and stir. Add ginger, raisins, walnuts, and orange juice. Place in glasses, garnish with yogurt, and sprinkle with cinnamon.

Raspberry and Blueberry Soup

Vegan

A delicacy in all its simplicity, with a flavor of Swedish summer. Raspberry and blueberry soup is also an appreciated drink in a thermos during a hike. The soup is tasty even without vanilla and star anise.

4 SERVINGS

3 cups water (700 ml)
2 tbsp apple juice concentrate (30 ml)
1 cinnamon stick
3–4 star anise
½ vanilla bean
17.6 oz raspberries and blueberries (500 g)
2 tbsp potato starch (15 g)
2 tbsp water (30 ml)
½ lemon
3–4 tbsp palm sugar (37–50 g)

Sides:
yogurt or vanilla ice cream
mint leaves
grated lemon zest

■ Bring water with apple juice, cinnamon, and star anise as well as a cut vanilla bean to a boil. Let simmer on low heat for about 15 minutes.

■ Add the berries but save a few for garnishing. Bring to a boil. Stir the potato starch into the water and add to the soup while beating. Quickly bring the soup to a boil and remove the pan from the stove when you see the first bubble.

■ Grate some zest from the lemon and squeeze the juice. Add sugar and lemon juice to taste. Serve the soup lukewarm or cold with a little yogurt or vanilla ice cream. Garnish with whole berries, mint, and lemon zest.

Melon Soup *Raw*

A simple and delicious dessert. Cantaloupe melons can be replaced with other melons. Serve the soup with ice cream, Almond Cream, p. 116, or Cashew Cream, p. 117.

4 SERVINGS

2 ripe refrigerator-cold cantaloupe melons
1 lemon
2–3 tbsp finely chopped lemon balm leaves (20–30 g)
½–1 tbsp honey (7.5–15 ml)

■ Peel and cut the melon in pieces. Grate the lemon zest. Mix melon pieces to a smooth soup. Dilute with some water if it is too thick. Add lemon zest and lemon balm and add lemon juice and honey to taste.

Honey Marinated Strawberries *Vegan or Raw*

4 SERVINGS

1 quart ripe strawberries (1 liter)
1 tbsp balsamic vinegar (15 ml)
3–4 tbsp honey (45–60 ml)

■ Clean and slice the strawberries. Carefully mix with vinegar and honey and carefully add the berries. Let stand for about 10 minutes. Serve with ice cream, softly whipped cream, Almond Cream, p. 116, or Cashew Cream, p. 117.

Honey Marinated Strawberries with Basil

Follow the recipe above and mix the strawberries with finely chopped basil.

◀ APPLE STIR-FRY with Cinnamon

▲ RASPBERRY and Blueberry Soup

Spelt Waffles *Lacto or Vegan*

10 WAFFLES
3.5 oz butter or coconut oil (100 g)
¾ cup soy or oat milk (200 ml)
1 cup water (250 ml)
3⅓ cup sifted spelt flour (365 g)
2 tsp baking powder (15 ml)

■ Melt butter and coconut oil and let cool off. Mix milk, water, sifted spelt, and baking powder to a smooth batter. Add the butter or coconut oil.

■ Heat the waffle iron and grease with butter or coconut oil the first time and add more if needed. Place the waffles in the oven if they are not going to be eaten freshly made. Serve with berries and cream, Almond Cream, p. 116, or Cashew Cream, p. 117.

Fruit Compote *Vegan*

A plate of old-fashioned fruit compote goes well with milk or a spoon of yogurt.

4 SERVINGS
2½ cup apple juice concentrate (600 ml)
1 cinnamon stick
½ tsp grated ginger (1 g)
5 star anise
5 dried figs
1 cup pitted plums (150 g)
⅔ cup dried apricot (100 g)
1 lemon (zest)
2½ tbsp potato starch (22.5 g)

■ Boil apple juice, cinnamon stick, and star anise for about 10 minutes. Clean and cut the figs in smaller pieces. Add figs, plums, apricots, and lemon zest and let boil for another 5 minutes.

■ Mix potato starch with an equal amount of water. Slowly add the potato starch to the mixture while stirring. Remove the pan from the stove when you see the first bubbles.

▲ FRUIT COMPOTE

Cottage Cheese Cake with Almond and Cardamom *Lacto-Ovo*

Serve the cottage cheese cake with Strawberry Sauce, see below, or with berries and whipped cream.

4 SERVINGS
½ cup sifted spelt flour (55 g)
1¼ cup soy or oat milk (300 ml)
17.6 oz cottage cheese (500 g)
3 eggs
2–3 tbsp palm sugar (25–37.5 g)
½ tsp cardamom (1 g)
⅓ cup chopped almonds (50 g)
Oven temperature: 392°F

■ Whip flour and milk until smooth. Add cottage cheese, eggs, sugar, cardamom, and almonds while whipping. Place the batter in a greased baking pan. Bake in the middle of the oven for about 25 minutes. Serve the cake lukewarm with fresh berries or Strawberry Sauce, see below.

Cottage Cake with Almonds and Saffron

Follow the basic recipe above but replace cardamom with 1 pinch (1 ml) saffron that first is crushed with some of the sugar.

Cottage Cheese Cake with Almond and Lemon

Follow the basic recipe above but replace cardamom with ½ tablespoon grated lemon zest.

Strawberry Sauce *Vegan*

Strawberries can be replaced with other berries like blueberries and raspberries.

4 SERVINGS
3⅓ cup strawberries (500 g)
½ cup water (100 ml)
½–1 tbsp honey (7.5–15 ml)
1–2 tsp lemon juice (5–10 ml)

■ Mix berries and water; season with honey and lemon.

▲ MANGO TORTE with Raspberries

PASTRIES

Mango Torte with Raspberries *Raw*

A delicious torte that is easy to make and has a wonderful flavor. It only contains healthy ingredients. Does it get any better than that?

8 SERVINGS

Torte cake:
⅔ chopped dates (100 g)
2 cups walnuts (300 g)
¼ cup water (50 ml)
2 cups coconut flakes (200 g)
1 tbsp honey (15 ml)
2 tsp cinnamon (6 g)
1 pinch of salt (1 ml)

Filling:
1 ripe mango
⅔ cup cashew nuts (100 g)
1 tbsp coconut oil, preferably virgin (15 ml)
1 tbsp honey (15 ml)

Garnish:
1 ripe mango
1⅓–2 cups raspberries (200–300 g)

■ First mix the dates. Add walnuts and continue to mix until the walnuts are fairly finely mixed. Add water, coconut flakes, honey, cinnamon, and salt. Only mix for another few seconds. The texture should still be crumbly. Place the mixture on a dish.

■ Peel mango fruit for both filling and garnish. Cut one in pieces and the other in fine wedges. Save the small pieces.

■ Mix the cashew nuts until they turn into a flour. Add all the mango pieces, coconut oil, and honey. Mix the filling until smooth. Spread the filling on the "torte cake" and garnish with mango wedges as well as raspberries.

Tip! Do not mix the torte cake for too long or the texture will end up too compact. However, the torte will be the most tasty if the cashew nuts for the filling are very finely mixed.

▲ CHOCOLATE TORTE

Strawberry Torte *PHOTO P. 272
Follow the above recipe but replace mango with strawberries and garnish the torte with strawberries, blueberries, currants, and/or blackberries.

Chocolate Torte *Lacto-Ovo*

I4 PIECES
5.3 oz dark chocolate, 70% (150 g)
3.5 oz butter (100 g)
3 eggs
I cup raw sugar (200 g)
I quart finely grated carrot (I liter, fluffy)
2 ¾ cup sifted spelt flour or regular flour (300 g)
I tsp baking powder (3 g)
I⅔ cup chopped dates (250 g)

Icing:
¼ cup cream (50 ml)
I tbsp butter (15 ml)
I–2 tbsp palm sugar (12.5–25 g)
3.5 oz dark unsweetened chocolate (100 g)
Oven temperature: 347°F

■ Melt the chocolate in the butter. Beat eggs and sugar until fluffy. Add the melted chocolate as well as carrots, a little at a time, and continue to beat.

■ Mix flour, baking powder, as well as dates and stir into the batter. Pour the batter in a greased and floured baking form, about 9.8 inches in diameter. Bake at the bottom of the oven for about 50 minutes. The cake should still be a little sticky in the middle. Let it cool off.

Icing:
■ Heat cream, butter, and sugar. Remove the pan from the stove. Add the chocolate and stir until it has melted. Spread the icing over the cake and place in a cool place until the icing has cooled off.

Apples Under Almond Cover

Lacto-Ovo

4–5 SERVINGS

4–5 large, tart apples
½ cup water (100 ml)
2–4 tbsp palm sugar (25–50 g)
1 tsp lemon juice (5 ml)
1 vanilla bean, scraped off seeds or ½ tsp vanilla (1 g)
1 tsp potato starch (3 g)
½ tbsp water (7.5 ml)

Almond Cover:

⅔ cup blanched almonds (100 g)
1 cup oats (100 g)
3.5 oz butter (100 g)
⅓ cup palm sugar (65 g)
1 egg

Oven temperature: 392°F

■ Cut unpeeled apples in wedges and remove the core. Cook the apple pieces with peel in water into a fairly loose sauce. Season with sugar, lemon juice, and vanilla. Mix the potato starch with water and stir the mixture into the sauce. Bring everything to a quick boil and set the pan aside. Spread the apple sauce in a greased baking form.

■ Mix almonds and oats in a food processor. Add butter and sugar. Continue to mix the batter and add the egg toward the end. Spread the batter over the apple sauce. Bake in the middle of the oven for 15–20 minutes.

Raspberry and Blueberry Pie *Raw*

6–8 SERVINGS

Pie crust:

2 cups almonds (300 g)
5⅓ cup chopped dates (800 g)
2–3 tbsp water (30–45 ml)
1 tbsp honey (15 ml)
1 tsp cinnamon (3 g)
1 tsp ginger (3 g)
1 pinch salt (1 ml)
⅔ cup walnuts (100 g)

Filling:

1–1½ quart fresh raspberries and blueberries (1–1½ liters)

■ First mix the almonds finely. Add dates and water and continue to mix. Add honey, cinnamon, ginger, cloves, as well as salt and continue to mix the dough. Chop the walnuts and add to the pie dough by hand. Spread the dough into a pie form. Fill the pie form with raspberries and blueberries. Serve with Almond Cream, p. 116, or Cashew Cream, p. 117.

Lingonberry Tosca Pie *Lacto or Vegan*

Lingonberries can be replaced with other berries like blueberries, raspberries, or red or black currants.

8 SERVINGS

1 quart lingonberries (1 liter)
⅓ cup raw sugar (65 g)
1 tbsp potato starch (15 g)

Tosca cover:

4.4 oz butter or coconut oil (125 g)
1 cup raw sugar (200 g)
¼ cup light syrup (50 ml)
2½ cup oats (300 g)
1⅓ cup sifted spelt flour (145 g)
½ tsp baking powder (1 g)
½ tsp cinnamon (1 g)

Oven temperature: 347°F

■ Mix lingonberries with sugar and potato starch and spread in a greased pie form.
■ Melt butter, sugar, and syrup in a sauce pan. Remove the pan from the heat and add oats. Let sit for five minutes.
■ Mix flour, baking powder, and cinnamon. Add the mixture to the batter. Spread the batter over the berries.
■ Bake in the middle of the oven for 20–25 minutes.

Rhubarb Tosca Pie

Follow the recipe above, but replace lingonberries with about 1 quart thinly sliced rhubarb.

▲ CHEESECAKE with Cherries

Cheesecake with Raspberries *Lacto*

10 SERVINGS

Pie crust:

15 Digestive crackers

1 tsp ground cinnamon (5 ml)

2.6 oz melted butter or margarine (75 ml)

Filling:

2 boxes Philadelphia cream cheese (7 oz/200 g each)

1 can quark (8.8 oz/250 g)

2–3 tbsp honey (30–45 ml)

1–2 tsp vanilla (3–6 g)

Icing:

¾-1¼ cup raspberry jam

■ Crush the crackers in a food processor. Mix with cinnamon and melted butter. Press the batter into a greased pie form and let sit in the refrigerator for half an hour.

■ Mix cream cheese and quark in a food processor. Add honey and vanilla to taste. Spread the filling in the pie crust. Let sit in the refrigerator for at least an hour.

■ Spread the jam on the pie and keep in the refrigerator.

Cheesecake with Cherries

Follow the recipe above but replace raspberry jam with cherry jam.

Apple Pie *Raw*

Lovely flavors meet in this wonderful apple pie. The flavor of the apples is enhanced and becomes something above the ordinary…

6–8 SERVINGS

Pie crust:

2 cups cashew nut pieces (300 g)
5⅓ cup chopped dates (800 g)
2–3 tbsp water (30–45 ml)
1 tbsp honey (15 ml)
1 tsp cinnamon (3 g)
1 tsp ginger (3 g)
1 pinch ground cloves (1 ml)
1 pinch salt (1 ml)
⅔ cups walnuts (100 g)

Filling:

3 apples
1 tbsp coconut oil, preferably virgin (15 ml)
½–1 tsp vanilla (1–3 g)
½–1 tbsp honey (2.5–5 ml)

Garnish:

3–4 apples
cinnamon

■ First mix cashew nuts into a fine powder. Save two tablespoons of the mixed cashew nuts. Add dates and continue to mix. Add honey, cinnamon, ginger, cloves, as well as salt and continue to mix the dough. Chop the walnuts and mix the pie dough by hand. Spread the dough out in a pie form.

■ Cut the apples in wedges for the filling and leave the peel on. Remove the core and cut the apples in pieces. Mix apple pieces, coconut oil, and vanilla. Season with honey. The apple sauce will be the most tasty if not too finely mixed. Stir the saved cashew nuts into the sauce. Spread the apple sauce over the pie dough.

■ Slice the apple pieces thinly. Leave the peel. Garnish the pie with the apple slices and sprinkle with cinnamon.

Pear Pie

Follow the recipe above but replace the apples with pears and ground cloves with cardamom. Also sprinkle cardamom over the finished pie instead of cinnamon.

Carrot Cake with Nuts *Lacto-Ovo*

A juicy and tasty cake. Hazelnuts can be replaced with walnuts or almonds.

8–10 SERVINGS

3⅓ cup finely grated carrots (measured with air, 500 g)
3.5 oz butter, canola, or coconut oil (100 g)
1 cup palm sugar (200 g)
2 eggs
1 ¾ cup sifted spelt flour (190 g)
2 tsp baking powder (6 g)
⅔ cup chopped hazelnuts (100 g)
1 tsp cinnamon (3 g)
½ tsp ginger (1 g)
½ tsp cardamom (1 g)

Icing:

4.4 oz Philadelphia cream cheese (125 g)
2 tbsp honey (30ml)
2–3 tsp lemon juice (10–15 ml)
½–1 tsp vanilla sugar (3–6 g)

Garnish:

⅔ cup hazelnuts (100 g)
lemon zest

Oven temperature: 347°F

■ Grate the carrots finely. Mix butter or coconut oil with palm sugar. Add one egg at a time. Add carrots.

■ Mix flour with baking powder, nuts, and spices. Stir the flour mixture into the carrot batter. Spread in a greased baking pan. Bake at the bottom of the oven for 30–35 minutes. Let the cake cool off.

■ Mix all the ingredients for the icing and spread over the cake. Let sit in the refrigerator until the icing has hardened.

■ Chop the nuts coarsely. Garnish the cake with nuts and lemon zest.

▲ RASPBERRY TARTLETS

Raspberry Tartlets *Lacto or Vegan*

The forms can be kept in the freezer and filled when needed. Good to keep at home if you have unexpected guests. Raspberries can be replaced with blueberries, strawberries, or currants.

12–15 PIECES
⅔ cup hazelnuts (100 g)
3.5 oz butter or coconut oil (100 g)
1 tsp cinnamon (3 g)
1 ¾ cup oats (200 g)
1 tbsp raw sugar (25 g)

Filling:
½ quart raspberries (½ liter)
1–2 tbsp palm sugar (25–37.5 g)
2 cans vanilla quark or soy dessert with vanilla or chocolate flavor (8.8 oz/250 g)
Oven temperature: 437°F

■ Roast the vegetables in a frying pan while stirring on low heat. Rub the peels off and chop the nuts. Melt butter or coconut oil and add cinnamon, oats, nuts, and sugar. Press the batter into muffin cups. Bake in the middle of the oven for about 6–8 minutes and let them cool off.
■ Save raspberries for garnish. Mash the rest of the raspberries lightly with sugar, before they are defrosted if they are frozen. Spread the mashed raspberries in the forms and leave a couple of hours until the forms have softened. Garnish the tartlets with quark or soy dessert and decorate with raspberries.

Old-Fashioned Soft Gingerbread
Vegan

10–12 PIECES
3.5 oz coconut or canola oil (100 g)
¾ cup brown sugar (135 g)
1 cup finely grated zucchini (measured with air, 150 g)
¼ cup lingonberry jam (50 g)
¾ cup yogurt (200 ml)
⅔ cup small raisins (100 g)
⅓ cup soy flour (50 g)
2 ¾ cup sifted spelt flour (300 g)
1½ tsp cinnamon (4 g)
1½ tsp ginger (4 g)
1½ tsp cardamom (4 g)
1½ tsp cloves (4 g)
1½ tsp baking soda (4 g)
Oven temperature: 347°F

■ Stir coconut oil or canola oil with sugar until fluffy. Add zucchini, lingonberry jam, yogurt, and raisins.
■ Mix soy flour and spelt flour with spices and baking soda. Mix all well and pour the batter in a greased and floured form (1½ quarts). Bake the cake in the lower part of the oven for about 55 minutes. Let the cake cool off.

Energy Bars, Snacks, and Candy

Joy is when snacks, energy bars, and candy are healthy and taste as good! Here are the recipes for wonderful nut and chocolate balls filled with antioxidants and lovely truffle.

Raw Food Candy

Nut, almond and chocolate balls are perfect as both candy and snack. They are full of antioxidants, good fatty acids, fiber, and other nutrients. They all stay fresh in the refrigerator for about a week, but can also be stored in the freezer.

Dark chocolate belongs to one of the most antioxidant-rich food we can eat, and raw cacao tops the ORAC list. Above that, raw cacao has a wonderful flavor. It can be bought in some natural health food stores as well as online. Licorice powder, virgin coconut oil, and crystal salt can be bought in natural health food stores.

Datecoupe with Cottage Cheese
Vegan

Luxury to have a snack that tastes like dessert.

PER SERVINGS
1 orange
1–2 fresh dates
walnuts
3–4 tbsp cottage cheese (30–40 g)
goji berries
cinnamon

■ Peel and chop the oranges. Cut the dates into small pieces and chop the nuts. Mix cottage cheese with orange, dates, and nuts. Sprinkle with cinnamon and garnish with walnuts, goji berries, and orange.

Nut and Seed Candy *Raw*

A mix of nuts, almonds, and seeds like almonds, cashew nuts, pumpkin seeds, walnuts, pecan nuts, coconut chips, and/or hazelnuts are both simple and tasty to eat as candy or a snack. It is also always easy to bring with you.

Nut and Seed Candy with Dried Fruit
Follow the recipe above but add dried fruit in pieces like cranberries, apricots, goji berries, and apples.

Energy Bars *Raw*

Wonderful balls with pumpkin seeds.

30 PIECES
10 fresh pitted dates
¼ cup coconut oil (virgin (50 ml)
1–2 tbsp honey (15–30 ml)
1 tsp cinnamon (3 g)
1 tsp ginger (3 g)
1 pinch ground clove (1 ml)
1 pinch crystal salt (1 ml)
1 cup sesame seeds (150 g)
⅓ cup pumpkin seeds (50 mg)
⅓ cup sunflower seeds (50 g)

Garnish:
⅔ cup seeds from sesame, pumpkin, and sunflower

■ Mix dates, coconut oil, honey, as well as spices and salt in a food processor. Add all the seeds by hand. Form into balls and roll in the garnish.

Energy Bars with Cardamom
Follow the recipe above but replace ginger and clove with 1–2 tsp ground cardamom.

Almond Balls with Lemon and Coconut *Raw*

20–25 PIECES *PHOTO P. 288
1⅓ cup almonds (200 g)
5 pitted dates
2–3 tbsp coconut oil, virgin (30–45 ml)
1 tbsp honey or agave syrup (15 ml)
1–2 tsp organic vanilla powder (3–6 g)
1 pinch crystal salt (1 ml)
1 lemon (zest as well as 1 tsp juice)
coconut flakes

■ Mix the almond until a fine powder in a food processor. Add coarsely chopped dates, coconut oil, honey or agave syrup, vanilla, as well as salt and continue to mix until the batter is smooth. Add lemon juice and zest to taste. Form small balls and roll in coconut flakes.

▲ DATECOUPE with Cottage Cheese And Orange

Chocolate Fudge *Raw*

20–25 PIECES

1⅓ cup almonds (200 g)
8 pitted dates
⅓ cup raw cacao powder or regular cacao (50 g)
3–4 tbsp coconut oil, virgin (45–60 ml)
1 tbsp agave syrup or honey (15 ml)

■ Mix almonds to a fine powder in a food processor. Add dates, cacao, coconut oil, agave syrup or honey, as well as salt and continue to mix the batter until smooth. Form small balls or squares.

Chocolate Balls with Cranberries

Follow the recipe above but add ⅔–1⅓ cups dried cranberries in the batter (100–200 g).

Chocolate Balls with Licorice Root

Follow the recipe above but add 2–3 tbsp licorice root powder in the batter as well as ½ pinch extra crystal salt.

Mint Chocolate Balls

Follow the recipe above but season the batter with a few drops of mint oil as well as finely chopped fresh mint. Fresh leaves lower the perishability, but make the balls much tastier.

Spirulina Balls

Follow the recipes above but add 1–2 tbsp nettle, wheat grass, or spirulina powder.

Chocolate Candy *Lacto or Vegan*

5–6 PIECES

dried fruit like raisins, cranberries, goji berries, apricots, mango, apple rings, as well as nuts, seeds, and almonds

1.75 oz butter or coconut oil (50 g)

5.3 oz dark chocolate, 70% (150 g)

a pinch of salt

optionally 1 tbsp grated orange zest

■ Spread dried fruit, nuts, and almonds on a piece of greaseproof paper, about 5 to 8 inches big. Melt the butter or the coconut oil. Break the chocolate into pieces. Remove the pan from the stove and add chocolate and salt as well as grated orange zest.

■ Spread the chocolate batter over the fruit and nuts. Let harden and then break into smaller pieces.

Ice Chocolate *Vegan*

25 PIECES *PHOTO P. 288

3.5 oz coconut oil (100 g)

4.4 oz dark chocolate, 70% (125 g)

■ Melt the coconut oil in a pan on lowest heat. Break the chocolate in pieces, add to the pan, and stir until everything has melted. Pour the chocolate into a pastry bag or container with a spout, and then fill in small foil candy cup.

Ice Chocolate with Mint

Follow the basic recipe above, but season the batter with 1–2 drops mint oil as well as ⅔ cups finely chopped mint leaves.

Ice Chocolate with Orange and Cardamom

Follow the basic recipe above, but flavor the batter with 1 tsp finely grated orange zest and ½ tsp freshly ground cardamom.

Ice Chocolate with Raisins and Roasted Hazelnuts

Add a few raisins and chopped roasted hazelnuts in the cups and then pour the chocolate batter over it, according to the basic recipe.

Chocolate-Dipped Strawberries *Lacto or Vegan*

4 SERVINGS
1 cup dark chocolate (150 g)
2 tbsp butter or coconut oil (30 ml)
14 oz strawberries (400 g)

■ Bring water to a boil in a pan. Break the chocolate into pieces and place in a deep plate that covers the pan. Place the plate on the pan and make sure no steam reaches the chocolate. Melt the chocolate while stirring and add butter or coconut oil. Dip the strawberries in the chocolate. Then place them on parchment baking paper and let harden for 2–3 hours.

Chocolate Truffle *Lacto or Vegan*

Seductive truffles!

ABOUT 38 PIECES *PHOTO P. 288
½ cup whipped cream or oat cream (100 ml)
1.75 oz butter or coconut oil (50 g)
7 oz dark chocolate, 70% (200 g)
1–2 tbsp honey (15–30 ml)
1 pinch salt (1 ml)
1–1½ tbsp grated orange zest (3–4 g)

■ Bring cream and butter or coconut oil to a boil. Break the chocolate in pieces. Remove the pan from the heat and add chocolate, honey, salt, and orange zest. Let the batter harden a little in the refrigerator for one hour.
■ Pipe the batter in foil candy cups or form balls.

Chocolate Truffle with Almond and Cinnamon

Follow the basic recipe above but exclude orange zest. Form balls of the somewhat firm chocolate batter. Then stick a blanched almond in the middle of each ball.

■ Mix 1 tbsp cacao with 2 tbsp cinnamon and place on a plate. Roll the balls in the mixture until they are covered in powder.

Fig Truffle *Lacto or Vegan*

ABOUT 52 PIECES
⅔ cups almonds (100 ml)
3.5 oz dark chocolate, 70% (100 g)
12 coarsely chopped figs
¼ cup soy or oat milk (50 ml)
1–2 tbsp honey (15–30 ml)
1 tbsp butter or coconut oil (15 ml)
¼ cup red wine or orange juice (50 ml)
cacao or dark chocolate

■ Mix the almonds into a flour in a food processor. Add the chocolate in pieces and continue to mix. Add figs and continue to mix.
■ Add milk, honey, butter or coconut oil, as well as red wine or orange juice. Mix the batter until smooth. Let it sit in the refrigerator for a couple of hours until is somewhat firm.
■ Form small balls and roll in cacao or dip them in melted dark chocolate. See Chocolate-Dipped Strawberries, left.

Indian Nut and Fruit Balls *Lacto*

Candy similar to fudge.

15 PIECES *PHOTO P. 144
about ¾ cups mixed cashew nuts (100 g)
1⅓ cup finely chopped dates (200 g)
2 tbsp coarsely chopped sunflower seeds (20 g)
3–4 tbsp honey (45–60 ml)
1 cup milk powder (150 ml)
⅔ cup coconut flakes (100 g)
1 tsp rose water (5 ml)

■ First mix the cashew nuts into a fine powder in a food processor. Add dates, sunflower seeds, honey, as well as milk powder and continue to mix into a smooth batter.
■ Form round balls. Mix the coconut flakes with the rose water. Roll each ball in coconut flakes and keep in the refrigerator.

Breakfast Dishes

Oatmeal is a good way to start the day. There are many new, exciting kinds of cereals, grains, and seeds to choose, like buckwheat, quinoa, and amaranth. Here are suggestions on tasty porridges full of fiber and other nutrients.

The more nuts and seeds a porridge and muesli have, the lower the GI value and the better the taste. Other tasty things to sprinkle on your porridge are ground cinnamon, cardamom, and ginger, as well as fresh berries.

Muesli *Vegan*

It is both easy and fun to create your own muesli and it is much tastier than the store-bought kind. Vary with flakes of buckwheat, wheat, and rye and/or protein-rich soy flakes. If you would like to increase the nutritional value, add 3/4 cup flour of dried blueberries, rose hips, and/or cloudberries.

I BATCH
5 cups spelt flakes (500 g)
3 cups quinoa flakes (300 g)
2 cups oats (200 g)
1⅓–2 cups almonds, hazelnuts, cashew nuts, and/or walnuts (200–300 g)
1⅓ cup hampa seeds (200 g)
1⅓ cup pumpkin seeds and/or sunflower seeds (200 g)
1⅓ cup flax seeds (200 g)
1⅓ cup coconut chips or coconut flakes (200 g)
2⅔ cups chopped dried apricots, figs, plums, apples, cranberries, mango, and/or goji berries (400 g)
Oven temperature: 302°F

■ Spread the flakes in a baking pan. Roast in the middle of the oven for 15 minutes. Stir occasionally.

■ Coarsely chop almonds and/or nuts. Add to the flakes and continue to roast for another 10–15 minutes. Be careful not to burn. Add hampa seeds, pumpkin seeds, flax seeds, coconut, and dried fruit. Store the muesli in a can with a lid.

Gluten-Free Muesli

Follow the recipe above but replace spelt flakes and oats with buckwheat flakes, soy flakes, and quinoa puffs.

Spelt Porridge with Apricots *Vegan*

Spelt porridge can be varied in many ways. Try to make the porridge with flakes from rye, wheat, oat, buckwheat, and/or quinoa. Apricots can be replaced with other dried fruit.

PER SERVING
1 cup spelt flakes (150 g)
1¼ cup water (300 ml)
1 tbsp pumpkin seeds (10 g)
1 tbsp flax seeds (10 g)

Season the Porridge

Eat porridge with soy or oat milk and sprinkle with ground cinnamon, cardamom, as well as ginger. It is both tasty and good for digestion. Cinnamon, nuts, and seeds also lower the GI value of a meal. Other tasty things to add to your porridge are chopped nuts and berries.

2–3 chopped dried apricots
1 pinch salt (1 ml)

■ Place flakes, water, pumpkin seeds, flax seeds, apricots, and salt in a pan and bring to a boil. Lower the heat and let the porridge simmer on lowest heat for a couple of minutes and then turn off the stove and leave the porridge to swell.

Oatmeal with Apple *Vegan*

Follow the recipe above but replace spelt flakes and apricots with oats and a chopped apple.

Porridge Mix with Pumpkin Seeds *Vegan*

To make your own porridge mix is simple and perfect to use in the morning. Take ⅔ cup of the mix per serving and cook in 3/4 cup water and a pinch of salt for about 5 minutes on low heat. Add more water if necessary.

I BATCH *PHOTO P. 294
4 cups spelt flakes (400 g)
4 cups oats (400 g)
4 cups rye flakes (400 g)
1⅓ cup flax seeds (200 g)
1⅓ cup pumpkin seeds (200 g)
1⅓–2 cups chopped dried fruit (200–300 g)

■ Mix all the ingredients and store in a jar with a lid.

Tip! If you soak all the ingredients the night before, you only need to bring it to a quick boil in the morning.

◀ MUESLI

Buckwheat Porridge with Goji Berries and Almonds *Vegan*

Porridge from buckwheat is delicious. It has a similar flavor to rice pudding. You can buy steam prepared whole buckwheat in the stores which will cook in about 10 minutes.

4 SERVINGS
1⅓ cup whole buckwheat (200 g)
2–3 tbsp chopped almonds (20–30 g)
⅔ cup goji berries (100 g)
2½ cup water (600 ml)
½ tsp salt (1 g)

■ First rinse the buckwheat in hot water and then in cold water. Cook buckwheat, almonds, and goji berries in salted water for about 10 minutes or until the buckwheat is soft.

Bran with Figs and Almond *Vegan*

Bran has a long cooking time, but is fine to save and reheat later.

4 SERVINGS
1⅓ cup crushed rye, oats, or wheat (200 g)
⅔ cup oat bran (100 g)
⅔ cup chopped figs (100 g)
⅓ cups chopped almonds (50 g)
½ tsp salt (1 g)

■ Mix all the ingredients and let simmer on low heat for about 10 minutes. Turn off the stove and let the porridge swell for about 2 hours.

Sprouted Spelt with Goji Berries *Raw*

PER SERVING
⅔ cup sprouted spelt (100 g)
½ orange
1 apple
½–1 tsp grated ginger (1–3 g)
2 tbsp dried goji berries (20 g)
2 tbsp chopped nuts (20 g)
1–2 tbsp pomegranate seeds (10–20 g)

■ Soak the spelt for one night. Rinse morning and night for one day until they start to sprout, see p. 14.
■ Squeeze juice from the half-orange. Coarsely grate the apple. Mix sprouted spelt, apple, ginger, raisins, and orange juice. Sprinkle with chopped nuts and pomegranate seeds.

Amaranth Porridge with Cranberries *Vegan*

Delicious porridge that both young and old will love. Amaranth seeds have a long cooking time, but the porridge is fine to reheat later.

2 SERVINGS
1⅓ cup amaranth seeds (200 g)
⅓ cup dried cranberries (50 g)
2 cups water (500 ml)
½ tsp salt (1 g)

■ Cook amaranth and cranberries in water and salt for about 30 minutes.

▶ SPROUTED SPELT with Goji Berries

Bread

Bread has been highly esteemed throughout the ages. The knowledge of bread baking is very old. As early as 9,000 years ago, unleavened bread was baked. Today, bread baking has become a luxury that few people indulge in. People often lack time and energy. Still, it is like pure meditation to knead a dough and let the house fill up from the lovely aroma of baking bread.

THERE ARE MANY DIFFERENT METHODS to use when baking bread. You can use sour dough, regular yeast, or baking powder. It is also possible to bake unleavened bread or to let dough self-rise.

The rising process makes the dough fluffy and increases the volume. Regular yeast contains live yeast bacteria. They are sensitive to high heat and can be destroyed if the dough liquid is warmer than 98.6°F (body temperature). The yeast bacteria transform the starch to sugar, carbonic acid, carbon dioxide, and alcohol.

In regular wheat, spelt, rye, and barley there is gluten, mostly found in regular wheat flour and sifted spelt flour. From gluten, coatings are produced and blown into small air bubbles from the carbonic acid. The more yeast the dough contains, the faster it will rise. The problem is that it usually happens too fast.

The phytic acid does not have time to decompose and not enough aroma substances are formed. Long rising time gives the bread a completely different aroma, flavor, and perishability. It also makes the bread easier to digest.

The smaller amount of yeast you use and the longer time the dough is allowed to rise, the tastier the finished bread will end up. In bakeries cold liquid and a very small amount of yeast is used and the dough is then allowed to rise in a refrigerator overnight, for about 8 hours.

Sourdough bread. Sourdough is the predecessor of yeast. It can partly or completely replace yeast. If you want to bake a bread entirely on sourdough, the rising process will be longer.

Baking with sourdough has many advantages. The bread will have a greater volume, longer perishability, be more moist, and the taste will turn out richer and more aromatic. The uptake of minerals, like zinc and iron, also increases and the bread has a lower GI value.

Tips! In all bread recipes you can replace ¼-½ cup of the dough liquid with ½ cup sourdough and follow the rest of the recipe. However, calculate ¾-1 ⅔ cup less flour.

Baking powder dough. It is fast and simple to bake with baking powder. But baking powder bread is tougher to digest and baking powder needs B vitamins to develop, which is taken from the flour. In natural health food stores there is

Baking tips
The more sourdough, crushed and whole grains, and seeds you add to the dough, the lower the GI value!

When you follow a recipe, especially when it comes to baking, it is important to use leveled measurements, otherwise the finished bread can end up with a completely different texture.

Heat the oven well before so that the bread can be baked as soon as it is done rising. If the dough has risen for too long, it may have to be kneaded again.

natural baking powder, like cream of tartar, to buy. Cream of tartar is a by-product of wine making. To have the same effect as regular baking powder, you need to use the double amount of cream of tartar.

Baking powder will not activate until it comes in contact with heat. If you use hot (melted) fat in the dough the bread needs to be baked immediately. If you use cold liquids in your dough, it can sit for up to 2 hours before baking. Unlike yeast doughs, the doughs with baking powder should be kneaded as little as possible.

Baking by hand. When you bake by hand, the dough is worked with a wooden spoon or the hands until it feels smooth and does not stick to the bowl. Then the dough should rise under a cover until it has doubled in size. Then the dough is thoroughly kneaded and baked according to the recipe.

Baking with a mixer. The most simple way of baking is to use a mixer and work the dough for 4 to 5 minutes. If the dough contains a large amount of whole grain flour it is important that the dough be fairly loose in the first rising process, in order for the flour to swell enough. Then let the dough rise under a cover until it has doubled in size.

Knead the dough for one more minute in the machine before placing it on a floured table and baking it according to the recipe. Place the bread on a baking sheet, cover with a kitchen towel, and place in a warm, draft-free place. The dough will rise the most when the weather is nice and less when there is thunder in the air.

Right

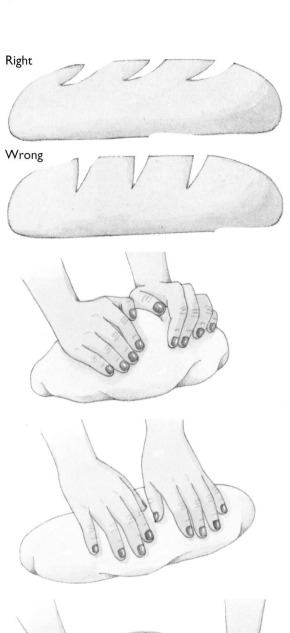

Wrong

◀ WHEN THE BREAD RISES in the oven, the gas evolution is often too strong and the bread starts to crack. If you make a few cuts before the last rising on the baking sheet, the gas can be released through the cuts. Cut with a razor blade or sharp knife.

◀ PLACE THE DOUGH on a floured table. Always knead the bread in the same direction, away from yourself. Swing forward with your whole body instead of only using your arms.

◀ FORM A LONG ROLL from the dough.

◀ FLATTEN THE DOUGH, fold the outer ends, and bake a ball from the dough. Turn the ball in the other direction, so that the dough can be worked in a new direction.

◀ KEEP KNEADING, rolling, folding, and turning the dough with rhythmical movements until it is smooth and does not stick to your hands or the table.

The dough should rise until it has doubled in size. If the dough rises when you press it gently, it is done rising. It is important to not let the dough rise for too long during the second rising, since large breads can collapse while baking in the oven.

Sourdough

Sourdough culture (starter) only needs to be made one time. The sour dough rises the best on coarse, freshly milled organic flour.

ABOUT 1½ QUART (1½ LITER)

Day 1:
¾ cup coarse rye flour (90 g)
½ cup water (100 ml)

■ Heat the water to 104°F. Mix flour and water in a glass jar. Place the lid on top but do not tighten it.
■ Let the jar stand in a warm place, 77–86°F for 2–3 days. The top of the refrigerator is usually a good spot. Carefully shake the jar in the morning and at night. The finished sourdough should smell fresh and tart.

Day 4:
1 quart water (1 liter)
1 quart coarse rye flour (1 liter)

■ Heat the water to 104°F. Stir water and flour into a stainless-steel bowl. Add the sourdough and let the bowl sit, covered with a kitchen towel, in a warm place for about one day. The sourdough is done when it smells freshly tart and the dough is filled with bubbles.
■ If you are unsure of whether or not the sourdough is done, you can mix ⅔ cup each of sourdough, rye flour, and water and let stand in a warm place. After 6–10 hours the dough starts to rise and the surface becomes bubbly.

Tip! Freeze sourdough in serving size packages of 1⅓ cup. Then all you have to do is take out a package of sourdough when you are about to bake. When you are almost out of sourdough, you rejuvenate it by mixing one package of sourdough with 1 quart water and 1 quart rye flour in the same way as Day 4.

Estonian Sourdough Bread *Vegan*

This is a wonderful juicy rye bread with a tart and aromatic flavor of rye.

2 LOAVES *PHOTO P. 309

Day 1:
3 cups water (700 ml)
1⅓ cup sourdough (150 ml)
4 cups crushed rye (600 g)
3⅓ rye flour (420 g)

Day 2:
0.9–1.7 oz yeast (25–50 g)
1 tbsp salt (20 g)
1 tbsp whole caraway (15 g)
6⅔–7⅓ cup sifted spelt flour or wheat flour (730–205 g)
Oven temperature: 482°F

Day 1:
■ Heat the water to 98.6°F. Mix water with sourdough, crushed rye, and rye flour. Let the dough stand at room temperature covered with a kitchen towel for about 1 day.

Day 2:
■ Carefully heat the sourdough to 98.6°F in a water bath. Dissolve the yeast and add salt, caraway, and most of the flour. Knead the dough in a KitchenAid for about 5 minutes. Let it rise covered with a kitchen towel until it doubles its size, for about 1–2 hours in a warm place.
■ Knead the dough again. Divide the bread into two loaves on a floured table.
■ Place the dough in greased forms and let rise to double size in a warm place for about one hour.
■ Bake in the lowest part of the oven. Immediately lower the temperature to 347°F and bake for about 50 minutes.
■ Brush the loaves with oil and let them cool off, wrapped in cloths. Let the loaves sit for one to two days in order to let the flavors mature.

Finnish Rivekakor *Lacto*

20 PIECES *PHOTO P. 306

■ Follow the basic recipe above but split the dough into 20 pieces. Flatten each piece into a round cake, about 0.4 inches thick. Place the cakes on a baking sheet with parchment baking paper. Poke small holes in the cakes with a fork. Let rise in a warm place for 1–1½ hour to its double size.

■ Heat the oven to 437°F. Place the baking sheet in the middle of the oven and bake for 12–15 minutes.

■ Brush the cakes with 1.75 oz melted butter and ¼ cup milk. Make a thin cut all along the cake's edge and split the cake in two pieces. Place the pieces on top of each other with the cut side facing up. Let cool off wrapped in a cloth.

Karelian Potato Pierogies *Lacto*

12 PIECES *PHOTO P. 306

■ Make one batch mashed potatoes. Follow the recipe of Estonian sourdough bread and use one fourth of the dough. Split the dough into 12 pieces. Roll out every piece into a thin oval cake about 5–3 inches big.

■ Heat the oven to 482°F. Place a spoon of mashed potatoes in the middle of the dough and fold and wrinkle the edges toward the filling.

■ Bake the pierogies in the middle of the oven for 10–12 minutes on baking sheets with parchment baking paper.

■ Melt 0.9–1.75 oz butter and mix with ¼ cup milk. Brush the pierogies with the milk mix. Stack the pierogies on top of each other and let them cool off under a cloth.

Tip! In Finland, people mix boiled, mashed eggs with butter and garnish the pierogies with the mixture. Pierogies can also be stored in the freezer and are perfect to bring on the picnic.

Potato Cakes *Vegan*

They are the very tastiest when freshly baked, but you can also store them in the freezer.

24 PIECES
¾ cup soy or oat milk (200 ml)
¼ cup canola or olive oil (50 ml)
1½ tsp salt (4 g)
2⅔ cups freshly cooked mashed potatoes (400 g)
5 cups rye flour (600 g)
2 ¾-3 ¾ cup sifted spelt flour (300–400 g)
Oven temperature: 482°F

■ Mix milk, oil, salt, and mashed potatoes. Add flour, but save some for baking. Work the dough until smooth.

■ Place the dough on a floured table and roll into two lengths. Split each length into 12 pieces and form round balls. Roll each ball into a

thick cake and finish the rolling with a textured rolling pin.

■ Bake the cakes in a well-heated frying pan or wok for a couple of minutes on each side. You can also bake them on a greased baking sheet at 482°F in the oven for 3–5 minutes. Let them cool off on an oven rack.

Sesame Flatbread With Sourdough *Vegan*

Is there anything more tasty than crispy baked sesame flatbreads? The thinner you roll, the tastier the bread will be!

20 PIECES
0.9 oz yeast (25 g)
⅔ cup sourdough, room temperature (100 ml)
2 cups water (500 ml)
1 tsp salt (5 ml)
1–2 tbsp freshly ground bread spices (anise, fennel, caraway, and coriander) (15–30 g)
1 tbsp canola oil (15 ml)
2 cups oats and spelt grains (300 g)
10–10⅔ cup whole grain spelt flour (1.2–1.3 kg)
17.6 oz sesame seeds (500 g) and sifted spelt flour for baking
Oven temperature: 482°F

■ Stir the yeast into the sourdough. Heat the water to about 104°F. Add sourdough, spices, oil, oats, and most of the flour. Work the dough until it does not stick to the bowl. Let the dough rise under a towel for one hour.

■ Place the dough on a floured table and knead until shiny and smooth. Roll two lengths and split every length into 10 pieces. Roll every piece in sesame flour and sifted spelt into round cakes of about 10 inches in diameter. Turn the cake while rolling. Finish by using a textured rolling pin.

■ Bake without rising first in the top of the oven on floured baking sheets for about 5 minutes. Let the bread cool off separately, otherwise they turn too soft.

Fruit and Almond Bread *Vegan*

A juicy and tasty bread that goes perfectly with a cup of tea.

2 LOAVES
1⅔ cup water (400 ml)
12 figs in pieces
2 cups sultans (300 g)
2½ cup coarse rye flour (300 g)

In the morning:
⅔ cup water (150 ml)
0.9 oz yeast (25 g)
¼ cup oil (50 ml)
1½ tsp salt (4 g)
1 lemon (zest)
2 tsp cinnamon (10 ml)
1⅓ cup almonds (200 g)
2½ cup whole grain spelt flour (300 g)
about 5 cups sifted spelt or wheat flour (600 g)
Oven temperature: 392°F

■ Bring water to a boil and place in a bowl. Add figs, raisins, and flour. Let sit covered during night.

In the morning:
■ Bring water to a boil and add the blanched mix. Dissolve the yeast in the liquid. Add oil, salt, lemon zest, cinnamon, almonds, and whole grain spelt as well as most of the sifted spelt. Knead the dough for about 4 minutes in a machine. Let the dough rise covered for one hour. Knead the dough for an additional one minute.
■ Place the dough on a floured table, form the dough in two loaves, and place them in two greased forms. Let them rise covered to the double size for 40–50 minutes. Heat the oven to 482°F.
■ Place the forms at the bottom of the oven and reduce the heat to 392°F.
■ Take the bread out of the forms and brush them with some water. Let the breads cool off wrapped in a kitchen towel.

◀ ON THE TOP LEFT: Fruit and almond bread; to the right, Finnish Rivekakor; under that, a spelt bread and Karelian potato pierogies.

Annelund Loaves *Vegan*

This great bread is extra juicy thanks to the apples and a loose dough. The dough is so big that it should be kneaded in a KitchenAid. If you knead the dough by hand, you have to use more flour.

4 LOAVES *PHOTO P. 309
At night:
3¼ cup water (750 ml)
2 cups crushed barley (300 g)
1⅓ cup raisins (200 g)
1 cup flax seeds (150 g)
⅔ cup brans (100 g)

In the morning:
1⅔ cup water (400 ml)
2.6 oz yeast (75 g)
2 cups coarsely grated carrots or ⅔ cup apple sauce (300 g/150 g)
1 tbsp salt (10 g)
2.2–2.6 quarts sifted spelt flour or wheat flour (2.2–2.6 kg)
Oven temperature: 482°F

At night:
■ Bring water to a boil and add crushed barley, raisins, flax seeds, and brans. Let soak under a lid during the night.

In the morning:
■ Warm the water and soak to 98.6°F. Dissolve the yeast in the lukewarm water. Add the grated apples, salt, and most of the sifted spelt flour.
■ Knead the dough for 4–5 minutes in a KitchenAid. Let rise under a kitchen towel for about 40 minutes.
■ Knead the dough an additional few seconds in the KitchenAid. Place the dough on a floured table. Split the dough in four pieces and form round loaves.
■ Place all four loaves on a greased baking sheet. Sprinkle with some flour on top and in between the breads. Let rise for about 30 minutes or until it doubles its size.
■ Place the baking sheet in the bottom of the oven at 482°F. Lower the heat to 392°F and bake for about 50 minutes. Let the loaves cool off wrapped in a baking cloth.

Spelt Bread, Basic Recipe *Vegan*

2 LOAVES

At night:

2 cups water (500 ml)

1⅓ cup crushed spelt, barley, wheat, rye, or buckwheat (200 g)

1⅓ cup oats or spelt grain (200 g)

In the morning:

1 cup water (250 ml)

0.9 oz yeast (25 g)

½ tbsp salt (5 g)

11 ¾-12⅔ cup sifted spelt or wheat flour (1.4–1.5 kg)

Oven temperature: 392°F

At night:

■ Bring the water to a boil and stir crushed barley and grains. Let sit overnight.

In the morning:

■ Bring the water to a boil and stir the parboiled barley and grains into the water. Let sit until the temperature is 98.6°F. Dissolve the yeast in the fluid. Add salt and most of the flour. Knead the dough by hand for at least 10 minutes or in a machine for 4–5 minutes. Let the dough rise under a kitchen towel for an hour.

■ Place the dough on a floured table and knead for a few minutes. Form two round loaves. Let rise covered until it has doubled in size on a greased baking sheet for about 40–50 minutes.

■ Bake in the bottom of the oven for 30–40 minutes.

Baguettes

3 BREADS

Follow the recipe above, but split the dough into three chubby loaves. Let them rise covered on a greased baking sheet until it has doubled in size, for 40–50 minutes.

Heat the oven to 482°F. Place the baking sheet in the middle of the oven and reduce the heat to 392°F. Bake for 25 minutes.

Ciabatta

12 BREADS

Follow the basic recipe above and let the dough rise for one hour. Let the dough rise on an oiled baking sheet under a baking cloth for about 1½ hour.

Place the dough on a floured table and cut it into 5- to 6-inch-large pieces by using a sharp knife. Pull the pieces of dough a little to make them thinner in the middle. Avoid pressing the dough together. Bake in the middle of the oven for about 17 minutes at 437°F.

Filled Ciabatta

Follow the recipe above and let the dough rise. Place the dough on a floured table and knead it for a few minutes. Split the dough into 12 pieces. Let the pieces of dough rest and then pull them out a little.

Place a strip of filling consisting of 2 cups coarsely chopped, pitted, black olives; 2 cups chopped, marinated tomatoes; 7 oz (200 g) coarsely grated Parmesan; as well as 2–2 ⅔ cup coarsely chopped basil in the middle of each piece of dough. Fold the sides, press together, and place them on a greased baking sheet. The shape of the breads should be a little thinner in the middle and the seam should be facing down.

Let rise under a cloth for about 1½ hour. Bake in the middle of the oven for about 17 minutes at 437°F.

Spelt Buns with Sunflower Seeds

12 BUNS

Follow the basic recipe above but let the dough rise for 1 hour. Place the dough in a flours table and knead for a couple of minutes.

Split the dough into twelve pieces. Shape into buns and dip them in sunflower seeds and press a little to make them stick. Place on a greased baking sheet. Let the buns rise covered with a cloth until it doubled in size for about 40 minutes.

Heat the oven to 437°F. Place the plate in the middle of the oven and bake the buns for about 15 minutes.

Pan Rolls with Olives

Make half a batch of the basic recipe, which is allowed to rise for 1 hour. Then work coarsely shredded basil leaves, ⅔ cup black olives in

▶ ANNELUND LOAF, Buns with Sunflower Seeds, Pan Rolls with Olives, Sweet Sour Rye Loaf, Estonian Sourdough Bread, and Spelt Buns.

▲ JUICY WHOLE GRAIN BREAD **with apricot and walnuts**

pieces, and 1 cup grated Parmesan cheese into the dough. Split the dough into 16 pieces and bake buns. Place the buns in a greased spring-form pan about 10 inches in diameter. Sprinkle with some flour. Let rise to double size in a warm place.

Heat the oven to 482°F. Place the form at the bottom of the oven and reduce the heat to 392°F. Bake the bread for about 30 minutes.

Sweet Sour Rye Loaf *Vegan*

These large, lovely loaves turn out juicy and tasty. Since the dough is large it should be kneaded in a KitchenAid.

3 LARGE LOAVES *PHOTO P. 309

At night:
3 cups water (700 ml)
2⅓ cup crushed rye (280 g)

In the morning:
¾ cup water (200 ml)
1¼ cup sourdough, room temperature (300 ml)
1.75 oz yeast (50 g)
⅓ cup malt or molasses (100 ml)
1 tbsp salt (20 g)
2–3 tbsp freshly grounded anise, fennel, caraway, and/or coriander (20–30 g)
1–2 tbsp oil (15–30 ml)
6⅔ cup coarse rye flour (800 g)

6⅔ cup whole grain spelt flour (800 g)
about 6⅓ sifted spelt flour and/or sifted wheat flour (700 g)
Oven temperature: 482°F

At night:
■ Bring the water to a boil. Remove the pan from the stove and pout the crushed rye into it. Let it soak overnight.

In the morning:
■ Bring the water to a boil and add the parboiled rye and heat to 98.6°F. Add the sourdough and crumbled yeast. Add malt, salt, spices, oil, rye flour, whole grain spelt, and most of the sifted spelt flour.
■ Knead the dough in a KitchenAid for about 5 minutes. Let rise covered with a cloth for about 1 hour in a warm place.
■ Knead the dough for a short while in the KitchenAid again. Place the dough on a floured table. Split the dough in three pieces and shape into loaves.
■ Place the loaves crosswise on a greased baking sheet. Poke holes with a fork.
■ Heat the oven to 482°F. Brush with oil between the loaves and let them rise under a cloth 40–50 minutes until they have doubled in size.
■ Place the baking sheet at the bottom of the oven and lower the heat to 392°F. Bake for 50 minutes.

▲ SPELT BREAD with Flax Seeds

Spelt Bread with Flax Seeds *Vegan*

Soy or chickpea flour gives the bread a higher nutritional value.

I BREAD

At night:
1⅔ cup water (400 ml)
⅔ cup crushed spelt (100 g)
⅓ cup flax seeds (50 g)

In the morning:
⅔ cup soy or chickpea flour (100 g)
1.75 oz yeast (50 g)
1 tsp salt (3 g)
3 ¾-4⅔ cup sifted spelt flour and/or sifted wheat flour (410–510 g)
Oven temperature: 482°F

At night:
■ Bring water to a boil and add the crushed spelt and flax seeds. Let sit in a pot overnight.

In the morning:
■ Heat the soaked mixture to 98.6°F. First add the soy or chickpea flour. Then crumble yeast into the mixture and add other ingredients. Work the dough for 7–8 minutes by hand or 4–5 minutes in a KitchenAid. Sprinkle with some flour and let the dough rise covered for about 40 minutes.
■ Work the dough on a floured table and shape a round loaf. Place the loaf on a greased baking sheet or parchment baking paper. Sprinkle with some flour and let rise to the double size under a cloth for about 30 minutes in a warm place.
■ Place the baking sheet at the bottom of the oven. Reduce the temperature to 257°F after 15 minutes and let the bread bake for an additional 40–45 minutes. If you would like a crispy crust, you can let the bread cool off on an oven rack without a baking cloth.

Juicy Whole Grain Bread *Lacto*

A tasty and juicy wholegrain bread that quickly becomes the family favorite. It is fast to bake—all you need to do is stir the ingredients together.

2 LOAVES
5½ cup sifted spelt flour (600 g)
2⅔ cup spelt flakes (400 g)
1⅓ cup crushed 4-grain or buckwheat (200 g)
⅔ cup amaranth or quinoa (100 g)
⅔ cup flax seeds (100 g)
1 tbsp baking soda (15 g)
1 tsp salt (3 g)
1 tsp cinnamon (3 g)
¼ cup canola oil (50 ml)
⅓ cup dark syrup (75 ml)
1 quart sour milk (1 liter)
Oven temperature: 302°F

■ Mix sifted spelt, flakes, crushed spelt, amaranth, and flax seeds with baking soda, salt, and cinnamon. Add oil, syrup, and sour milk. Spread the dough out in two greased forms. Bake the bread at the bottom of the oven for about 1 hour and 15 minutes in 302°F.
■ Remove the loaves from the forms and let them cool off wrapped in a baking cloth.

Tip! To succeed with the bread, it is extra important to use leveled measurements of all the ingredients. Remove excess flour from the cup by using a knife.

Wholegrain Bread with Apricot and Walnuts

Healthier and tastier bread cannot be found. Perfect with a cup of tea.

■ Follow the recipe above but increase the amount of syrup to ⅔ cup and cinnamon to 2 tsp, and add 1⅓ coarsely chopped walnuts as well as 1⅓ coarsely chopped apricots.

CRACKERS AND RUSKS

Seed Crackers *Vegan*

Tasty and crispy crackers that are easy to make! Keep in a jar with a lid. Gluten-free.

I BAKING SHEET
¼ cup coconut oil (50 ml)
I cup water (250 ml)
⅔ cup sesame seeds (100 g)
⅓ cup flax seeds (50 g)
⅓ cup pumpkin seeds (50 g)
⅓ cup sunflower seeds (50 g)
2 tbsp potato fiber (15 g)
I tbsp psyllium seed husks (15 g)
½ tsp salt (I g)
optionally salt flakes
Oven temperature: 392°F

■ Heat the coconut oil in the water. Mix all dry ingredients except for the flake salt and stir into the water. Spread the batter on a baking sheet with parchment baking paper. Sprinkle with salt flakes if you want to. Bake in the middle of the oven for about 20 minutes. Break into pieces.

Crispy Spelt Rusks *Lacto or Vegan*

56 PIECES
3.5–4.4 oz butter or coconut oil (100–125 g)
2 cups regular or vegetarian milk (475 ml)
1.75 oz yeast (50 g)
½–I tsp salt (1–3 g)
3–4 tbsp honey (45–60 ml)
3–4 tsp cinnamon (9–12 g)
2 cups soy flour (300 g)
9–10 cups wholegrain spelt flour (1.1–1.2 kg)
Oven temperature: 437°F

■ Melt the butter and heat the milk until lukewarm. Dissolve the yeast in the lukewarm milk. Add salt, honey, and cinnamon. Add soy flour and spelt flour, but save some of the spelt flour for later. Work the dough with a wooden fork until smooth. Cover with a kitchen towel and let it rise in a warm place for about 30 minutes.

■ Place the dough on a floured table and knead it well. Split into four pieces, which are rolled into lengths. Divide each length into 7 pieces that are shaped into round buns and let them rise on a greased baking sheet for about 30 minutes.

■ Bake them for about 10 minutes in the oven at 437–482°F. Let them cool off and then split with a fork. Roast the rusks until light yellow at 482°F for about 5 minutes and then let them dry at 212°F for about 1–2 hours with the oven door a little bit open.

Flaxseed Crackers *Raw*

Delicious, rich in antioxidants, and crispy, crackers are an alternative to regular crisp bread! Let the crackers dry on a warm place like, for example, on top of the refrigerator. Then store them in a jar with a lid.

2 BAKING SHEETS
2 cups flax seeds (300 g)
½ cup sesame seeds, preferably black (75 g)
½ cup pumpkin seeds (75 g)
½ cup sunflower seeds (75 g)
¾ cup water (200 ml)
I tsp salt (4 g)
Oven temperature: 104–113°F

■ Mix the flaxseeds, sesame, pumpkin, and sunflower seeds with water and salt. Stir for a while and then allow the batter to swell for 30 minutes.

■ Spread the batter over two baking sheets with parchment baking paper. Dry the crackers in the sun, in a drying cabinet, or in the oven. If you dry the crackers in the oven, you have to open the oven door occasionally in order to let the moisture evaporate. It takes 6–10 hours.

■ The crackers are done when they break into pieces easily. Serve the crackers with Cashew Sour Cream, p. 178.

Nettle Crackers *Raw*

Follow the basic recipe above but add 2–3 tablespoons ground nettles, wheat grass, or spirulina.

▶ SEED CRACKERS

Drinks

Wonderful, refreshing drinks for all occasions as well as for strengthening the body and for detox. Delicious antioxidant-rich smoothies are mixed in no time and can be used for breakfast, a snack, or dessert.

▲ ORANGE SMOOTHIE

Black Currant Smoothie *Raw*

Delicious smoothie, fortified with rose hips.

2 GLASSES
6–7 almonds
2 dates
½ tbsp rose hip flour (7.5 g)
2–3 tbsp black currants (20–30 g)
1 banana
¾–1¼ cup water (300–400 ml)

■ First mix the almonds into a fine flour. Add dates and rose hip flour and continue to mix. Add black currant and banana and dilute with water while mixing.

Orange Smoothie *Vegan or Raw*

Oranges are the most tasty after Christmas.

1–2 GLASSES
2 large oranges
½ banana
½–1 tsp grated ginger (1–3 g)
about ⅔ cup yogurt, vegetarian milk, or almond milk (150 ml)

■ Remove all the peel and white parts of the orange. Cut it in slices and remove the seeds. Mix orange, banana, ginger, as well as yogurt or milk.

Tips! Mix with a small piece of the outer orange peel for a more aromatic flavor. The banana can be replaced with a pear.

Orange and Passion Fruit Smoothie
Follow the recipe above but add the inside of one passion fruit.

Blood Grape Smoothie
Follow the basic recipe above but exclude ginger and replace one orange with one squeezed blood grapefruit.

Peach Smoothie
Follow the basic recipe above but replace the oranges with 2 pitted peaches or nectarines.

▲ PROTEIN-RICH Smoothie with Raspberry

Chocolate Smoothie *Vegan or Raw*

Imagine that something so healthy can be so nutritious! The drink will turn out the best if all the ingredients are room temperature, otherwise the coconut oil will end up too firm in the texture. The banana can be replaced with a pear.

I LARGE GLASS (300 ML)
½ banana
1–2 tbsp cacao, preferably raw cacao (15–30 g)
½–I tbsp coconut oil, preferably virgin (7.5–15 ml)
I tsp honey or agave syrup (5 ml)
½–I pinches cardamom (0.5–I ml)
a pinch of salt, preferably crystal salt
¾ cup soy, oat, or almond milk (200 ml)
½ tsp green powder from nettles, wheat grass,
   or spirulina (I g)

■ Mix banana with cacao, coconut oil, honey or agave syrup, cardamom, salt, milk, and green powder.

Mint Chocolate Smoothie

Follow the recipe above, but replace the cardamom with 2–3 tbsp coarsely chopped mint leaves.

Protein-Rich Smoothie With Raspberry *Lacto or Vegan*

Creamy and protein-rich smoothie that is perfect to replace a whole meal with when you have little time or want to lose weight. Raspberries can be replaced with strawberries, blueberries, and black currants. The banana can be replaced with pears.

I–2 GLASSES
⅔ cup raspberries (100 g)
½ banana
¾ cup soy or oat milk (200 ml)
⅓ cup quark or soy cream cheese (50 ml)

■ Mix raspberries and banana with milk and quark or soy cream cheese.

Protein-Rich Smoothie With Apple And Cinnamon

Follow the recipe above but replace raspberries and banana with one cored sweet apple. Season with cinnamon.

Boost Your Smoothie!

If you would like to further increase the nutritional value in your smoothie:
• Hempseed flour: primarily contains essential fatty acids and is rich in complete protein.
• Maca: for extra power and endurance. Maca is a very nutritional root that has been used for thousands of years in Peru.
• Antioxidant rich berry powder: like acai, alma, rose hip, or berries like cloudberries, blueberries, or cranberries.
• Green powder: like wheat grass, nettles, and spirulina, which are very rich in chlorophyll, antioxidants, minerals, and micronutrients and also have a cleansing effect.
• Protein powder: can be based on whey or soy without any unnatural additives.

Blueberry Smoothie *Vegan and Raw*

Blueberries can be replaced with strawberries, raspberries, black currants, or kiwi. If you would like a more creamy texture, you can mix with half a banana or a pear.

1–2 GLASSES

1⅓ cups blueberries (200 g)

1¼ cup yogurt, soy yogurt, or almond milk (300 ml)

1 tsp honey or agave syrup (5 ml)

■ Mix the berries with yogurt or almond milk and honey or agave syrup.

Raspberry Smoothie with Melon *Raw*

1–2 GLASSES

½ honeydew

⅔ cup raspberries (100 g)

½ cup soy, oat, or almond milk (100 ml)

■ Scoop out the melon pulp and mix melon with raspberries and milk.

Strawberry Smoothie with Melon

Follow the recipe above but replace raspberries with strawberries and some lemon zest.

Pineapple and Mango Smoothie *Vegan*

2 GLASSES

2⅔ cup mango pieces (400 g)

¾ cup coconut milk (200 ml)

water or ice

1 tsp honey or agave syrup (5 ml)

1–2 tsp grated ginger (3–6 g)

½–1 lime, juice

■ Mix mango with coconut milk. Dilute with water or ice until the texture is good. Add honey, ginger, and lime juice to taste.

Mango Smoothie with Passion Fruit

Follow the recipe above but replace half of the mango with the pulp from a couple of passion fruit.

▲ BLUEBERRY SMOOTHIE

Strawberry Milkshake with Ice Cream *Lacto or Vegan*

Delicious as a snack or dessert on a lovely summer day. Strawberries can be replaced with other berries like raspberries or blueberries.

2 SERVINGS

6–7 strawberries

1¼ cup soy or oat milk (300 ml)

3 scoops vanilla ice cream or tofu ice cream, vanilla flavor

■ Clean the strawberries and cut off the tops. Mix them with the milk. Pour into two glasses and garnish with ice cream.

Citrus drink *Raw*

1–2 GLASSES *PHOTO P. 320

1½ orange

½ lime fruit

½ blood grapefruit

■ Cut the peel and white parts off the orange and lime fruit. Cut the fruit in pieces and remove the seeds. Squeeze the juice from the orange half that is left as well as the grapefruit.

▲ GREEN SUPER SMOOTHIE

Green Super Smoothie *Raw*

Carrot leaves can be replaced with sprouts, sunflower shoots, or lettuce. The younger the leaves, the milder the taste will be. Other tasty things to add are apples or pears. If you want a more creamy texture, you can add a piece of avocado.

1–2 GLASSES
1⅓ cup young and fresh carrot leaves (200 g)
⅔ cup lemon balm leaves (100 g)
4 inches sliced cucumber
2/4–1¼ cup water (200–300 ml)

- Mix green leaves with cucumber and water

Green Smoothie with Celery
Follow the recipe above but add one chopped celery.

Green Smoothie with Mint
Follow the basic recipe above but replace lemon balm with mint leaves.

Green Smoothie with Parsley
Follow the basic recipe above but replace lemon balm with ⅓-⅔ cup parsley.

Green Smoothie with "Spirulina"
*PHOTO P. 320
Follow the basic recipe above but replace fresh leaves with 2–3 tsp "spirulina" nettles, or wheat grass powder.

Mix orange and lime pulp together with the squeezed juice in a food processor.

Strawberry Lassi *Vegan*

Refreshing lassi can be found everywhere in India and is a common beverage with any meal. The drink can be seasoned with any fruit or berries you want.

3 GLASSES
⅔ cup sliced strawberries (100 g)
¾ cup mild yogurt (200 ml)
1¼ cup water (300 ml)
½ tbsp honey (7.5 ml)
optionally ½ tsp rose water (international stores)

- Mix all the ingredients in the mixer until the drink is smooth and foamy.

Watermelon Lassi
Follow the recipe above, but replace the strawberries with pieces of watermelon.

Green Super Drinks
Green leaves contain all the nutrients we need if the soil is in balance. All the amino acids and omega-3 are found, although in small amounts, as well as chlorophyll, antioxidants, vitamins, minerals, and micronutrients. Most fresh leaves like sprouts, sunflower shoots, spinach, and lettuce, as well as wild plants like nettles, goosefoot, and common chickweed (see p. 94) are perfect for green smoothies. Beetroot greens as well as leaves and peeled stems from different cabbage like kale and broccoli also go well in drinks.

Hot Tomato Cocktail *Raw*

1–2 GLASSES
2 tomatoes
½ red bell pepper
½–1 Spanish pepper fruit
¼ cup water (50 ml)

■ Clean and cut the vegetable fruit in pieces. Mix them and dilute with water.

Raspberry Drink *Raw*

Raspberries can be replaced with strawberries, blueberries, and black currants and be sweetened with honey if you want to.

2 GLASSES
1⅓ cup raspberries (200 g)
1¼ cup soda water or regular water (300 ml)

■ Mix the raspberries with some of the water. Strain the raspberries. Dilute the drink with soda water or regular water.

Lingonberry Drink *Raw*

Fresh and tasty! Replace lingonberries with cranberries, red currants, or other berries.

1–2 GLASSES
1⅓ cup lingonberries (200 g)
½ tsp grated ginger (1 g)
½-⅔ cup water by choice (100–150 ml)
½ tbsp honey or agave syrup (7.5 ml)

■ Mix lingonberries, ginger, and water. Season with honey or agave syrup.

Lemon Drink *Raw*

2 CUPS (500 ML)
1½ lemon
2 cups water (500 ml)
1 tsp honey (5 ml)

■ Slice half a lemon and squeeze the juice from the other lemon. Mix the lemon juice with water and lemon slices. Season with honey.

Infused Water!
Regular water is tasty when you infuse it with one of the following additives:
• squeezed lemon or lime
• squeezed grapefruit
• lingonberry or cranberry juice
• thinly sliced, fresh ginger
Other decorative ingredients for the water jug are whole radishes and cherry tomatoes or lemon balm, mint, or parsley as well as sliced orange, lemon, lime, or cucumber.

Lemon Drink with Lemon Balm

Follow the recipe above but mix the drink together with ⅔ cup lemon balm leaves.

Ginger Drink with Honey and Lemon *Raw*

A lovely thirst quencher that is as tasty cold as it is at room temperature.

1 QUART (1 LITER)
1 quart water (1 liter)
1–2 tbsp grated ginger (10–20 g)
1 lemon (juice)
1 tbsp honey or agave syrup (15 ml)

■ Season the water with ginger, lemon, and honey or agave syrup.

Ginger Drink with Honey and Lemon Balm

Follow the recipe above, but add a few twigs of lemon balm in the drink.

Ginger Drink with Honey and Mint

Follow the recipe above but add a few twigs of mint in the drink.

◄ CITRUS DRINK, Hot Tomato Cocktail and Green Smoothie with "Spirulina"

▲ CHAI

Chai *Vegan*

Chai is without a doubt the most popular drink in India and can be bought at any street corner. Try to vary the seasoning with cinnamon, star anise, and black pepper.

1–2 GLASSES
2 cups water (500 ml)
1 slice ginger
½ tsp cardamom seeds (1 g)
5 whole cloves
1 tbsp tea leaves (15 g)
1 cup soy or oat milk (250 ml)
cinnamon

■ Let the water simmer together with ginger and other spices for about 15 minutes. Remove the pan from the stove and add the tea leaves. Let the tea steep for five minutes.

■ Warm the milk until it starts to smoke. Whip it with an electric mixer or milk frother. Strain the tea and pour into big glasses. Garnish with milk foam and cinnamon dust.

Iced Tea

Follow the recipe above and place sliced lemon in the tea when it is done. Add ice cubes or store the tea in the refrigerator.

Ice rooibos tea with vanilla *Vegan*

1 QUART (1 LITER)
1 quart water (1 liter)
2–3 tbsp rooibos tea (30–45 g)
1 sliced lemon
1 tsp vanilla powder (5 ml)

■ Bring water to a boil. Add the tea leaves and steep for about 10 minutes. Strain the tea and pour into a jug. Add lemon slices and season with vanilla. Add ice cubes or keep the tea in the refrigerator.

COFFEE, TEA, AND CACAO

Coffee contains a lot of caffeine, see below, and is a diuretic. Coffee also contains a lot of tannic acids. Besides that, coffee contains antioxidants, but does not have the same protecting effect as tea.

Tea originally came from the tea bush *Camellia sinensis* and has been used for thousands of years in Asia. The leaves of the tea bush—and, in some cases, twigs—are picked at different stages. The tea that we call regular black tea goes through a fermenting, roasting, and drying process.

Caffeine can be found in both coffee and tea. Caffeine makes you more alert. A large cup of tea contains between 20 and 60 mg caffeine, depending on how long the tea is allowed to steep, while a small cup of coffee contains about 100 mg.

More than 1 to 2 cups of coffee each day causes the body to constantly run on high energy, which can cause negative side effects. One of the most common causes of insomnia is a too high caffeine level in the body. Many coffee drinkers also experience palpitations, extra beats, and unbalanced rhythms in the heart. Caffeine is addictive and gives withdrawal symptoms if the body does not get its regular dose of caffeine.

Tip! If you want to lower your intake of caffeine, start by decreasing your coffee intake incrementally. Drink a small or a half cup instead of a large and so on. Avoid drinking coffee later than 3 PM.

Green tea is made from dried leaves that have been neither fermented or roasted.

White tea is made from dried leaves from the top shoots on the tea bush, and they have been neither fermented or roasted. The white tea is consider to be more exclusive than the green tea.

How to brew tea:
Regular tea will have the best flavor and aroma if it is brewed in the right temperature.
- Regular black tea is brewed in 194°F water. Let the tea steep for 4 to 5 minutes.
- White and green tea will turn out the most aromatic at 158 to 176°F water. Let the tea

Health effects from white, green, black, and red tea:
- Rich in antioxidants. Green tea has 831 in ORAC value, see p. 48.
- Protective dose: 2–3 cups green tea per day. (Green tea is the most documented.)
- Has antibiotic effects.
- Contains high levels of natural fluorine that can prevent caries.
- Reduces the risk of heart and vascular diseases.
- Can protect against cancer, primarily stomach and colorectal cancer.
- Can increase the body's metabolism.

steep for 2 to 3 minutes, otherwise it will turn bitter.

Red tea is also known as rooibos tea or massai tea. Rooibos is Afrikaans and means "red bush." The tea has been used by Africans for many centuries and is considered to be anticonvulsant and good for allergies.

Red tea has a rich flavor that is similar to regular tea but is free from caffeine and lacks regular tea's iron-binding effect. The leaves contain some vitamin C as well as small amounts of iron, magnesium, and potassium. Red tea should be made with 176°F water and needs to steep for 4 to 10 minutes.

Yerba maté is a tea made from a South American plant that has somewhat of a woody and smoked flavor. Yerba maté has been the holy drink of the Indians. The tea increases alertness, but only contains traces of caffeine. Yerba mate is rich in antioxidants and minerals. The tea stimulates digestion and bile, increases metabolism and body temperature.

Cacao used to be part of an energizing drink that the Maya people and Aztecs originally drank. Cacao quickly gained popularity after Columbus brought the cacao beans to Europe. It was not until the middle of the 1800s that today's chocolate pralines started being produced.

Cacao contains theobromine which has a stimulating effect just like caffeine, but without the negative side effects of caffeine.

Cacao is one of the most antioxidant-rich things we can eat. Unprocessed raw cacao is on the top of the ORAC levels. Dark chocolate with at least 70 percent cacao is also high up on the top. Cacao is also rich in vitamins B and E, as well as iron, phosphorus, magnesium, and selenium.

Carob is the flour you get from grinding seeds from the Carob tree capsules. Carob is similar to cacao in flavor, but the content of theobromine and oxalic acid is lower. Carob powder can also be used as a sweetener thanks to its naturally high sugar levels, which are around 46 percent.

Herb Tea

At all times, tea has been brewed from different herbs. Leaves, roots, flowers, and seeds have been used. Many herbs have been used for their medicinal effects and others have been used as beverages when having company. Herbs with medicinal effects should not be taken regularly. The following suggestions of herb teas are considered similar to everyday tea and can be taken more regularly. But it is always good to vary different types of herbs and leaves.

Suggestions of Herb Teas:

Cinnamon and Apple Tea. Boil one cinnamon stick in water 15 minutes. Place dried apple peel in the pot and let steep 10 minutes.

Ginger and Lemon Tea. Boil sliced ginger for 15 minutes. Add lemon slices and sweeten with apple juice concentrate.

Ginger and Star Anise Tea. The same as above but let the star anise boil with the ginger.

Lemongrass Tea. Use the leftovers after cooking with lemongrass and let steep together with green tea.

Lemon Verbena Tea. Let fresh or dried lemon verbena steep 10 minutes in hot water.

Black Currant Tea with Lemongrass. Boil black currant leaves and lemongrass for about 10 minutes.

Green Tea with Lemon, Orange, or Lime Peel. Season green or white tea with peel from lemon, orange, or lime.

Star Anise Tea with Licorice Root. Boil star anise and licorice root for about 15 minutes. Place lemon slices in the tea.

Rose Hip Tea with Apple and Cinnamon. Boil rose hip peel and apple pieces with a cinnamon stick for about 15 minutes.

Nettle Tea with Peppermint. Let fresh or dried nettles and peppermint steep 10 minutes in hot water.

Spearmint Tea with Nettles. Let fresh or dried nettles and spearmint steep 10 minutes in hot water.

Spearmint Tea with Rose Hip. Boil rose hip peel 10 minutes and then let the tea steep with fresh or dried spearmint.

Common Heather Flower Tea. Take the flowers of Common heather and let steep 5–10 minutes in hot water. Common heather flowers are considered to have a calming effect.

Herb Tea as a Folk Medicine

Herb tea can be drunk separately or mixed according to your own taste. Herbs can also be found as a tincture in a bottle. (Licorice root should not be used in conjunction with potassium deficiency, high blood pressure, diabetes, edema, and if you are using blood thinners.)

Detox, Diuretic, and Cleansing: European goldenrod, St. John's wort, linden, marshmallow, dandelion, Kinnikinnick, nettle, parsley, celery seeds, cleavers, and sorrel.

Detox, Liver, and Cleansing: blueberries (the berries), Marian thistle, dandelion, turmeric, rosemary, and schisandra.

Diarrhea: dried blueberries and Kinnikinnick.

Reduces Sugar Cravings: anise, cardamom, cayenne pepper, cinnamon, fennel, green tea, licorice root, and stevia.

Colds: echinacea (root), elderflower, ginger, hyssop, pau d'arco, pot marigold, thyme, and meadowsweet.

Cough: elder, cowslip (mucus), marshmallow, thyme, and heartsease.

Immune System: licorice root and pau d'arco.

Gas: lemon balm, ginger, chamomile, cloves, peppermint, and parsley salvia.

Headache: chamomile and hop cones.

Menopause Problems: salvia, St. John's wort, and black cohosh.

Anticonvulsant: fennel.

Vomiting and Nausea: ginger, meadowsweet, and carnation.

Calming: cowslip, hop cones, hyssop, St. John's wort, chamomile, linden, parsley, celery seeds, black cohosh, and valerian.

How to Brew Herb Tea:
Most herb teas should not be boiled, but only steeped in hot water under a lid. An exception from this rule is seeds and roots as well as field horsetail, rose hip peel, and black currant leaves, which sometimes need to boil for 10 to 30 minutes in order for the flavor to really blossom.

Calculate about one-half tablespoon dried leaves per teacup of water. Heat the water to right under the boiling point (194°F). Place the tea leaves in the teapot and pour the hot water over them or place them right into the pan. Let sit for 5 to 10 minutes before straining and serving.

Tip! Season the tea with cinnamon, ginger, star anise, cardamom, or apple and lemon peel. Fresh herbs like lemon balm or mint as well as thyme and salvia give the tea a nice aroma, and licorice root adds a sweetness to herb teas.

Digestion Problems: peppermint, parsley, salvia, and celery seeds.

Muscle and Joint Problems: dandelion, nettle, celery seeds, heartsease, valerian, and meadowsweet.

PMS: black cohosh.

Sleeping Problems: lemon balm, hop cones, St. John's wort, chamomile, linden, black cohosh, and valerian.

Stimulating: ginger and licorice root.

Urinary Tract Infection: heartsease and cranberry (berries).

VITAMIN GUIDE

Vitamins	Function	Deficiency symptoms
A (retinol) Beta-carotene is a preliminary stage of vitamin A as well as an antioxidant, see p. 28. Recommended daily need of vitamin A Women: 0.8 mg Men: 1 mg 70–80 g carrot in a meal covers the daily need.	Important for growth, some hormones, and the immune system as well as the functions of the eye, skin, and mucus membrane. Vitamin A can only be find in animal products. In vegetables we find beta-carotene which transforms into vitamin A.	Night blindness (trouble seeing in poor lighting and in the dark). Dry skin, keratinized goosebumps, and eye irritations.
D (calciferous) Recommended daily need: 5 mg	Mostly needed for calcium and phosphorus metabolism in the body, as well as for bones and teeth, but also for immune system, reproduction, and insulin function.	Ache, muscle weakness, problem focusing, depression and irritability. A long-term deficiency can give rickets to children and brittle bones to adults. A vitamin D deficiency is also associated with diabetes type 1 and 2, multiple sclerosis, brittle bones, heart failure, stroke, and depression.
E (tocopherol) Antioxidant Recommended daily need: Women: 8 mg Men: 10 mg	Strengthens the capillary walls, improves circulation, and prevents thrombosis formation.	
K Recommended daily need: 0.1 mg	Needed for blood's ability to coagulate, mineralization of skeleton, and is important for the brain cells.	
Thiamin (B1) Recommended daily need: 1.2–1.5 mg	Needed for carbohydrate metabolism, functions of the nervous system, as well as the heart's functions.	Tiredness, impaired ability to focus, poor nerves, irritability, bad appetite, constipation, and digestion disorders. Major deficiency can lead to beriberi (nervous ailment).
Riboflavin (B2) Recommended daily need: 1.3–1.7 mg	Needed for fat, carbohydrates, and protein metabolism as well as energy production.	Sores on lips, eye irritations like sensitivity to light, red-purple lips, and tongue.
Niacin Recommended daily need: 15–20 mg	Helps the functions of the nervous system, the gastrointestinal tract, and healthy skin.	Insomnia, lack of appetite, and irritability. Later symptoms are nervous changes through serious depressions. Major deficiency cause pellagra.

Cause of deficiency	Other	Sources
Poor fat absorption. Carotene intake is facilitated if there is fat in the diet, when about one third of the carotene is absorbed.	Is sensitive to light, air, and high frying temperatures. Is stored in the body. Overdose of vitamin A (not carotene) can cause nausea, hair loss, and headache.	Vitamin A is found in egg, milk, and dairy products. Yellow-red and dark green vegetables like carrots, red bell peppers, mango, persimmon, rose hips, nettles, kale, and other green leaves are rich in beta-carotene which is transformed into vitamin A.
About 80 percent of vitamin D needs are normally covered by the skin's own production, but aging as well as dark skin reduces the body's ability to produce the vitamin. During November through March, the sunlight on our latitudes is not enough, and we become completely dependent on vitamin D in food (supplements) as well as the body's storages built up during the summer.	A vitamin D deficiency during the winter is fairly common in Scandinavia. All vegetarians, especially vegans, should make sure to find suitable vitamin D sources—for example, enriched food and supplements—and get enough sunlight during the summer. Overdose (supplements) can cause reduced appetite, calcification in tissues and organs.	Vitamin D is mainly produced in the body by sunlight and is also found in animal products like fat fish, milk, dairy products, egg, and chanterelles.
Problems with fat absorption and exaggerated intake of omega-6 oils.	Is destroyed when frozen as well as any other long-term storing.	Vegetable oils, almonds, nuts, seeds, wheat germs, soy, dried apricots, oats, whole grain, dark green leaves like spinach and kale, broccoli, as well as peas and beans.
Long-term diarrhea and antibiotics as well as poor fat absorption.	Normally enough vitamin K is produced by bacteria in the intestines.	Cauliflower, brussels sprouts, broccoli, spinach, green leaves, and white cabbage.
Alcohol abuse, smoking, absorption disorders, and long-term diarrhea. Increased need with stress, fever, and infections as well for elderly people.	Destroyed by baking powder and baking soda. Sensitive to oxygen and heating and often disappears with the boiling water.	Nutritional yeast, whole grain products, wheat germs, nuts, peas, and beans.
The need is increased by alcohol abuse, smoking, contraceptive pills, fever, and stress.		Nutritional yeast, egg, milk, whey cheese, green leaves, whole grain products, wheat germ, bran, peas, and beans.
Stress, fever, and infections increase the need.	A diet with enough protein also covers the need for niacin, since the amino acid tryptophan transforms to niacin in the body.	Nutritional yeast, peas, beans, milk, whole grain products, and wheat bran.

VITAMIN GUIDE (cont.)

Vitamins	Function	Deficiency symptoms
Pantothenic acid	Needed for fat metabolism.	Deficiency not yet discovered in humans.
B6 (pyridoxin) Recommended daily need: 1.5–2 mg	Contributes to the metabolism of amino acids and is needed to produce signal substances like serotonin, dopamine, and adrenalin.	Irritability, depression, and changes in skin.
Folic acid, folacin, folate: Recommended daily need: 0.3 mg Pregnant and nursing women: 0.4 mg	Needed to build new cells and produce serotonin, dopamine, and other signal substances.	Worsened immune system can increase the risk of heart and vascular diseases, some types of cancer, anemia, and depression. Lack of folic acid in pregnant women can cause miscarriage or damages in the fetus.
B12 (cobalamin) Recommended daily need: 2 mg	Needed for production of DNA, function of the nervous system, as well as to produce signal substances in the brain.	Tiredness, weakness, irritability, depression, and dyspnea as well as a burning and red tongue. Major deficiency can cause pernicious anemia and major damage to nerves.
Biotin Recommended daily need: 0.14 mg	Needed for protein, carbohydrate, and fat metabolism.	Blushing, dry skin, hair loss, tiredness, and nausea.
C (ascorbic acid) Antioxidant Recommended daily need: 75 mg Many scientists consider a daily need of 100–200 mg	Strengthens the immune system, blood vessels, skin, teeth, and skeleton. Contributes to producing collagen in connective tissue and some stress hormones. Contributes to the livers detox system.	Tiredness and irritability, bleeding gums. Deficiency causes easy bruising and impaired wound healing. Major deficiency can cause scurvy.
Coenzyme Q10 (vitamin-like substance) Antioxidant	Needed for cells' energy production and strengthens the immune system. It is, however, not a recognized nutrient.	
Choline (vitamin-like substance) Recommended daily need: Not established.	Important for liver activity, contributes to metabolism.	
Inositol (Vitamin-like substance) Rec. daily ration: Not defined	Plays a role in fat metabolism.	
PABA (vitamin-like substance)	Is likely to be important to the vitamin production of intestinal bacteria.	

Cause of deficiency	Other	Sources
	Intestinal bacteria can produce the vitamin.	Generally occurring in different food.
Long abuse of alcohol, contraceptive pills, and some other medicine.	Deficiency can increase the risk of heart and vascular diseases. Stress and protein-rich diet increases the need. Sensitive to heat and light as well as long-term storage.	Nutritional yeast, whole grain products, wheat germ, wheat bran, soybeans, potatoes, bananas, nuts, egg, milk, beans, as well as vegetables, which contain a lesser amount.
Alcohol abuse, poor intestinal absorption, contraceptive pills. 10–15 percent of the population have a genetic effect that causes the need for folic acid to increase.	Reduces the risk of heart and vascular diseases. Very sensitive to light, heat, and keeping warm. The vitamin is also produced by intestinal bacteria. Depression is more common with folic acid deficiency.	Fruit and berries—for example, kiwi, orange, green leaves like lettuce and kale, peas, beans, lentils, and all root vegetables except for carrot.
Hydrochloric acid deficiency. Lack of so-called inner factors, some intestinal disorders, poor gut flora, and poor absorption. Alcohol abuse.	Stored in the liver, the storage last for about 3 years and it takes about 5 years for the symptoms to occur. Vegans should take B12 supplements. Vegetarians, especially vegans, are recommended to regularly check their B12 status.	Egg and dairy products. Very small amounts can be found in sprouts, fermented vegetables, soy sauce, and miso but these sources are both enough as a B12-source.
Poor intestinal bacteria—for example, after an antibiotic treatment.	Produced by intestinal bacteria and deficiency is rare.	Nutritional yeast, grains (especially oats), nuts, beans, peas, milk, cheese, and bananas.
Smoking, stress, some contraceptive pills, and some medicines.	High vitamin C intake can protect against heart and vascular diseases. It is very sensitive to light, oxygen, and heat and easily dissolves in water. Increases the intake of iron in the diet.	Nettles, kale, brussels sprouts, cauliflower, broccoli, white cabbage, bell pepper, parsley, rose hip, black currants, strawberries, and citrus fruit.
Some diseases, like heart and some muscle diseases, as well as aging, reduces the production.	Normally the body can produce enough Q10, but aging reduces the production.	Oils and to a lesser extent in vegetables—for example, green leaves and broccoli, as well as whole grain products.
Diabetes and alcoholism.	The liver produces colin and deficiency is rare.	Nutritional yeast, citrus fruit, leafy vegetables, whole grain products, nuts, beans, and fruit.
	Intestinal bacteria create inositol.	Nutritional yeast, citrus fruits, leafy vegetables, whole grains, nuts, beans, and fruit.
	Produced by intestinal bacteria.	Nutritional yeast, wheat germ, and wholegrain products.

MINERAL GUIDE

Mineral	Function	Deficiency symptoms
Calcium (Ca) Recommended daily need: Adults: 600 mg Older women have an increased need Pregnant and nursing women: 1000 g	Regulates the function of muscles and nerves, hormone production, coagulation of blood, and heart activity. Needed to build skeleton and teeth.	Dry and inelastic skin, dry and brittle hair, brittle nails, poor mucus membranes, difficulty focusing, depression, numbness, stinging, and convulsions. The concentration of cramps in the blood is constant. If there is too little calcium in the blood it is taken from the skeleton which leads to brittle bones. Especially common in older people.
Phosphorus (P) Recommended daily need: 600 mg	Plays an important role in the cell membranes. Needed for building of bones and energy production. Contributes to the fat transportation in the body. Phosphate is also connected to calcium in the skeleton.	Phosphorus deficiency caused by poor diet has yet not been proven.
Magnesium (Mg) Recommended daily need: Men: 350 mg. Women: 300 mg Pregnant and nursing women: 450 mg	Needed for nerve and muscle functions as well as to activate the about 300 enzymes that are needed in order for the cells to work.	Problems with focusing, depression, numbness, stinging, and convulsions. Magnesium deficiency causes blood pressure and the blood fat triglyceride to rise.
Sodium (Na) Recommended need: 2 g	Works together with potassium. Needed to regulate water balance and for pH values as well as the functions of the nerves.	Lack in appetite, muscle cramps, and circulationsdisorders. Extremely strong perspiration (very unusual in our climate), long-term vomiting and diarrhea. Small children are extra sensitive.
Potassium (K) Recommended daily need: 1–4 g	Needed to regulate the pH values as well as the osmotic pressure. Important for nerve and muscle functions, kidney function, as well enzyme function.	Muscle weakness.

Cause of deficiency	Other	Sources
Too little vitamin D and magnesium. Hydrochloric acid deficiency in the stomach. Damaged intestinal mucosa prevents absorptions as well as kidney functions.	Limestone is especially important for children and teenagers as skeleton and teeth are developed, as well as for women in menopause. Phytic acid and oxalic acid prevents the intake of calcium. Caffeine as well as a large consumption of animal protein and salt increases the calcium excretion. Exercise, vitamin D, milk sugar, milk acid, and protein (in lesser amounts) increase the calcium intake.	Canihua seeds, chia seeds, hemp seeds, amaranth, unpeeled sesame seeds, and cheese are very good sources, but also leafy greens, white cabbage, kale, broccoli, rose hip, legumes, milk, fruit, nuts, and seeds. Extra calcium supplements should be taken at nighttime. The hormone systems that regulate the limestone balance are the most active during night. 1¼ cup sour milk or milk as well as 2 slices of cheese every day gives 70 percent of the limestone need.
Insufficient vitamin D intake and impaired kidney functions as well as diabetic coma and long-term alcoholism.	Phosphorus and calcium go hand in hand.	Cheese, egg, milk, whole grain products, nuts, kale, beans, and potatoes.
Poor diet, diuretic medicines, intestinal diseases, long-term diarrhea, as well as a large alcohol consumption.	Vitamin D stimulates the intake.	Green vegetables, bananas, figs, dates, cacao, almonds, nuts, whole grain products, brussels sprouts, beans, and peas.
Often we have a too large intake of sodium through salt, which can lead to high blood pressure.		Sodium is found naturally in all vegetables, like green leaves, cabbage, root vegetables, peas, beans, fruit, and berries. Regular salt consists of sodium chloride. Most industry-produced food contains salt, like bread, canned food, cheese, ketchup, and pre-made food.
Diuretic medicines, long-term vomiting, and diarrhea as well as uncontrolled diabetes.	Potassium is water-soluble and is wasted if the cooking broth is thrown away.	Potatoes, root vegetables, whole grain products, vegetables (primarily green), both fresh and dried fruit.

Mineral	Function	Deficiency symptoms
Iron (Fe) Recommended daily need: Women 11–50 years: 18 mg Other adults: 10 mg Increased need when pregnant	The red-colored substance hemoglobin in blood binds oxygen with the help of iron. Iron deficiency gives oxygen deficiency in cells. The general condition and resistance is reduced.	Pallor, tiredness, lethargy, irritability, and reduced physical efficiency. Impaired learning ability as well as protection against infection.
Zinc (Zn) Antioxidant together with enzymes (SOD) Recommended enzymes: 12 mg Pregnant and nursing women: 15 mg	Is needed for the function of about 70 different enzymes, among others, then transporting carbon dioxide from tissues to lungs, gene formation, and protein production. Zinc helps with detoxing heavy metals.	Impaired growth and immune system, poor wound healing ability, sensitive skin, eczema, unbalanced sense of taste—reduced appetite and disturbed sense of smelling.
Copper (Cu) Antioxidant together with enzymes (SOD) Recommended daily need: 2–3 mg	Needed for many of the body's enzymes—for instance, those that affect intake of iron and oxygen.	Deficiency is rare among healthy persons. Can give anemia.
Manganese (Mn) Antioxidant together with enzymes (SOD) Recommended daily need: Women 1.8 mg Men 2.3 mg	Needed for growth as well as fat and carbohydrate metabolism.	
Selenium (Se) Antioxidant together with enzymes (GPx) Recommended daily need: 50–200 mg	Important for the immune system. Protects against heavy metals. Works together with vitamin E.	Increased sensitivity to cadmium and mercury poisoning. The so-called Keshan disease is a heart and vascular disease that is connected to deficiency of selenium.

Cause of deficiency	Other	Sources
One-sided diet. Blood loss. Sulphuric acid deficiency in the stomach and poor intestinal absorption.	Vitamin C increases the uptake of non-heme iron: 100 grams of vitamin C in a meal can more than double iron intake. Lacto-fermented vegetables and molkosan also help to increase absorption. Inhibiting factors are phytic acid, black tea, coffee, milk, cocoa, and chocolate.	Whole wheat products, almonds, nuts, seeds, cocoa, beans, soybeans, kale and green leaves, parsley, brussels sprouts, potatoes, dried fruit, and green beans. Strawberries and other berries contain small amounts of iron.
Hydrochloric acid in the stomach, malabsorption, and alcoholism. Zinc also helps with detoxing heavy metals, so the more exposed we are to heavy metals—for example, through mercury poisoning (dental work from both amalgam and gold)—the greater is our deficiency.	Phytic acid in whole grain products prevents intake. Sprouting grains before making sourdough, decreases the rising time and reduces the amount of phytic acid. Protein (mostly animal protein like eggs, milk, and cheese) increases the intake. Zinc deficiency during pregnancy can cause skeletal malformations in the child.	Cheese, cacao, whole grain products, wheat germs, nettles, legumes, nuts, and seeds. Small amounts can also be found in most root vegetables, vegetables, and berries.
Some intestinal diseases and long-term overdosage of zinc which prevents the intake of Cu.	Can be found in higher levels in water from the warm water tap and water that has been still in copper pipes during night. Do not use warm water from tap for gruel and drinks.	Nuts and raisins contain high levels of copper. Small amounts are found in almost all food.
	Manganese deficiency can lead to weakened and disrupted cell breathing.	Whole grain products, nuts, vegetables, root vegetables, especially beetroots, fruit, and berries.
Low selenium levels in Nordic soils and thus in the food.	Organic selenium is easier for the body to absorb than non-organic. Selenium is poisonous in high dosages—maximum 500 mg/day. Too high an intake gives a metal flavor in the mouth and garlic smell from sweat and exhaled air.	Brazil nuts contain very high levels. Egg and cacao have high levels and lesser amounts are found in cheese, cottage cheese, aubergine, white button mushrooms, grains, buckwheat, dried dates, nuts, and almonds. Imported food, like beans, contain selenium in varying amounts. The U.S., Canada, and Japan have high levels of selenium in the soil.

Mineral	Function	Deficiency symptoms
Iodine (J) Recommended daily need: Adults: 0.15 mg Pregnant: 0.175 mg Nursing: 0.2 mg	A part of the metabolism hormones that are produced in the thyroid, that among other things stimulate metabolism and protein production. Prevents goiter and unbalanced metabolism.	Deficiency is rare in Sweden thanks to iodine-enriched feed for milk cows and enriched cooking salt.
Chromium (Cr) Recommended daily intake: Women: 25 mg Men: 30 mg	Needed for blood sugar metabolism.	Less efficient use of blood sugar. Low blood sugar levels causes a craving for sweets.
Molybdenum (Mo) Recommended daily need: 150–500 mg	Needed for different enzyme systems.	No documented deficiency with humans.
Nickel (Ni) Recommended daily need: unknown	Likely to protect the cell membranes from damage.	Impaired reproduction and growth in animals.
Silica (si) Recommended daily need: unknown	Silica is among other things part of the connective tissue and needed for production of collagen and elastin, which gives the connective tissue elasticity.	Impaired reproduction with animals, impaired growth, and less collagen in bone tissue, as well as less elasticity in the walls of blood vessels.

Cause of deficiency	Other	Sources
Vegans and vegetarians who live off a diet very low in salt should pay attention to their iodine intake. Iodine deficiency with pregnant women increases the risk of congenital hypothyroidism in the child.	Some algae like arame and hijiki contain very large amounts of iodine and should not be eaten more than once a week. Kombu should not be eaten more than once a month. Nori and wakame, on the other hand, can be eaten more often.	Seaweed and iodinated cooking salt are the best sources. Sea salt and rock salt contain half the amount of iodine as enriched iodine salt. Herb salt usually contains algae. Cheese and milk contain iodine since cow's feed are iodinated. Most food contain small amounts of iodine, primarily celery, but also grains, root vegetables, vegetables, potatoes, and fruit.
Deficiency is common in a diet that has a high content of refined food. Diabetics likely have an increased need.		Beer yeast, nettles, dried fruit, whole grain products, cheese, nuts, and seeds are good sources for chromium. Most vegetables and root vegetables as well as fruit and berries only contain small amounts of chromium.
Phytic acid inhibits absorption.		Soy flour, grains, beans, peas, root vegetables, fruit, and berries as well as most vegetables contain molybdenum.
		Oats, soy flour, buckwheat, nuts, almonds, whole grain products, broccoli, nettles, beans, and peas.
	Silica also strengthens nails and hair.	Field horsetail, whole grain products, especially barley, beans, potatoes, honey, milk, and cheese.

STUDY PLAN, ECO-FRIENDLY DINING DELIGHT

Today eco-friendly food is more relevant than ever before. How can you as an individual reduce your carbon dioxide emissions? What food additives should be avoided? How do you cook climate-smart food and how do you eat all the nutrients you need as a vegetarian?

There is a lot to discuss and learn in a eco-friendly study circle and a lot of tasty food to cook. The following suggestion is a schedule with questions to discuss for a study circle of 10 meetings. The ideal plan is to have 2 to 3 meetings during summer and autumn, winter and spring. But it is fine to only have a few meetings and choose the most important questions for the group to discuss.

Suggested schedule for a meeting

1. Start each meeting with theory and questions to discuss.
2. Practical cooking: salad, soup, and main course as well as herb tea or any other drink. Vary between small dishes, spreads, bread, pastries, desserts, and healthy candy depending on the size of the group.
3. Finish the meeting by eating together and a general discussion as well as an evaluation of the meeting. Also plan the next meeting, both the theory and the cooking.

Choose dishes after one season at a time for each meeting, also see food suggestions on p. 61. The group can also choose to ferment vegetables, see p. 20, or pick edible wild plants and cook a meal from these.

Food cost

Divide the participants into groups of two people each. Create a rolling schedule of practical cooking. Each group chooses a suitable recipe and is responsible for buying all the ingredients that is needed for the meal on the next meeting. Eventual leftovers are taken care of by respective group.

The final cost for each group is usually the same by the end of the circle study. Each group also has a possibility of adjusting the costs by choosing a dish with cheaper ingredients for the next meeting, if the previous dish was expensive. If the group wants to, some ingredients like vegetarian stock, herb salt, and oil can be paid for together.

General advice

In a study circle, all participants should be heard. Both circle leader and the rest of the group are responsible for making sure that everyone's views are heard. Preparation and homework are divided between the participants.

Each participant reads the specific theory for every meeting. At least one computer is needed for the first two meetings. Bring interesting new articles and books; borrow books at the library. Collect material to make an exhibition about eco-friendly dining delight. Schools, libraries, work sites, and other public facilities are usually interested in exhibitions.

Since the time in a study circle is limited, it can be difficult to bake bread during a meeting. Someone or a few people might have the responsibility to bake at home and invite the rest of the group. Or each participant can bring a home-baked bread for a special bread meeting. During this meeting, there might be more time to discuss questions and theory. Another possibility to make more time for discussing questions is that each group mixes a smoothie or other drink at a meeting.

STUDY PLAN

Meeting 1

Presenting the leader and participants. Make yourselves acquainted with each other and let all the participants introduce themselves and their expectations of the circle. Discuss expectations and the purpose of the circle and adjust the schedule according to the group's demands. Look at the possibilities to do a study visit or work with an expert.

Theory: Course chapter, p. 12–14.

Practice: Make different kinds of snacks, see p. 194, as well as tea, see p. 324. The circle leader buys ingredients and brings a computer. The expenses are split between all participants.

Questions for discussion:

- Why is it dangerous with too many greenhouse gases in the atmosphere?
- How much carbon dioxide does each person contribute every year?
- How many tons should we contribute if we want to show solidarity with the rest of the populations on the planet?
- What percentage of carbon dioxide does animal farming contribute globally?
- What kind of carbon footprints does the group have?
- Discuss how to reduce the carbon footprints.

Preparing for next meeting: Divide the participants into food groups and each group plans what dish should be cooked for next time. See suggestion above.

Meeting 2

Repetition from previous meeting as well as possible questions and thoughts.

Course chapter: p. 12–14

Questions for discussion:

- Continue to discuss how the group can reduce carbon footprints and what is reasonable.
- Browse for climate-smart addresses. Also see p. 339.
- Discuss the tips in an eco-friendly guide. Are they reasonable?

- Look at the seasonal guide on p.16. What season brings the biggest challenge of cooking eco-friendly food?

Practice: Cooking.

Preparing for next meeting: The groups plan what dish should be cooked next time. See suggestion above.

Meeting 3

Theory: Repeating previous meeting and possible questions and thoughts.

Course chapter: p. 30–33

Questions for discussion:

- What does it mean if food is KRAV-labeled.
- What advantages can be found by eating organic or KRAV labeled food?
- Can you trust KRAV labeling? Feel free to look at the regulations for KRAV on their site.
- Are there other individuals or groups that make a profit off us eating KRAV-labeled food?
- How many food additives are approved by KRAV?
- Why?
- Are there any "natural" additives?
- How come the azo dyes that were earlier regulated in Sweden are once again allowed?

Practice: Cooking.

Preparing for next meeting: The groups plan what dish should be cooked next time, see suggestion above.

"Homework": Each group bring different food packages for the next meeting.

Meeting 4

Theory: Repetition of previous meeting and possible thoughts or questions.

Course chapter: p. 30–33

Questions for discussion:

- Discuss additives from the food packages that the group has brought.
- Why is food irradiated?
- What type of food is irradiated here in the country?
- What does GMO mean?
- What types of food can be GMO-labeled?
- In what food can you find dioxins?

- How many pesticides are registered in our country?
- Why is it important to have good quality water?

Practice: Cooking.

Preparing for next meeting: The groups plan what dish should be cooked for next time.

Meeting 5

Theory: Repetition of previous meeting and possible thoughts and questions.

Course chapter: p. 52–54.

Questions for discussion:
- What amino acids can the body not produce by itself?
- How much protein do we need?
- How can we obtain enough protein from a lacto-vegetarian as well as a vegan diet?
- What factors affect GI value?
- Why do you become addicted to sugar?
- Do you dare to eat potatoes?
- What about other root vegetables?
- What should you think about to maintain the most even blood sugar level possible?

Practice: Cooking.

Preparing for next meeting: The groups plan what dish should be cooked for next time.

Meeting 6

Theory: Repetition of previous meeting and possible thoughts and questions.

Course chapter: p. 54–57.

Questions for discussion:
- Why do we need to eat fat?
- What type of fat do we need?
- What fat should we choose for cooking?
- What fatty acids are essential?
- Does everyone that eats, for example, flaxseed oil obtain enough EPA and DHA?
- How to you know if you have a deficiency?

Practice: Cooking.

Homework: Everyone should sprout one kind of seed, see p. 14.

Meeting 7

Theory: Repetition of previous meeting and possible thoughts and questions.

Course chapter: p. 14–15.

Questions for discussion:
- What seeds can be sprouted?
- What happens during sprouting?
- What can be cultivated indoors?

Practice: Cooking.

Preparing for next meeting: The groups plan what dish should be cooked next time.

Meeting 8

Theory: Repetition of previous meeting and possible thoughts and questions.

Course chapter: p. 46–49.

Questions for discussion:
- How many known vitamins are there?
- Why do we need vitamins?
- What vitamins are particularly sensitive? In what way?
- Why are free radicals produced?
- Where can we find antioxidants?
- Where can we find plant chemicals?

Practice: Cooking.

Preparing for next meeting: The groups are planning what dish should be cooked next time.

Meeting 9

Theory: Repetition of previous meeting and possible thoughts and questions.

Course chapter: p. 56–57.

Questions for discussion:
- What is the difference between minerals and micronutrients?
- What minerals and micronutrients are especially important to lacto-vegetarians as well as vegans? Where can we find these nutrients?
- Is there any risk of minerals and micronutrients disappearing during the cooking process?

Practice: Cooking.

Preparing for next meeting: The groups plan what dish should be cooked next time.

Meeting 10

Finish with a feast and make a conclusion and evaluation of the course.

ALPHABETICAL INDEX

INDEX OF RECIPES BY CHAPTER

RECIPES AND FOOD BY ALPHABET

VOLUME AND WEIGHT

Volume

1 teacup = 1¹⁄₁₆ cups (250 ml)
1 coffee cup = ⅝ cup (150 ml)
1 glass = ⅘ cup (200 ml)
1 lemon = 3 tbsp lemon juice

Measurement Kits

1 deciliter (dl) = 100 ml = ⁷⁄₁₆ cup
1 tablespoon = 15 ml
1 teaspoon = 5 ml
1 pinch = 1ml

All dimensions in the Recipes refers to noted measurements

• Always use noted measurements!
• Taste first—then sprinkle!

English and American Weight Measurements

1 pound (lb) = 16 ounces = 453.6 grams (g)
1 ounce (oz) = 28.3 g
1 kilogram (kg) = 2.188 lb
1 g = 0.035 oz
3.5 oz ~ 100 g

Volume Weights for Certain Foods

	1 liter	1 dl	1 table-spoon	1 teaspoon graham
flour	600 g (l)	60 g (dl)	10 g (tbsp)	3 g (tsp)
country wheat	600 g (l)	60 g (dl)	10 g (tbsp)	3 g (tsp)
almonds		65 g (dl)	10 g (tbsp)	
margarine		90 g (dl)	15 g (tbsp)	5 g (tsp)
hazelnuts		65 g (dl)	10 g (tbsp)	
oil		90 g (dl)	15 g (tbsp)	5 g (tsp)
cheese, grated		40g (dl)		
rye flour	500 g (l)	50 g (dl)	7 g (tbsp)	
salt, rough		115 g (dl)	15g (tbsp)	6 g (tsp)
butter	90 g (l)	15 g (dl)	5 g (tbsp)	

An Easier Way to Measure

Small amounts of dry food can be taken out of their box fully measured from the box's dimensions. Level off excess with the flat edge of a knife. By shaking a measure of flour, it becomes tightly packed and can be easily poured directly into a graduated measuring cup.

Average Weights for Common Fruits and Vegetables

orange	160 g
banana	175 g
onion, yellow	100 g
carrot	100 g
potato	100 g
apple	100 g

Average Weight for 1 Liter of Berries

blueberries	600 g
lingonberries	600 g
raspberries	600 g
cloudberries	600 g
strawberries	600 g
currants	500 g

American Measurements

1 gallon = 4 liquid quarts = 3.8 liters
1 liquid quart = 2 liquid pints = 9.5 deciliters
1 liquid pint = 2 cups = 4.7 deciliters
1 cup = 16 tablespoons = 2.4 deciliters
1 cup = 8 fluid ounces = 2.4 deciliters
1 fluid ounce = 29.6 milliliters
1 tablespoon = 3 teaspoons = 15 milliliters
1 teaspoon = 5 milliliters
1 liter = 0.264 gallon = 1.06 quarts
1 milliliter = 0.34 fluid ounces

Oven

572	degrees F grill
527	degrees F very strong oven
482	degrees F strong oven
392–437	degrees F moderate oven
347–392	degrees F rather weak oven
302	degrees F weak oven
212	degrees F very weak oven